A Historical Study of Referent Honorifics in Japanese

Hituzi Linguistics in English

No. 1   Lexical Borrowing and its Impact on English   Makimi Kimura-Kano
No. 2   From a Subordinate Clause to an Independent Clause
                                                        Yuko Higashiizumi
No. 3   ModalP and Subjunctive Present   Tadao Nomura
No. 4   A Historical Study of Referent Honorifics in Japanese
                                                        Takashi Nagata

Hituzi Linguistics in English No. 4

A Historical Study of Referent Honorifics in Japanese

Takashi Nagata

Hituzi Syobo Publishing

Copyright © Takashi Nagata 2006
First published 2006

Author: Takashi Nagata

All rights reserved. Except for the quotation of short passages for the purposes of criticism and review, no part of this publication may be reduced, stored in a retrieval system, or transmitted in any form or by any means, electronic, mechanical, photocopying, recording or otherwise, without the written prior permission of the publisher.
In case of photocopying and electronic copying and retrieval from network personally, permission will be given on receipts of payment and making inquiries. For details please contact us through e-mail. Our e-mail address is given below.

Book Design © Hirokazu Mukai (glyph)

Hituzi Syobo Publishing
5-21-5 Koishikawa Bunkyo-ku Tokyo, Japan 112-0002

phone +81-3-5684-6871 fax +81-3-5684-6872
e-mail: toiawase@hituzi.co.jp
http://www.hituzi.co.jp/
postal transfer 00120-8-142852

ISBN4-89476-271-4
Printed in Japan

Contents

Preface   xiii
STYLE NOTES   xviii

1 INTRODUCTION   1

   1. Politeness and honorific expressions   1
   2. Outline of Japanese honorifics   2
   3. Brief overview of Japanese history and sources used in this study   8
   4. Historical changes in the referent honorific expression system   11
   5. From absolute to relative honorifics   13
   6. Criteria for honorific expression   16

2 REFERENT HONORIFIC EXPRESSION IN GENJI-MONOGATARI   21

   1. Introduction   21
   2. Methodology   22
   3. Analysis   26
      3.1 Kinship relationship   26
         3.1.1 about the inferior by kinship relationship (Table 1)   26
         3.1.2 about wives (Table 2)   35
         3.1.3 about husbands (Table 3)   38
         3.1.4 about the superior by kinship relationship (Table 4)   39
      3.2 Hierarchical relationships   44
         3.2.1 about servants (Table 5)   45
         3.2.2 between servants (Table 6)   46
         3.2.3 about masters (Table 7)   48
      3.3 Social status relationships   52
         3.3.1 about the inferior by social status relationship (Table 8)   53
         3.3.2 about the same by social status relationship (Table 9)   55

   3.3.3 about the superior by social status relationship (Table 10) 57
  3.4 Humble form of dual honorifics, and humble
    form plus respectful form 59
 4. Conclusion 66
Proposal of the term Status Honorifics 68
APPENDIX 70

3 REFERENT HONORIFIC EXPRESSION IN HEIKE-MONOGATARI 75

 1. Introduction 75
 2. Data 75
 3. Methodology 76
 4. Analysis 81
  4.1 Referent who is inferior to a speaker 81
  4.2 Referent and speaker of the same status 84
  4.3 Referent who is superior to a speaker 85
 5. Conclusion 95
Proposal of the term Hierarchical Honorifics 99

4 REFERENT HONORIFIC EXPRESSION IN TORAAKI'S KYŌGEN PLAYS 103

 1. Introduction 103
 2. Data 104
 3. Classification of honorific words toward a referent 105
 4. Honorific expression toward a referent from the view-point
  of human relations 107
  4.1 a wife talks about her husband (Table 2) 109
  4.2 a husband talks about his wife (Table 3) 111
  4.3 a child or a grandchild talks about a parent or
    a grandparent (Table 4) 112
  4.4 a parent or a grandparent talks about a child or
    a grandchild (Table 5) 114

4.5 a younger brother talks about an elder brother	115
4.6 an elder brother talks about a young brother	115
4.7 a son-in-law talks about a father-in-law (Table 6)	116
4.8 a father-in-law talks about a son-in-law (Table 7)	117
4.9 a servant talks about his master (Table 8)	117
4.10 a master talks about his servant (Table 9)	120
4.11 a servant talks about a servant	121
4.12 a teacher talks about an apprentice	121
4.13 an apprentice talks about a teacher (Table 10)	122
4.14 a bridegroom talks about a teacher (Table 11)	123
4.15 a monk talks about parishioners (Table 12)	124
4.16 a parishioner talks about a monk (Table 13)	125
4.17 about a person of high social rank with whom a speaker has no personal connection (Table 14)	126
4.18 about a person of ordinary social rank with whom a speaker has no personal connection (Table 15)	128
4.19 about a visitor (Table 16)	130
5. The honorific system toward a referent from the viewpoint of lexicon	131
5.1 ōseraru (Table 17)	132
5.2 mausu (Table 18)	134
5.3 ihu (Table 19)	136
5.4 mausaru (Table 20)	137
5.5 iharu (Table 21)	139
5.6 oshiyaru (Table 22)	140
5.7 ihaseraru	141
5.8 ihasu	141
5.9 nukasu	141
5.10 ihiyaru	141
5.11 Flow chart (Table 23)	142
6. Conclusion	143

5 REFERENT HONORIFIC EXPRESSION IN THE SHŌKAISHINGO — 151

    1. Introduction — 151
    2. Data — 152
    3. Analysis — 153
        3.1 Honorific expression in the first edition of the *Shōkaishingo* — 153
        3.2. Summary of honorific expression in the first version of the *Shōkaishingo* — 165
        3.3. Revisions in the last edition — 167
        3.4. Conclusion about the revisions in the last edition — 170
    4. Conclusion — 171

6 REFERENT HONORIFIC EXPRESSION IN THE KAMIGATA DIALECT OF THE EARLY EDO PERIOD: IN KYŌGEN AND JŌRURI DOMESTIC PLAYS — 175

    1. Introduction — 175
    2. Data — 176
    3. An analysis — 181
        3.1 self-introduction — 181
        3.2 a wife about her husband (Table 2) — 183
        3.3 a son about his parents (Table 5) — 186
        3.4 a daughter about her parents (Table 9) — 189
        3.5 a younger brother about his elder brother or sister — 190
        3.6 a younger sister about her elder brother or sister — 192
        3.7 a servant about his master (Table 11) — 193
    4. Conclusion — 198

7 REFERENT HONORIFIC EXPRESSION IN THE EDO DIALECT OF THE LATE EDO PERIOD: IN NANBOKU'S KI-ZEWA-MONO — 201

1. Introduction	201
2. Data	201
3. Analysis	204
3.1 about parents	205
3.1.1 about his parents	205
3.1.2 a daughter about her parents	209
3.2 a wife about her husband	210
3.3 about an elder brother or sister	212
3.3.1 about his elder brother or sister	212
3.3.2 about her elder brother or sister	215
3.4 a servant about his master	216
3.5 synthetic analysis	219
3.6 analysis of respectful predicates	221
4. Comparison with other kinds of data	221
5. Summary	222

8 REFERENT HONORIFIC EXPRESSION IN CHŌNIN-KOTOBA OF THE LATER EDO PERIOD: IN SHARE-BON, KOKKEI-BON AND NINJŌ-BON   225

1. Introduction	225
2. Data	225
3. Analysis	227
3.1 about a kinship superior	228
3.1.1 about her husband	228
3.1.2 a younger brotehr or sister about his or her elder siblings	230
3.1.3 a son about his parents	230
3.1.4 a daughter about her parents	232
3.2 a servant about his master	232
3.3 about a *yūjo*	234
3.4 about a superior in social stratum	236
3.5 total analysis	237
4. Conclusion	241

9 REFERENT HONORIFIC EXPRESSION IN THE FORMAR MEIJI PERIOD: IN ZANGIRI-MONO OF MOKUAMI   245

   1. Introduction   245
   2. Data   246
   3. Analysis   247
      3.1 a servant about his master   247
      3.2 a wife about her husband   249
      3.3 a daughter about her parents   252
      3.4 a son about his parents   254
      3.5 a young sister about elder brother or sister   258
      3.6 about a colleague   259
   4. Conclusion   259

10 REFERENT HONORIFIC EXPRESSION IN THE PRESENT DAY   263

   1. Introduction   263
   2. Data   264
   3. Analysis   270
      3.1 about a superior by kinship relation   270
      3.2 about a husband   281
      3.3 about a superior within a military   283
      3.4 about a master from a servant or about a one's superior official   286
   4. Summary   289

11 REFERENT HONORIFIC EXPRESSION IN REGIONAL DIALECTS   293

   1. Survey of the honorific expression toward a referent in regional dialects   293
   2. History of the honorific expression toward a referent based on the distribution of regional forms   294
   3. Respectful expression toward in-group members   297

12 CONCLUSION 309

    1. The shift in the honorific system used toward a referent 309
    2. Words to be used for the honorific expression toward a referent 316
    3. The provenance of relative honorifics 318
    4. The honorific system—in literary Japanese 321

Reference 323
INDEX 331

Preface

This book examines the history of honorific expression in the Japanese language. Any language has its own device to show a speaker's politeness towards a hearer, but this device differs from one language to another. In general, Asian languages have developed a rich linguistic device to show politeness on a lexical and grammatical level, while European languages only display politeness on a pragmatic level. Japanese language also has developed honorifics on a grammatical level. There are two categories of honorific expressions: 1. honorifics toward the hearer (addressee-oriented honorifics); and 2. toward the person being spoken about (referent-oriented honorifics). Japanese honorifics can show deference not only toward the hearer but also toward the person being spoken about. In this book I focus on the second category of honorific expression. In classical literature any person who is superior to a speaker is referred to using respectful expression by the speaker. However, in modern Japanese the person being spoken about is treated in consideration of the relationship between a speaker and a hearer. On the one hand, any person who belongs to the speaker's side should not be referred to using respectful expressions. One the other hand, any person who belongs to the hearer's side should be referred to with respectful expressions. The classical honorific system is named absolute honorifics because a person being spoken about is treated according to his/her absolute social status, while the modern honorific system is named relative honorifics because one is treated based on the relative relationship among speaker and hearer. It is agreed among scholars on honorifics that the most important shift from classical to modern honorifics is the shift from absolute to relative honorifics. But there is no fixed theory explaining how and when Japanese honorifics changed from absolute to relative honorifics. In this book I clarify this process.

This is the first Japanese book to investigate the shift of honorifics from the viewpoint of sociolinguistics. There are many books on the history of Japanese honorifics but all of these books are lexical or grammatical studies. There are some studies on honorifics from the viewpoint of sociolinguistics, but they all focus on modern Japanese. The practical use of honorifics depends heavily on the society in which they are used. Therefore, the methodology that has developed under sociolinguistic study is useful for investigating the shift of honorific usage taking social factors into consideration. The attempt to investigate historical documents from the viewpoint of sociolinguistics started in Japan quite recently. As a result, the publication of this study in the English language will be a valuable contribution to the fields of Japanese language and sociolinguistics.

This book is an English version of a Japanese book that was accepted by Sophia University in 2005 as a Ph.D. thesis on linguistics. When I published the original Japanese book in 2001, Dr. Akira Ishikawa, a professor in the Department of Foreign Studies at Sophia University in Tokyo, from which I had graduated about fifteen years ago, recommended that I submit it as a doctoral dissertation. According to the regulations of the department, a doctoral dissertation should be written in the language that a candidate had majored. As I specialized in English linguistics, I had to translate my Japanese book into English. I translated the Japanese version into English while conducting research as a visiting fellow both at the Australian National University (ANU) and Monash University for one year in 2004. I was sent to Australia for one year by my employer Kinki University under the overseas research personnel program. Sophia University changed its rules regarding doctoral dissertations; they now accept a Japanese thesis when the subject is related to Japanese linguistics. However, I decided to finish translating the thesis because I discovered that while there were some studies on Japanese linguistics, these were quite biased. The Australian government designated ANU as the center for Japanese study among all Australian universities and consequently ANU had the biggest collection of Japanese and English books on Japanese studies in its library. But I could not find any English books on the historical study of Japanese honorifics. English books examining Japanese language were written by two kinds of linguists: one is Japanese linguists who established their academic discipline based on western linguistics and the other is western linguists who studied linguistics and applied western methodologies to Japanese language. That is, the authors conducted their research from the perspective of linguistic methodologies developed in Europe or the U.S.A. and examined modern Japanese based on arguments derived from European or American linguistics. But there is a vast literature on Japanese honorifics in Japan and its methodology has developed independently from western linguistics. In general, Japanese people are very eager to learn what happens abroad and to try to adapt themselves to it, but are very lazy when it comes to introducing their own traditions abroad. The term 'international' sounds quite fascinating for Japanese who believe they need to be judged based on international standards, and who, at the same time, disparage themselves because of their insularism. I believe that Japanese possess many valuable cultural traits that can be introduced overseas and Japanese linguistics is one of them.

At the beginning, when I started translating, I could not imagine who the book's English readership might be. It is quite obvious that most native English speakers have no background knowledge on Japanese honorifics. It is quite technical and doesn't seem to attract the attention of non-native Japanese scholars. I decided to target the following people as potential readers of the book: scholars interested in Japanese literature and linguists who are interested in honorifics or polite expression in general. Therefore, example sentences will be given in full Japanese script, followed by a romaji rendering of the pronunciation. This will be explained by a partial linguistic gloss, highlighting only features of interest to the current example, and finally, an English translation. Therefore, scholars who major in Japanese literature can read the original Japanese text, and scholars who don't read Japanese can understand the example sentences through a partial linguistic gloss and English translation. I added a brief introduction to Japanese honorifics and the history of Japanese society for those unfamiliar with either Japanese language or society in the first chapter. This will allow them to obtain some basic knowledge that will be useful for reading later chapters.

In Western countries people can come in contact with Japanese literature through translation. Both classical and modern Japanese literature has been translated into European languages such as English, French and Spanish. Honorifics are important in understanding Japanese society and a correct understanding of Japanese literature cannot be attained without knowledge of Japanese honorifics.

For example, The Tale of Genji has been translated into English by three translators; Arther Waley, Edward Seidensticker and Royall Tyler. In Japanese the subject or object of a sentence, the agent or patient, can be omitted grammatically but we can make inferences to it through context. In the Tale of Genji the usage of honorifics makes it easier to ascertain who the agent or patient of each sentence is. There are some grades of honorific expressions and the proper honorifics are determined according to the social status of each character. Royall Tyler tried to translate the original as faithfully as possible while Arther Waley tried to transplant the Japanese story into a European Court context. The former translated honorific expressions in the original text into English, but the latter neglected to translate it into English. When people want to enjoy the Tale of Genji as a classical story of Japanese aristocratic society, they need to study honorifics.

I hope that this book will be useful from the perspective of linguistics, especially sociolinguistics. There are some works on honorifics but these only explore modern Japanese since without the knowledge of honorifics nobody can speak correct Japanese. There is a practical need for books on contemporary Japanese honorifics. There are very few studies examining historical Japanese. While honorifics did not develop in the European languages, polite expression still exists. Brown and Levinson developed their 'politeness' theory from a pragmatic viewpoint in order to explain polite expression from a speaker to a hearer. Linguists who are familiar with sociolinguistics should find it easier to understand this book.

No words can fully express my gratitude for the kindness and patience of the following linguists who kindly read my paper and examined it as doctoral thesis: Prof. Fumio Inoue, Dr. Akira Ishikawa, Dr. Tatsushi Motohashi and Prof. Akio Tanaka. I also must thank Dr. Meredith Mckinney, who is experienced in translating Japanese classical literature into English, and gave me valuable suggestions on how to introduce Japanese honorifics to an English audience. I am also indebted to Dr. Brad Williams and Ms. Teresa Anile for proof-reading the English manuscript.

This book is an English revision of the Japanese original text, *Daisansha taigū-hyōgen-shi no kenkyū (A Historical Study of Referent Honorifics in Japanese)* published by Izumi shoin in 2001, and is published with a grant from Kinki University.

I am sure that introductory books should be published in English for the Japanese linguistics and especially for the historical study of Japanese language. There are many books on Japanese but most of these books are published for the practical purpose of speaking and writing modern Japanese. There also are a few books on Japanese linguistics, but these books are written on the basis of western linguistics, and, therefore, it is quite important to publish introductory books on Japanese linguistics in English. And linguists who are interested in studying more on Japanese linguistics can carry on their study in Japanese afterwards. I hope this book becomes a foothold for the further propagation of Japanese linguistics.

2006 March   Takashi Nagata

STYLE NOTES

This study is expected to be of use to a variety of readers, including students of the Japanese language, scholars and translators of historical Japanese literature, and linguists with an interest in the development of honorifics or systems of politeness.

Bearing this broad audience in mind, examples sentences will be given in full Japanese script, followed by a *romaji* rendering of the pronunciation. This will be explained by a partial linguistic gloss, highlighting only features of interest to the current example (e.g. honorific verbal morphology and grammatical relation of referent), and finally, an English translation. For example,

(Ichizjō Haven→a servant)

何の用意もなく、軽らかに、人に見え給ひけむこそ、いといみじけれ（夕霧、5.36）

nani no youi mo naku, karuraka ni hito ni miye *tamahi* 'ORA' kem koso, ito imizikere

'But she(=the second princes, her daughter) let him (=Yūgiri) see her, nothing alters that horrid fact' (Evining Mist, 685)

This is an example that Ichizjō Haven refers her daughter, the second princes, to her servant. The italicized part *tamahi* indicates the honorific expression toward a referent, the second princes in this case. The quoted part 'ORA' indicates the honorific meaning of italicized word, Ordinary Respectful Auxiliary verb in this case. The abbreviation is shown at the end of this note in a list. Another example is such as follows.

(Tō no Chūjō→Consort (=his daughter))

かの人参らせむ（常夏、3.204）

kano hito *mawira* 'come(HVN)' se m

'I will make you a gift of her (=Ōmi no kimi, his daughter of humble birth).' (Wild Carnations, 448)

This is an example that Tō no Chūjō refers his daughter of humble birth, Ōmi no kimi, to his another daughter, Consort. The italicized part *mawira* indicates the honorific expression toward a referent, Ōmi no kimi in this case. The quoted part 'come (HVN)' indicates the honorific meaning of italicized word, the lexical meaning is 'come' and humble verb(nominative) in this case. Humble expression has opposite meanings depending on the referent of humble expression is subject or object. For example,

    X ga   mairu

    X NOMINATIVE   'come (HVN)'

A speaker expresses the behaviour of the agent, X, by humble verb for 'come'. The speaker makes X humble in this case. But on the contrary,

    X ni   mairu

    X OBJECTIVE   'come (HVO)'

A speaker expresses the behaviour of unspecified agent to the recipient, X, by humble verb for 'come'. The speaker respects X by making the unspecified agent humble to X in this case. For example,

(Aksashi Empress→Kaoru)

宮は出で給ひぬなり。あさましくいとほしき御様かな。いかに人見奉るらむ。（総角、6.59）

Miya ha ide *tamahi* 'ORA' nu nari. Asamashiku itohosiki *ohom* 'RP'-sama kana! Ikani hito mi *tatematuru* 'HAO' ram?

'So he (=Prince Niou) has run off again. I cannot understand him. Has he no notion of what people will be thinking? (Trefoil Knots, 845)

Tatematuru is a humble auxiliary to show the actor's humbleness toward a patient or to show the addresser's humbleness toward a patient. In this sentence, the patient is Prince Niou.

    The method of romanization used is the Hepburn method, which indicates long vowels with a macron (bar) over the vowel like ā, ī, ū and ō. The Hepburn method is the method that was invented by James Curtis Hepburn (1815-1911), who came to Japan as a mission and published a Japanese-English Dictionary. There are few methods for Romanization used in Japan, but the Hepburn method is one of the most popular one. I tried to transcribe the pronunciation of each time as much as possible, but there are still some phones that all linguists don't agree for their real pronunciation.

The list of abbreviations

DE	dual expression
EE	equal expression
FN	first name
HAN	humble auxiliary verb(nominative)
HAO	humble auxiliary verb(objective)
HE	humble expression
HN	humble noun
HP	humble prefix
HPA	humble particle
HTE	humble title expression
HVN	humble verb(nominative)
HVO	humble verb(objective)
IE	inferior expression
ISE	insulting expression
LN	last name
NE	neutral expression
NPE	non-polite expression
ORA	ordinary respectful auxiliary verb
ORE	ordinary respectful expression
ORV	ordinary respectful verb
OSE	ordinary superior expression
PE	polite expression
RA	respectful auxiliary verb
RARU	auxiliary 'raru'
RARUE	'raru' expression
RE	respectful expression
RN	respectful noun
RP	respectful prefix
RPA	respectful particle
RS	respectful suffix
RTE	respectful title expression
RV	respectful verb
SE	superior expression
SRA	supreme respectful auxiliary verb
SRE	supreme respectful expression
SRV	supreme respectful verb
SSE	supreme superior expression
TN	title name
V	verb

1

INTRODUCTION

1. Politeness and honorific expressions

Human societies employ various strategies to promote social harmony within their communities. Politeness in language is one such strategy, with different languages encoding politeness in a variety of ways. In English, for example, a speaker may choose from a number of directive/request forms, such as the following, depending on their judgement of a social situation:

Pass the salt.

Can you pass the salt?

Could you pass the salt?

Would you mind passing the salt?

Social factors influencing the speaker's choice can include: participants in the spoken exchange, other people present during the exchange, the location of the exchange and the formality of the occasion. In other words, the social context of the exchange affects the level of politeness employed. Here the honorific expression does not appear on a lexical level but on a pragmatic level. Brown and Levinson (1987) developed their 'politeness' theory from this viewpoint.

Whilst this applies to any European language, there are some languages whose honorific expressions are located on a lexical level: among Asian languages, Korean, Javanese, Vietnamese, Tibetan and Mongolian are well known for this, as is Japanese. Modes of politeness encoded in a language's grammar, lexicon and pronunciation are termed 'honorifics'. This terminology is especially important in languages like

Japanese, where the honorific system is extensive and quite elaborate. English, on the other hand, can be said to have no true honorifics; most modes of politeness are, instead, encoded through auxiliary routines such as 'Would you mind…' as in the example above. English terms of address (first name only; Mr/Mrs plus surname; Sir/Madam; Professor) resemble some aspects of an honorific system, but remain relatively isolated from other structural aspects of the language. Central European languages are well known for the honorific system exhibited in their use of intimate/distant (or formal/informal) second person pronouns. This is often referred to as the T/V distinction, after the French second person pronouns *tu* and *vous*, the Italian *tu* and *voi*, and other European languages. Brown and Gilman (1960) refer to the way in which, in European languages, these two kinds of second-person pronouns are code-switched according to the interpersonal relationship between a speaker and an addressee.

2. Outline of Japanese honorifics

In general, linguistic expression can be divided into three categories: honorific, neutral and disdain expressions. The latter is not so developed in Japanese, while the neutral expression is commonly used; therefore, as a custom of Japanese linguistics, we represent all these expressions by honorific expression. Disdain expressions can therefore be interpreted as negative honorific expressions.

The Japanese honorific expression system is both syntactic and lexical. In school education, honorifics are divided into three categories: *teineigo* 丁寧語 'polite form'; *sonkeigo* 尊敬語 'respectful form'; and *kenjōgo* 謙讓語 'humble form'. In Japanese, there is a distinction between the informal and formal style. When a speaker speaks to an addressee in a polite way, he uses the polite form. For example, to change the informal *watashi ga hanasu* (I speak) to a formal style, one should affix *masu*, as in *watashi ga hanashi masu*. To the informal style *kore wa hon da* (this is a book), should be affixed *desu*, as in *kore wa hon desu*. These *desu* and *masu* forms are named *teineigo*, and require that a speaker varies his language according to his addressee. *Teineigo* is sometimes translated as addressee honorifics, because its main function is to express politeness toward an addressee. In Japanese, this stylistic distinction between formal and informal is located in the sentence-final predicate. *Sonkeigo* should be used to refer to actions performed by a respected person and also in speaking about the possessions of that respected person. For example:

sensei	*ga*	*watakushi*	*ni*	*o-hanashi ni naru*
teacher	(nominative)	I	(objective)	speak
noun	(case marker)	noun	(case marker)	verb

'A teacher speaks to me'

When a speaker refers to the action of a superior, the verb, sometimes called an exalting verb, is conjugated *o-V-ni-naru*. There are three ways to generate an exalting verb. One is by using the conjugation *o-V-ni-naru*; another is by inflecting the verb by adding the respectful auxiliary *reru* at the end, as in *hanasa-reru*. Particular respectful vocabularies are utilized for frequently used verbs: for example, *irassharu* for 'come' and 'go'; *meshi-agaru* for 'eat'; and *nasaru* for 'do'. *Sonkeigo* includes not only exalting verbs but also respectful prefixes and respectful suffixes such as *sama*, as in *o-isha-sama* (doctor)—all these forms are used by a speaker to express respect to a referent. Various forms are used effectively as the second-person pronoun according to the degree of respect: *anata, omae, kimi, otaku*. *Sonkeigo* is sometimes translated as subject referent honorifics, or subject honorifics, because it is the agent or subject who is respected.

When a speaker refers to actions performed by others or oneself that impinge on the respected person, *kenjōgo* should be used:

watakushi	*ga*	*sensei*	*ni*	*o-hanashi suru*
I	(nominative)	teacher	(objective)	speak
noun	(case marker)	noun	(case marker)	verb

'I speak to a teacher'

The construction *o-Verb-suru*, called a humble verb, should be used. Specific humble vocabularies are utilized for frequently used verbs: for example, *itasu* for 'do'; *mairu* for 'come' and 'go'; and *itadaku* for 'eat' and 'receive'. *Kenjōgo* includes not only humble verbs but also humble prefixes, and humble suffixes like *domo* of *watakushi-domo* 'we'. With *kenjōgo* a speaker expresses his humility to a referent. *Kenjōgo* is sometimes translated as directive referent honorifics, or object honorifics, because the recipient or object of the action is respected through humiliating the actor or subject.

Further categories are indicated by other scholars. *Bikago* 美化語 'beautifying form' is used to decorate a word and, like euphemism in English, is a linguistic device commonly used in order to avoid saying unpleasant or offensive words. For example, *o* is prefixed to a noun *hana* 'flower' like *o-hana* just like 'pass away' is used instead of 'die' in English. When a speaker wants to show regard toward an addressee, he intentionally keeps the speech level polite. In Japanese, the beautifying form is a positive way to show politeness, whilst, in English, euphemisms have negative connotations. As an honorific expression, the prefix *o* has many functions: prefixed to the thing belonging to an addressee, it becomes a respectful prefix; prefixed to the thing belonging to a speaker, it is a humble prefix. But the prefix *o* can be attached to something that belongs to neither of them. For example, a speaker talks to an addressee about a flower that blossoms alongside the road they walk. This flower belongs to neither of them, but the speaker can use *o-hana*, which is a beautifying form. Its function is as an honorific expression that retains the speaker's dignity. Beautifying forms are part of polite forms for, by making an utterance polite, a speaker indirectly shows his regard to an addressee.

Teichōgo 丁重語 'courteous form' is a term coined by Miyaji (1971) that defines 'honorifics in which a speaker shows deference to an addressee through the expression of topics.' In modern honorifics, humble forms such as *zonzu*, *itasu* and *mairu* are never used independently, but always with the polite form *masu* to construct such courteous form as *zonzimasu, itashimasu, mairimasu*. Here I should mention the theory of Motoki Tokieda, which greatly influenced the development of Japanese linguistics. Tokieda believes that language itself is a human behavior and does not exist externally to human beings. He lists three factors that constitute a language: a speaker, an addressee and an expressive content. A speaker conceptualizes external material—or an expressive content—according to the situation, and expresses it to an addressee in accordance with the relationship to the addressee. Tokieda (1941) classifies words into two groups: *shi* 詞, expressed through the process of conceptualization, and *ji* 辞, used to express the speaker's personal idea directly. While he insists that there is a clear demarcation between *shi* and *ji*, more discussion is still needed to resolve the effectiveness of this distinction. According to Tokieda, humble forms such as *zonzu*, *itasu* and *mairu* are classified as *shi*, whilst the polite form *masu* is classified as *ji*. Miyaji classified the honorific expression that contains features of both *shi* and *ji* by a new term: *teichōgo*. There is more to say about the Japanese honorific system, but due to space limitations, I refer readers to the following articles in English: Prideaux (1970), Martin (1964), Mizutani (1989) and Neustupný (1978).

There is a clear difference between *teineigo*, *sonkeigo* and *kenjōgo* from the viewpoint of their functions. That is to say, *teineigo* is an honorific expression whereby a speaker shows respect toward an addressee. In contrast, *sonkeigo* and *kenjōgo* are honorific expressions that show a speaker's respect toward a referent. The honorific expression system can be divided into two: addressee-oriented honorific expressions, which show deference by using polite language out of respect for the person addressed; and referent-oriented honorific expressions, which show deference to the person mentioned or talked about. *Teineigo* is addressee-oriented honorifics, whilst *sonkeigo* and *kenjōgo* are referent-oriented honorifics. In European languages with honorific expressions, these appear only when an addressee and a referent is the same person. In English 'his highness' shows respect to the third person, but it is a *cliché* and its use is very limited. In this sense, the honorific expression of

	Nara (710-794)	Heian (794-1192)	Kamakura (1192-1333)	Muromachi and Edo (1336-1867)	After Meiji (1868-)
sonkeigo	+	+	+	+	+
kenjōgo	+	+	+	+	+
teichōgo	-	+	+	+	+
teineigo	-	±	+	+	+
bikago	-	-	±	+	+

Table 1: the usage of each honorific forms
   + means affirmatively used
   - means negatively used
   ± means slightly used

European languages is an addressee-oriented honorific expression. But in almost all Asian languages, a speaker can show respect not only to an addressee but also to a referent who may not always be the same person as the addressee. It is quite common for Japanese to mention a respectable third person using an honorific expression. In this sense, Japanese has a referent-oriented honorific expression system.

In Table 1, where Miyaji (1981) indicates the usage of each honorific form in each period, we find that Japanese honorifics have moved toward an addressee-orientation. That is, the group of *ji*—courteous, polite and beautifying forms—did not exist in the Nara period, with the polite form developing only since the Heian period. The *shi* group of respectful and humble forms were completed in the Nara period. This signifies that Japanese honorifics started with deference toward the person who was the subject of a topic, and moved towards politeness to an addressee. The process of movement toward addressee-orientation is reflected in the development of lexical features.

In this book, I will focus on a referent-oriented honorific expression system, which is nevertheless tightly interwoven with an addressee-oriented honorific expression system. That is, when a person mentioned belongs to an addressee—for example, the addressee's mother—the speaker needs to bear the addressee in mind. Also, when the person mentioned belongs to a speaker—for example, the speaker's mother—the speaker needs to bear the addressee in mind. In Japanese honorific expression, both speaker and addressee can be a referent, as in *watakushi ga anata-sama no uchi ni mairi masu* 'I shall come to your house'. According to school grammar, the speaker's polite expression toward an addressee is expressed by using *teineigo*, *-masu*, and by the content of the topic *watakushi ga anata-sama no uchi ni mairu*. The topic itself includes both a speaker and an addressee, and the speaker expresses his respect to the addressee as a referent of the topic by using both *kenjōgo* (*watakushi* and *mairu*) and *sonkeigo* (*anata-sama*). But in this book, 'referent' means the third person mentioned, other than a speaker and an addressee.

In this book, there is a clear distinction between honorific form and honorific expression. Honorific form refers to the lexical forms—respectful, humble, polite, beautifying and courteous—whereas honorific expression refers to the pragmatic meaning that is actualized through using honorific forms. As explained in the Style Notes, the same humble form *mairu* has different pragmatic meanings depending upon whether it is used to refer to a subject or an object: for example, *X ga mairu* 'X comes' vs *X ni mairu* '(somebody) comes to X'.

In Japanese, factors such as social hierarchical order, intimacy and the public or private conversational situation between a speaker and a person to be mentioned determine the use of honorific expressions. Numerous factors influence determination of superiority: age, gender, seniority, debt, social position. In traditional Japanese society, elders were respected by the young because experience was valued as offering good life lessons. The man of higher rank in a company had the right to give orders to the man of lower rank; the debtor could not raise his head before a creditor. Seniority, that usually coincides with age, also influences honorific expression within a closed community like a company, school or club. For example, all graduates generally enter a company at the same age and, therefore, the elder by age is senior to the newcomer. But it can happen that a newcomer who moves from another company may be older than senior workers. In such a case, there is a conflict between age and seniority in determining superiority. The most favorable condition for the use of honorific expression is the superiority and non-intimacy of the person mentioned, and a public domain where conversational behavior takes place. When the situation is coincident with these factors, honorific expression is easily determined. That is, the person mentioned is superior and not an intimate of the addresser and the field of conversation is public. But when these factors compete with each other—if a referent is superior but quite intimate—honorific expressions cannot be determined easily and fluctuate according to the addressers and the contexts. The order of importance of these factors differs from one era to another. In the feudal age, when social hierarchy was paramount, honorific expression was determined solely by hierarchical superiority. In contrast, in modern democratic society, intimacy is the main factor that determines honorific expression. In Japanese linguistics, the honorific expression system is determined by a combination of these factors . Compare Minami (1987) and Neustupný (1978) if you would like to study this in more detail.

3. Brief overview of Japanese history and sources used in this study

As early as the third century AD, several powerful kingdoms were present in Japan, but it was not until the seventh century that these regions came under the control of a single powerful group. Their leader was called the *tennō* 天皇 'emperor,' and under his rule a complex centralized administration was established. The *ritsuryō* 律令 'legal codes' employed by the administration were based on the Chinese model, and a large aristocracy grew up around the *tennō* court bureaucracy, which lasted until the twelfth century. During this period, the Japanese language had no writing system. Under the influence of mainland China, in the Nara period (710–794) the imperial court had adopted classical Chinese as its language of literature and learning.

In the Heian period (794–1192) new phonetic *kana* scripts derived from Chinese characters began to be employed for the writing of colloquial Japanese. *The Tale of Genji* 源氏物語, perhaps Japan's most well-known piece of literature, was written in Japanese during the eleventh century. The novel is a collection of tales documenting the life and loves of an imperial prince known as Shining Genji. The work is attributed to an aristocratic woman, and sometimes lady-in-waiting, known only as Murasaki Shikibu 紫式部 (Murasaki, after the commonly used epithet for Genji's principal wife, and Shikibu, which was her father's rank at court). At the time of its writing, fictional 'tale' literature was incredibly popular. *The Tale of Genji* thus includes many instances of reported speech within the narrative, allowing the reader to observe colloquial honorific expressions within their social context (i.e. where the relative status and relationships between the characters are well established).

Under the *ritsuryō* system, all land was owned and managed by the central government. In time, a system of private land-holding was developed, where newly cleared lands were approved as private property. These estates were predominantly owned and maintained by religious orders and the aristocracy, *kuge* 公家. As the warrior caste, originally employed for the protection of these estates, gradually came into power, a feudal system developed. There were two main *samurai* 侍, *buke* 武家,

or *bushi* 武士 allegiances in the twelfth century: the Genji and the Heike clans. While the Heike had originally held political power over the settled lands, after a series of battles, the Genji clan rose to power and established the shogunate system of governance in 1192. Under this system, the shogun, a military ruler from the *samurai* caste, officially held power over the emperor, whose role was thus reduced to a mainly symbolic and spiritual function. *The Tale of the Heike* is an epic narrative describing the changing fortunes and gradual tragic demise of the eponymous clan. It contains numerous instances of dialogue and quoted speech, again providing a useful resource for observing honorific expressions during this time—called the Kamakura period (1192–1333)—when battles raged among the *samurai*, and the common people, *chōnin* 町人, started to unite and develop industries. During the Muromachi period (1336–1573), *kyōgen* 狂言, a form of comic theatre, was born from the peasant class. It was considered public entertainment for the common people, rather than an elitist art form such as the *Noh* 能 theatre. *Kyōgen* scripts thus contain the vernacular language spoken at the time, and they too include useful instances of honorific expressions in their social context.

After the breakdown of the Ashikaga Shogunate in 1537, warring factions spread throughout Japan until in 1590 Hideyoshi 秀吉 was able to establish a new government, under which he attempted to centralize the nation's political and economic power. His rule was succeeded by the Tokugawa 徳川 Shogunate, and the capital was moved to Edo (now Tokyo) in 1603. Hideyoshi had attempted to conquer Korea and the resultant commercial relationship continued well into the Edo Period (1603–1867). During this time, textbooks were produced for the instruction of Korean traders, and their descriptions of how Japanese honorifics should be employed are of immense value. *The Shōkaishingo* 捷解新語 is one such textbook included in this study.

The Edo Period is typically divided into early and late Edo. In the early Edo period, when the land was not yet settled, the language spoken tended to be that of the new settlers from Kyoto, the site of the former capital. In the late Edo period, scholars began to recognize the developing Edo vernacular as the official language of the capital. The Edo period lasted for nearly three hundred years, during which time there was no major conflict, and the economy, arts and culture of the capital flourished. Many people, including a growing merchant class, relocated to the capital. The public entertainment industry burgeoned during this time, giving rise to *jōruri* 浄瑠璃 recitation, a chanted narrative that accompanies *bunraku* 文楽 puppet theatre, and also to *kabuki* 歌舞伎 dance-theatre. Scripts from both these genres provide useful honorific resources. Although both forms of theatre are quite stylized and elite today, at the time of their birth they were in touch with the lives of the common people of Edo. The print-making industry also flourished, producing not only the *ukiyo-e* 浮世絵 wood-block prints so well-known in the West, but countless *sharebon* 洒落本, *kokkeibon* 滑稽本 and *ninjōbon* 人情本 books for popular consumption. These also reflect the vernacular language of the people, and contain examples of honorific use.

Japan closed its door to foreign countries from 1635, and it was not until 1853 that the military might of the United States of America forced its re-opening. At that time the Edo government had lost the power to control unsatisfied local *samurai*, and in 1867 it surrendered its power to the emperor who regained his ruling status. The name of this new era was Meiji 明治 (1868–1912). In the Edo period, all citizens' social status (and therefore their life cycle) had been determined at birth. But from the Meiji period, all people were deemed to be equal and citizens of the country Japan. The Meiji government had essential work to do in order to build a democratic country. Previously, there had been no common Japanese language that was understood by all. In the Edo period, a centralised government had controlled all the territory, but the common people spoke their own dialects; despite a common written language, not all Japanese could read and write. A common standard language was necessary and it had to be a language that all Japanese could speak, understand, read and write. The first twenty years of Meiji was an admixture of the remnants of the Edo period and the birth of democracy. The *kabuki* plays by Mokuami 黙阿弥 show the daily life of the people living in Tokyo during this transition. The Meiji period lasted forty five years; the Taishō period 大正 fifteen years (1912–1926); and the Shōwa period 昭和 sixty five years (1926–1989). In 1941 Japan went to war against the allied powers of America, England,

Holland and China, and was defeated in 1945. After this occurred the biggest change for the society and the language. The inborn hierarchical social order was abolished but there was a big gap between the rich and the poor. Especially in the countryside, a handful of rich farmers occupied almost all of the farms, and a majority of poor farmers were engaged in tenant farming. But after the defeat in the Second World War, the general headquarters of the allied powers liberated the farms and surrendered them to tenant farmers. They also broke up financial combines. The Japanese experienced financial equality. In a hierarchical society, honorifics were important factors for an harmonious social life, but this new society changed the character of the old honorific system. The hierarchical social order was lost, but honorifics could still serve a new function.

We are expected to treat strangers politely, and degree of intimacy has become a new standard for the usage of honorifics. Influenced by Confucianism, Japanese society thinks highly of the order imposed by age whereby precedence is given to older people. This system is applied equally to chronological age and to the length of work experience. For example, a senior worker has precedence to a newcomer in a factory. Nowadays, with technology changing rapidly, a newcomer with recent technological experience takes the leadership role, and old experience is of little value. This tendency has also impacted greatly on the use of honorifics. The existence till the recent past of discrimination based on gender cannot be denied, but since the Equal Employment Opportunity Law was promulgated in 1986, women have had more employment opportunities, and relations between the sexes have changed. This too has affected the use of contemporary honorifics. Almost all Japanese are bilingual, employing both Standard Japanese and their regional dialect, but due to the development of transportation and telecommunication, it is feared that the time will come when regional dialects, together with their honorific systems that differ from that of Standard Japanese, will disappear.

4. Historical changes in the referent honorific expression system

Almost all Japanese researchers agree that the referent honorific expression system has shifted from an absolute honorific expression system to a relative honorific one. According to Tsujimura (1971), who studied the history of Japanese honorifics, 'The shift from an absolute honorific expression system to a relative honorific expression system cannot be neglected in the history of Japanese honorifics'. Let us look at the definition of both these systems, as coined by Kindaichi (1941):

> Honorifics today are different from those of the old days. The referent term for 'father' should change depending on the person to whom a speaker mentions his father: within a family, *otōsama* (*sama* is a respectful suffix), to people outside the family, *chichi* or *guhu* (stupid father). Therefore I name today's honorifics 'relative honorifics'.

In relative honorifics the expression about a referent is controlled by the relationship between referent and addressee. In contrast, Tsujimura (1992a) defines the absolute honorific expression system: 'In ancient times, a fixed expression was used to a specific person regardless of context and addressee. In that sense, it is an absolute system'. Tamagami (1955) also uses the technical term 'absolute honorifics', but his definition differs from the ordinary meaning. He defines absolute honorifics as a referent term which is uniquely to be used towards a certain class of people. In ancient times, the verbs *sōsu* 'tell' and *keisu* 'tell' were used by the common person to describe a deed to the family of the emperor. He called these fixed expressions, which were used only to a certain class of people, 'absolute honorifics'.

Kindaichi (1941) argues that the main historical change in Japanese honorifics was the shift from absolute honorifics to relative honorifics. He further argues that honorifics originated from superstitions and taboos held towards the female gender or the gods, and shifted to absolute honorifics before becoming today's relative honorifics. Not all researchers agree with his hypothesis of the origin of honorifics, but all of them agree that the main shift has been from absolute to relative honorifics.

5. From absolute to relative honorifics

There is no established theory about when absolute honorifics became relative honorifics. Self-respectful expressions used by an emperor can be found in the earliest extant document, *the Manyoshu* 万葉集, which is a collection of poems published during the eighth and twelfth centuries. Kindaichi (1941) states, 'The salient characteristic of absolute honorifics is a self-respectful expression, where the respect form is used in the first person pronoun'. But a lot of the discussion about the existence of self-respectful expressions is unresolved, and Nishida (1995), who denies their existence, argues that self-respectful expressions were found in the *Manyoshu* because of confusion about direct and indirect speech. Even if we accept the existence of self-respectful expressions, there is no established theory about how long they survived.

Nor is there any established theory about when relative honorifics came into being. No one has found that relative honorifics were used in the Nara period, that is, the eighth century, but we have many documents from the Heian period, between the ninth and twelfth centuries. Drawing evidence from the story of *Genji-monogatari*, Ishizaka (1960) argues that relative honorifics were already used in the Heian period. In the novel, a servant refers to her master with the honorific suffix *dono* to an emperor's family, and is ridiculed for that usage. Ishizaka (1960) writes:

> At the time when relative honorifics were commonly used, people were expected to change the honorific expression according to the situation. Therefore, the servant made a mistake and the author used that passage to show the girl's ignorance to readers.

But Morino (1971) argues differently:

> In the Heian period, hierarchical social order is foremost in determining the honorific expression, so only in a private situation like the treatment of a family member might relative honorifics be used. But in general, the characteristics of present-day relative honorifics are quite faint.

He believes that in the Heian period, relative honorifics were not commonly used, though there can be a difference between private and public situations.

Iwabuchi (1937) suggests that absolute honorifics prevailed until modern times, drawing evidence from the *kyogen* play *nushi* 塗師 'the plasterer', in which a plasterer's wife uses honorifics to mention her husband to his master. But, Toyama (1977) writes:

> It is quite hard to find when the honorific system changed from an absolute to a relative one. But, it cannot be supposed that an honorific system shifts all of a sudden at a certain period. Even in the Kamakura period, stretching for a period of about 150 years from 1333, the characteristics of relative honorifics survived; and in the Edo period (1600–1867), those of absolute honorifics still remained. We can reasonably assume that the use of relative honorifics had been growing since the Muromachi period (1392–1573) to the Edo period as a result of the growing complexity of human relationships in these societies.

Nobody has clearly specified how relative honorifics spread after the Edo period. According to Miyaji (1981):

> The honorific system in the Edo period had dual characteristics: one situated in earlier times and based on the hierarchical relation between a ruler and an obedient; and the other situated in modern times and based on a society whose common citizens, living in big cities, began to acquire power. The present honorific system, especially since the Second World War, developed from the latter character.

In conclusion, Miyaji (1981) conjectured that relative honorifics were supported and spread by citizens who lived on commercialism. Yamazaki (1964) argues that regional dialects have only absolute honorifics:

> Historical documents describe only the honorific expression of superiors such as rulers or gods, who were at the center of cultural life at that time. Honorifics that were taught as good manners by these people could not have grown up naturally, but they were mindful to maintain them. Human life has a dual character: a public and a private life. Linguistic behavior also has a dual character: a public and a private language. It is easily supposed that many of the common people could not properly use public language and that honorifics in private life could be different from that of public life.

He reached the opposite conclusion to Miyaji (1981): that relative honorifics were used by rulers, while absolute honorifics were used by the common people, and that relative honorifics eventually displaced absolute honorifics.

To summarize the outcome of contemporary studies, there are no established theories to support the existence of either relative honorifics or absolute honorifics in any period. The biggest problem is that researchers have tried to draw their conclusions only from the documents they studied; they did not have a bird's-eye view across each period. What was lacking was the concept of situation. In modern Japanese, it is quite usual for honorific expressions to vary according to such situations as regional variation, gender, public or private. Modern language can be investigated through interview, but historical language can only be investigated through historical documents. However, it is still possible to conduct research applying the concept of situation. Especially, it is possible to suppose that in past hierarchical societies various honorific expressions co-existed according to social class. And, we cannot ignore regional differences. Though relative honorifics are popular in Standard Japanese, absolute honorifics are still popular in the dialects of eastern Japan. For example, in the Kansai area, people speaking of their father to others in a private situation use the Kansai dialect *Otōsan ite hari masen* 'My father is out' (*san* is an respectful suffix, and *hari* is an respectful auxiliary) But in a public situation they use the Standard Japanese *chichi wa gaishutsu itashite orimasu* (*chichi* is a humble noun, and *itasu* is a humble auxiliary). Absolute honorifics and relative honorifics are switched. The sociolinguistic method seems quite important. There is one more obstacle to solving how absolute honorifics became relative honorifics. Tsujimura (1971) writes:

> The studies on honorifics focused only on lexical features and, therefore, historical studies were also limited within lexicon. But, the big difference between the study of the history of honorifics, and that of syntax and phonology, is that the latter is the history of language, whilst the former cannot be solved within the problem of language. That is, what is more important for the study of the historical change in honorifics is the change in the degree of deference and, more than that, the relationship between honorific expression and the

human relationship among speaker, addressee and the subject of the topic. He insisted on the importance of sociolinguistic method for the study of honorifics, for it is only when a referent is mentioned that we can find whether the honorific system is absolute or relative. The criterion to determine absolute or relative honorifics is how a referent is treated in relation to a speaker and an addressee, and it is necessary to check this dual relation from the viewpoint of both speaker and addressee. That is, factors such as: whether the referent belongs to the speaker's side or to an addressee's side; whether the referent is superior to a speaker; and whether he is superior to an addressee. There has been a good deal of work done about the relation only between a speaker and an addressee, and we can easily find out about the first and second-person pronouns for each period. This is because these questions can be solved only when the unitary relation between a speaker and an addressee is fixed. For this, we can utilize the quantitative method of sociolinguistics.

6. Criteria for honorific expression

There are four possible criteria to determine the honorific expression used toward a referent:

① The social status of a referent from the standpoint of a speaker.

② The social status of a referent from the standpoint of both a speaker and an addressee.

③ Whether a referent is superior or inferior from the standpoints of both a speaker and an addressee.

④ Whether a referent belongs to the in-group of either a speaker or an addressee.

Criterion ① means that the honorific expression toward a referent is determined only by the superiority between a speaker and a referent, and the addressee does not participate in any way. This is termed absolute honorifics by Kindaichi (1941) and is supposed to be a system used in ancient times. Criterion ② means that the honorific expression toward a referent is determined by a referent's status within the society constituted by speaker, addressee and referent. I termed the honorific system functioning in *Genji-monogatari* 'status honorifics'. The term 'status' used here covers not only social status but also hierarchical status like that of owner and worker, and a relationship status like that of father and son. The difference between absolute honorifics and status honorifics is the participation of an addressee. Criterion ③ means that the honorific expression toward a referent is determined not by the relation between a speaker and an addressee, but by the hierarchical order between them. I termed the honorific system functioning in *Heike-monogatari* 'hierarchical honorifics'. It is not easy to draw a line of demarcation between status and hierarchical honorifics, but let us use an example. In *Genji-monogatari*, a father treats his son with a respectful expression when speaking to his vassal, because his son is also a master from the vassal's perspective. His son is treated according to the status between master and vassal. But in *Heike-monogatari*, a father never mentions his son to his vassal using the respectful form, because his son is inferior according to the hierarchical order between father and son. Also, in *Genji-monogatari*, a vassal uses the respectful form when referring to his master to any addressee, but in *Heike-monogatari*, he does not use a respectful form if an addressee is superior to his master. Status honorifics determines the honorific expression for the referent by the status of the referent in relation to both speaker and addressee. On the other hand, hierarchical honorifics determines the honorific expression to be used for the referent according to the hierarchical order in relation to a speaker and an addressee. Criterion ④ is that of the honorifics of modern Standard Japanese, and Kindaichi (1941) named it 'relative honorifics'. In modern Standard Japanese, whether a referent belongs to the in-group of a speaker or an addressee is the most important function. The shift from ① to ④ means the shift from referent-orientation to addressee-orientation. But this does not mean that all the criteria of the preceding period were displaced by that of the following period. For example, in the present time, criterion ④ does not take the place of criterion ③ in any situation. Today also, there are referents who do not belong to either a speaker or an addressee, in which case, present-day honorifics takes criterion ③ into consideration. But when criterion ④ conflicts with criterion ③, the former has priority in general. However, in the very conservative field of the honorific expression of the imperial family just before the Second World War, an empress referred to an emperor to an out-group using the respectful form.

In order to interpret the honorific system, terms like 'status', 'hierarchy', 'relative', and 'absolute' are used. But in most cases, these terms have been used without definition and their meanings differ from one researcher to another—a problem that arose from the digital classification of 'absolute' or 'relative' by Kindaichi (1941). A classification of quasi-absolute and quasi-relative honorifics was proposed by researchers who wanted to include the notion of a gradual transition but admitted the shortcomings of alternative classifications. That is, only two honorific systems, absolute or relative honorifics, are assumed. And it is supposed that if it is not a relative one, it should be an absolute one, or the other way around. What is important here is to make a clear definition of the terms. A new term is needed to interpret the honorific system of Standard Japanese. I have named this: in/out-group honorifics. That is, the honorific expression toward a referent is determined by criterion ④— whether a referent belongs to the in-group of either a speaker or an addressee. In/out-group honorifics make the consideration for an addressee the most important factor. In modern honorifics, a referent that belongs to the in-group of the addresser is not treated with the respectful form even if he is superior to a speaker. He is referred to by a humble form. On the contrary, a referent that belongs to the in-group of the addressee should be treated by a respectful form even if he is inferior to a speaker. For example, the child of an addressee should be treated by a respectful form even if he is much younger than a speaker because the child is part of the addressee's in-group. The use of honorifics toward a referent who does not belong to the in-group of either a speaker or an addressee has been disappearing in recent honorific usage. In my youth, the appropriate form for a referent to be respected was chosen by applying criterion ③. This kind of honorific expression, in which people speak in a refined manner, is named self-oriented honorifics because its principal function is to maintain a speaker's dignity. This use of in/out-group honorifics has been gaining influence recently because the system places consideration for an addressee as the highest the most important factor. I can conclude that 'in-group' functions as the most important factor in modern honorifics. As a result of my research on modern honorifics I have concluded that in/out-group honorifics spread all over Japan with the proliferation of Standard Japanese.

2

REFERENT HONORIFIC EXPRESSION IN GENJI-MONOGATARI

1. Introduction

All researchers indicate that the major historical change in referent honorifics has been the change from absolute to relative honorifics, but it is not clear how and when that change occurred. There has been no established theory about whether the honorific system in *Genji-Monogatari*, which is that used in aristocratic society, is either an absolute or a relative one. Generally, the following theories are believed about the honorific system of the Heian period. From the syntactic point of view, Watanabe (1973) states that it was in a transitional stage from absolute to relative honorifics, because dual honorifics were possible at that time. That is, a referent could be referred to with both the respectful and humble forms at the same time. When an in-group referent performed an action to a much superior person, that referent was mentioned with a combined respectful and humble form like *mausi-tamahu* (*mausu* is the humble form of 'say' and *tamahu* is the respectful auxiliary form). Anybody superior to a speaker should be treated respectfully, using the absolute honorific system, and anybody belonging to the speaker's in-group should be treated humbly, using the relative one. From the point of view of language usage, Morino (1971) states that the relative honorific system was used in private life, but the absolute honorific system was used in public life. Both systems could coexist according to the situation. In this chapter, I investigate quantitatively the honorific system used to mention referents in *Genji-Monogatari*.

Genji-Monogatari is an epic tale written in the Heian period by Murasaki-

Shikibu, an aristocratic lady who worked at the imperial court. The main character is a son of the emperor, Hikaru Genji, and the story centres on the events that occur around Hikaru. The language of *Genji-Monogatari* reflects one that was daily used in court. We cannot forget, however, that it only reflects the honorifics used in the aristocratic strata of society, and that it differs markedly from that used among the common people of the time.

2. Methodology

First of all, we need to classify the honorific expressions, and because a good deal of work has already been done on the meaning of respectful and humble forms, it might be reasonable to utilize these. We can list the words that have a functional load as honorific expressions: verbs that show respect or humility—like *notamahu* 宣ふ, *ohosu* 仰す, *mausu* 申す, which are all variants of the verb *ihu* 言ふ 'say'; auxiliaries that show respect, like *tamahu* 給ふ ; respectful prefixes like *ohm* 御 ; humble suffixes like *tachi* 達 and *domo* 共 ; and respectful suffixes like *dono* 殿. We can classify honorific expressions into five categories:

1. supreme respectful expressions (SRE)

2. ordinary respectful expressions (ORE)

3. *raru* expressions (RARUE)

4. neutral expressions (NE)

5. humble expressions (HE)

In fact, these categories are flexible, because words categorized differently can in fact coexist in the same conversation. For example, the supreme respectful expression *se-tamahu* せ給ふ and the ordinary respectful expression *tamahu* can be used to refer to the same referent and, in this case, I categorize it as a supreme respectful expression because that referent can be qualified as a person deserving a supreme respectful expression. But this does not mean that a referent that is treated by an ordinary respectful expression cannot also be treated by a supreme respectful one. Duplicate uses of honorifics like *meshi-tamahu* (*mesu* is a respectful verb and *tamahu* is a respectful auxiliary) are categorized as supreme respectful expressions. I count *raru* expressions as an independent category because the respectful auxiliary *raru* has a very peculiar feature. It can be combined with humble verbs like *mausa-ru* (*mausu* is the humble form of *ihu* 'say') and is used interchangeably with neutral expressions. *Raru* is used in the following cases: a speaker's superior relative is mentioned to a much superior out-group addressee; an addressee's relatives to an inferior addressee; a speaker's superior out-group to a much superior out-group. The degree of respect is supposed to be low, so I categorize *raru* below ordinary respectful expressions. A humble expression means that the status of a referent is lowered by a speaker, as in X *ga mausu* 'X speaks'. In this case the referent X is never a person to whom a speaker needs to show respect. In most cases X belongs to an in-group, and some researchers believe that a speaker shows his respect to an addressee indirectly by humbling his in-group[1]. These categories are not maintained consistently so, in some cases, a respectful prefix like *go* is used with a neutral verb, and a respectful verb is used without a respectful prefix[2]. I have therefore analyzed utterances in the context of the same speaker talking about the same referent to the same addressee. And when different expressions are used for the same context, I have chosen the most frequently used expression.

Honorific expressions in *Genji-Monogatari* are usually determined by the social status of a referent, who can be positioned in any of the following three relationships: between a speaker and an addressee; between a speaker and a referent; and between an addressee and a referent. These relationships are defined in accordance with relational, hierarchical and social superiority. For example, when a son speaks of his father to a socially superior person, the position of the referent is defined as superior to the speaker in kinship status, but inferior to the addressee in social status. Kinship status excludes relations-in-law. In the matrilineal society common at that time, polygamous marriages were the norm. A man would only visit his wife at night, and their children were raised by the maternal family. The bridegroom was not considered to be a member of the wife's family, yet grandchildren were members of the wife's family[3]. That is to say, children of daughters counted as relatives, but those of sons did not. As for the relationship between man and wife, only the legal wife counted as a relative, whilst those who were not acknowledged by legal marriage were not counted. Children born to the same mother were considered siblings, whilst those sired by the same father but born to different mothers were not. Hierarchical status is the vertical relationship between a master and a servant, but because not all human relationships can be characterised by either a kinship or hierarchical relation, social status should be also considered. The positional hierarchy of government officials is easy to determine, but the social status of others is not so easy to decide. Tamagami (1952) states that honorific expressions toward fictional characters can be dominated by the emotional judgement of an author, so I have decided to judge the social status of the characters by the honorific expressions that they use. The four categories of social status, in descending order, are: imperial family; higher aristocracy; lower aristocracy and others[4]. The imperial family includes emperors, retired emperors, and imperial princes. The aristocracy consists of aristocrats above the third court rank and the lower aristocracy of the fourth or the fifth court rank. Others includes aristocracy below the sixth court rank. If necessary, the imperial family can be subdivided into three categories: emperor and retired emperor; empress and quasi-emperor; and quasi-empress and prince. A minister is sometimes more elevated than other aristocrats so, if necessary, he is given special treatment. As for the ladies at court, their rank before marriage is determined by their status at birth, and by the social status of their husbands after their marriage. It can be seen, then, that kinship status and social status are intertwined and quite complicated. I therefore make use of much of the work that has been done on the ranking of social hierarchy (cf. Watanabe, 1974; Watanabe, 1978; and Akita, 1976) and subdivide social status as follows:

1. emperor, retired emperor and prince who is to succeed emperor
2. empress and quasi-emperor
3. quasi-empress and prince who is not to succeed emperor
4. minister
5. aristocracy above the third court rank
6. aristocracy of the fourth or the fifth court rank
7. aristocracy below the sixth court rank; servant and upper servant
8. lower servant

I analyze the linguistic aspects of honorific expressions toward referents by combining social and hierarchical relationships, such as between a speaker and an addressee; between a speaker and a referent; and between an addressee and a referent. I select only conversational parts, because in the narrative parts the social factor is fixed between only a narrator and a referent. In conversational parts there is no space for a narrator's viewpoint and, consequently, these parts reflect the linguistic usage that was activated by the social relationships of the period.

Genji-Monogatari is supposedly a story that is narrated by a gentlewoman[5] to her mistress. The narrator is acutely aware of social rank and assumes that the reader is, too. Most women did not use their personal names, but were instead named according to the government organ or post associated with a male relative. Because it was quite abrupt to call a nobleman by his name, men were known by their government organ or post. If a man was promoted, he would be re-named according to his new post; it is also possible that the same post name might refer to different men at different times. For example, Tō no Chūjō is the title of a main character who is subsequently promoted to general and, finally, to minister. Another man succeeds him and is named Tō no Chūjō. *Genji-Monogatari* depicts the story of two generations of characters that are promoted and change their names, therefore, it can be quite confusing trying to remember all the human networks among the characters throughout the volumes. In Japanese texts, there is a genealogy of the characters that appears in each volume either at the beginning or the end of the book. Here I use the naming of principal characters as listed in the introduction of the popular English translation by Seidensticker (1977), and the glossary of offices and titles listed in an appendix by Tyler (2001). The original text is *Aobyōshi-hon*. I use Ikeda (1954) as a text[6] and when I quote an example, I show the name of its volume and its page. At the beginning of each example, I list a speaker and an addressee as: (speaker→addressee). Words that are loaded with honorific value are in italics and the honorific value is shown in brackets by the abbreviations listed in the style notes. As for verbs, I write: *notamahu* 'say (ORV)'; this means that *notamahu* is the ordinary respectful verb meaning 'say'. I use Seidensticker (1977) for the translation and list its page at the end.

3. Analysis

The numbers in tables show the frequencies of not token but type. That is to say, even when someone speaks of the same referent to the same addressee by using more than one utterance, it is counted once. But when either a speaker, an addressee or a referent changes their social status, it counts as a different situation; consequently, expressions are analyzed according to each situation. Relations between addressees and referents are shown on a horizontal level in accordance with kinship, hierarchical and social status; and on a vertical column in accordance with superiority. For example, Table 1 shows honorific expressions for referents that are inferior by kinship status. The number in the cell that crosses 'kinship status' and 'superior' indicates the frequency of the use of honorific expressions towards referents when addressing a superior to the referent. A concrete example is when a speaker's kinship inferior (eg, a son) is mentioned to an addressee who is superior to that referent; or, to be more concrete, it shows how children are treated between fathers and mothers. Hierarchical status is the relationship to a servant, and social status is the relationship to an addressee who is not connected by either kinship or hierarchical status. The number in each cell indicates both the frequency and percentage of respectful expressions used. Supreme respectful expressions, ordinary respectful expressions and *raru* expressions are all counted as respectful expressions, but neither neutral nor humble expressions are counted as respectful expressions. In 33 out of 48 cases (68.8%) parents refer to their children using a respectful expression.

3.1 Kinship relationship

3.1.1 about the inferior by kinship relationship (Table 1)

	kinship	hierarchical	social
superior	33/48(68.8)	0/0	5/24(20.8)
equal	2/3(66.7)	0/0	8/16(50.0)
inferior	5/7(71.4)	13/13(100.0)	21/25(84.0)

Table 1   respectful expression to kinship inferior

Table 1 shows how a speaker treats a referent that is inferior by kinship, for example: father to son, or grandfather to granddaughter.

1. Tō no Chūjō→his wife
上につと侍はせ給ひて夜昼おはします（少女、3.65)[7]
uhe ni tuto saburaha *setamahi* 'SRA' te, yoru hiru *ohasimasu* 'be (SRV)'
'She (=Kokiden Consort[8]) is with the emperor constantly in spite of everything.'
(The Maiden, 372)

2. Tō no Chūjō→Consort (=his daughter)
かの人参らせむ（常夏、3.204)
kano hito *mawira* 'come (HVN)' se m
'I will make you a gift of her (=Ōmi no kimi, my daughter of humble birth).'
(Wild Carnations, 448)

In example 1 Tō no Chūjō is speaking about his daughter to his wife and uses the supreme respectful expressions *se-tamahu* and *ohasu*, but in example 2[9] he addresses his daughter and refers to her half-sister using the expression *mawiru*, meaning an inferior actor comes to visit a superior. Why does the speaker refer to his daughters using different expressions? Let us look at the factors that determine the honorific expression by checking the relationship between an addressee and a referent, itemizing the rules of honorific usage one by one.

①The inferior by kinship relationship is treated with a respectful expression when speaking to one's servant.

This is always the case when an addressee is inferior by hierarchical relationship. For example, the following two speakers refer to their daughters using respectful expressions.

3. Tō no Chūjō→wet nurse
若き人とはいひながら、心幼くものし給ひけるを知らで、いとかく人なみなみにと思ひける、われこそまさりてはかなかりけれ（少女、3.60)
wakaki hito to ha ihi nagara, kokoro-osanaku monosi *tamahi* 'ORA' keru wo sira-de, ito kaku hitonami-nami ni to omohi keru, ware koso masari te hakanakari kere.
'Kumoinokari (=my daughter) is still very young and innocent; but I fear that

in my own innocence, making my own plans for her, I failed to recognize the degree of her innocence.' (The Maiden, 370)

4. Ichizjō Haven[10]→servant

何の用意もなく、軽らかに、人に見え給ひけむこそ、いといみじけれ（夕霧、5.36)

nani no youi mo naku, karuraka ni, hito ni miye *tamahi* 'ORA' kem koso, ito imizikere

'But she (=the Second Princes, my daughter) let him (=Yūgiri) see her, nothing alters that horrid fact' (Evining Mist, 685)

②The inferior by kinship relationship is treated with a respectful expression within an imperial family.

There are 48 instances of this, of which 33 are treated by respectful expressions. That is, all eight examples of empresses, one example of an emperor and five examples of princes, and four out of five examples of princesses. We notice that because of their high social status, members of an imperial family are treated with respectful expressions even from a superior by kinship relation.

③Within the families of ministers and the aristocracy, daughters are treated with respectful expressions.

In aristocratic families, sons like Yūgiri and Kashiwagi are treated by respectful expressions only in two out of fifteen examples, whereas daughters like the Akashi Empress and Kumoinokari are addressed respectfully in nine out of twelve examples. This big difference between the treatment of sons and daughters might reflect the matrilineal trend of those days[11]. But it still depends on the social status of the daughters, as we saw in examples 1 and 2.

④It is common for the families of ministers and the aristocracy to treat their inferior by kinship relations with respectful expressions to an out-group, but when an addressee is high in social status (like the imperial family) respectful expressions are not used.

Let us look at the following cases where an out-group person is the addressee.

5. Suzaku Emperor→Reizei Emperor

三の宮なむ、いはけなき齢にて、ただ一人をたのもしきものとならひて、

うち棄ててむ後の世に、さすらへむこと、いといとうしろめたく悲しく侍る（若菜上、4.17,18）

sam-no-miya nam, ihakenaki yohahi ni te, tada hitori wo tanomosiki mono to narahi te, uti-sute te m noti no yo ni, sasurahe m koto, ito ito usirometaku kanasiku haberu

'The Third Princess—it is she I worry about. She is very young and she has been completely dependent on me. And now I am abandoning her. What will happen to the poor child?' (New Herbs: Part One, 538)

6. Suzaku Emperor→Genji

かくなむ進み宣ふを、今は限のさまならば、片時の程にても、その助あるべきさまにてとなむ、思ひ給ふる（柏木、4.236）

kaku nam susumi *notamahu* 'say (SRV)' wo, ima ha kagiri no sama nara ba, kata-toki no hodo ni te mo, sono tasuke aru beki sama ni te to nam omohi tamahuru

'But she (=San-no-Miya[12], my daughter) really does seem to mean it. If this is indeed her last hour, we would certainly not want to deny her the support and comfort of religion, however briefly.' (The Oak Tree, 642)

The referent is the same person, but in example 5 a neutral expression is used, whilst in example 6 a respectful expression is used; the only difference being the addressee. In example 5 the addressee is a son of the speaker, and a present emperor; in example 6 the addressee is a brother-in-law and a subject of the speaker. It is therefore the social status of the addressee that determines the honorific expression toward an inferior by kinship relation. To the addressee who is inferior by social status, respectful expressions are used as follows:

7. Akashi Empress→Kaoru

宮は出で給ひぬなり。あさましくいとほしき御様かな。いかに人見奉るらむ。（総角、6.59）

miya ha ide *tamahi* 'ORA' nu nari. asamashiku itohosiki *ohom* 'RP'-sama kana. ikani hito mi *tatematuru* 'HAO' ram

'So he (=Prince Niou) has run off again. I cannot understand him. Has he no notion of what people will be thinking? (Trefoil Knots, 845)

Tatematuru is a humble auxiliary to show either an actor's or a speaker's humility toward a patient. In this sentence, the patient is Prince Niou.

8. wife of the Lord Inspector (=mother of Kiritsubo Intimate[13])→Myōbu[14]

人げなき恥をかくしつつ、交ひ給ふめりつるを（桐壺、1.169）

hito-ge-naki hadi wo kakushi tutu, mazirahi *tamahu* 'ORA' meri turu wo

'She (=Kiritsubo Intimate) was the object of insults such as no one can be asked to endure'. (The Paulownia Court, 9)

In example 7 the referent is the speaker's son, but the addressee is the subject of the referent; and in example 8 the referent is the speaker's daughter, but the addressee is inferior to the referent[15]. To an addressee who is superior to a referent, a neutral expression is used as follows:

9. Kiritsubo Emperor→Suzaku Emperor

必ず世の中たもつべき相ある人なり。さるによりてわづらはしさに、親王にもなさず、ただ人にて、おほやけの御後見をせさせむ、と思ひ給へしなり。（賢木、2.73, 74）

kanarazu yononaka tamotu beki sau aru hito nari. saru ni yori te wadurahasisa ni, miko ni mo nasa zu, tadaudo ni te, ohoyake no ohm-usiromi wo se sasem m to, omohi tamahe si nari.

'There is no office of which he (=Genji) need feel unworthy and no task in all the land that is beyond his powers. I reduced him to common rank so that you might make full use of his services.' (The Sacred Tree, 190)

There are five examples where respectful expressions are used to a superior addressee, and in four of them the referents are daughters, and in three examples their respectful expressions are limited to *raru* expressions. We can see that when a speaker treats his inferior by kinship relation to a superior addressee, respectful expressions—when used—are confined to the lower level. In Table 1, in six out of eight respectful examples to an addressee of the same social status, the referents are daughters, but out of 21 respectful examples, daughters are referents only in eleven cases. We can see the frequency of respectful expressions used to out-group addressees in accordance with the social status of the referent: for the imperial family, 22 out of 24 examples (91.7%); for the upper aristocracy, 23 out of 25 examples (92.07%); for the lower aristocracy, three out of 21 examples (14.3%); and for other social classes, four out of fourteen examples (28.6%). Notice that a referent of a high social status is treated with a respectful expression even to an out-group addressee.

⑤When an addressee is of the same social status, a speaker uses a respectful expression towards the addressee's kin.

Concern for the addressee can be a factor in determining honorific expression when an addressee is of the same social status as a speaker. Let us look at the following examples. Genji holds a conjugal relationship with the family of the Minister of the Left. Yūgiri is Genji's son; Aoi, Genji's wife, is a daughter of the Minister of the Left; Tō no Chūjō is his son, and Ōmiya is the mother of Aoi. When she speaks to her son-in-law Genji, Ōmiya refers to Yūgiri, her grandson, with a respectful expression:

10. Princess Ōmiya→Genji

この中将の、いとあはれに怪しきまで思ひ扱ひ、心をさわがい給ふ、見侍るになむ（行幸、3.242）

kono tyuuzyau[16] no, ito ahare ni ayasiki made omohi atukahi, kokoro wo sawagai *tamahu* 'ORA', mi haberu ni nam

'Yūgiri has been the exception. He is wonderfully kind and attentive.' (The Royal Outing, 471)

To his servant, Genji refers to his brother-in-law Tō no Chūjō with a neutral expression in example 11 and with the *raru* expression in example 12, even after Tō no Chūjō's promotion to Minister:

11. Genji→female servant

幼き人惑わしたりと、中将の憂へしは、さる人や（夕顔、1.281）

wosanaki hito madohasi tari to, tyuuzyau no urehe si ha, saru hito ya

'He (=Captain, Tō no Chūjō) once told me of a lost child. Was there such a one?' (Evening Faces, 79)

12. Genji→female servant

父大臣には何か知られむ。いとあまたもて騒がるめるが（玉鬘、3.118）

titi-otodo ni ha, nani ka sira re m. ito amata mote-sawaga *ru* 'RARU' meru ga

'Why should we tell her father? His house swarms with children.' (The Jeweled

Chaplet, 402)

But Genji uses a respectful expression when talking about Tō no Chūjō to his mother Ōmiya:

> 13. Genji→Ōmiya
>
> 内の大臣は、日隔てず参り給ふことしげからむを、かかるついでに対面のあらば、いかにうれしからむ（行幸、3.243）
>
> uti-no-otodo ha, hi hedate zu mawiri *tamahu* 'ORA' koto sigekara m wo, kakaru tuide ni taimen no ara ba, ikani uresikara m.
>
> 'I suppose your son comes to see you every day. It would please me enormously if he were to come today.' (The Royal Outing, 472)

That is to say, an addressee's son is treated with a respectful expression, but when speaking of one's own son the neutral or *raru* expression is used:

> 14. Ōmiya→Genji
>
> 公事のしげきにや、私の志の深からぬにや、さしもとぶらひものし侍らず（行幸、3.243）
>
> ohoyake-goto no sigeki ni ya, watakusi no kokorozasi no hukakara nu ni ya, sasimo toburahi monosi habera zu
>
> 'I do not see a great deal of him (=Tō nō Chūjō), I fear, perhaps because he does not have an overwhelming sense of filial duty.' (The Royal Outing, 472)
>
> 15. Ōmiya→Genji
>
> この大将なども、「あまりひき違へたる御事なり」と、かたぶき侍るめるを（少女、3.45）
>
> kono daisiyau nado mo, amari hiki-tagahe taru ohom-koto nari to, katabuki haberu meru wo
>
> 'My sons (=Tō no Chūjō and other sons) have said that you are being very strict with him (=Yūgiri)' (The Maidens, 362)
>
> 16. Ōmiya→Genji
>
> かしこには様々にかかる名のりする人を、厭ふ事なくひろひ集めらるるに、いかなる心にて、かくひき違へかこち聞えらるらむ（行幸、3.245）
>
> kasiko ni ha, sama-zama ni kakaru nanori suru hito wo, itohu koto naku hirohi atumera *ruru* 'RARU' ni, ikanaru kokoro ni te, kaku hiki-tagahe kakoti kikoye

raru ram

'I know that he (=Tō no Chūjō) has been rather indiscriminately collecting children who have claimed to be his. It is astonishing that this one (=Tamakazura) went to the wrong father (=Genji).' (The Royal Outing, 473)

17. Genji→Ōmiya

いとおよずけてもうらみ侍るななりな。いとはかなしや、この人の程よ。（少女、3.45）

ito oyozuketemo urami haberu na nari na. ito hakanasi ya, kono hito no hodo yo

'He (=Yūgiri) is very grown-up for his age.' (The Maiden, 362)

These examples show that to an addressee of the same social status, a speaker controls the use of honorific expressions when referring to his own children but uses respectful expressions when referring to the addressee's children.

⑥Honorific expression changes in accordance with the change in a referent's social position.

A speaker modifies the honorific expression toward a referent when the referent's social position changes:

18. Akashi Novice[17]→Genji

女の童のいときなう侍りしより（明石、2.181）

me-no-waraha no itokinau haberi si yori

'Since she (=Akashi Lady) was very young' (Akashi, 256)

19. Nun of Akashi→Genji

荒磯かげに心苦しう思ひ聞えさせ侍りし二葉の松も、今はたのもしき御生先とはいはひ聞えさするを（松風、2.293）

ara-iso-kage ni kokoro-gurusiu omohi *kikoye* 'HAO' sase haberi si hutaba no matu mo, ima ha tanomosiki ohom-ohisaki to ihahi *kikoye* 'HAO' sasuru wo

'I worried about the seedling pine (=Akashi Lady) on those unfriendly coasts. Its prospects have improved enormously, and yet I am afraid.' (The Wind in the Pines, 325)

In example 18, the speaker refers to his daughter by a neutral expression because his social position is inferior to the addressee, Genji. But in example 19, after the same referent, the Akashi Lady, has become Genji's lover, her mother refers to her using a respectful expression. The humble auxiliary *kikoye* is used by the mother to lower herself and elevate her daughter. That is, one's public social standing is more important in determining honorific expression than the private kinship relationship. In this case, the speaker, a former Governor of Akashi, treats the Akashi Lady as his daughter in example 18, but once his daughter becomes Genji's lover, he and his wife treat her as the lover of the addressee, who belongs to a much higher social class. Further examples illustrate this:

20. Akashi Novice→Akashi Lady

なかなか身の程をとざまかうざまに悲しう歎き侍りつれど、若君のかうい出おはしましたる御宿世のたのもしさに（松風、2.288）

naka-naka mi no hodo wo tozama-kauzama ni kanasiu nageki haberi ture do, waka-gimi no kau ide *ohasimasi* 'SRA' taru *ohom* 'RP'-sukuse no tanomosisa ni

'(Then came that happy and unexpected event,) which had the perverse effect of emphasizing our low place in life. Determined to believe in the bond of which our little one here is evidence' (The Wind in the Pines, 321)

21. Akashi Novice→nun of Akashi

桐壺の更衣の御腹の、源氏の光君こそ、公の御かしこまりにて、須磨の浦にものし給ふなれ。あこの御宿世にて、覚えぬ事のあるなり（須磨、2.156）

kiritubo-no-kaui no ohom-hara no, genzi-no-hikarukimi koso, ohoyake no ohom-kasikomari ni te, suma no ura ni monosi tamahu nare. akono *ohom* 'RP'-sukuse ni te, oboye nu koto no aru nari

'I hear that the shining Genji is out of favor, and that he has come to Suma. What a rare stroke of luck—the chance we have been waiting for. '(Suma, 242)

22. Genji→ Akashi Empress

若君はおどろき給へりや（若菜上、4.98）

waka-miya ha odoroki *tamahe* 'ORA' ri ya

'And is he (=son of the Akashi Empress and the present prince) awake?' (New Herbs: Part One, 577)

All of these examples show a referent who is an inferior by kinship relation being treated with respectful expressions because of his social position. In example 20, a father talks to his daughter about his granddaughter; in example 21, a husband talks to his wife about their daughter; and in example 22, a father talks to his daughter about his grandson. Each referent is inferior by kinship, but either marries a person of high social rank or is born into a high social class[18].

3.1.2 about wives (Table 2)

	kinship	hierarchical	social
superior	4/4(100.0)	0/0	0/2(0.0)
equal	0/0	0/0	0/3(0.0)
inferior	2/2(100.0)	3/3(100.0)	9/11(81.8)

Table 2   respectful expression to a wife

Here we focus on the legal wife, because the marriage system in those times was matrilineal and very different from that of today.

⑦A husband treats his wife in accordance with her social status.

There are four examples in Table 2 of the superior by kinship relationship, where a husband refers to his wife when speaking to her family:

23. Kaoru→Akashi Empress

この里にものし給ふ皇女の、雲の上離れて、思ひ屈し給へるこそいとほしう見給ふれ（蜻蛉、7.133）

kono sato ni monosi *tamahu* 'ORA' *mi* 'RP'-ko no, kumo no uhe hanare te, omohi-kut'-si *tamahe* 'ORA' ru koso, itohosiu mi tamahure

'My princess at Sanjō (=Miko, the Second Princess) is rather despondent at having, as they say, descended from the clouds. I feel very sorry for her.'(The Drake Fly, 1033)

24. Genji→Suzaku Emperor

わづらひ給ふ御さま、ことなる御悩にも侍らず。ただ月頃弱り給へる御有様に、はかばかしう物なども参らぬつもりにや、かくものし給ふこそ（柏木、4.235）

wadurahi *tamahu* 'ORA' *ohom* 'RP'-sama, koto naru *ohom* 'RP' -nayami ni mo habera zu. tada tuki-goro yowari *tamahe* 'ORA' ru *mi* 'RP' -arisama ni, haka-bakasiu mono nado mo *mawira* 'eat (ORV)' nu tumori ni ya, kaku monosi *tamahu* 'ORA' ni koso

'I do not think it is anything serious, but for the last month and more she (=the Third Princess, Suzaku's daughter and Genji's wife) has been weak and has eaten very little.' (The Oak Tree, 642)

In these two examples, the referents are treated not according to their relationship as wives but according to their social positions as part of the imperial family.

Let us now look at how the same speaker talks of his wives to the same addressee:

25. Genji→Kashiwagi

重き病者のにはかにとぢめつるさまなりつるを（若菜下、4.186）

omoki byauzya no nihaka ni todime turu sama nari turu wo

'She (=Murasaki) was dangerously ill. This morning quite suddenly it appeared that she had breathed her last.' (New Herbs: Part Two, 620)

26. Genji→Kashiwagi

ここにものし給ふ御子の、法事仕うまつり給ふべくありしを（若菜下、4.214）

koko ni monosi *tamahu* 'ORA' *mi* 'RP'-ko no, hohuzi tukau-maturi *tamahu* 'ORA' beku ari si wo,

'Our princess (=the Third Princess) here has all along thought of doing something in honor of her father (=Suzaku Emperor)' (New Herbs: Part Two, 631)

Genji uses a neutral expression for Murasaki, but the Third Princess is referred to with the respectful expression *mi*-ko 'child of the emperor' because she is a daughter of the Suzaku Emperor.

Notice next how the honorific expression to the same referent, Murasaki, changes depending on the addressee:

27. Genji→Yūgiri

かの志しおかれたる極楽の曼陀羅など、この度なむ供養ずべき（幻、5.125）

ka no kokorozasi oka *re* 'RARU' taru gokuraku no mandara nado, kono-tabi nam kuyau-zu beki

'This is the time, I think, to dedicate the Paradise Mandala she (=Murasaki) had done' (The Wizard, 730)

28. Genji→Akashi Lady

ただこの御有様を、うち添ひてもえ見奉らぬおぼつかなさに、ゆづり聞えらるるなめり（若菜上、4.103）

tada kono ohom-arisama wo, uti-sohi te mo e mi tatematura nu obotukanasa ni, yuduri kikoye *raruru* 'RARU' na' meri

'She (=Murasaki) has wanted to have someone with the girl (=Akashi Empress, your daughter), and that is all.' (New Herbs: Part One, 579)

To Yūgiri and the Akashi Lady, Murasaki is treated with the *raru* expression, while to the servant, she is treated with the following respectful expression:

29. Genji→female servant

上も、年経ぬるどちうちとけ過ぎば、はたむつかり給はむ、とや（玉鬘、3.117）

uhe 'RN' mo, tosi he nuru doti utitoke sugi, hata, mutukari *tamaha* 'ORA' m to ya!

'Even we oldsters must be careful. There is jealousy abroad (= Murasaki).' (The Jeweled Chaplet, 401)

But to the Third Princess, Murasaki is treated with the humble expression *kikoye sasu*[19]:

30. Genji→the Third Princess

夕つ方、かの対に侍る人の、淑景舎に対面せむとて出でたつそのついでに、近づき聞えさせまほしげにものすめるを、ゆるしてかたらひ給へ（若菜上、4.69）

yuhutukata, kano tai ni haberu hito no, sigeisha ni taimen se m tote ide-tatu sono tuide ni, tikaduki *kikoye sase* 'HAN' mahosige ni monosu meru wo, yurusi te katarahi tamahe

'The lady in the east wing (=Murasaki) will be going to see the lady who has just come from court (=Akashi Empress), and she has said that she thinks it a good

3.1.3 about husbands (Table 3)

	kinship	hierarchical	social
superior	0/0	0/0	0/0
equal	0/0	0/0	0/0
inferior	6/6(100.0)	3/4(75.0)	4/4(100.0)

Table 3   respectful expression to a husband

⑧Within a family, a wife uses a respectful expression when speaking of her husband.

All the examples in this book are of a wife speaking of her husband to her children:

31. Ōmiya→Tō no Chūjō

故大臣の思ひ給ひて、女御の御事をも、ゐたちいそぎ給ひしものを、おはせましかば、かくもてひがむる事もなからまし（少女、3.54）

ko-otodo no omohi *tamahi* 'ORA' te, nyogo no ohom-koto wo mo, wi-tati isogi *tamahi* 'ORA' si mono wo, *ohase* 'be alive (ORV)' masika ba, kaku mote higamuru koto mo nakara masi

'Your father (=the late Minister) was all wrapped up in his plans to send your little girl to court, and he thought it extremely unlikely that an empress would be named from any house but ours. It is an injustice which would not have been permitted if he had lived.' (The Maidens, 367)

⑨To a servant, a wife uses a respectful expression when speaking of her husband.

32. Murasaki→female servant

御心にかなひて、今めかしくすぐれたる際にもあらずと、目なれてさうざうしく思したりつるに（若菜上、4.53）

mi 'RP'-kokoro ni kanahi te, imamekasiku sugure taru kiha ni mo ara zu to, me-nare te sau-zausiku *obosi* 'think (ORV)' tari turu ni

'We have had a full house, but I sometimes think he (=Genji) has been a little bored with us, poor man. None of us is grand enough to be really interesting.' (New Herbs: Part One, 555)

33. The Third Princess→a female servant

見し程に入り給ひしかば（若菜下、4.195）

mi si hodo ni iri *tamahi* 'ORA' sika ba

'He (=Genji) came in on me while I was reading it.' (New Herbs: Part Two, 624)

There is one example of a wife using the neutral expression when talking to a wet nurse, but this happens because the wife is angry with her husband[20], and it can be considered an exception.

34. Wife of the Governor of Hitachi→female servant

守のかくおもだたしきことに思ひて、受け取り騒ぐめれば（東屋、6.248）

kami no kaku omodatasiki koto ni omohi te, uketori sawagu mere ba

'Just listen to them (=the Governor) if you will—as if it were the greatest honor in the world.' (The Eastern Cottage, 943)

There are only four examples that show how a wife treats her husband to a member of an out-group:

35. Wife of the Lord Inspector (=mother of Kiritsubo Intimate) →myōbu

故大納言臨終となるまで、ただ「……」と、かへすがへすいさめ置かれ侍りしかば（桐壺、1.168）

ko-dainagon imaha to naru made, tada '…' to, kahesu-gahesu isame-oka *re* 'RARU' haberi sika ba

'Until he (=the late Grand Counselor, the Lord Inspector) died her father did not let me forget that …' (The Paulownia Court, 9)

In this case she mentions him to a messenger of the Kiritsubo Emperor by using the *raru* expression, but there is no case where she addresses someone who is superior to her husband.

3.1.4 about the superior by kinship relationship (Table 4)

Table 4 clearly shows that a speaker uses a respectful expression to refer to a kin superior when speaking to any addressee who is inferior to the referent either by

	kinship	hierarchical	social
superior	2/3(66.7)	0/5(0.0)	5/16(31.3)
equal	3/3(100.0)	0/0	13/13(100.0)
inferior	30/30(100.0)	7/7(100.0)	37/37(100.0)

Table 4　respectful expression to kinship superior

kinship, hierarchy or social status.

⑩Within a family, a superior by kinship relationship is treated with a respectful expression.

Within the imperial family, a father is treated with a respectful expression:

36. Suzaku Emperor→Genji

春宮をば今の皇子になしてなど、宣はせ置きしかば（賢木、2.95）

touguu wo ba ima no miko ni nasi te nado, *notamahase* 'say (SRV)'-oki sika ba

'Father (=Kiritsubo Emperor) did worry a great deal about the crown prince (=Reizei Emperor). Indeed one of his last requests was that I adopt him as my own son.' (The Sacred Tree, 203)

37. Genji→ Prince Hotaru (=brother of Genji)

いはけなき程より、学問に心を入れて侍りしに、すこしも才などつきぬべくや御覧じけむ。院の宣はせしやう（絵合、2.278）

ihakenaki hodo yori, gakumon ni kokoro wo ire te haberi si ni, sukosi mo zae nado tuki nu beku ya *go-ran-zi* 'find (SRV)' kem. win no *notamaha* se 'say (SRV)' si yau

'I worked very hard at my Chinese studies when I was a boy, so hard that Father (=Kiritsubo) seemed to fear I might become a scholar. He said, …' (A Picture Contest, 315)

And within aristocratic families also, fathers are treated with respectful expressions:

38. Kashiwagi→Tamakazura

なにがしを選びて奉り給へるは、人伝ならぬ御消息にこそ侍らめ（藤袴、3.272）

nanigasira wo erabi te tatematuri *tamahe* 'ORA' ru ha, hitodute nara nu *ohom* 'RP'-seusoko ni koso habera me

'I rather think that Father (=Tō no Chūjō) expected the message to go directly to my sister and not to travel these impossible distances. Why otherwise would he have chosen me for his messenger?' (Purple Trousers, 487)

⑪ To a servant, a superior by kinship relation is treated with a respectful expression.

A child addressing a servant treats a parent respectfully:

39. Princess Ochiba → her servant

自ら聞え給はざめるかたはらいたさに、代り侍るべきを、いと恐しきまでものし給ふめりしを（夕霧、5.21）

midukara kikoye *tamaha* 'ORA' za meru katahara itasa ni, kahari haberu beki wo, ito osorosiki made monosi *tamahu* 'ORA' meri si wo

'I am very sorry indeed that she (=Ichijō Lady, my mother) seems too ill to answer your kind inquiry in the way that it deserves. I shall try to answer for her. Whatever spirit it is that has taken possession of her, it seems to be of an unusually baneful sort' (Evening Mist, 678)

⑫ Even to members of an out-group, imperial and aristocratic families refer to their superior by kinship relations using respectful expressions.

When addressing members of an out-group, a referent that is superior to the addressee by social status is treated with a respectful expression:

40. Genji → the governor[21] of Kii

上にも聞こし召しおきて、「宮仕に出し立てむと漏らし奏せし、いかになりけむ」と、いつぞやも宣はせし（帚木、1.216）

uhe 'RN' ni mo *kikosimesi* 'hear (SRV)'-oki te, 'miyadukahe ni idasi-tate m to morasi souse si, ika ni nari ni kem' to, ituzoya mo *notamahase* 'say (SRV)' si

'My father (=Kiritsubo Emperor) had thought of inviting her (=Utsusemi) to court. He was asking just the other day what might have happened to her.' (The Broom Tree, 41)

41. Ōigimi and Nakanokimi[22] → the monk of Uji

亡き人になり給へらむ御様容貌をだに、今一度見奉らむ（椎本、5.264）

naki hito ni nari *tamahe* 'ORA' ra m *ohom* 'RP'-sama katati wo dani, ima hito-tabi mi *tatematura* 'HAO' m

'They (=Ōigimi and Nakanokimi) would like to see their father (=the Eighth Prince) again, even in death.' (Beneath the Oak, 808)

There are, however, variations between respectful and neutral expressions when an addressee is superior to a referent:

42. Kōbai→Genji

この春の頃ほひ、夢語りし給ひけるを、ほの聞き伝へ侍りける女の、われなむかこつべきことある、と、名のり出で侍りけるを、中将の朝臣なむ聞きつけて、まことに、さやうに触ればひぬべきしるしやある、と尋ねとぶらひ侍りける（常夏、3.191）

kono haru no korohohi, yume-gatari si *tamahi* 'ORA' keru wo, hono-kiki-tutahe haberi keru womna no, ware nam kakotu beki koto aru, to, nanori-ide haberi keru wo, tyuuzyau-no-asom[23] nam kiki-tuke te, makoto ni sayau ni hure-bahi nu beki sirusi ya aru to, tadune toburahi haberi keru

'There was a woman, it is true, who got wind of a dream Father (=Tō no Chūjō) had this Spring and made it known that she had certain relevant matters to bring to his attention. My brother Kashiwagi went to see her and asked what evidence she had to support her claims.' (Wild Carnations, 442)

Kōbai uses the respectful expression *tamahu* when speaking of his father, Tō no Chūjō, but for his brother adopts a neutral expression. And in the following, Tō no Chūjō's son uses the *raru* expression *mausaru*[24] for his father:

43. Kashiwagi→Genji

致仕の大臣思ひおよび申されしを、「……」と、もよほし申さるることの侍りしかば（若菜下、4.214-215）

tizi-no-otodo omohi oyobi *mausa re* 'say (RARU)' si wo, '...' to, moyohosi *mausa ruru* 'say (RARU)' koto no haberi sika ba

'Father (=the retired Minister, Tō no Chūjō) says, ... , he says,' (New Herbs: Part Two, 632)

Genji uses *tamahu* to speak of Tō no Chūjō to Tō no Chūjō's children, and they refer to their father by *tamahu* or *raru* to Genji. It is reasonable to think that they treat Tō no Chūjō with a respectful expression not because he is a superior by kinship relation but because he is a minister. Given that the addressee, Genji, is superior to their father, the less respectful expression *raru* is used. Let us look at all the cases where respectful expressions are used. There are three examples in which Kōbai, Kashiwagi and Yūgiri speak of Tō no Chujō to Genji, and there is one case when only a neutral expression is used together with the respectful prefix *mi* [25]:

44. Akikonomu Empress→Genji

亡き人の御有様の、罪浅からぬさまに、ほの聞く事の侍りしを（鈴虫、4.297）

naki hito no *mi* 'RP'-arisama no, tumi asakara nu sama ni, hono-kiku koto no haberi si wo

'I have been told, though I have no very precise information, that my mother (=Rokuzyō Haven) died carrying a heavy burden of sin.' (The Bell Cricket, 675)

In this last example Nakanokimi refers to her father when speaking to her lover. Let us look at the frequency with which respectful expressions are used to out-group addressees according to the social status of a referent: two out of two examples (100%) for the imperial family; three out of four examples (75%) for an aristocratic family above the third court rank; zero out of four examples (0%) for the aristocracy of the fourth or the fifth court rank, and zero out of six examples (0%) for other social classes.

There is one example of referring to one's own kin to a son-in-law:

45. Priest in Akashi→Genji

親大臣の位をたもち給へりき（明石、2.181）

oya daizin no kurawi wo tamoti *tamahe* 'ORA' ri ki

'My father was a minister.' (Akashi, 257)

In example 45, the respectful expression *tamahu* is used because the referent, the speaker's father, is the late minister; but there are other examples where one speaks of one's parents to a husband:

46. Akashi Lady→Genji

まだしき願などの侍りけるを、御心にも知らせ奉るべき折あらば、御覧じ置くべきやとて侍るを（若菜上、4.99）

madasiki gwan nado no haberi keru wo, mi-kokoro ni mo sira se tatematuru beki wori ara ba, go-ran-zi-oku beku ya tote haberu wo

'My father (=the priest in Akashi) has sent a list of prayers and vows from his cave in Akashi. He thought that I might perhaps ask you to look at them sometime.' (Spring Shoots: Part One, 577)

47. Akashi Lady→Genji

この度は、かく大方の響きに、立ち交わらむもかたはらいたし。もし思ふやうならむ世の中を待ち出でたらば（若菜下、4.132）

kono-tabi ha, kaku ohokata no hibiki ni, tati-mazira m mo kataharaitasi. mosi omohu yau nara m yononaka wo mati-ide tara ba

'It would not be a good idea to have her (=the nun of Akashi) join so public an event. Perhaps she might wait until things have really gone as one hopes they will.' (Spring Schoots: Part Two, 633)[26]

In these examples a neutral expression is used because the speaker's parent belongs to a low social class.

⑬ A servant refers to a superior by kinship relation using a neutral expression to his master.

48. Governor of Kii→Genji

私の主とこそは思ひて侍るめるを、すきずきしき事と、なにがしよりはじめて、うけひき侍らずなむ（帚木、1.217）

watakusi no syuu to koso ha omohi te haberu meru wo, suki-zukisiki koto to, nanigasi yori hazime te, uke-hiki habera zu nam

'He (=the governor of Iyo=Kii's father) quite worships her (=Utsusemi). The rest of us are not entirely happy with the arrangements he has made.' (The Broom Tree, 41)

49. Ukon (=a gentlewoman of Ukifune) →Ukifune

右近が姉の、常陸にても人二人見侍りしを（浮舟、7.73）

ukon ga ane no, hitati nite mo, hito hutari mi haberi si wo

'She (=Ukon's sister) had two men after her' (A Boat upon the Waters, 1003)

3.2 Hierarchical relationships

A hierarchical relationship —such as that between a wet nurse and a master, or a servant and a master—is one based on employment. In aristocratic families, workers were employed for various jobs, and many girls from lower aristocratic families came to work as *nyōbō*. A wet nurse was a mature woman who reared the child of her master while still living with her own family.

3.2.1 about servants (Table 5)

	kinship	hierarchical	social
superior	0/1(0.0)	0/10(0.0)	0/12(0.0)
equal	0/0	0/4(0.0)	0/2(0.0)
inferior	1/2(50.0)	0/0	0/4(0.0)

Table 5　respectful expression from a master to a servant

⑭A master always refers to his servant by using a neutral or humble expression.

50. Genji→Tō no Chujō

乳母にて侍るものの、この五月の頃ほひより、重くわづらひ侍りしが、頭剃り忌む事受けなどして、その験にや、蘇りたりしを、この頃またおこりて、弱くなむなりにたる、今一度とぶらひ見よ、と申したりしかば（夕顔、1.271-272）

menoto[27] ni te *haberu* 'be (HVN)' mono no, kono go-gwati no korohohi yori, omoku wadurahi haberi si ga, kasira sori imu koto uke nado si te, sono sirusi ni ya, yomigaheri tari si wo, konogoro mata okori te, yowaku nam nari ni taru, ima hito-tabi, toburahi mi yo, to *mausi* 'say (HVN)' tari sika ba

'My old nurse fell seriously ill and took her vows in the Fifth Month or so. Perhaps because of them, she seemed to recover. But recently she had a relapse. Someone came to ask if I would not call on her at least once more.'[28] (Evening Faces, 75)

51. Monk→Ichijō Haven

この法師ばらなむ、大将殿の出で給ふなりけり、昨夜も御車かへして泊り給ひにける、と口々申しつる（夕霧、5.34）

kono hohusi-bara nam, daisyau-dono no ide tamahu nari keri, yobe mo mi-kuruma mo kahesi te tomari tamahi ni keru, to kuti-guti *mausi* 'say (HVN)' turu

'Some of my colleagues were saying that it was definitely the general (=Yūgiri). He sent his carriage away yesterday evening, they said, and stayed the night.'[29] (Evening Mist, 684)

There are nine examples of using humble expressions such as *mausu*, *X-wo mesu* 'a superior summons an inferior X', and *X-ga mawiru* 'an inferior X goes to a superior'. Neutral or *raru* expressions are used when an addressee is part of the family of a servant:

52. Genji→Koremitsu (=Genji's servant)

少将の命婦などにも聞かすな。尼君ましてかやうの事などいさめらるるを、心はづかしくなむ覚ゆべき（夕顔、1.274）

seusyau-no-myaubu nado ni mo kikasu na. ama-gimi masite kayau no koto nado isame *raruru* 'RARU' wo, kokoro-hadukasiku nam oboyu beki

'You are not to tell your sister, and you must be very sure that your mother does not hear. I would not survive the scolding I would get from her.' (Evening Faces, 75)

In the following, the respectful verb *notamahu* is used when a mistress refers to her wet nurse when addressing the nurse's son:

53. Safflower Lady→jijū[30] of Safflower Lady

故ままの、宣ひ置きし事もありしかば、かひなき身なりとも、身はててむとこそ思ひつれ（蓬生、2.284）

ko-mama no, *notamahi* 'say (SRV)'-oki si koto mo ari sika ba, kahinaki mi nari tomo, mi-hate te m to koso omohi ture

'I am a useless person, I know, but there were your mama's last instructions, and I had thought you would stay with me.' (The Wormwood Patch, 297)

In this case the mistress's use of infantile language such as *mama* 'wet nurse' can be interpreted as a literary technique to show the childishness of the mistress.

3.2.2 between servants (Table 6)

⑮Servants treat each other with neutral or humble expressions.

When a servant speaks of co-workers to a master, it is common to use a neutral

	kinship	hierarchical	social
superior	0/0	1/5(20.0)	0/9(0.0)
equal	0/0	4/7(57.1)	0/0
inferior	0/0	1/2(50.0)	0/0

Table 6 respectful expression among servants

expression:

54. Gentlewoman→Utsusemi

下に湯におりて、「唯今参らむ」と侍る（帚木、1.218）

simo ni yu ni ori te, 'tada-ima mawira m' to haberu

'She (=another gentlewoman) went to have a bath. She said she'd be right back.' (The Broom Tree, 42)

However, there are examples of the use of respectful expressions in cases where the referent is a wet nurse or a young charge considered to have a more intimate relationship with their master than ordinary servants:

55. Gentlewoman→Ukifune

このおとどのいと急にものし給ひて、にはかにかう聞えなし給ふなめりかし（浮舟、7.26）

kono otodo no ito kihu ni monosi *tamahi* 'ORA' te, nihaka ni kau kikoye-nasi *tamahu* 'ORA' meri kasi

'The old woman (=wet nurse of Ukifune) here is much too quick with her good ideas.' (A Boat upon the Waters, 978)

To an addressee who is of a high social status, a servant refers to a co-worker using a word that can be either a polite or a humble form:

56. Gentlewoman→Kaoru

大輔がもとより申したりしは（宿木、6.203）

taihu ga moto yori *mausi* 'say (HVN)' tari si ha

'I have had a letter from Tayū' (The Ivy, 921)

57. Gentlewoman→Niou

宮の侍に平の重経となむ名のり侍りつる（東屋、6.271）

miya no saburahi ni tahira-no-sigetune to nam nanori *haberi* 'HAN' turu.

'A chamberlain to Her Majesty who announced himself as Taira no Shigetsune.'

(The Eastern Cottage, 956)

3.2.3 about masters (Table 7)

	kinship	hierarchical	social
superior	13/13(100.0)	0/0	10/10(100.0)
equal	9/9(100.0)	1/1(100.0)	14/14(100.0)
inferior	7/7(100.0)	42/42(100.0)	38/38(100.0)

Table 7　respectful expression from a servant to a master

All honorific expressions are either supreme respectful expressions or ordinary respectful expressions. Of 134 examples, 103 are references to female masters. ⑯Servants always refer to their masters by respectful expressions when speaking to anybody.

There are eleven cases where servants refer to their masters using a supreme respectful expression when speaking to the master's kin:

58. Nurse of Kumoinokari→Tō no Chūjō

世づきたる人もおはすべかめるを、夢に乱れたる所おはしまさざめれば、更に思ひよらざりけること（少女、3.61）

yo-duki taru hito mo ohasu beka meru wo, yume ni midare taru tokoro *ohasimasa* 'be (SRV)' za mere ba, sarani omohi-yora zari keru koto

'There are young gentlemen who take advantage of the fact that people still think them boys and do odd and mischievous things. But not the young master (=Yūgiri). There has not been the slightest suggestion of anything improper in his behavior. What you say comes as a surprise to us.' (The Maiden, 370)

59. Nurse of Ukifune→the mother of Ukifune

はかなきものも聞こし召さず、なやましげにせさせ給ふ（浮舟、7.61）

hakanaki mono mo *kikosi- mesa* 'eat (ORV)' zu, nayamasi-ge ni se *sase-tamahu* 'SRA'.

'She (=Ukifune) won't eat a bite, and she seems so tired and mopish all the time.' (A Boat upon the Waters, 997)

And it is appropriate that among themselves servants refer to their master using respectful expressions:

60. Gentlewoman→gentlewoman

殿は今こそ出でさせ給ひけれ。いづれの隈におはしましつらむ（少女、3.57）

tono 'RN' ha ima koso ide *sase tamahi* 'SRA' kere. idure no kuma ni *ohasimasi* 'be (SRV)' tu ram

'Just leaving? Where can he (=Tō no Chūjō) have been hiding himself?' (The Maiden, 368)

61. Servant→servant

待つとて起きおはしまし、また御らんずる程の久しきは、いかばかり御心にしむ事ならむ（椎本、5.268）

matu tote oki *ohasimasi* 'SRA', mata *go-ran-zuru* 'see (SRV)' hodo no hisasiki ha, ikabakari *mi* 'RP'-kokoro ni simu koto nara m

'They could see why he (=Niou) would wish to wait up until an answer came, whispered the women, but here he was still mooning over it. The sender must be someone who interested him greatly.' (Beneath the Oak, 810)

Even when a servant speaks with a member of an out-group who is of a lower social status than his master, a respectful expression is still used:

62. Koremitsu→ gentlewoman of Suetsumuhana

かはらぬ御有様ならば、たづね聞こえさせ給ふべき御志も、絶えずなむおはしますめるかし（蓬生、2.252）

kahara nu ohom-arisama nara ba, tadune kikoye *sase-tamahu* 'SRA' beki *mi* 'RP'-kokorozasi mo, taye zu nam *ohasimasu* 'be (SRV)' meru kasi

'If your lady (=Suetsumuhana) has not changed, then my lord's (=Genji's) wishes to call upon her have not changed either.' (The Wormwood Patch, 299)

And in the following response the addressee also refers to her master with a respectful expression:

63. Gentlewoman of Suetsumuhana→Koremitsu

かはらせ給ふ御有様ならば、かかる浅茅が原をうつろひ給はでは侍りなむや（蓬生、2.252）

kahara *se-tamahu* 'SRA' *ohom* 'RP'-arisama nara ba, kakaru asadi-ga-hara wo uturohi *tamaha* 'ORA' de ha haberi na m ya.

'Do you think that if she (=Suetsumuhana) had changed she would not have moved away from this jungle?' (The Wormwood Patch, 299)

To an addressee who is of the same social status, respectful expressions are used:

64. Guard of Uji→Kaoru

かくて女達おはしますことをば、隠させ給ひ、なべての人に知らせ奉らじと、おぼし宣はするなり（橋姫、5.225）

kakute womna-*tati* 'RS' *ohasimasu* 'be (SRV)' koto wo ba, kakusa *se tamahi* 'SRA', nabete no hito ni sirase tatematura zi to, *obosi* 'think (ORV)' *notamahasuru* 'say (SRV)' nari

'No one's supposed to know they (=daughters, Ōigimi and Nakanokimi) even exist. That's how His Highness (=the Eighth Prince) wants it.' (The Lady at the Bridge, 784)

There are ten instances where an addressee is superior to his master and in these cases respectful expressions are used:

65. Gentlewoman→Niou

あやしう日頃もの憂がらせ給ひて（東屋、6.266）

ayasiu hi-goro mono-ugara *se tamahi* 'SRA' te

'She (=Nakanokimi) has been putting it off and putting it off.' (The Eastern Cottage, 953)

66. Gentlewoman of Ukifune→Niou

あやしきまで言ずくなに、おぼおぼとのみものし給ひて、いみじと思すことをも、人にうち出で給ふことは難く、ものづつみをのみし給ひしけにや、のたまひ置くことも侍らず（蜻蛉、7.112）

ayasiki made koto-zukuna ni, obo-obo to nomi monosi *tamahi* 'ORA' te, imizi to *obosu* 'think (ORV)' koto wo mo, hito ni uti-ide *tamahu* 'ORA' koto ha kataku, mono-dutumi wo nomi si *tamahi* 'ORA' si ke ni ya, *notamahi* 'say (SRV)'-oku koto mo habera zu.

'My lady (=Ukifune) had been in low spirits for some time and she was weeping when she went to bed that night. She seemed so wrapped up in herself, she had even less to say than usual.' (The Drake Fly, 1022-1023)

67. Gentlewoman of Ukifune→Kaoru

おのづから聞し召しけむ。もとより思すさまならで生ひ出で給へりし人の、世離れたる御住ひの後は、いつとなくものをのみ思すめりしかど（蜻蛉、7.115）

onodukara kikosi-mesi kem. moto yori *obosu* 'think (ORV)' sama nara de ohi-ide *tamahe* 'ORA' ri si hito no, yo-banare taru *ohom* 'RP'-sumahi no noti ha, itu to naku mono wo nomi *obosu* 'think (ORV)' meri sika do

'You will have heard all about it, I am sure. She (=Ukifune) was unlucky from the beginning, and after she came here to live, so far away from everyone, she seemed to slip deeper and deeper into herself. (The Drake Fly, 1024)

Ukifune is an unrecognized daughter of the Eighth Prince. Let us further appreciate the importance of social status by looking at the following:

68. Nun of Uji→Kaoru

中将の君とてさぶらひける上臈の、心ばせなどもけしうはあらざりけるを、……その君たいらかにものし給ふよし（宿木、6.202）

tyuuzyau-no-kimi tote saburahi keru zyaurahu no, kokorobase nado mo kesiu ha ara zari keru wo, …sono kimi tahiraka ni monosi *tamahu* 'ORA' yosi

'Among his (=the Eighth Prince) attendants was a woman named Chūjō, of good family and an amiable enough... she let it be known that the girl (=Ukifune) was in good health.' (The Ivy, 920)

69. Kaoru→Kogimi=half brother of Ukifune

いとたしかにものし給ふなれ。……母には、まだしきに言ふな。……その親のみ思ひのいとほしさにこそ、かくもたづぬれ（夢浮橋、7.232）

ito tasika ni monosi *tamahu* 'ORA' nare….haha ni ha, madasiki ni ihu na.…sono oya no *mi*[31]-omohi no itohosisa ni koso, kaku mo tadunure

'Well, I had resigned myself to the fact that she (=Ukifune) was no longer among us, but now it seems quite clear that I was wrong. … You are not to tell your mother (=Chūjō no Kimi), not for the moment, at least. … My main reason for wanting to find your sister (=Ukifune) is that I feel so sorry for your mother.' (The Floating Bridge of Dreams, 1085)

Although Chūjō no Kimi is the mother of Ukifune, she is treated with a neutral expression, whereas Ukifune can be treated with the respectful expression *tamahu* only because she is a daughter of the Eighth Prince. In nine out of ten cases servants refer to their female mistress, and this can be interpreted as a symptom of the afore-mentioned matrilineal trend. There is only one case of a servant referring to his male master (while praying to Buddha), and so it is hard to draw conclusions about how servants referred to male masters in a public situation.

70. **Servant of Chūjō no Kimi→Niou's servants on the street**

常陸殿のまかでさせ給ふ（東屋、6.265）

hitati-*dono* 'RP' no makade *sase-tamahu* 'SRA'

'One of her (=Chūjō no Kimi) attendants identified her as "a noble person from Hitachi".' (The Eastern Cottage, 953)

After hearing these words, the servants of Prince Niou laugh, saying *dono koso azayakanare* '*dono* is quite conspicuous'. From this example, Ishizaka (1960) infers that relative honorifics are commonly used, but Morino (1971) argues that *dono* is a suitable title only for the high noblility, and the reason for the derision is that *dono* was used for the regional director Hitachi no Suke and his family. In *Genji Monogatari*, the only people who are referred to by *dono* are Genji, Azechi Dainagon, Tō no Chūjō, Kokiden, Yūgiri and Kaoru, who all belong to a social class that is higher than the aristocracy above the third court rank. Sakon Shōshō and his father are also treated by *dono*, but the context of these examples is a rural society, among rural officers and a go-between. I believe the use of *sase-tamahu* is not suitable either. Hitachi no Suke is the chief officer in a rural community, but in the capital he is only the chief of a rural office. The reason for the mocking laughter is that his attendents still maintained their regional custom, and their behavior reflected their countrified origins.

3.3 Social status relationships

In the Heian period, everyone was born within a pre-established social status, according to which their occupation was determined.

3.3.1 about the inferior by social status relationship (Table 8)

	kinship	hierarchical	social
superior	3/6(50.0)	0/2(0.0)	6/60(10.0)
equal	6/8(75.0)	0/3(0.0)	0/16(0.0)
inferior	10/17(58.8)	1/2(50.0)	8/21(38.1)

Table 8   respectful expression to inferior by social status

⑰An emperor or minister, even if he is inferior to the speaker, is referred to with a respectful expression when addressing their kin.

When the kin of an addressee is mentioned, a speaker uses a respectful expression even if the referent is inferior. But its object is limited to the upper social classes with the following number of examples: six of ministers, four of Yūgiri, two of the imperial family, one of Murasaki, Empress[32] and one of the father of the Akashi Novice. Let us consider the importance of social status by comparing the pair of references contained in the following exchange:

71. Genji→Akashi Lady

かの先祖の大臣は、いと賢くあり難き志をつくして、おほやけに仕うまつり給ひける程に、ものの違目ありて、その報に、かく末は無きなり、と人いふめりしを、女子の方につけたれど、かくていと嗣なしといふべきにはあらぬも、そこらの行のしるしにこそはあらめ（若菜上、4.101）

kano senzo no otodo ha, ito kasikoku arigataki kokorozasi wo tukusi te, ohoyake ni tukau-maturi *tamahi* 'ORA' keru hodo ni, mono no tagahime ari te, sono mukuyi ni, kaku suwe ha naki nari, to hito ihu meri si wo, womna-go no kata ni tuke tare do, kaku te ito tugi nasi to ihu beki ni ha ara nu mo, sokora no okonahi no sirusi ni koso ha ara me

'He (=the Minister, Akashi Lady's ancestor) is a very learned and a very talented man, and all that has been lacking is a certain political sense, a flair for making his way ahead in the world. There was a minister in your family, an extremely earnest and intelligent man, I have always heard. People who speak of him in such high terms have always asked what misstep may have been responsible for bringing his line to an end … though of course we have you, and even though you are a lady we cannot say that his line has come to a complete end. No doubt your father's (=Akashi novice's) piety and devotion are being rewarded.' (New Herbs: Part One, 578)

Genji talks to the addressee about her grandfather, who was a minister, using the respectful auxiliary *tamahu*. For her father, who is only a chief regional officer, he uses a neutral expression, in both here and other passages.

⑱A referent such as an emperor or minister who belongs to a high social class is referred to using a respectful expression, even if he is inferior to a speaker.

But such respectful expressions are limited to *raru* expressions in most cases.

72. Kiritsubo Emperor→Genji

いとほしく大臣の思ひ歎かるなること（紅葉賀、1.385）

itohosiku otodo no omohi-nageka *ru* 'RARU' naru koto

'I am sorry to learn that the Minister of the Left is unhappy with you,' (An Autumn Excursion, 143)

73. Genji→Koremitsu

大納言の、外腹の娘を奉らるなるに（少女、3.72）

dainagon[33] no, hoka-bara no musume wo tatematura *ru* 'RARU' naru ni

'People pointed out that the Lord Inspector was offering a daughter by an unimportant wife' (The Maiden, 375)

74. Genji→Kiritsubo Empress

太政大臣のかくれ給ひぬをだに（薄雲、2.318）

ohoki-otodo[34] no kakure *tamahi* 'ORA' nuru wo dani

'The chancellor's death is a great blow' (A Rack of Cloud, 339)

Their social positions are limited to the high social class with the following examples: five of ministers, five of grand counselors, one of a prince, one of the imperial family, and one of a *nyōgo*. In general, a referent that is on a lower strata than a speaker is treated with a neutral expression, and when a referent belongs to a high social class, he is sometimes treated by a *raru* expression, which is the lowest respectful form. When the Suzaku Emperor talks about his daughter, *chūgū*, who has a high social status, to her wet nurse, he uses *tamahu*. But for the *nyōgo*, who has a low social status, *raru* is used:

75. Suzaku Emperor→a nurse

内裏には中宮侍ひ給ふ、次々の女御達とても、いとやむごとなき限ものせらるるに、はかばかしき後見なくて、さやうの交いとなかなかならむ（若菜上、4.23）

uti ni ha tyuuguu saburahi *tamahu* 'ORA', tugi-tugi no nyougo-*tati* 'RS' tote mo, ito yamgotonaki kagiri monose *raruru* 'RARU' ni, haka-bakasiki usiromi naku te, sayau no mazirahi ito naka-naka nara m

'His Majesty (=Reizei Emperor) has the empress (=Akikonomu, Chūgū), and his other ladies (=Nyōgo) are all so very well favored that I would fear for her (=the third Princess) in the competition and worry about her lack of adequate support.' (New Herbs: Part One, 541)

This example clearly illustrates the importance of social status in determining the honorific expression.

3.3.2 about the same by social status relationship (Table 9)

	kinship	hierarchical	social
superior	8/9(88.9)	0/2(0.0)	2/16(12.5)
equal	2/2(100.0)	0/0	23/32(71.9)
inferior	12/12(100.0)	9/9(100.0)	14/17(82.4)

Table 9 respectful expression to equal by social status

⑲A respectful expression is used when speaking to the family of a referent who has the same social status as the speaker.

This is commonly used out of consideration for the addressee when speaking about relatives such as husbands, wives or parents:

76. Nun→Kogimi

御文御覧ずべき人は、ここにものせさせ給ふめり。見証の人なむ、いかなることにか、と、心得がたく侍るを、なほのたまはせよ（夢浮橋、7.237）

ohom-humi *go-ranzu* 'see (SRV) beki hito ha, koko ni monose *sase-tamahu* 'SRA' meri. kensyou no hito nam, ika naru koto ni ka, to, kokoro-e gataku haberu wo, naho notamaha se yo

'Yes, here she (=Ukifune) is, the person the letter is for. We outsiders are somewhat puzzled by it all. Have a talk with her yourself.' (The Floating Bridge of Dreams, 1088)

⑳ For a referent who has the same social status as the speaker, a respectful expression is used when addressing the referent's servant.

77. Kaoru→guard of Uji

しか限りある御おこなひの程を、まぎらはし聞えさせむにあいなし。かく濡れ濡れ参りて、いたづらに帰らむうれへを、姫君の御方に聞えて、あはれと宣はせばなむなぐさむべき（橋姫、5.224）

sika kagiri aru *ohom* 'RP'-okonahi no hodo wo, magirahasi *kikoye* 'HAO' sase m ni ahinasi. kaku nure-nure mawiri te, itadura ni kahera m urehe wo, hime-gimi no *ohom* 'RP'-kata 'RS' ni *kikoye* 'say (HAO)' te, ahare to *notamahase* 'say (SRV)' ba nam nagusamu beki

'Please do not bother. It would be a pity to interrupt his (=the Eighth Prince's) retreat when it will be over soon in any case. But do tell the ladies (=Ōigimi and Nakanokimi) that I have arrived, sodden as you see me, and must go back with my mission unaccomplished; and if they are sorry for me that will be my reward.' (The Lady at the Bridge, 784)

The humble auxiliary *kikoyu* in this sentence means that the speaker, Kaoru, denigrates the addressee in relation to the referents, consequently demonstrating respect towards Ōigimi and Nakanokimi.

There are sixteen examples in which a referent that is inferior to an addressee is mentioned. Of these, two use respectful expressions: when the Minister of the Right refers to the daughter of the Minister of the Left to his daughter; the other is the following example.

78. Nakanobu (=subordinate of Kaoru) →Kaoru

みづから会ひ侍りたうびて、いみじく泣く泣くよろづのことをのたまひて、「……」となむものし侍りつる（蜻蛉、7.122）

midukara ahi *haberi-taubi* 'RARU' te, imiziku naku-naku yorodu no koto *notamahi* 'say (ORV)' te, '…' to nam monosi *haberi* 'HAN' turu

'She (=Chūjō no Kimi, Ukifune's mother) made me come in and between her sobs she told me … she said…' (The Drake Fly, 1027)

The honorific expression fluctuates between *haberitaubu*[35], the respectful verb *notamahu* and the humble auxiliary *haberu*.

㉑A referent that is in a high social class, like the imperial family or a minister, is referred to with a respectful expression even if he has the same social status as a speaker.

When a referent is in the same social class as the speaker and the addressee, it is common for an honorific expression to fluctuate between respectful and neutral. The following frequency rates are for respectful expressions used for referents of a high social status: nine out of nine examples (100%) for the imperial family; twelve out of thirteen examples (92.3%) for an aristocratic family above the third court rank; two out of four examples (50%) for an aristocrat of the fourth or fifth court rank; and zero out of five examples (0%) for other social classes.

3.3.3. about the superior by social status relationship (Table 10)

	kinship	hierarchical	social
superior	20/20(100.0)	0/0	36/39(92.3)
equal	9/9(100.0)	0/0	12/14(85.7)
inferior	26/26(100.0)	15/15(100.0)	186/188(98.9)

Table 10 respectful expression to superior by social status

㉒To any addressee, a speaker uses a respectful expression for a superior by social status relationship.

There are two exceptions that do not follow this convention:

79. Gentlewoman→gentlewoman
この殿の姫君の御傍には、これをこそさし並べて見め（竹河、5.171）
kono tono no hime-gimi no ohom-katahara ni ha, kore wo koso sasi-narabe te mi me
'Oh, that Kaoru. Put him beside our young lady here and you would really have something.' (Bamboo River, 754)

80. Gentlewoman→gentlewoman

かれぞこの常陸の守の婿の少将な（東屋、6.254）

kare zo kono hitati-no-kami no muko no seusyau na

'That's the lieutenant, the governor of Hitachi's son-in-law.' (The Eastern Cottage, 947)

Example 79 is uttered as gossip among servants and in the next sentence the author comments *kikinikuku ihu* 'It may have sounded just a little cheeky'. Also, in example 80 the following comment is made: *onogadoti ihu kikuramu tomo sirade* 'only half listening, the governor's wife was suddenly attentive'. Nowadays it is also common to deviate from the usual linguistic pattern in the context of gossip, so these cases can be interpreted as exceptions. The more important issue is how a speaker treats a referent that is superior to himself, but inferior to an addressee. There are three such examples:

81. Soldier→Niou

中務の宮参らせ給ひぬ。大夫は唯今なむ、参りつる道に、御車引き出づる、見侍りつ（東屋、6.271）

nakatukasa-no-miya, mawira *se-tamahi* 'SRA' nu. daibu ha tada ima nam, mawiri turu miti ni, *mi* 'RP'-kuruma hiki-iduru, mi haberi tu

'Prince Nakatsukasa is already at court, and I saw Her Majesty's chamberlain leaving his house.' (The Eastern Cottage, 956)

82. Nurse of the Third Princess→Suzaku Emperor

中納言は、もとよりいとまめ人にて、年頃もかのわたりに心をかけて、外様に思ひ移ろふべくも侍らざりけるに、その思ひかなひては、いとど動く方侍らじ。かの院こそ、なかなかほ、いかなるにつけても、人をゆかしく思したる心は、絶えずものせさせ給ふなれ（若菜上、4.23）

tyuunagon ha, motoyori ito mame-bito nite, tosi-goro mo kano watari ni kokoro wo kake te, hoka-zama ni omohi uturohu beku mo habera zari keru ni, sono omohi kanahi te ha, itodo yurugu kata habera zi. kano win koso, naka-naka naho, ika naru ni tuke te mo, hito wo yukasiku *obosi* 'think (ORV)' taru kokoro ha, taye zu monose *sase-tamahu* 'SRA' nare

'But he (=the Counselor, Yūgiri) is such a steady, proper young man. Through all those years he thought only of the girl who is now his wife (=Kumoinokari), and nothing could pull him away from her. He will doubtless be even more unbudgeable now that they are married. I should think that the chances might be better with his father (=Genji). It would seem that Genji still has the old acquisitive instincts and that he is always on the alert for ladies of really good pedigree.' (New Herbs: Part One, 541)

In example 81, Prince Nakatukasa is referred to with the respectful expression *se-tamahu*, but the chamberlain is referred to with a neutral expression. The social status of referents is reflected in the honorific expression. In example 82, Genji is referred to with the supreme respectful auxiliary *sase-tamahu*, but Yūgiri is referred to with a neutral expression. The reason might be that Yūgiri is the counselor, but not of the royal family, while Genji has become quasi-emperor. Respectful expressions are used for other cases such as the following:

83. Akashi Empress→gentlewoman of the First Princess

大将のそなたに参りつるは (蜻蛉、7.135)

daisyau no sonata ni *mawiri* 'come (HVN)' turu ha

'But the general (=Kaoru) seems to be over in your wing,' (The Drake Fly, 1033)

84. Gentlewoman of the First Princess→Akashi Empress

人よりは心よせ給ひて、局などに立ち寄り給ふべし (蜻蛉、7.135)

hito yori ha kokoro-yose *tamahi* 'ORA' te, tubone nado ni tati-yori *tamahu* 'ORA' besi

'It's always Kosaishō's room that he (=Kaoru) goes to.' (The Drake Fly, 1034)

In example 83, the Akashi Empress uses the humble expression *mawiru* for her brother-in-law Kaoru, whereas in example 84 a servant uses a respectful expression to refer to him.

3.4 Humble form of dual honorifics, and humble form plus respectful form

Honorific expressions that combine the humble form and the respectful form are considered a characteristic feature of the honorific system of the Heian period. There has been much lively discussion about the character of the humble form. Tokieda (1954) insists that it is 'an honorific to express the mutual relationship between the object of a topic and the person who participates in the topic'. For example, *kikoyu* (a humble verb meaning 'tell') in *X ga Y ni kikoyu*, 'X tells to Y', should express the mutual relationship between X and Y. According to this concept, the agent X should be treated as inferior to the patient Y by a speaker because *kikoyu* is a humble verb that relates to agent X. But in *Genji Monogatari*, the humble form is used even when X is superior to Y, and Matsushita (1928) argues that this form is an honorific with which a speaker shows his respect toward a patient Y[36]. There are many examples of the use of *kikoye tamahu* in *Genji-Monogatari*, and this indicates that it is possible to respect an actor whom a speaker makes humble to a patient. Much work has been done on the narrative sections to solve this issue, with much of the interest focused on whether any rule can be applied in cases when an actor is superior to a patient. If the conclusion is negative, it may support the theory that the humble form is the honorific form that a speaker uses to show his respect toward a patient. Although some articles have been published on this, there is no established theory[37]. Let us now turn to the conversational sections. I limit my survey to those cases that use humble forms—such as *tatematuru, kikoyu, mawiru, mousu*—to which the respectful form *tamahu* or *se-tamahu* has been appended.

Firstly let us look at the examples to which Tokieda's theory apply. There are 351 in total, but 47 of them have either a monologue or a speaker, an addressee, a referent, an actor or a patient who is not clearly defined. Therefore the object of the study is limited to 304 examples, of which 104 (34.2%) show an actor who is inferior to a patient by either kinship, hierarchy or social status. There are 72 examples (23.7%) where the same person is both an addressee and an actor.

85. Gentlewoman of Suetsumuhana→Koremitsu

ただおしはかりて聞こえさせ給へかし（蓬生、2.252）

tada osihakari te *kikoye sase tamahe* kasi

'Please imagine for yourself, sir, the situation of which you inquire, and report it to your lord (=Genji).' (The Wormwood Patch, 299)

This is an expression used to make the addressee, Koremitsu, humble to the actor, Genji, who is superior. There are 101 examples (33.2%) where the relationship between an actor and a patient is that of husband and wife, or lovers.

In the following, a mother talks to her son the emperor about his wife, with an expression intended to make both humble:

86. Fujitsubo Empress→Reizei Emperor

かくはづかしき人参り給ふを、御心づかひして見え奉らせ給へ（絵合、2.267)

kaku hadukasiki hito *mawiri tamahu* wo, mi-kokoro-dukahi si te miye *tatematura se-tamahe*

'Yes, she (=Akikonomu Empress) is splendid. You must be on your best behavior when you meet her.' (A Picture Contest, 309)

Here a servant speaking of Genji uses a humble verb:

87. Controller→nurse of the Third Princess

院は、あやしきまで御心ながく、仮にも見そめ給へる人は、御心とまりたるをも、又さしも深からざりけるをも、方々につけても尋ね取り給ひつつ、あまたつどへ聞え給へれど（若菜上、4.25)

win ha, ayasiki made mi-kokoro nagaku, kari ni mo mi-some tamahe ru hito ha, mi-kokoro tomari taru wo mo, mata sasimo hukakara zari keru wo mo, katagata ni tuke te mo tadune-tori tamahi tutu, amata tudohe *kikoye tamahe* re do

'Genji is a more reliable man than you would imagine. When he has had an affair, even the most lighthearted sort of adventure, he ends up by taking the lady in and making her one of his own. The result is that he has a large collection.' (New Herbs: Part One, 542)

In those days, the conventions of honorifics allowed a speaker to treat men (as actors) with the humble form if their discussion was with the actor's wife or lover (as patients) and the conversation focused on the relationship of actor and patient[38]. But, there are 34 examples where a servant treats an actor by humbling him in order to elevate his master:

88. Gentlewoman of Uji→Kaoru

かく山深く尋ねきこえさせ給ふめる御志（総角、6.20)

kaku yama hukaku tadune *kikoye sase-tamahu* meru mi-kokorozasi

'She (=Ōikimi) has watched you climb over these mountains year after year' (Trefoil Knots, 825)

Remembering rule ⑯ 'Servants always refer to their masters by respectful expressions when speaking to anybody', the 34 examples should then be interpreted as a respectful expression towards one's master. In 58 examples (19.1%) an actor who is supposed to be superior to a patient is still treated with a humble expression, and these should be counted as exceptions to the Tokieda theory. There are 49 examples (16.1%) where an actor is superior to a patient by kinship; within these, there are 40 examples (13.2%), like the following, where the patient is the daughter of an actor:

89. Murasaki→Genji

などて返し給ひけむ。書きとどめて、姫君にも見せ奉り給ふべかりけるものを（玉鬘、3.131）

nadote kahesi tamahi kem. kaki-todome te, hime-gimi ni mo mise *tatematuri tamahu* bekari keru mono wo

'And why did you send them back? We could have made copies and given them to the little girl (=Akashi Empress).' (The Jewel Chaplet, 408)

These cases comply with rule ③ 'Within the families of ministers and the aristocracy, daughters are treated with respectful expressions'. There are, however, eight examples of actors who are superior to patients by social status. In one example, the speaker uses humiliative language for an emperor when addressing the daughter of an addressee:

90. Genji→Rokujō Haven

故院の御子たちあまたものし給へど、親しく睦び思ほすもをさなきを、上の同じ御子たちの中にかずまへ聞え給ひしかば、さこそは頼み聞え侍らめ（澪標、2.229）

ko-win no miko tati amata monosi tamahe do, sitasiku mutubi omohosu mo wosanaki wo, uhe no onazi miko-tati no uti ni kazumahe *kikoye tamahi* sika ba, sa koso ha tanomi kikoe haberame

'I have many brothers, but I have never felt close to them. My father (=Kiritsubo Emperor) looked upon the high priestess (=Akikonomu Empress) as one of his daughters, and to me she shall be a sister.'(Channel Buoys, 286-287)

Here, the honorific expression is used toward the patient either because the actor (Kiritsubo Emperor) treated her as his own daughter, or the honorific expression is directed toward the addressee, Rokujō Haven, who is a parent of the patient, the Akikonomu Empress. There are three examples where a patient is also the addressee, and these examples should be seen as honorific expressions toward an addressee. There are two examples where an addressee who is also an actor is made humble to a patient:

91. The present Emperor→Suzaku Emperor

かの六条の院にこそ、親ざまに譲り聞えさせ給はめ（若菜上、4.32）

kano rokudeu-no-win ni koso, oya-zama ni yuduri *kikoye sase tamaha* me

'But if Genji is to be your choice, then I think he should be asked to look after her (=the Third Princess) as a father looks after a daughter.' (New Herbs: Part One, 545)

In this case the patient, Genji, is a young brother of the actor and belongs to a high social class, like the quasi-emperor, so it is an appropriate expression. There is also a case where a wet nurse humbles an actor to her master, and this can be interpreted as a respectful expression toward her master:

92. Nurse of Yūgiri→Ōmiya=mother of Tō no Chūjō

あなづり聞えさせ給ふに侍るめりかし（少女、3.69）

anaduri *kikoye sase-tamahu* ni haberu meri kasi

'His Lordship (=Tō no Chūjō) dismisses the young master (=Yūgiri) as beneath his contempt.' (The Maiden, 373)

To summarize all of these examples, the humble verb can be used in the following situations: when an actor is inferior to a patient; when an actor and a patient are of equal status (eg, husband and wife); and when a speaker treats a patient with a respectful expression even though the actor is superior to the patient. The honorific expression reflects not only the relationship between an actor and a patient, but also the relationship among a speaker, an addressee and a patient.

Let us analyze the honorific expression from the point of view of the humble form as a respectful expression from speaker to patient. There are 304 examples that demonstrate the social hierarchy between a speaker and a patient. First of all, there are 221 examples (72.7%) where a speaker is inferior to a patient:

93. Myōbu→Genji

上の、まめにおはします、と持てなやみ聞えさせ給ふこそ、をかしう思う給へらるる折々侍れ（末摘花、1.340）

uhe no, mame ni ohasimasu, to mote-nayami *kikoye sase-tamahu* koso, wokasiu omou tamahe raruru wori-ori habere

'It amuses me sometimes to think that your royal father (=Kiritsubo Emperor) believes you to be excessively serious.' (The Safflower, 115)

In this case the actor is an emperor and the father of the patient. There are 29 examples (9.5%) where an actor is superior to a patient, but in 26 of them (8.6%) the actor is a superior by kinship relation. In the remaining three examples, an actor is superior by social status and addressee and patient is the same person, as in example 93. Therefore these cases can be interpreted as respectful expressions toward an addressee. There are 14 examples (4.6%) where the patient is either the husband, wife or lover of a speaker; and in these cases the addressee is himself a patient or inferior to a patient, as in the following:

94. Genji→the Third Princess

いと幼き御心ばへを見置き給ひて、いたくはうしろめたがり聞え給ふなりけりと、思ひ合せ奉れば（若菜下、4.209）

ito wosanaki mi-kokorobahe wo mi-oki tamahi te, itaku ha usirometagari *kikoye tamahu* nari keri to, omohi ahase tatemature ba

'He (=Suzaku Emperor) worries about leaving you behind when you are so very young and innocent. I fear that I worry too.' (New Herbs: Part Two, 629)

These cases can be interpreted as respectful expressions toward an addressee. There are 27 examples (8.9%) of speakers and patients of the same social status; and there are a problematic 38 examples (12.5%) of speakers that are superior to patients. In 32 examples (10.5%) there are speakers who are superior to patients by a kinship relationship, and 10 examples where a patient is the same person as an addressee:

95. The Fifth Princess=aunt of Asagao→Asagao

この大臣の、かくいとねんごろに聞え給ふめるを、（少女、3.41）

kono otodo no, kaku ito nengoro ni *kikoye tamahu* meru wo,

'Such lovely notes as the Genji minister is always writing.' (The Maiden, 361)

The above is a respectful expression toward an addressee who is a niece of the speaker. There also are 10 examples of conversations within families:

> **96. Murasaki→Genji**
>
> この折に添へ奉り給へ（藤裏葉、3.351）
>
> kono wori ni sohe *tatematuri tamahe*
>
> 'Suppose you send the Akashi Lady with the child (=Akashi Empress),' (Wisteria Leaves, 531)

It is quite appropriate for a daughter to be treated with a respectful expression because these cases comply with rule ③ 'Within the families of ministers and the aristocracy, daughters are treated with respectful expressions'. There are nine examples of a speaker using humiliative language for an addressee's father when addressing a patient who is the speaker's son:

> **97. Suzaku Emperor→Yūgiri**
>
> 東宮などにも心をよせ聞え給ふ（若菜上、4.19）
>
> touguu nado ni mo kokoro wo yose *kikoye tamahu*
>
> 'It would seem that he (=Genji) has the warmest feelings towards the crown prince.' (New Herbs: Part One, 538)

In these cases, all of the patients are of an elevated social status (eg, an emperor, a prince or an empress) and the importance of their social status is reflected by the speaker's use of honorifics. There are seven examples where humble expressions are used even when a patient is inferior to a speaker:

> **98. Genji→Tamakazura**
>
> かのおとどに知られ奉り給はむことも、まだ若々しう何となき程に、ここら年経給へる御中にさし出で給はむことは如何、と、思ひめぐらし侍る。
> （胡蝶、3.160）
>
> kano otodo ni sira re *tatematuri tamaha* m koto mo, mada waka-wakasiu nani to naki hodo ni, kokora tosi he tamahe ru ohom-naka ni sasi-ide tamaha m koto ha ikaga, to, omohi-megurasi haberu.
>
> 'But I think you would have a difficult time if you were dropped down in that enormous family of your father's (=Tō no chūjō), all of them as good as strangers.' (Butterflies, 425)

In these cases, too, addressees and actors are the same people, and the actor and patient have a kinship relationship. These cases are interpreted as respectful expressions toward an addressee. We can conclude that a situational factor like the relationship with an addressee cannot be ignored when interpreting honorific expressions from the point of view of humble forms as a speaker's respectful expression toward a patient.

It is hard to determine the right answer. Is the humble form an honorific that expresses the mutual relationship between the object of the topic and the person who participates in the topic; or is it an honorific that a speaker uses to show respect toward a patient? My answer is that there are examples that support both theories, while at the same time there are examples that cannot be explained by either. There is, however, one theory that compromises both theories. When the relationship between an actor and a patient is that of kinship, the humble form is used even when the patient is inferior. This is also true when relations are very intimate, like those between husband and wife. And when a patient is an addressee, the humble form is used even when an actor is superior to a patient. In any case, the question cannot be solved only by the hierarchical relationship between an actor and a patient, or by that between a speaker and a patient. What must also be considered is the situational factor such as the standpoint of an addressee or the kinship relationship.

4. Conclusion

1. Within a family, kinship hierarchy is maintained but acquired social status may disrupt this.

Within a family, kinship hierarchy is maintained, and the superior by kinship relationship is acknowledged by the use of respectful expressions. Therefore, both husbands and wives treat each other with respectful expressions to their children. The inferior is usually treated with a neutral expression, and it is common for sons to be treated with neutral expressions. But aquired social status can alter this. For example, a daughter who is married to an emperor is treated with a respectful expression as a superior by social status rather than as an inferior by kinship. The daughter of the Akashis is married to Genji and her parents speak of her respectfully to Genji, in deference to her new status as part of his in-group. Parents also shift the honorific expression used for a son, according to his social status. These examples show the importance of social status as a determinant of honorific expression.

2. The hierarchical order is always maintained.

Servants treat their masters, especially female ones, with respectful expressions when talking to any person. In contrast, a master always treats his servant with a neutral expression, even when the addressee is a relative of the servant. A master treats his own child, who is an inferior by kin, with a respectful expression when talking to his servant—thereby emphasising his position as a master from the standpoint of his servant. In this way, the hierarchical order is always maintained.

3. A referent is treated according to his social status.

The honorific expression is determined according to the social status of a referent. A member of the imperial family or the aristocracy is treated respectfully not only by those belonging to his out-group, but also by his family. And when speaking to the emperor, who is superior to the aristocracy, about an aristocrat, one uses a respectful expression, taking the referent's high social status into consideration.

4. Concern for an addressee is not sufficient to disrupt the social hierarchy.

A speaker sometimes uses a slightly higher honorific expression than usual in cases when an addressee is a relative or the master of a referent. Yet despite any feelings of concern toward an addressee, it never happens that a master uses a respectful expression when speaking of his servant to a servant's relative. Concern can only function within the limits of social order.

5. Gradations of respectful expressions are adapted to specific situations.

I have divided respectful expressions into three classes, but in fact there are further intermediary classes adapted to the domains of their use. There are some expressions—such as *keisu* and *sousu* 'tell'—that are used exclusively for the imperial family. In most cases, an honorific expression is not absolute; rather, it is adapted within a given social setting according to its hierarchical order. The earlier example where the use of the title '*Hitachi dono*' is laughed at by metropolitan aristocracy shows how a chief officer located at the highest social strata in his local society is nevertheless in a much inferior class when compared with the imperial family in metropolitan society. As a result, *dono* is used to describe the rustic appearance of Hitachi. The proper usage of honorific expressions is determined by its situation. For example, any person who is treated with a respectful expression within a family may be treated by a neutral expression by members of an out-group.

Proposal of the term Status Honorifics

By which criteria are honorific expressions determined in *Genji-monogatari*? Technical terms such as 'absolute' or 'relative' honorifics are commonly used to designate the honorific expression toward a referent. Let us take the examples listed here. In the system of 'absolute' honorifics an honorific expression (toward a referent) is determined only by the relationship between a speaker and a referent, with the addressee being irrelevant. In *Genji-Monogatari* there are examples of someone who is inferior to a speaker being treated with a respectful expression. For example, a son who is technically an inferior by kinship relation is treated with a respectful expression by his father when the addressee is his servant. These show that the honorific system used is not one of absolute honorifics, and that the position of an addressee is important in determining the honorific expression. In 'relative' honorifics an honorific expression toward a referent is determined only by the relationship among speaker, addressee and referent. This is the kind of Japanese honorifics used today. When a referent belongs to an addressee, he is treated with a respectful expression even if he is inferior to the speaker; so the position of the addressee is the first criterion to determine the honorific expression. But in *Genji-Monogatari*, a servant is never treated with a respectful expression by his master even when the addressee is the servant's relative. And a noble person from either the imperial family or the aristocracy treats his child with a respectful expression even to an out-group addressee. These show us that the honorific system used in *Genji-Monogatari* is not a system of 'relative' honorifics; and that the criteria of in-group and out-group did not function like today's honorific system.

I propose a new term—'status' honorifics—for a system in which the honorific expression toward a referent is determined according to the status of a referent in a 'society' that is composed of a speaker, an addressee and a referent. Within a family, the honorific expression is determined by the status among its members. For example, when a husband speaks about his wife to their child, he uses a respectful expression because she is superior to her child based on her status as a mother. Honorific usage is the same for hierarchical relationships. That is to say, a master is always treated with a respectful expression by his servant, and a servant is always treated with a neutral expression by his master, even to the servant's family. Within a society, social status determines the honorific expression toward a referent. For example, a member of the imperial family treats his child with a respectful expression when speaking to an out-group person; although a child is inferior by kinship, as a child of the noblility he has an elevated social status. It is the same for the aristocracy, where a father may use different honorific expressions for his son. For example, when speaking of him to his wife he uses a neutral expression because of their kinship relationship; to his servant, he uses a respectful expression because of their hierarchical relationship; and to an out-group person, an appropriate expression. When a son belongs to a high social stratum like the aristocracy, he is treated with a respectful expression, but when he is of low social status, a neutral expression is used.

In *Genji-Monogatari*, there are different levels of respectful expressions, and the proper one is chosen in accordance with the social status of a referent. Humble expressions are used only when there is a social or hierarchical distance between speaker and referent, like a master and a servant. In modern Japanese, there is not much difference among the various respectful expressions, whereas the humble expression has become more developed. On the contrary, in the Heian period, the range of each respectful expression was wide, but the humble expression was underdeveloped. When an addressee was much superior to a referent, and an honorific expression toward a referent therefore needed to be controlled, a speaker could show his regard to the addressee by downgrading the level of respectful expression. As the term 'dual' honorifics shows, the honorific system of the Heian period allowed respectful expressions for both an addressee and a referent to coexist.

APPENDIX

There is one chapter in *Makuranosōshi* 枕草子 'The Pillow Book' that refers to an aspect of the honorific expression of the Heian period.

をとこ、しゅなどなめくいふ、いとわるし。わが使ふものなど「何とおはする」「のたまふ」などいふ、いとにくし。ここもとに、「侍り」などいふ文字をあらせばやと聞くこそ多かれ

wotoko nusinado namekuihu ito warusi. waga tukahu mononado, 'nani to ohasuru' 'notamahu' nado ihu, ito nikusi. 'haberi' nado ihu mozi wo arase baya to kiku koso oho kare.

'It is very rude to say bad things about one's husband and master. I hate to hear my servants say *nani to ohasuru* and *notamahu*. I feel *haberi* should be used in such cases.'

The author, Seishō-Nagon, admonishes her servants for their usage of honorifics. She would prefer them to use the humble verb *haberi* instead of the respect verbs *ohasu* and *notamahu*. But there is no description in the book about the context, nor about whom and to whom the servant speaks. There are different interpretations about this chapter. Some believe that the referent is the husband of the servant; that is to say, the context is when a servant speaks of her husband to her master. Some insist that the referent is her master. In this case it would be natural to interpret the passage as a servant referring to her master when speaking to an out-group person. *Makuranosōshi* was written at the same time as *Genji-Monogatari*, and the settings of both stories are that of aristocratic society. As rule ⑯ 'Servants always refer to their masters by respectful expressions when speaking to anybody' shows in *Genji-Monogatari*, the latter interpretation cannot be correct. Therefore, it seems more reasonable to see the referent in the above passage as the husband of her servant. As rule ⑬ 'A servant refers to a superior by kinship relation by neutral expression to his master' shows in *Genji-Monogatari*, the referent in *Makuranosōshi* should be the husband of her servant. Some researchers argue that relative honorifics already prevailed in the Heian period; they infer that a servant addressing her master treats her husband with a neutral expression because the master belongs to her out-group. I see a different rule at work from that of today's relative honorifics. That is to say, a servant's husband is far inferior to her master, and a neutral expression reflects the difference in social status between them. More interesting is the fact that there was a servant who used a respectful expression for her husband when speaking to her master. Absolute honorifics, the honorific system whereby a speaker should respect whoever is superior to himself, was commonly used in private among common people, and some of them applied their private honorific system to a public situation. It was for just such a reason that the utterance '*Hitachi-dono*' was laughed at by aristocratic society. That is to say, status honorifics—the honorific expression toward a referent as determined by an addressee—was used in a public situation in an aristocratic society, but there were those among the common people who misused their private honorific system in a public situation. It is supposed that absolute honorifics prevailed in regional and common society, and that status honorifics were confined to the upper classes. There is in *kyōgen* of the Muromachi period an example of a wife who speaks of her husband to his master using a respectful expression; however I believe that absolute honorifics may have already been used as early as the Heian period. I would like to emphasize that status honorifics, used in aristocratic society in a public situation, and absolute honorifics, commonly used among common people in a private situation, coexisted in the Heian period.

(Endnotes)

1. Miyaji (1971) names these kinds of words *teichōgo*, and Sugisaki (1988) names them *kashikomari no gohō*, 'expressions of sincerity'.
2. Ōkubo (1995) refers to a case where a respectful verb is omitted because a respectful prefix is already used.
3. Takamure (1963) defines the marriage system in the Heian period as a matriarchy, but it is still debated among scholars whether women had most of the authority and power.
4. Tyler (2001) gives a brief survey of the hierarchical system of this time in the introduction of volume one.
5. Gentlewoman is *nyōbō*女房, a woman of good family who serves a higher-ranking lord or lady.
6. I try to reflect the pronunciation of the time in the transcription of the text. Proper names for the translation are in accordance with contemporary pronunciation, so there is some incongruence between the romanized transcription and translation. As for romanization, I use

a text by Eiichi Shibuya downloaded through http://www.sainet-or.jp/~eshibuya/.
7   The quoted parts are shown within parentheses. The names of chapters are shown and the number indicates the quoted pages of each text.
8   I use the term 'consort' for *nyōgo* 女御—one of the top ranking candidates for empress in the palace.
9   As for the neutral honorific form, I omit to write it in italics for it is quite troublesome to do so in all cases of the neutral form. Italics are used for either the respectful or humble forms because the neutral form itself is unmarked. It is obligatory to choose the proper honorific expression to refer to someone, so if the neutral expression is used, it means that a referent is an ordinary person belonging to the speaker's side.
10 Haven in this case is *miyasundokoro* 御息所, a lady who bore a child to an emperor. Ichizjō is the place she lived.
11 Morino (1971) states that the matrilineal trend influences the usage of honorific expression. Kamitani (1976) offers an example of even an emperor addressing and referring to his daughter by a respectful expression.
12 *Miya* 宮 is a title for children of the Emperor, prince or princess. San-no-Miya 三の宮 is the third (=san) child.
13 I use the term 'intimate' for *kaui* 更衣, one of the rank of candidates for empress in the palace. *Kaui* is one rank below *nyōgo*.
14 *Myōbu* 命婦 is a title for middle-ranking gentlewomen who work in the royal court.
15 Prof. Takasumi Waragai, who wrote a review of this book, suggests that the referent married the master of the addressee; therefore, the speaker treats her daughter as an in-group member of the addressee.
16 Captain is *Chūjō* 中将, the second-level officer in the Palace Guards of Left or Right.
17 Novice is *Nyūdō* 入道, a man or woman of noble birth who has taken preliminary vows as a monk or nun.
18 Tamagami (1952) states that the Akashi Lady is treated with a respectful expression in the narrative parts only when she is recognized as the mother of Akashi Empress. Social status factors such as the person with whom the speaker's relative has a marital relation should be counted when determining the honorific expression.
19 *Kikoye sasu* implies stronger humility than *kikoyu* and can be categorized as a supreme humble expression.
20 Morino (1971) points out that emotional factors can violate the normal pattern of honorific usage.
21 Governor is *Kami* 守, an official appointed by the Emperor to govern a province.
22 Ōigimi and Nakanokimi are the eldest and second daughter respectively of the Eighth

Prince.

23 *Asom* 朝臣 is a respectful title for aristocracy above the third rank.
24 There is no fixed theory about the honorific value of *mausaru* 申さる. Sugisaki (1988a) interprets it as a dual honorific usage, like the combination of the humble expression *mausu* used by a speaker toward an addressee, and the respectful expression *raru* used by a speaker toward a referent.
25 The respectful prefix *mi* 御 has a few phonological variants that do not seem to derive from the same suffix. When it is followed by a word of Japanese origin, it is pronounced as *mi* or *ohm*; but when followed by a borrowed Chinese word, it is pronounced *gyo* or *go*.
26 This translation is by Tyler (2001). The translation by Seidensticker (1977) is as follows: "Are you quite sure you should be showing yourself on such a public occasion?" the lady asked her mother. "Perhaps when the very last of our prayers has been answered" (New Herbs: part Two, 593). I use Tyler because in Seidensticker's translation the utterance is only by the Akashi Lady to the nun of Akashi, her mother.
27 *Menoto* 乳母 is a woman who nurses a highborn infant in place of its mother; the relationship between a highborn child and its nurse is lasting and intimate.
28 According to Seidensticker's translation, the actor of *mausu* is an anonymous person who is an intimate of the wet nurse, but it is more reasonable to interpret the actor as the wet nurse.
29 According to Seidensticker's translation, the actors of *mausu* are the speaker's colleagues, but there also exists a hierarchical order in clerical society. In this case, the speaker is the master and the referents are his followers. Tyler (2001) translates the speaker as 'the Master of Discipline' and the referents as 'my monks'.
30 *Jijū* 侍従 is a gentlewoman.
31 In the original text, this *mi* is written in *hiragana* (Japanese character) as み. The respectful prefix *mi* is usually written in *kanji* (Chinese character) as 御. *Mi* written in *hiragana* is an expression of endearment, not of respect (cf., Mochizuki,1970 and Seki, 1976).
32 Here I use the term Empress for *Chūgū* 中宮, the Emperor's highest-ranking wife.
33 *Dainagon* 大納言 is Grand Counselor, the office below Minister in the Council of State.
34 *Ohoki-Otodo* 太政大臣 is the highest possible civil post, one not provided for in the government's nominal table of organization. Here I translate it as Chancellor.
35 Sugisaki (1988a) and Sugisaki (1988b) state that *taubu* has not as high an honorific value as *tamahu* and its function is to show a speaker's sincerity toward an addressee.
36 According to Kikuchi (1994), the only function of this kind of humble form in the dual honorific system of the Heian period is for a speaker to show respect to Y, and not for a speaker to denigrate X. The respectful form shows a speaker's respect for X.
37 Watanabe (1981) posits a compromising theory.

[38] Negoro (1992) interprets these kinds of expression as reflecting the emotional sphere of the characters. For example, the regard that Fujitsubo Empress has for both Reizei Emperor and Akikonomu Empress is reflected in Example 86.

3

REFERENT HONORIFIC EXPRESSION IN HEIKE-MONOGATARI

1. Introduction

Let us use *Heike-Monogatari* to analyze the honorific expression in the Kamakura period (1192–1333 AD). *Heike-Monogatari* depicts a samurai society where males dominate, and it reflects the public language of that society. About the honorific system of this time, Toyama (1977) writes that 'though the political power shifted from aristocracy to samurai, it seems that the regard for social status did not change and the hierarchical order of the aristocratic class was built on and maintained by the samurai class'. Nishida (1998) argues that addressee-oriented honorifics had come into existence because of the development of the polite form. That is to say, in *Heike-Monogatari* the polite form *saburahu* is used even when a speaker must pay their regards in order to make a request to a socially inferior addressee. Most researchers believe that the time of *Heike-Monogatari* is a transition period from absolute to relative honorifics, when both intermingled.

Heike-Monogatari is a narrative epic from the thirteenth century. Its main theme, based on the Buddhist sense of life's impermanence, is the rise and fall of a powerful warrior clan, the Heike. Originally a *biwa* 琵琶 minstrel narrated this epic to a tune, but a number of texts survive.

2. Data

I use Kajiwara & Yamashita's (1991) text, which is based on *Kakuichi–hon* 覚一

本, believed to have been written during the *Nanbokuchou* 南北朝 period (1333-1392). It is said that many manuscripts of this are extant, amongst which Okamura (1957) finds wide and differing descriptions of honorific expressions. These differences are believed to reflect each author's attitude towards the characters, which might also depend on the social background of each time. Due to scarcity of materials, I also use *Hogen-Monogatari* 保元物語, based on *Nakarai-bon* 半井本; and *Heiji-Monogatari* 平治物語, based on *Kotai-hon* 古態本. I use Tochigi, Kusaka, et al. (1992) as the text. For the English translation, I use Kitagawa & Tsuchida (1975).

I limit the range of enquiry only to the conversational parts. It is considered that the honorific expression toward a referent in *Heike-Monogatari* varies according to the evaluation of an author (cf., Shinoda, 1978 and Okumura, 1989). The honorific expressions used towards Kiyomori, one of the main characters, are not fixed, but decrease as the tale progresses. For example, there is a different level of honorific expression used toward Kiso Yoshinaka before and after his evil-doing in Kyoto. These shifts are based on an author's changed evaluation of the referent. We can expect the author's attitude toward a referent not to intervene in the conversational parts. While the narrative sections may reflect an author's personal feeling about the honorific expression used toward a referent, in the conversational parts the honorific expression used by one character toward another is based on the relationship between them. Therefore, these parts reflect more directly the honorific expression of the day. It is sometimes difficult to distinguish where the dialogue ends and the narrative passage begins[1]. In these cases, I rely on the annotation of the researcher, and I refer to the monologue segments.

3. Methodology

The honorific expression toward a referent is determined by the triad relationship of speaker, addressee and referent, and the dual relationships contained therein— between a speaker and a referent, and between an addressee and a referent—should be taken into consideration. In absolute honorifics, the expression used toward a referent is determined only by the relationship between the speaker and the referent, regardless of the addressee. That is to say, a referent that is superior to a speaker is treated with a respectful expression; one who is inferior is treated with a humble expression; and one who is equal is treated with a neutral expression. These are speaker-oriented honorifics. In contrast, in relative honorifics, the expression toward a referent is determined by the relationship that the referent has with both speaker and addressee. In this chapter, I classify the relationship between a referent and a speaker, and between a referent and an addressee, from three relational viewpoints: kinship, hierarchy and social status. A kinship relationship is between blood relatives such as a parent and a child; an example of a hierarchical relationship is that of lord and vassal; and a social status relationship refers to the social strata one belongs to, such as the aristocracy or the common people. I further classify these relations into superior, equal and inferior, keeping in mind that superiority can be fluid and not always consistent. For instance, a Minister of the Right talks about his daughter, who became an empress, and his grandchild using a respectful expression. By kinship, the Minister of the Right is superior to his daughter and his grandchild, but by social status he is inferior to her because she has married into the imperial family. This example shows the importance of social status at that time. It also shows why most researchers think that absolute honorifics was the honorific system used at this time. It was common during this time for communication between the upper and lower classes to take place not face-to-face but through messengers; in this case, we have to consider the honorific expression not of the messenger but of the speaker who wants to convey the message.

Observing how a speaker treats a referent is the best method to judge the honorific system in *Heike-Monogatari* and so I try to classify a referent from the point of view of a speaker.

During this period, the honorific expression is determined mainly by the social status of a referent. Sakurai (1966) classified the level of social class from the honorific usage in *Konjaku-Monogatari*, and Nishida (1978) applied Sakurai's classification to sort them into three categories. Here I use Nishida's classification:

1. emperor, retired emperor, empress, prince, regent, and chief advisor to

emperor

2. minister and aristocracy above the third court rank

3. aristocracy below the third court rank

Now we need to classify the honorific expressions used toward a referent. Nishida's (1974) research on the honorific expressions in the conversational parts focuses on the honorific expressions of speaker to addressee. My research indicates that there is little difference between honorific expression toward an addressee and a referent, so we can use his classification. There are three types of sentences where honorific expressions toward a referent can appear.

A. a referent's X, or the X of a referent

B. a referent does X

C. somebody does X to a referent

The honorific expression that a speaker uses toward a referent reflects one of these three types. For instance, 'the sword of a referent' is type A; 'a referent comes' is type B; 'somebody says to a referent' is type C. And we can find another type: 'referent 1 does X to referent 2', but this is a combination of types B and C. We can list the linguistic features that express honorifics as follows: reference terms, case particles, nouns, verbs, and others. Let me give more concrete examples. For reference terms, there are honorific titles such as *dono* 殿, *kyou* 卿, *kou* 公, *kimi* 君; humble suffixes *domo* 共 and *me* め; status titles *houwau* 法皇, *sammi* 三位, *suke* 守 and *niudau* 入道; kinship terms *titi* 父 and *haha* 母; and pronouns *kore* これ, *are* あれ and pronoun is attached to nouns *konoko* この子. As for case particles, *no* の and *ga* が. For the prefix, *go* 御. As for verbs: *asobasu* あそばす, *shiroshimesu* しろしめす, *ohashimasu* おはします, *kikoshimesu* きこしめす, *oboshimesu* おぼしめす, *ohosu* おほす and *tamahasu* 給はす are supreme respectful verbs; *ohasu* おはす, *obosu* おぼす, *notamahu* のたまふ, *tamahu* 給ふ and *mesu* めす are ordinary respectful verbs; *mausu* 申す and *mawiru* 参る are humble verbs; *se-tamahu* せ給ふ, *mashimasu* まします and *shimetamahu* しめ給ふ are supreme respectful auxiliary verbs; and *tamahu* 給ふ, *ari* あり, *raru* らる are ordinary respectful auxiliary verbs.

Words that are loaded with honorific value are in italics, and honorific value is shown in brackets by the abbreviations listed in the style notes. Verbs are written as follows; *notamahu* 'say (ORV)' to indicate that *notamahu* is the ordinary respectful verb meaning 'say'.

The case particles *no* and *ga* have honorific value; in the following, *no* is used for the lieutenant, who is the son of the grand counsellor, and *ga* is used to mention the local officer by his first name, Yasuyori.

少将の取ッてよむにも、康頼入道が読みけるにも（巻3、足摺）[2]

seusiyau *no* 'RPA' totte yomunimo yasuyori niudau *ga* 'HPA' yomi kerunimo[3]

'Now Naritsune (= the lieutenant, *Seusiyau*) and Yasuyori appeared. Each of them in turn read the letter' (163)

Titles range from one's position in office or one's social status, to given names and Chinese names. For example, Kiyomori is sometimes called *niudau siyaukoku*. *Siyaukoku* is the Chinese word for chancellor, and Rodriguez (1955)[4] tells us that a Chinese name is a term of deep respect. Yoritomo is called either *kamakura dono* or by his first name *Yoritomo*, which is used only with humble expressions. The respectful suffix *dono* is used mainly for ministers like Moromichi, Narichika, Motofusa, Kiyomori, Shigemori and Munemori, but the head of a family also has *dono* (*Kawasaki dono*) attached to his family name even he is not a minister.

Dual honorifics include expressions such as *X ga Y ni hon wo sashiage rare mashi ta*, 'X gave a book to Y'. *Sashiage* is a humble verb, and *rare* is a respectful auxiliary verb, yet both forms can coexist in speaking of the same referent. This was quite common in the Heian period but is rare today. In dual honorific expressions a speaker makes referent X humble to another referent Y and then respects X. This apparent contradiction has developed into a focus of writings that deal with the characteristics of the humble verb. Watanabe (1981) concludes that 'Honorifics in the Heian period have the character of both relative honorifics (but less so than modern honorifics) and absolute honorifics (but not so much as in the previous Nara period). It must be understood as an honorific system that possesses both characteristics in the process from absolute to relative honorifics'. In Rodriguez (1955) there is the following description: 'When two referents are both worthy of respect, we make the lower referent humble to the higher one by *marasuru*, and show respect to the lower referent by adding the respectful *rare* or *ari*, preceded by *vo*'. It can be understood that dual honorifics survived until early modern times[5].

Dual honorifics also exist in *Heike-Monogatari*.

In the following, the messenger Toshinari speaks about Yorinaga, the Minister of the Left, to Yorinaga's father, Tadami:

富家殿ニ、今一度、御対面申サセ給ハンㇳテ渡セ給テ候（保元物語、中）

huka-*dono* 'RP' ni ima-ichido *go*-taimen-*mausa* 'HAN' *se-tamaha* 'SRA' n to te watara *se-tamahi* 'SRA' te saurou.

'(Yorinaga) came to meet Fuka (=Tadami)'

He uses the humble verb *o-mausu* for Yorinaga when addressing Tadami, but is at the same time respectful to Yorinaga by using *se-tamahu*. It is the most appropriate expression because they are son and father, and the speaker needs to respect both of them. The next example shows how a messenger of Minamoto Yorimasa treats his master when addressing monks.

衆徒の御中へ、三位殿の申せと候（巻1、御輿振）

siyuto no on-naka he minamoto sammi-*dono* 'RP' *no* 'RPA' *mause* 'say (HVN)' to saburahu.

'Most honorable priests, I pray you to hear the message of Minamoto Yorimasa, the lord of the third court rank.' (68)

He respects his master by using *dono* and the case particle *no*, but makes him humble in relation to those he is addressing. The context of the above example is that the other referent is an addressee himself.

In sum, I classify honorific expressions into five categories:

1. supreme respectful expression (SRE)
2. ordinary respectful expression (ORE)
3. dual expression (DE)
4. neutral expression (NE)
5. humble expression (HE)

I have not found any contradictions in the use of nouns as humble expressions or verbs as respectful expressions, therefore all expressions fall into one of the above categories.

4. Analysis

The term 'superiority' used here is of three types: kinship, hierarchy and social status. Within a family, superiority is determined by a kinship relationship such as that of father and son; and in a battle field, superiority is determined by the hierarchical relationship between a commander and his followers. But when these three relationships compete with each other, social status becomes the most important determinant of superiority, followed by hierarchy and kinship, in that order.

In itemizing the rules, those that follow the main rule are shown as ①, whilst the exceptions are shown as ❶.

4.1 Referent who is inferior to a speaker

Because social standing was strictly observed during this period, a referent that was inferior to a speaker was commonly treated by use of a humble expression.

① **The inferior by kinship is treated with a humble expression.**

Kiyomori refers to his grandson, Sukemori, when speaking to his followers who are inferior to Sukemori:

前駆、御随身どもがもとゞりきッて、資盛が恥すゝげ（巻1、殿下乗合）

sengu mi-zuijin domo ga motodori kitte *sukemori* 'FN' *ga* 'HPA' hazi susuge

'Cut off the topknots of van couriers and attendants. Thus Sukemori's honor will be avenged.' (47)

② **An inferior by hierarchy is treated with a humble expression.**

A master uses the humble expression when speaking of his follower to anybody. Here a high ranking monk, Keishu, refers to his disciple when speaking to a member of the imperial family:

弟子で候刑部房俊秀をまいらせ候（巻4、大衆揃）

desi de sarauhu giyaububau *shunsiu* 'FN' *wo maira* 'come (HVN)' *se sarauhu*

'I will have my disciple Shunsiu go with you.' (262)

And below, when Koremori talks to his follower, using the humble pronoun *onore*, but also uses a neutral expression for the follower's father, we see the importance of hierarchical order.

をのれが父、斎藤別当、北国へくだッし時（巻7、維盛都落）

onore-ra ga titi saitou bettau kitagunihe kudasshi toki

'When your father, Sanemori (=Saitou bettau), went forth to do battle in the Northern provinces.' (435)

③ **An inferior by social status is treated with a humble expression.**

Kiyomori speaks of Yukitsuna, who is his inferior by social status, to his other followers and uses the humble expressions *ga*, *sanzu* and *mairu*.

常に参らぬ者が参じたるは何事ぞ（巻2、西光被斬）

tuneni mo *maira* 'come (HVN)' nu mono *ga* 'HPA' *sanji* 'come (HVN)' taru ha nani goto zo

'He (=Yukitsuna) is not a regular visitor here. Go and ask on what business he has come.' (89)

And Minamoto Yorimasa refers to Watanabe Kihohu to the other Watanabe clan:

いま見よ、只今参らうずるぞ（巻4、競）

ima miyo tada ima *maira* 'come (HVN)' u zuru zo

'Let us wait. He (=Kihohu) will surely come.' (251)

Kiyomori uses the humble verb *mairu* to describe the act of the referent coming to his place. People who belong to classification 2 never use self-respectful expressions as would the emperor or the retired emperor. Instead they describe the deeds of their inferiors using humble verbs, and, in this way, respect themselves.

In the following, Kiyomori attaches no honorific title to Yukitsuna's name when addressing his followers.

さればこそ、行綱はまことを言ひけり（巻2、西光被斬）

sareba koso *yukituna* 'FN' ha makoto o ihi keri

'That is what I supposed. Yukitsuna spoke the truth.' (90-91)

And in the case of an addressee who is superior to the speaker, Yoritomo refers to his follower, Tomoyasu, by humble expression when addressing a retired emperor:

まづ鼓判官知泰が不思議事申出して、御所をも焼かせまいらせ、高僧、貴僧をもほろぼしたてまッたるこそ寄怪なれ（巻8、法住寺合戦）

madu tudumi hangan *tomoyasu* 'FN' *ga* 'HPA' husigi no koto *maushi-idashi* 'speak to'(HVN) te go-sho wo mo yakase *mairase* 'HA', kausou kisou wo mo horoboshi *tatemat* 'HAN' taru koso kikkai nare

'First, Captain Tsuzumi is to be accused of causing the burning of the Cloistered Palace and the death of the noble priests by his presumptuous agitation.' (501)

Next, Yoritomo addresses Yorimori, the captain of his enemy.

宗清は御共して候か（巻10、三日平家）

munekiyo 'FN' ha on-tomo shi te saurau ka

'Where is Munekiyo? Is he not escorting you?' (630)

He refers to Munekiyo, the follower of Yorimori, using his first name but also uses the polite verb *saurau*. In modern times it is common for the employee of an addressee to be treated by respectful expression, because he is considered part of the addressee's in-group. As we have examined so far, it is common to treat an inferior to a speaker by humble expression.

❶ **A referent who is of a high social status can sometimes be treated with a respectful expression even if he is inferior by kinship. In particular, a person who belongs to classification 1 is usually accorded a supreme respectful expression.**

Shigemori talks to his son, Koremori, in the following.

御辺は人の子共の中には、勝て見え給ふ也（巻3、無文）

gohen ha hito no kodo-mono no naka ni ha sugurete mie *tamahu* 'ORA' nari

'I must tell you that you are the finest of all my children.' (199)

He respects his son by using the respectful expression *tamahu* when addressing his follower:

この盃をば、先少将にこそとらせたけれ共、親より先にはよものみ給はじなれば、（巻3、無文）

kono sakaduki o ba madu seushiyau ni koso tora se takere domo, oya yori saki ni ha yomo nomi *tamaha* 'ORA' zi nare ba

'I wish to give you this cup. But you may hesitate to drink before your father does.' (199)[6]

This expression indicates that Koremori's social status is more important than the kinship relationship.

It is also the same if a referent belongs to classification 1. Toba Emperor's daughter, Hachijō Nyoin, addresses Yorimori:

> まッたく此御所にはわたらせ給はず（巻4、若宮出家）
>
> mattaku kono gosho ni ha watara *se tamaha* 'SRA' zu
>
> 'He (=Prince Takakura) is no longer here (=the palace).' (275)

She is the adoptive mother of Prince Takakura, but he is treated with a supreme respectful expression because of his high social status. And in the following, the retired Emperor Goshirakawa also uses a supreme respectful expression for his grandson, the fourth prince of Takakura.

> 是ぞ我まことの孫にてましましける。故女院のおさなをひに、すこしもたがわせ給はぬ物かな（巻8、山門御幸）
>
> kore zo makoto no mago ni te *mashimashi* 'be (SRV)' keru. ko-niyouin no osana ohi ni sukoshi mo tagaha *se tamaha* 'SRA' nu mono kana
>
> 'Oh, he is my grandson! He is the perfect image of his father, the late emperor, in his childhood' (459-460)

4.2 Referent and speaker of the same status

④ **A referent who is of the same hierarchical status as a speaker is usually treated either by a neutral or a humble expression.**

Among *samurai* 'warriors', a comrade is treated as follows:

> すはや源氏の大ぜいのよするは、斎藤別当が申つる様に（巻5、富士川）
>
> suha-ya genji no ohozei no yosuru ha saitou bettau *ga* 'HPA' *moushi* 'say (HVN)' turu yauni
>
> 'It is the Genji coming to attack us! Yesterday Sanemori (=Saitou bettau) said,' (331)

The humble verb is used without any honorific title. And among chieftains of *samurai* also, each is treated without any honorific title.

> 成田もつゞひて出できたり（巻9、一二之懸）
>
> *Narita* 'LN' mo tudui te ide-kita ri
>
> 'But that deceitful Gorō (=the first name of Narita) gained on me and passed by.' (544)

Their enemies are treated as follows:

越中次郎兵衛はないか、上総五郎兵衛、悪七兵衛はないか、能登殿はましまさぬか（巻9、一二之懸）

ecchiyuu jiroubehe 'FN' ha nai ka, *kazusa goraubehe* 'FN', *akushichibiyaue* 'FN' ha nai ka, noto-*dono* 'RP' ha *mashimasa* 'be (SRV)' nu ka

'Is there one among you named Etchū no Jirōbyōe? Are Kazusa no Gorō and Akushichibyōe here? Is there in your midst the governor of Noto Province, Noritsune?' (545)

Samurai who are of the same rank are treated without any honorific title and by the neutral verb *nai* 'not to be here', but a leader is treated with the honorific title *dono* and the respectful verb *mashimasu*, 'be here'. Ecchiyuu, Kazusa and Noto are the place names of the *samurai's* home provinces.

Yorinaka addresses Gen Kurando's followers[7]:

ここなる馬は、源蔵人の馬とこそ見れ。はや討たれけるにこそ（巻8、法住寺合戦）

Koko naru koko naru uma ha gen no kurando no uma to koso mi ture. haya uta re keru ni koso

'I understand this chestnut belongs to my master. He (=Gen Kurando) must be dead by now.' (498)

Yorinaka treats Kurando, who is of the same rank, with a neutral expression, but the followers reply using a respectful expression.

川原坂の勢のなかへこそ懸入らせ給ひ候つるなれ。やがてあの勢の中より御馬も出きて候（巻8、法住寺合戦）

kawahara-zaka no sei no naka he koso kake ira *se-tamahi* 'SRA' saurahi turu nare. yagate ano sei no naka yori *on* 'RP'-uma mo ide-ki te saurahu.

'He (=Kurando) must have charged upon the enemy at Kawara-zaka, because it is from that direction that his horse has come.' (499)

The hierarchical order is clearly reflected in these expressions.

4.3 Referent who is superior to a speaker

It is common for a referent who is superior by any relationship—kinship, hierarchical or social status—to be treated with a respectful expression.

⑤ **Referent who is superior by kinship is treated with a respectful expression within the family.**

For example, Shigemori addresses one of his sons, Sukemori, and uses a respectful expression to refer to his father Kiyomori.

たとひ入道いかなる不思議を下知し給ふとも、など重盛に夢をば見せざりけるぞ（巻1、殿下乗合）

tatohi nihudau ika naru hushigi o geti shi *tamahu* 'ORA' tomo, nado shigemori ni yume o ba mise zari keru zo.

'Even though the Priest-Premier issued an order, and however exciting that order may have been, why did you not let me, Shigemori, know about it?' (48)

Let us look at the honorific expression used toward a referent related by marriage. In the first example, Norimori speaks of his half-brother to his son-in-law, Naritsune, using a respectful expression.

入道あまりに腹を立てて、教盛には終に対面もし給はず（巻2、少将乞請）

nihudau amari ni hara o tate te, norimori ni ha tuhini taimen mo shi *tamaha* 'ORA' zu

'The Priest-Premier was so angry that I was not even allowed to see him.' (105)

Naritsune addresses his father-in-law, Norimori:

大納言が事をば、いかゞきこしめされ候……ちゝを今一度見ばやと思ふため也（巻2、少将乞請）

dainagon *ga* 'HPA' koto o ba ikaga kikosimesa re saurahu. …titi wo ima itido mi baya to omohu tame nari.

'But what have you heard of my father, the new councillor? … it is only so that I may see my father but once more.' (105)

He refers to his father Naricchika with a neutral expression, using the case particle *ga*. This usage can be understood in terms of one of the following reasons: a neutral expression is the official expression of aristocracy toward an out-group addressee, or Norimori is indebted to Kiyomori because Narichika had rebelled against Kiyomori.

And in another example, Tomomori refers to his son, Tomoakira, when addressing his brother, Munemori.

> 武蔵守にをくれ候ぬ（巻9、知章最期）
>
> musashi no kami ni okure saurahi nu
>
> 'I have outlived my son Tomoakira.' (565)

He refers to his son by his official title—*Musasi no kami* 'the governor of Musashi'—a polite usage at that time.

In the following, Munemori talks with his brother Tomomori about both their sons.

> 武蔵守の、父の命にかはられるこそありがたけれ。手もきゝ、心もかうに、よき大将軍にておはしつる人を。清宗と同年にて、今年は十六な（巻9、知章最期）
>
> musashi no kami no 'RPA', titi no inochi ni kaha rare 'ORA' keru koso arigata kere. te mo kiki, kokoro mo kauni yoki dai-shiyaugun ni te *ohashi* 'be (ORV)' turu hito wo. *kiyomune* 'FN' to dounen ni te kotoshi ha jihuroku na.
>
> 'What a faithful son he was! Tomoakira was indeed a great general, skilled in the arts of bow and sword and valiant of heart. He would be just sixteen years of age if he were still alive. As young as my son Kiyomune !' (566)

He makes a clear distinction between his own family and that of his brother, by not using any honorific title for his own son whilst using a respectful expression for his brother's son.

⑥ **Referent who is superior by kinship is treated with a respectful expression to a speaker's vassal or to an inferior addressee.**

Shigemori addresses his follower and is referring to his father, Kiyomori, using the respectful auxiliary *tamahu*.

> 入道腹の立のまゝに、ものさはがしき事し給ひては、後に必くやみ給ふべし（巻2、小教訓）
>
> nihudau hara no tati no mama ni mono sawagashiki koto shi *tamahi* 'ORA' te ha noti ni kanarazu kuyami *tamahu* 'ORA' besi
>
> 'When the Priest-Premier is angry, he is apt to do rash things that he afterward regrets.' (99)

Sukemori addresses his brother Koremori's vassal:

御詞にて仰らるる事はなかりしか（巻10、三日平氏）

on 'RP'-*kotoba ni te ohose-raruru* 'say (SRV)' *koto ha nakari shi ka*

'Did he (=Koremori) give you any more words for us besides this letter?' (628)

A superior by kinship relation is treated with a respectful expression when the addressee is one's vassal. This applies even when an addressee is not a vassal, if he is clearly inferior by social status. For example, when Tokitada addresses the warrior Koremura, the messenger of his enemy, he refers to his brother-in-law Kiyomori with a respectful expression:

就中に故太政大臣入道殿は、保元、平治両度の逆乱をしづめ、其上鎮西の者どもをば、うち様へこそ召されしか（巻8、大宰府落）

nakannduku ni ko-dajyaudaijin nihudau-dono 'RS' *ha hougen heidi riyau-do no gekiran o shidume sono uhe tinzei no mono domo o ba uti zama ni koso mesare* 'call (ORV)' *si ka*

'Above all, our late Priest-Premier destroyed the rebels both in the Hōgen and Heiji eras. And it was he who summoned you, the men of Kyushu, to the capital and gave you the opportunity to serve at court.' (471–472)

Social status is an important factor in determining honorific expression.

❷ **Referent who is superior by kinship is treated with a neutral expression when an addressee is his lord.**

For example, the warrior, Beppu Kotarou, addresses his lord Yoshitsune as follows:

父で候し義重法師がおしへ候ひしは（巻9、老馬）

titi de saurahi shi yoshishige 'FN' *hohushi ga* 'HPA' *oshihe saurai shi ha*

'My father, Priest Yoshishige, once told me' (540)

The referent who is superior by kinship is treated with the case particle *ga*, and a neutral expression.

❸ **In an official ceremony, a speaker introduces oneself by referring to a superior by kinship using a neutral expression.**

足利太郎俊綱が子、又太郎忠綱、生年十七歳（巻4、宮御最期）

ashikaga tarou[8] *toshituna* 'FN' *ga* 'HPA' *ko matatarou tadatuna shiyaunen jihunanasai*

'I am Matatarō Tadatsune, aged seventeen, the son of Ashikaga no Tarō Toshitsune.' (269)

佐々木三郎秀義が四男、佐々木四郎高綱（巻9、宇治川先陣）

sasaki saburou *hideyoshi* 'FN' *ga* 'HPA' yonnan sasaki shirou takatuna

'I am Sasaki no Shirō Takatsuna, the fourth son of Sasaki no Saburō Hideyoshi.' (512)

In these cases, the *buke* 武家 'warrior' announces his name in the fixed humble pattern, *X ga Y, Z*, 'I am Z, who is Y (=kinship relation e.g. a son or daughter) of X'. A daughter of *kuge* 公家 'aristocrat' also introduces herself to a retired emperor as follows.

故少納言入道信西がむすめ、阿波の内侍と申ししものにてさぶらふなり（灌頂巻、大原御幸）

ko-seunagon nihudau *shinsei* 'FN' *ga* 'HPA' musume, Aha no naishi to maushi shi mono nite saburahu nari

'I am a daughter of the late priest Shinzei. I am Awa-no-Naishi.' (771)

These examples show that in a formal occasion social status is more important than kinship.

❹ **To an addressee who is very high in social status, like an emperor or a retired emperor, a referent that is superior by kinship is treated with a humble expression.**

Munemori addresses the retired emperor Goshirakawa, and refers to his father, Kiyomori:

鳥羽殿へ御幸なしまいらせんと、父の入道申候（巻3、法皇被流）

toba-dono he miyuki nashi *mairase* 'HAN' n to titi no nihudau *maushi* 'say (HVN)' saurahu

'He (=Kiyomori) says that he wishes Your Majesty to stay at the North Palace of Toba.' (216)

And Yoshitsune addresses an emperor and mentions his brothers, Yoritomo and Noriyori:

義仲が謀叛の事、頼朝大おどろき、範頼、義経をはじめとして（巻9、河原合戦）

yoshinaka ga muhon no koto, *yoritomo* 'FN' ohoi ni odoroki *noriyori* 'FN', yoshitune o hazime to shi te

'The lawless conduct of Yoshinaka greatly surprised my brother, Yoritomo, and so he has sent Noriyori and Yoshitsune.' (517)

⑦ **Referent who is superior by hierarchical relationship is treated with a respectful expression.**

Whether addressing friend or foe, a lord is always treated with a respectful expression. A warrior speaks of his lord to his friend:

河原殿おとゝい、只今城の内へまッさきかけて討たれ給いひぬるぞや（巻9、二度之懸）

kahara-*dono* 'RS' ototoi tadaima jiyau no uti he massaki kake te uta re *tamahi* 'ORA' nuru zo ya

'The Kawara brothers made the first strike into the enemy position, but they have been killed!' (548)

A warrior speaks of his lord to his enemy:

鎌倉殿の、「相構てよくよくなぐさめまいらせよ。懈怠にて頼朝うらむな」と仰られ候（巻10、千手前）

kamakura-*dono* 'RS' no 'RPA' 'ahikamahe te yoku-yoku nagusame mairase yo. kedainite yoritomo uramu na' to *ohose rare* 'say (SRV)' saurahu

'He (=Yoritomo) ordered me to wait upon you most cordially so that you would feel comfortable here. If you feel sad because of my negligent service, he will not forgive me.' (605)

清和天皇十代の御末、鎌倉殿の御弟、九郎大夫判官殿ぞかし（巻11、嗣信最期）

seiwa tennou jihu dai no *on* 'RP'-suwe, kamakura-*dono* 'RS' no *on* 'RP'-otouto, kurou taihu haugwan-*dono* 'RS' zo kashi

'Our commander is the captain of the Police Commissioners Division, Yoshitsune, a young brother of Lord Yoritomo, a tenth-generation descendant of Emperor Seiwa.' (655)

In such cases, a warrior treats his lord with a respectful expression regardless of whom he is addressing.

The warrior Takiguchi Kiohu addresses his enemy, Taira no Munemori and treats his lord with a respectful expression:

> 何と思はれ候けるやらむ、かうともおほせられ候はず（巻4、競）
>
> nanto omoha *re* 'ORA' saurahi keru ya ramu kau to mo *ohose-rare* 'say(SRV)' sauraha zu
>
> 'though I do not know why, my master (=Yorimasa) did not summon me.' (249)

But, he changes the honorific expressions in accordance with the social status of the referent. For example, elsewhere he refers to Yorimasa as *neudau-dono*; he refers to a monk as *Miidera hohusi* 'the monks of Mii temple'; and calls his colleagues as *Watanabe no sitasii yatu-bara* 'the men of the Watanabe clan'. For this, we can understand how important the social status of referents is in determining the choice of expression. The examples we have examined so far are all of a type. That is to say, the addressees are all warriors and are inferior to the speaker's lord, or they belong to the same social rank if the addressee is also a lord. There is only one example of an addressee who is superior to a speaker's lord—Iesada speaks of his lord, Taira no Tadamori, to a messenger who is an aristocrat below the sixth court rank—but there too a respectful expression is used for the lord[9].

> 相伝の主備前守殿、今夜闇討にせられ給べき由（巻1、殿上闇討）
>
> sauden no shiyu bizen no kau no *tono* 'RN' konya yamiuti ni serare *tamahu* 'ORA' beki yoshi
>
> 'It has been reported that my master, the governor of Bizen (=Tadamori), is to be attacked in the dark tonight.' (8)

Women also use the same honorific expression. Yoshimune's wet nurse addresses Yoshitsune and uses the respectful prefix *on* to refer to her master:

> 御頸ばかりをば給はッて、後世をとぶらひまいらせん（巻11、副将被斬）
>
> *on* 'RP'-kubi bakari o ba tamahat te gose o tobirahi *mairase* 'HAO' n
>
> 'We pray you to allow us to take back his (=Yoshimune's) head with us. We wish to pray for his afterlife.' (700)

⑧ **A warrior uses a respectful expression when referring to the head of his enemy.**

> 平家の御方に聞えさせ給ひつる薩摩守殿をば、岡辺の六野太忠純が討ちたてまッたるぞや（巻9、忠教最期）

heike no on-kata ni kikoe sase *tamahi* 'ORA' turu satuma no kami-*dono* 'RS' o ba, okabe no rokuyata tadasumi ga uti *tatemat* 'HAO' taru zo ya

'The head of one of the most prominent Heike courtiers, a lord named Tadanori, governor of Satsuma Province, has been obtained by Okabe no Rokuyata Tadazumi.' (558)

A warrior addresses his lord, Yoshinaka, using the respectful title *dono* to refer to the head of his enemy.

甲斐の一条次郎殿とこそ承候へ（巻9、木曽最期）

kahi no itideu jirou-*dono* 'RS' to koso *uketamari* 'hear (HVO)' saurahe

'I hear that it is Tadayori's army, my lord.' (520)

A warrior treats a superior person, even if he is a foe, with a respectful expression.

Yoshitsune refers to his brother, Yoritomo, addressing a retired emperor:

東国より前兵衛佐頼朝が舎弟、九郎義経こそ参ッて候へ（巻9、河原合戦）

tougoku yori saki no hiyauwe no suke *yoritomo* 'FN' ga 'HPA' shiyatei, kurou yoshitune koso maitte saurahe

'Kurō Yoshitsune, a brother of the former aide to the chief of the Imperial Guard, Yoritomo, has come from the east.' (516)

Yet, he uses a humble expression because the addressee is superior to Yoritomo. However, when the addressee is a warrior, Yoshitsune uses a respectful expression to refer to Yoritomo:

いかに鎌倉殿より御文はなきか（巻12、土佐房被斬）

ikani kamakura-*dono* 'RS' yori on 'RP'-humi ha naki ka

'Tosa-bō, have you brought a letter from Lord Yoritomo?' (727)

In conclusion, a referent that is superior to an addressee is treated with a respectful expression, and one that is of the same rank is treated with a neutral expression.

⑨ **Dual honorifics can be used when either an addressee or a referent is superior to a speaker's lord.**

福原より大将殿の御参り候（巻5、月見）

hukuhara yori taishau-*dono* 'RS' no 'RPA' on 'RP'-*mairi* 'come (HVN)' saurahu

'It is the general, come from Fukuhara.' (297)

A warrior refers to his lord and uses the humble verb *mairu*, but also the respectful title *dono*.

⑩ Those who belong in classification 1—like emperors or retired emperors—are always referred to with a supreme respectful expression.

Kiyomori has come to power yet affords the retired emperor, Goshirakawa, the following supreme respectful expressions.

To his son, Shigemori 重盛:

かねても思食より仰らるゝ旨のあればこそ、かうは聞ゆらめ（巻1、清水寺炎上）

kanetemo *oboshimeshi* 'think (SRV)' yori *ohose-raruru* 'say (SRV)' mune no are ba koso kau ha kikoyu rame

'This is why the rumor sprang up that he (=Goshirakawa) invited the mob to come down from Mount Hiei.' (41)

To his foe, Tada Ikituna 多田行綱:

さてそれをば法皇もしろしめされたるか（巻2、西光被斬）

sate sore wo ba houwau mo *shiroshimesa-re* 'know (SRV)' taru ka

'Does the cloistered emperor (=Goshirakawa) know of this?' (89)

And to his follower, Abe Sukenari 安陪資成:

それをば君もしろしめさるまじう候（巻2、西光被斬）

sore o ba kimi mo *shiroshimesa-ru* 'know (SRV)' majiu saurahu

'I hope that the cloistered emperor (=Goshirakawa) will not stand in my way.' (90)

Kiyomori describes the behavior of the retired emperor using supreme respectful expressions like *oboshimesu*, *ohoseraru* and *shiroshimesu*.

He addresses his brother, Munemori 宗盛 in the following:

成親卿が謀反は、事の数にもあらず、一向法皇の御結構にてありけるぞや（巻2、教訓状）

narichika kiyau *ga* 'HPA' muhon ha koto no kazu ni mo ara zu, ikkau houwau *no* 'RPA' *go* 'RP'-ketukou ni te ari keru zo ya

'If Narichika alone had been responsible for this plot, it would be no importance. But the cloistered emperor (=Goshirakawa) himself is the chief conspirator.' (109)

He uses a different honorific expression toward the two rebels, Narichika and Goshirakawa. That is, Narichika who is only of the second court rank is described with the case particle *ga*, and Goshirakawa who is a retired emperor by the case particle *no* and the respectful prefix *go*.

We have seen that those who belong to classification 1 are treated with supreme respectful expressions both by other people and among themselves in accordance with their social status. As shown in rule ❶, an emperor or a retired emperor treats his inferior by kinship relation with a supreme respectful expression because regardless of kinship hierarchy his kin also belongs to a high social status. Self-respectful honorifics are conceptually linked to the above illustrated honorific system. That is, an emperor respects himself because of his elevated social status as a member of imperial family.

⑪ **Regents and chief advisors to the emperor are treated with respectful expressions.**

Kiyomori is speaking to his son, Shigemori:

たとひ殿下なりとも、浄海があたりをば、憚り給ふべきに、おさなきものに、左右なく恥辱を与へられけるこそ、遺恨の次第なれ（巻1、殿下乗合）

tatohi *tenga* 'RN' nari tomo jiyaukai ga atari wo ba habakari *tamahu* 'ORA' beki ni,

osanaki mono ni saunaku tijiyoku wo atahe *rare* 'ORA' keru koso, ikan no sidai nare

'However high a rank the prince (=Motohusa) may enjoy, he should pay special attention to my concerns, for I am Jōkai[10]. Instead, he has not hesitated to dishonor this beloved grandchild of mine. Now I bear him a grudge.' (46)

Although Kiyomori is angry with Motohusa, he uses the respectful auxiliaries *tamahu* and *raru* above and the humble auxiliary *tatematsuru* below:

殿下御出あるべかむなり。いづくにても待ちうけ奉り（巻1、殿下乗合）

tenga 'RN' *giyo* 'RP'-shutu aru bekamu nari. iduku ni te mo mati-uke *tatematuri* 'HAO'

'the prince (=Motohusa) is scheduled to attend court. Choose a good hiding place and wait for his procession.' (47)

Motohusa's social status as the chief advisor to the emperor determines the proper honorific expression, whether or not he is a foe.

5. Conclusion

The general rules that are listed as ① are the rules of absolute honorifics, but the exceptions that are listed as ❶ cannot be interpreted according to the rules of absolute honorifics. Let us find a system that can explain both the general rules and the exceptions.

1. The social status relationship is the most important factor determining honorific expression, followed by the hierarchical and kinship relationship.

In order to distinguish the levels of the superiority between referents, I took three vertical relationship into consideration; kinship, hierarchical and social status. It is common for a referent who is superior by kinship to be treated with a respectful expression, and for a referent who is inferior by kinship to be treated with a humble expression. But if a referent is of a high social status, he can be treated by respectful expression even by a speaker who is his superior by kinship, as when Shigemori uses a respectful expression to refer to his son, Koremori. And behavior can also be a factor in determining the honorific expression. For example, Kiyomori uses a humble expression for his uncle Tadamasa, who has been executed, but towards his father Tadamori, he adopts a respectful expression. Kin'yoshi treats his daughter, an empress, and his grandchild with respectful expressions. By their kinship relationship, his daughter and grandchild are inferior, but they are superior by social status because the daughter married an emperor. This example shows that social status is more important than kinship.

In a hierarchical relationship such as a lord and vassals, it is easily understood who is to be treated with a respectful expression and who is to be treated with a humble expression. A self-respectful expression like *kochira he maire* 'come here!', (which elevates the speaker), is commonly used by a lord when talking to his vassals. Even parents of a vassal are treated using a humble expression. A humble expression is used when a vassal refers to his superior by kinship to his lord. When addressing his enemy, a vassal will adopt a respectful expression to refer to his lord and a humble expression to speak of his superior by kinship relation. Even when addressing his own lord, a vassal uses a respectful expression for the chief of his foe because respect is accorded to the enemy's status as a leader. In all cases, we can see that social status is the most important factor in determining honorific expression.

2. Superiority by social status is not linear but stepped.

In classifying social status into three groups, I conclude that superiority by social status is not linear but stepped. That is to say, differences in superiority within the same group are quite small and can be ignored. Using as an example the aristocracy that belongs to classification 2, third rank court aristocrats are not considered to be superior to the fourth rank, because they are of the same social class. However, there is a difference between the imperial family on the one hand, and the regent or chief advisor to the emperor on the other, who can be placed in the quasi-1 classification.

3. Dual honorifics are sometimes used when both a referent and an addressee are superior to a speaker.

For example, a messenger refers to his lord to a member of the lord's family with *hukuhara yori taisiyau-dono no on-mairi saurahu* 'it is the general, come from Fukuhara'. He uses the honorific title *dono*, the case particle *no* and the respectful prefix *on*, but at the same time uses the humble verb *mairu* to elevate his lord's family. In this way, he respects both his lord and his lord's family. It would be quite interesting to discover whether or not these dual honorifics have inherited from those of the Heian period.

4. The degree of superiority between a referent and an addressee influences the honorific expression toward the referent.

The honorific expression used toward a referent seems to be controlled only by the superiority between a referent and a speaker, although the superiority between a referent and an addressee is also influential. It is common for a humble expression to be employed in both the following situations: when speaking of one's kin superior to one's master; and speaking of anybody, even a parent or lord, when addressing a person of classification 1.

Let us compare some treatments of a superior by kinship relationship and a superior by hierarchy relationship. The levels of social status follow the classification chart, and those who belong to the same classification are counted as the same rank. The horizontal line shows superiority between a referent and an addressee, and the vertical line shows the honorific expression. For example, the superior on the horizontal line means that an addressee is superior to a referent. The number that is shown on a table means the frequency by not token, but type. That is to say, however many times the same speaker refers to the same referent when addressing the same addressee, it is counted as one case. In Table 1, frequency is shown in the upper section of each column, and the percentage within vertical lines is shown in the lower section.

	superior	equal	inferior	total
SRE	0	1(33.3)	2(66.6)	3
			(10.0)	(7.7)
ORE	1(3.3)	12(40.0)	17(56.7)	30
	(25.0)	(80.0)	(85.0)	(76.9)
DE	2(40.0)	2(40.0)	1(20.0)	5
	(0.0)	(13.3)	(5.0)	(12.8)
NE	0	0	0	0
HE	1(100.0)	0	0	1
	(25.0)			(2.6)
total	4(10.3)	15(38.5)	20(51.3)	39

Table 1 honorific expression
to a hierarchical superior
$x^2 = 0.0133$

Table 1 shows how a lord is treated by his vassal based on the relative status of both lord and addressee. A lord is treated with a respectful expression only when he is the same rank as, or superior to, an addressee. The only case where a respectful expression is used even to an addressee who is superior to his lord is the example of Iesada. There is another text, *Yoshino-bon*, where a neutral expression is used for the same passage. It is clear then that the honorific expression toward a lord is determined by the status differential between a lord and an addressee.

	superior	equal	inferior	total
SRE	0	0	3(100.0) (11.5)	3 (5.2)
ORE	1(3.7) (7.7)	3(11.1) (17.6)	23(85.2) (88.5)	27 (48.2)
DE	0	0	0	0
NE	3(27.3) (23.1)	8(72.7) (47.1)	0	11 (19.6)
HE	9(60.0) (69.2)	6(40.0) (35.3)	0	15 (26.8)
total	13(23.2)	17(30.7)	26(46.4)	56

Table 2 honorific expression to a kinship superior
$\chi^2 = 1.310$

Next, we will look at the superior by kinship relationship in Table 2. The superior by kinship relationship is treated with a respectful expression when he is of the same rank as, or superior to, an addressee. A humble expression is frequently used when one makes a self-introduction, and here also the honorific expression toward a superior by kinship relationship is determined by status differential between a referent and an addressee. Let us use the Chi-square (χ^2) statistical means of comparing when the relative status between a referent and an addressee is more important. The value of a superior by kinship relationship is higher than that of a lord, and this shows that status differential that exists between a superior by kinship relationship and an addressee is more important than that which exists between a lord and an addressee.

In answer to whether the honorific system in *Heike-Monogatari* is absolute or relative honorifics, all articles suggest that the superior by hierarchy relationship is treated by absolute honorifics whilst the superior by kinship relationship is treated by relative honorifics. But there is only one example to support the absolute honorifics hypothesis. That is when Iesada treats his lord, Tadamori, to an addressee who is Tadamori's superior with a respectful expression. There is also only one example to support the relative honorifics hypothesis. Yoshitsune uses a neutral expression to speak of his brother, Yoritomo, to a retired emperor. It would be quite useful if we could find examples of how Yoshitsune treats Yoritomo when speaking to the other warriors' leader.

5. **The in-group or out-group criterion that is important for modern honorifics doesn't apply in *Heike-Monogatari*.**

A parent, as a superior in-group member, is treated with a neutral or humble expression to an out-group person, but a lord, who also is a superior in-group member, is treated with a respectful expression. Therefore, most researchers conclude that the honorific system in *Heike-Monogatari* is in some aspects absolute honorifics and in others relative honorifics. But as we have seen, an honorific expression toward a referent is determined by the difference in social status between a referent and an addressee. It might therefore be appropriate to view in the same way the superiority of both the kinship and the hierarchical relationship. Let us look at the case of a superior by kinship relationship in which a parent is usually treated with a neutral or humble expression when a warrior introduces himself or refers to his lord. For a parent to be treated with a respectful expression, an addressee has to be of the same rank as, or lower than, a speaker. The same context has to apply for a superior by hierarchical relationship to be treated with a respectful expression. A superior by hierarchical relationship is necessarily high in social status and a speaker's lord is superior to an addressee; as a result a warrior treats his lord with a respectful expression when speaking to the chief of his enemy because both lord and chief are the same social class. A lord is treated not as in-group person, but according to his social status.

In conclusion, in *Heike-Monogatari* an honorific expression toward a referent is determined by the difference in social status between a referent and an addressee[11].

Proposal of the term Hierarchical Honorifics

Kindaichi (1941) presented the main issue of this book, absolute and relative honorifics:

The honorifics used today are different from those of old. The referent term for father changes relative to the person to whom a speaker mentions his father: within the family, *otōsama* (Mr. Father, *sama* being an honorific title); to people outside the family, *chichi* or *guhu* (stupid father). Therefore I name today's honorifics 'relative honorifics'.

Kindaichi defined relative honorifics as the honorific expression that is determined by the relationship between a referent and an addressee; in contrast, he defined absolute honorifics as the honorific expression where an addressee's position is irrelevant:

> The characteristic of absolute honorifics is that a respectful expression is also used when a speaker refers to his own behavior.

He states that self-respectful expression is the defining characteristic of absolute honorifics. There still exists a dispute about the existence of self-respectful expressions in the history of Japanese honorifics, but my question then is how is it possible to connect self-respectful expressions with absolute honorifics when an addressee's position never play a role. Scholars who insist on the existence of self-respectful expressions argue that these are used to show the power and authority of emperors and God to the common people. I think that self-respectful expressions are used to clarify the status of superiority of speaker over addressee and, as such, they are very much a speaker-oriented expression. Hierarchical honorifics are sometimes used for absolute honorifics, with the same meaning. Hereafter, I define hierarchical honorifics and in/out-group honorifics in the following way. That is, hierarchical honorifics belongs to an honorific system wherein the honorific expression toward a referent is determined not by the relationship between speaker and referent but by the hierarchical order between addressee and referent. A referent that is superior to a speaker cannot be treated by a respectful expression if the addressee of that communicative event is superior to the referent by hierarchical order. And in/out-group honorifics are part of an honorific system where the honorific expression toward a referent is determined by the referent's position as a member of either a speaker or an addressee's in-group. So the question, 'Are the honorifics in *Heike-Monogatari* absolute or relative honorifics?' should instead be, 'Are the honorifics in

Heike-Monogatari hierarchical or in/out-group honorifics?' My answer is that they are hierarchical honorifics. The honorific expression toward a referent is determined by the hierarchical order between an addressee and a referent, but whether a referent belongs to a speaker's in-group or out-group is not a consideration at all in *Heike-Monogatari*. Kindaichi did not provide a clear-cut definition, and scholars use the same term with different meanings. I propose that now is the time to elucidate a clear definition.

What seems more important to understand, though, is that the honorific expression shown in *Heike-Monogatari* is that of the ruling classs—the *buke* and *kuge*. As I will show from Chapter 6, the public honorifics of the ruling class must be different from the private ones used by the common people. It would be problematic to imagine that the latter might be the same as those contained in *Heike-Monogatari*. And there needs to be a distinction of honorific usage according to gender. My conclusion is that men make use of relative honorifics more often than women, but this might be because men have more opportunities to be in the public domain than women. The characters in *Heike-Monogatari* are overwhelmingly men and the honorific examples are also those of public usage. It might be necessary to investigate how the honorific expression was used in private circumstances, but it is almost impossible to find this literature.

(Endnotes)

1 Tomioka (1959) suggests that there are some discrepancies between direct and indirect speech within the text.
2 The quoted parts are shown within parentheses. The number of volumes and its title are shown.
3 As for the neutral honorific form, I omit to write it in italics. I use italics for either the respectful or humble forms but the neutral form itself is unmarked. It is obligatory to choose the proper honorific expression, so if a neutral form is used, it means that either the referent or the addressee is an ordinary person belonging to the speaker's side.
4 Joan Rodriguez came to Japan in 1578 and stayed as a Christian missionary until exiled in 1610. During his stay, he left books on Japanese language for his fellow Portuguese. He compiled a Japanese grammar book titled *Arte da lingoa de Iapam* from 1604 to 1608. This book was translated into Japanese by Tadao Doi in 1955 and is used by Japanese linguists to

understand the Japanese language of that period. When I refer to this book, I quote Rodriguez (1955).

5   I interpret as 'dual' honorifics those expressions for a referent that use both humble and respectful forms both within the same predicate and the same sentence.
6   It is rather common to interpret that this utterance is spoken to his follower, Sadayoshi, in front of his son, Koremori.
7   Kurando is the name of the position at court, but his given name is Nakakane.
8   It was common to name sons by the order of birth. For example, the first son is named Tarō, the second Jirō, and the third Saburō.
9   In the *Yashiro-hon* text, considered to be older than the *Kakuichi-hon*, a respectful expression is not used in this passage. This could be a reflection of the historical shift in honorific expression between the time when the *Yashiro-hon* and the *Kakuichi-hon* were written.
10 Kiyomori's Buddhist name.
11 Mikami (1953) mentions an honorific system where a respectful expression is used only when a referent is superior to an addressee.

4

REFERENT HONORIFIC EXPRESSION IN TORAAKI'S KYŌGEN PLAYS

1. Introduction

I will use *kyōgen* plays in order to get an overviews of the honorific expressions that were used during the Muromachi period (1336–1573). The characters in *kyōgen* plays cover a wide range of social classes; from *daimyō* 大名[1] 'feudal lord' to common people like servants, merchants, and farmers. A *daimyō* at this time was only the head of a village, and did not yet part of the elite class that would rule during the Edo period. The dialogue in *kyōgen* 狂言 plays therefore serve as good material for the study of the language of the *buke* class in its incipient stage, and the language of the common people. There are many studies about the language that appears in *kyōgen* plays to verify their value as material for the colloquial language of the Muromachi period. *Kyōgen* originated as improvised plays with no scenarios, but as it became popular, plots were written and groups of professional players were formed, each developing their own storylines. Much of the research on the lexical and honorific expressions in *kyōgen* plays focused on the honorific expression between a speaker and an addressee, but none looked at the honorific expression toward a referent. Studies were done on the first and second person pronoun, because these honorific expressions are unitary relations between a speaker and an addressee. But in order to research the honorific expression toward a referent, we need to observe a dual relation: a referent from the view-points of speaker and addressee. In this chapter I will classify the honorific lexicon used toward a referent, then move on to a sociolinguistic survey, focusing on the lexicon of the verb *iu* 'say'.

2. Data

Kyōgen plays commenced in the Muromachi period and have been performed without interruption. But questions remain about which era in Japanese history is reflected in the lines spoken by *kyōgen* comic players. There are many original *kyōgen* texts still in use today. Toraaki's *kyōgen* plays, which I use in this chapter, were recorded in 1642, but by then *kyōgen* had long been an accomplished classical entertainment. Whilst one might expect that the dialogue reflects the colloquial language used when *kyōgen* began, the plays were improvised entertainment from an oral tradition, on the other hand, and it is quite possible that the actors' improvised lines reflected each era's audience. Koyama (1960) classifies the historical development of *kyōgen* into three periods: 1. the formation of the plays; 2. the establishment of plots; 3. the stabilization and transmission of scenarios. He states that Toraaki's plays were recorded during stage two, a time when *kyōgen* was transiting from an improvised unscripted entertainment to a classical one and players spoke the colloquial language of the time. But when *kyōgen* developed into a classical refined art, players tried to transmit its original features in recorded scenes. Kamei (1980) and Hachiya (1970, 1998) both show that Toraaki's *kyōgen* texts mixed two languages, the original from the Muromachi period and the improvised lines of the Edo period.

I use Ikeda & Kitahara (eds.) (1972) as a text and a later index by Kitahara et al (eds.) (1984). Comparative studies of the plays of Torakiyo, Toraaki and Torahiro were done by Hikosaka (1975), Sakaguchi (1978) and Sasaki (1970) who all concluded that the lines are stereotyped and fixed in this order. *Kyōgen* is traditionally performed by successive generations of a family, and Torakiyo, Toraaki and Torahiro were actors who each progressively formalized the texts transmitted by their predecessors. Whilst it might be best to use the oldest text by Torakiyo, he left only eight plays, and so I use those of Toraaki.

3. Classification of honorific words toward a referent

While there has been much scholarship on the honorific expression of a speaker and an addressee (cf., Yamazaki, 1963; Sakaguchi, 1978; Kojima, 1979; Kurano, 1967; and Ikegami, 1977), no work has been done on the honorific expression toward a referent. There are other important historical documents of the Japanese language of that time. Many Christian missionaries who came to Japan from Portugal in the 16th and 17th centuries in order to spread Christianity had to study Japanese in order to preach and they left grammar books and a dictionary of Japanese. One catholic priest, Joãn Rodriguez, compiled two Japanese grammar books: *Arte da Lingoa de Iapam* and *Arte Breve da Lingoa de Iapam*.

Here I classify the honorific words based on three types of methodology.

A: inductive method from social status

B: judgment by co-occurrence

C: judgment by co-reference

The inductive method from social status (A) induces words from an outer criterion like social status and is quite objective. But various honorific expressions can be used by an addresser to the same addressee, with the addresser adapting his manner of speaking to suit the occasion; consequently other external factors should also be counted. When the object of research is a modern language, a scholar is familiar with and understands the contextual use of the honorifics. When exceptional examples emerge, he tries to discern the reason for a speaker's choice of words, and this creates a deeper connotation to the literature. It is, however, quite difficult to fully understand the social background in the case of classical literature and one's judgment can be subjective. A judgment by co-occurrence (B) groups together words that co-occur, but this method shares the same weaknesses as (A): the possibility of a speaker changing speech to suit the occasion, and the possibility that various honorific expressions might co-mingle. Here I try to classify honorific expression by applying judgment by co-reference (C), a method of classifying words both from a syntagmatic and paradigmatic relation.

There are the following honorific expressions for a referent: nominative and genitive case particles *no* and *ga*; honorific titles *dono*, *sama* and *domo*, and respectful verbs. There are descriptions of nominative and genitive case particles *no* and *ga* in *Arte da Lingoa de Iapam* and *Arte Breve da Lingoa de Iapam* by Rodriguez, but Yasuda (1977) points to the discrepancies between both books, while it can be supposed that case particles *no* and *ga* fluctuated at that time, even among modern researchers, there are disputes about their honorific value. Yamazaki (1963) denies their honorific value and concludes that there is only a difference of nuance. Jugaku (1958) insists that the function of the case particles is to express a speaker's emotional value, whilst Kuwayama (1972, 1973) argues that they are in the transitional stage from honorific to grammatical expression. Here I divide them into three cases: nominative case particle, genitive case particle, and nominative case particle within a noun clause. To sum up the opinions of all the researchers: *ga* is only used as a nominative case particle and loses its honorific value within a main clause, and genitive and nominative case particles within a noun clause still maintain their honorific value. Case particles are sometimes determined by the verbs that follow them except with the verb *gozaru*, when it is always *ga gozaru*. As for suffixes, the respectful suffix, *dono*, *sama* and *tachi*, and the humble *domo*, are used. Respectful verbs such as *irassharu*, *mesu*, and humble ones like *mausu*,[2] and *itasu*, are used; with respectful auxiliaries also added to verbs to express honorific speech acts.

As a result, expressions are classified into five categories.

1. supreme respectful expressions (SRE)
2. ordinary respectful expressions (ORE)
3. neutral expressions (NE)
4. humble expressions (HE)
5. insulting expressions (ISE)

Table 1 shows the expressions in each classification. For example *iu(ga)* means *X ga iu* 'X says', and *mikado ga ōseraru* 'an emperor says' using a supreme respectful expression. And *iu(ni)* means that *X ni iu* 'say to X', and *mikado ni mausiagu* 'say to an emperor' using a supreme respectful expression. This division doesn't necessarily mean that there are such strict classifications, for expressions are sometimes interchangeable.

	SRE	ORE	NE	HE	ISE
iu(ga)	ooseraru	oshiyaru mausaru ihiyaru	ihu	mausu	nukasu
iu(ni)	maushiagu	mausu	ihu	maushitsuku	
suru(ga)	nasaru	itasaru	su	itasu	
iku(ga)		mairaru	iku	mairu	
iku(ni)	mairu	mairu	iku	iku	
yaru(ni)	agu tatematsuru sasagu	shinzu	yaru	kudasu	
kureru	kudasaru	kudasaru	kuru	kuru	
morau	itadaku	itadaku	morahu	morahu	
kuru		wasu mairaru ojaru gozaru	ku	mairu	
kangaeru	oboshimesu		kangahu	kangahu	
yobu	mesaru	mesu	yobu	yobu	
taberu	kikoshimesu		tabu	tabu	kurahu
iru	mashimasu oide ohasu	ojaru gozaru	iru	iru	
auxiliary	setamahu seraru tamahu	asobasu o-V-yaru raru			oru
suffix	sama	dono			me yatsu
plural	tachi	shū		domo	
nominative case	no	no/ga	ga	ga	ga
noun clause	no	no	no	ga	ga
genitive case	no	no	no	ga	ga

Table 1 : classification of honorific forms

4. Honorific expression toward a referent from the view-point of human relations

The honorific expression toward a referent is dependent on, and changes according to, the relationship between a speaker and a referent, or between an addressee and a referent. Supposing that a referent is a feudal lord, a husband and a master; his wife and his servant will naturally choose different honorific expressions when speaking of him. Understandably a wife referring to her husband will change her honorific expression depending on whether she is addressing his parent or his child. Toraaki's 231 plays are sub-divided into seven categories: *waki-kyōgen* 'celebration plays', *daimyō-kyōgen* 'feudal lord plays', *muko/yamabushi-kyōgen* 'bridegroom/Buddhist monk plays', *oni/shōmyō-kyōgen* 'ghost/servant plays', *onna-kyōgen* 'women plays', *shukke/zatō-kyōgen* 'Buddhist priest/blind man plays', and *atsume-kyōgen* 'miscellaneous fashioned plays'. The characters in each play are one-dimensional, with relationships among them categorized into stereotypes to a certain extent. Despite this, there are still many characters through which the system of honorific expression toward a referent can be analyzed. It would be too complicated to simultaneously consider each of the three participants in a conversational exchange for each of the subsequent group (4.1–4.19). Therefore, firstly I will look at the human relation between a speaker and a referent, and investigate how the honorific expression may change according to an addressee. For example, I focus on the changing honorific expression used by a wife toward her husband, according to each addressee like her child or a servant. I analyze human relations among kin, first of all, then hierarchical relations like those between master and servant, and lastly social status relations. Each table lists addressees on the horizontal line and honorific expressions on the vertical line. The number on the intersection of the horizontal and vertical line shows the frequency of an utterance. When 'introduction' is listed on the horizontal line it refers to a character's self-introduction. When each player enters the stage, he introduces his character to the audience; therefore, we count the audience as an addressee. I count as monologue an utterance to oneself. When a referent (e.g. a visitor) doesn't have any particular relation with a speaker, the honorific expression doesn't change according to the addressee, and therefore I count only the frequency, ignoring the addressee. On the vertical line, I list items in order of suffix, case particle, auxiliary and verb. And within each sub-category, we list from the higher honorific value to the lower. I include those compound verbs that are never used independently such as *ōseraru* (*ōsu* is used only with the auxiliary *raru*) in the verb category. Neutral verb means a verb like *ihu* that has a neutral honorific value.

4. REFERENT HONORIFIC EXPRESSION IN TORAAKI'S KYŌGEN PLAYS

Hereafter I utilize the notion of in-group and out-group. This is the attitude of a speaker toward a referent, taking into consideration the standpoint of an addressee. When a speaker views a referent as a person that belongs to his side, the referent is treated as an in-group person in the presence of the addressee. Conversely, when a speaker views a referent as a person that doesn't belong to his side, the referent is treated as an out-group person in the presence of the addressee. That is to say, whether a referent is either in-group or out-group depends on their relation with the addressee. For example, in modern honorifics, a worker refers to his immediate superior X to a much superior official Y, using either *X ga mōshi-mashi-ta* or *X ga osshai-mashi-ta* 'X said'. In the former case, he treats X as belonging to his in-group, and in the latter case, as belonging to his out-group.

4.1 a wife talks about her husband (Table 2)

On the horizontal line, I list monologue and introduction first, and the more a referent belongs to an in-group, the more to the right I list the referent. Table 2 shows that supreme respectful expressions *mesaru* and *seraru* are used when an addressee is an in-group person, such as a father-in-law or servant, and that neutral or ordinary respectful expressions are used when an addressee is an out-group person such as a go-between, a visitor or a teacher. The humble verb *itasu* is used only in one case to a go-between. Humble expressions are the preferred form in modern honorifics, but in Toraaki's plays, ordinary respectful expressions are commonly used.

	monologue	introduction	go-between	visitor	teacher	ghost	lover	father-in-law	servant
dono	3	1		3			1		
me	2								
no(genitive case)	1	1			2			1	
no(noun clause)		1							1
no(nominative case)	1								1
ga(genitive case)	1	4	2		2		2		
ga(noun clause)	1						1		
ga(nominative case)	2		1			2	1		
seraru	1								1
raru	4	1			2		1		
o-V-yaru							2		
su							1		1
ōseraru	1								
mesaru	1							1	
mausu(ni)	1		1				1		
oshiyaru	1						1	1	
ojaru	1								
mausaru	1					1	1		
mairaru	1			1				1	
neutral verbs	9		4				1		1
itasu(ga)			1						

Table 2   honorific expression
from a wife about her husband

Cited quite often as evidence of absolute honorifics, a wife refers to her husband when speaking to his master.

なかなか、こなたにいつも御目にかゝりたいと申されて御ざる、その執心がのこつて、ま見えられたと存る程に、跡をともらふてくだされひ（塗師）³

naka-naka konata ni itsumo o-me ni kakari tahi to *mausare* 'say (ORV)' te gozaru. sono shihushin ga nokotsu te ma mie *rare* 'RARU' ta to zonzuru hodoni ato o tomorau te kudasarehi

'(My husband) always said that he wanted to meet you, and that attachment made him come here. Please pray for the repose of his soul.'

She uses the ordinary respectful expression *mausaru* and *raru*.

But there is a case where, instead of the ordinary respectful expression more commonly used, the genitive case particle *ga* is used when a wife visits a go-between to consult him about a divorce and expresses anger towards her husband.

あれが心も直らふかと存ずれども（いしがみ）

are *ga* 'HPA' kokoro mo naworau ka to zonzure domo

'I had hoped he would get rid of his bad habit, but…'

And to an in-group person such as a servant, father-in-law and a lover, the supreme respectful expression is also used.

4.2 a husband talks about his wife (Table 3)

	monologue	introduction	go-between	young people	messenger	monk	teacher	lender	father-in-law	servant
domo	8	10	1	1	1		2		3	4
me		1								1
no(genitive case)	2	1								
no(noun clause)	1									
ga(genitive case)	2	2								4
ga(noun clause)	2	2	1						1	2
ga(nominative case)	3	4	3		1		2		2	7
mausu(ga)		1	1							
zonzu								1		
neutral verbs	10	2	3		1		1			2
mairu(ga)	2	2	1							
mausu(ga)	1	2	2			1	1			
itasu(ga)		1				1	1	1	2	
hoeru	1									

Table 3   honorific expression
      from a husband about his wife

Table 3 shows that a husband refers to his wife using neutral verbs or the humble verb *mairu(ga)*. The nominal case particle *ga* is mainly used in noun clauses, and in an introduction a husband refers to his wife in the following manner:

かやうの事も、女共に談合いたさひではならぬ程に、呼び出さう（かはかみ）

kayau no koto mo onna-*domo* 'HS' ni dankau itasa hi de ha nara nu hodoni yobi idasa u

'I even have to talk with women about such trivial things, so I'll call her out.'

The suffix *domo* is commonly used. Rodriguez (1955) writes, '*domo* is very derogatory, and is used for a low social class, animals and inanimate objects'. So, a husband treats his wife with a humble expression in most cases, but when an addressee is an inferior by hierarchical relation, such as a servant, he uses a neutral expression.[4]

4.3 a child or a grandchild talks about a parent or a grandparent (Table 4)

	monologue	introduction	swindler	merchant	teacher	master	parents	sibling	wife	servant	monologue	husband	servant
sama												4	1
me	2	1		1		3		1		3	1		
no(genitive case)	1	1		1								1	
no(noun clause)	1							3		1		1	
no(nominative case)	1												
ga(noun clause)				1									
ga(nominative case)	1	1	1					1					
seraru		2								5		1	
o-V-itasu(ni)								1					
raru	6	1		3	1	3		3	7	4			
o-V-yaru	1							6					
nasaru										1			
ōseraru	1									3			
mairu(ga)	4			1		3		3		6	9		
mausu(ni)	1							1					
V-mausu(ni)								3					
shinzu		1								2			
kudasaru										1			
mesaru										2			
oshiyaru								1					
ojaru								2					
gozaru		1								1			1
narasu								1					
maushi-V-raru	1												
mausaru		1		2		3							
itasaru	2	1										1	
mairaru										1			
neutral verbs		1		3				1		1			

Table 4　honorific expression
　　　　from a child or grandchild about parents or grandparents

We have seen from previous studies about different periods that there is a difference in honorific expression based on the gender of a speaker, so in Table 4 and 5 I list male to the left and female to the right. Table 4 shows that a child and a grandchild treat parents and grandparents by ordinary respectful expressions. *No* is used as a nominative case particle within a noun clause and as a genitive case particle. The following shows how children speak of their parents to servants.

毎度の御合戦にさぞくたびれさせられうず（武悪）

maido no go-kasen ni sazo kutabire sa *serare* 'SRA' uzu,

'(My father) might be tired of the frequent fights.'

When an addressee is a servant or another grandchild, grandparents are treated with a supreme respectful expression such as *seraru* or *ōseraru*. There are not many cases that show how parents are treated to an out-group person, but the following is an example of how a grandfather is treated among merchant class:

それがしが先祖のおうぢが罷出て、あの馬を只今此所へ引よせて参らせんと申されたれば、……息をしかけて、するすゑと言はれたれば（かうやくねり）

soregashi ga senzo no oudi ga makari de te, ano uma wo tadaima koko he hiki-yose te maira se n to *mausare* 'say (ORV)' tare ba,…iki o shikake te suwe-suwe to iha *re* 'RARU' tare ba

'My old ancestor came to say that he would drag that horse out,…blew his breath, and said, "Inhale, inhale".'

Ordinary respectful expressions such as *mausaru* and *iharu* are used when talking to out-group. There are cases where parents are discussed with both in-group and out-group members. In either case, a respectful expression is used; to the former, it would be a supreme respectful expression, and to the latter, an ordinary respectful expression.

4.4 a parent or a grandparent talks about a child or a grandchild (Table 5)

	monologue	introduction	feudal lord	mediator	borrower	gambler	step-mother	son-in-law	grandson	servant	monologue	father
domo	1							1		1		2
no(genitive case)	1					1		1		1		2
ga(genitive case)	1											
ga(noun clause)								1				
ga(nominative case)		2			1	1	1			3	1	1
tamahu												2
neutral verbs	2			1				1		1	1	
maushiagu(ga)		1										
itasu(ga)	2				1							

Table 5 honorific expression
from a parent or grandparent about child or grandchild

Table 5 shows that it is common for parents or grandparents to treat children or grandchildren by neutral or humble expression. In *Genji-Monogatari*, children and grandchildren are treated by respectful expressions when an addressee is inferior to both speaker and child or grandchild, but, in Toraaki's plays, they are treated by humble expression regardless of the addressee. In *Heike-Monogatari*, too, they are treated by neutral or humble expression regardless of the addressee. There is also a difference according to gender:

きやうの殿のむなしくなり給ひて候（まゝこ）

kiyau no tono *no* 'RPA' munashiku nari *tamahi* 'ORA' te saurau

'Mr Kiyau passed away.'

さて息子がむなしくなりたるとや（まゝこ）

sate musuko *ga* 'HPA' munashiku nari taru to ya

'Well, you say, my son has passed away.'

In the first, a step-mother is speaking of her son-in-law to her husband and she uses the supreme respectful expression *tamahu*. In the second, his own father uses a neutral expression when speaking of him to his wife. It might be possible that the step-mother uses a respectful expression because he is a son-in-law. However she introduces her own son to an audience in the following way:

わらはにも息子が御いり候へども（まゝこ）

waraha ni mo musuko *ga* 'HPA' *on* 'RP'-iri saurahe domo

'I also have a son, though.'

She uses the nominative case particle *ga* and the respectful prefix *on* at the same time. This might indicate that a mother chooses a high honorific register for her son because of the prevailing social climate of male chauvinism, but I can't be certain because there is no other example to support this.

4.5 a younger brother talks about an elder brother

A younger brother mentions his elder brother when introducing himself to the audience:

某は兄を一人持つてござるが、某が名をば申さいで、しやていしやていとばかりいつも申す（しやてい）

soregashi ha ani wo hitori motsu te gozaru ga, soregashi ga na o *mausa* 'say (HVN)' i de, siyatei-siyatei to bakari itsumo *mausu* 'say (HVN)'

'I have one elder brother, but he doesn't call me by first name but always calling me, "Brother, brother".'

It is common to treat parents and grandparents by respectful expression to any out-group addressee, but for an elder brother, a humble expression is used. Because there are only two examples in the text, where the younger brother is angry with his elder brother and uses *mausu(ga)*, they might be considered uncommon examples.

4.6 an elder brother talks about a young brother

There are several examples, of which two use the neutral verbs *mausu(ga)* and *mairu(ga)* to the audience, and one uses a neutral verb to a monk. In the following exchange with a nun, an elder brother speaks about his younger brother.

かなぼうしも、久しう参らぬ程に、連れて参つて御ざる（びくさだ）

kanabōshi mo hisashiu *maira* 'come (HVN)' nu hodoni, tsure te maitsu te gozaru

'(My younger brother) Kanabōshi has not been here for a long time, so I have brought him along.'

It is common to treat a younger brother by either a neutral or a humble expression and accordingly he uses the humble verb *mairu(ga)* and one neutral verb.

4.7 a son-in-law talks about a father-in-law (Table 6)

	monologue	teacher	wife	servant
no(genitive)	1	2		
raru	2	3	6	
ōseraru				2
mairu(ni)	1	2		2
oshiyaru				1
mausaru	1			

Table 6 honorific expression from a son-in-law to a father-in-law

A *muko* 'bridegroom' is a person connected by marriage to one's daughter. During this time, a matrilineal social system still prevailed, and it was common for a bridegroom to marry into a household who would inherit. The honorific expression used toward a father-in-law is different from that used toward ones real father. As the following shows, a son-in-law treats his father-in-law with a supreme respectful expression when talking to a servant:

今日参れと仰せられたほどに、聟が参つたとおしやれ（おか太夫）

kehu *maire* 'come (HVO)' to *ōse rare* 'say (SRV)' ta hodoni, Muko ga *maitsu* 'come (HVO)' ta to oshiyare

'As (father-in-law) asked me to come, tell him (his) son-in-law is here.'

Yet he uses ordinary respectful expressions such as *raru, mausaru* and *no* when talking to his teacher in the following:

定めて待ちかねられうほどに、はや参りまらする（音曲聟）

sadame te machikane *rare* 'RARU' u hodoni haya *mairi* 'come (HVO)' marasuru

'As (father-in-law) must be waiting impatiently for me, I'll come in a hurry.'

4.8 a father-in-law talks about a son-in-law (Table 7)

	monologue	introduction	servant
dono	4	3	7
no(noun clause)	1	3	2
no(nominative)			3
seraru			1
raru			1
nasaru	1		
oide	3		1
gozaru	1		1
shinzu(ni)			1
wasu			1
oneutral verb			1

Table 7 honorific expression from a father-in-law to a son-in-law

Table 7 shows that a different honorific expression is used for a son-in-law and for ones real son. It is quite common to choose a humble expression when speaking of ones real son, but to use an ordinary respectful expression to refer to a son-in-law. The honorific title *dono*, which according to Rodriguez (1955) is the third most respectful after *sama* and *kou* 公, is used for a son-in-law, who although inferior by kinship relation should be given due respect.

4.9 a servant talks about his master (Table 8)

There is much variation of the honorific expression. I list addressees, officers and merchants who are superior to a master on the left side of Table 8. In the following, a servant is talking to a merchant to whom his master owes a debt, and he refers to his master using *itasaru* and *mairu*:

久々かよひの算用も致されひて、わたくしまで面目もござらぬによつて、おのつからゑ参らぬ（ちどり）

	monologue	feudal lord	merchant	Shinto priest	passer-by	visitor	Mr.So-and-so	swindler	woman	uncle of a master	son-in-law	parent of a son-in-law	wife	newcomer	servant
no(genitive case)	10		1											1	13
no(noun clause)	6		2				1		2	1				1	9
no(nominative case)	1		1				1	1					1		1
ga(noun clause)	1	1													1
ga(nominative case)													1		
seraru	4					1	1						1	1	2
nasaru													1		2
o-V-itasu(ni)	1					1									
o-V-yaru	5							2							4
raru	5	1		1	1			1	2		1	1		3	9
oboshimesu	1														
ōse-V-raru	10														8
ōseraru	11					1								4	8
mesaru	1														2
mesu															4
maushiagu(ni)						2									
mausu(ni)	8								1	1				6	4
oshiyaru	4							2						2	1
ojaru	1													1	
gozaru			1						1				1	1	
kudasaru	1														
te	1					1									
maushi-V-raru	7		1												
mairaru			1		1					2					
itasaru			2						1						
mausaru	3		4	1		7					1	3		6	
neutral verbs	3	12							1					1	4
mausu(ga)	1					1	1								
mairu(ga)			1												

Table 8 honorific expression from a servant about his master

hisa-bisa kayohi no sanyō mo *itasare* 'do (ORV)' hi te, watakushi made menboku mo gozara nu ni yotsu te, onotu kara we *maira* 'come (HVN)' nu.

'(My master) hasn't paid his credit for a long time, so I am also ashamed of him.

He never comes himself.'

Next, I list addressees who are the same rank as a master, that is, visitors, sons-in-law and relatives. A servant addresses a visitor and uses *mausu(ga)* and *mausaru*:

頼ふだもの申されまするは、各ござつて、渡り物の談合なされて下されひと申されまする（くじざい人）

tanohu da mono *mausaruru* 'say (ORV)' ha, ono-ono gozatsu te, watari-mono no dankau nasare te kudasarehi to *mausare* 'say (ORV)' masuru

'My master said, "Please come here to have a meeting about the parade".'

頼ふだもの申は、よそから珍しい御酒を得てござる程に、お隙でござらば、ちと出させられて、御酒をまいるかとのお事でござる（口まね）

tanohuda-mono *mausu* 'say (HVN)' ha, yoso kara medurashihi goshu o e te gozaru hodoni, o-himade gozaraba, chito de sase rare te, go-shu o meiru ka to no o-koto de gozaru

'My master said, "I've got some rare wine, so if you are free, please visit me for a drink".'

I list addressees who are employees of a master on the right side of the Table 8. That is, the honorific expression for a master among servants is as follows:

いつものことく腹をおたちやれども（武悪）

itsumo no kotoku hara wo *o-tachi-yare* 'ORA' domo

'(My master) got angry as usual.'

He uses *o-V-yaru* and also a supreme respectful expression:

迷惑すると仰せられたほどに（ぶす）

meiwaku suru to *ōserare* 'say (SRV)' ta hodoni

'My master said that he would be in trouble.'

The case particle *no* is commonly used. As the horizontal line moves to the right, the honorific expression toward addressees lowers. I list honorific expressions from top to bottom of the vertical line in the following order: supreme respectful expressions, ordinary respectful expressions, neutral expressions and humble expressions. We can see that numbers are distributed mainly in the upper left and the lower right of Table 8, which tells us that a servant changes his honorific expression toward his master according to the addressee. The more deference a servant needs to pay to an addressee, the lower the honorific expression used toward his master.

4.10 a master talks about his servant (Table 9)

	monologue	introduction	woman	feudal lord	visitor	mediator	thief	servant
domo	4	4						
me	3	1	1		1			1
no(genitive case)		1						
ga(genitive case)	1							5
ga(noun clause)	3							3
ga(nominative case)	6	2	1				1	3
mausu(ni)	7	1						
neutral verbs	11			1	1		1	
maushitsuku(ni)	3							
mausu(ga)	3					1		
mairu(ga)			3		1	1		
itasu(ga)	2							
useru	1							

Table 9 honorific expression
from a master about his servant

Table 9 shows that a master treats his servant by a humble expression to anybody. The case particle *ga* is commonly used. The problematic case to interpret is *mausu(ni)* which is used in eight cases of self-introductions or monologues:

のさものをよび出し、申す事がござる、有るかやい（しうくがらかさ）

nosa mono o yobi-dashi *mausu* 'say (PE)' koto ga gozaru. aru ka yai.

'I have to call the stupid fellow (=servant) to tell him something. Are you there?'

Mausu(ni) can be used as either the humble expression of an actor to a patient or the polite expression of a speaker to an addressee. So *X ga Y ni mausu* can mean that X shows respectful regard toward Y. But in these cases, a master always treats his servant with a humble expression, and therefore it might be more appropriate to interpret these usages as polite expressions to an audience.

4.11 a servant talks about a servant

All of the cases are situations in which a servant speaks of a colleague to his master:

かの者は傘を細工に致すものでござるに依て、紙気と申すも傘の事、ゑ申すまひと言ふも、傘の柄の事でござる（しうくがらかさ）

kano mono ha karakasa o sahiku ni itasu mono de gozaru ni yotsute, kamige to *mausu* 'say (HVN)' mo karakasa no koto, we *mausu* 'say (HVN)' mahi to ihu mo, karakasa no we no koto de gozaru.

'He makes his living by making umbrellas, so when he says 'kamige', he means umbrella, and when he says 'we mausu mahi', he means the handle of an umbrella.'

A servant treats his colleague with a humble expression by using the following: case particle *ga* (eight cases), *mausu(ga)* (seven cases) and neutral verb (one case).

4.12 a teacher talks about an apprentice

When a teacher mentions his apprentice in a self-introduction, he uses a humble expression such as *mausu(ga)* or a neutral expression. Introducing himself to the wife of his disciple in the following, he uses the disciple's first name without any honorific title and with a humble expression.

いや是は、都の塗師平八をしたてたる、師匠にて候（ぬし）

iya kore ha miyako no nushi *hēhachi* 'FN' o shitate taru, shishiyau ni te saurau.

'I am a painter from the capital. I am the teacher who trained Hēhachi.'

4.13 an apprentice talks about a teacher (Table 10)

no(genitive case)	5
no(noun clause)	3
no(nominative case)	5
seraru	1
raru	6
ōseraru	1
zonzeraru	1
mesaru	1
mausu(ni)	1
oshiyaru	2
ojaru	2
gozaru	2
mausaru	2

Table 10 honorific expression from an apprentice to a teacher

There are several examples where an apprentice refers to his teacher in the company of an artisan, a monk or a blind man. Almost all cases in Table 10 are of apprentices referring to their teachers to out-group addressees, so we list these numbers in a group. A young monk refers to his teacher when speaking to a supporter of their temple.

是は坊主の、さしぞめもせられぬ傘でござれども、貸しまらする（ほねかわ）

kore ha bouzu *no* 'RPA', sashi-zome mo se *rare* 'RARU' nu kasa de gozare domo, kashi marasuru

'This is an umbrella that our teacher has never used before, but I'll let you use it.'

In this case, a supreme or ordinary respectful expression is used, together with the case particle *no*.

4.14 a bridegroom talks about a teacher (Table 11)

no(noun clause)	1
ga(noun clause)	1
ga(nominative)	2
seraru	2
raru	4
nasaru	1
kudasaru	2
mairu(ni)	4
mausu(ni)	2
oshiyaru	1
gozaru	1

Table 11   honorific expression from a bridegroom about his teacher

In Toraaki's plays, a character called *oshiete* 'a person who teaches' appears. An old man considered to be a master of the precepts of life teaches a young bridegroom how to behave at the marriage ceremony. In the following *oshiete* is mentioned at the time of a self-introduction and monologue.

愛にわたしにお目をかけらるゝ人がござるが、是は又さいさい聟入りをなされて御ざる程に、あれへ参つて、聟入りのしつけようだい、習て参らふと存る（鶏聟）

kokon ni watashi ni o 'RP'-me o kake *raruru* 'RARU' hito ga *gozaru* 'be (ORV)' ga, kore ha mata sai-sai muko-iri wo *nasare* 'do (ORV)' te gozaru hodoni, are he *maitsu* 'come (HVO)' te, muko-iri no shitsuke youdai narau te *maira* 'come (HVO)' hu to zonzuru

'There is a man who takes good care of me here. He has married quite often, so I go to learn from him how to behave at the marriage ceremony.'

Table 11 is quite similar to Table 10.

4.15 a monk talks about parishioners (Table 12)

shū(plural suffix)	4
no(genitive case)	4
no(noun clause)	3
no(nominative case)	2
ga(nominative case)	2
o-V-yaru	1
seraru	6
ōseraru	1
mausu(ni)	2
mairu(ni)	1
oide	1
mausaru	1
neutral verb	1

Table 12 honorific expression from a monk to parishioners

Table 12 shows that when a monk talks to his apprentice about parishioners he uses a supreme respectful expression such as *ōseraru*.

旦那衆も一段よからふと仰らるゝ程に（ほねかわ）

danna-*shū* 'RS' mo ichidan yokara hu to *ōseraruru* 'say (SRV)' hodoni

'As the parishioners said, it was quite good,'

Rodriguez (1955) writes, '*Shū* 衆 is lower than *tachi* 達 in its honorific value and is used only for human beings'.

4.16 a parishioner talks about a monk (Table 13)

sama	1
no(genitive case)	1
no(nominative case)	4
ga(noun clause)	1
ga(nominative case)	3
tamahu	3
seraru	8
asobasu	1
raru	2
o-V-nasaru	1
ōseraru	3
oboshimesu	2
mausu(ni)	1
mairu(ni)	1
ojaru	1
ohasu	1
nasaru	2
mausaru	1
neutral verb	1
mairu(ga)	2

Table 13   honorific expression from a parishioner to a monk

Table 13 shows how a parishioner treats a monk. In a self-introduction, a parishioner refers to a monk using a supreme respectful expression.

旦那のお寺へ参り、此よし申て、御出なされ候やうに申さばやと存じ候（ふせなひきやう）

danna no 'RPA' o 'RP'-tera he *mairi* 'come (HVO)', kono yoshi *maushi* 'say (HVO)' te, *o*-ide *nasare* 'SRA' saurau yauni *mausa* 'say (HVO)' baya to zonji saurau

'I'll go to the temple of my parish, and explain the situation. I would like to ask (the monk) to come.'

4.17 about a person of high social rank with whom a speaker has no personal connection (Table 14)

tachi(plural suffix)	8
shū(plural suffix)	6
dono	3
no(genitive case)	40
no(noun clause)	23
no(nominative case)	25
ga(noun clause)	3
ga(nominative case)	2
tamahu	15
setamahu	3
seraru	34
raru	8
oboshimesu	17
nasaru	11
kudasaru	22
itadaku	2
itasu(ni)	1
kikoshimesaru	1
mashimasu	3
mairu 'eat'	1
kikoshimesu	1
mesaru	5
tatematsuru(ni)	1
ōseraru	36
maushiagu(ni)	30
sasagu	7
agu	7
shinzu(ni)	1
mairu(ni)	18
asobasu	2
mesu	3
mausu(ni)	6
gozonji	2
ōseidasaru	3
gozaru	4
oide	2
ohasu	1
neutral verbs	2

Table 14   honorific expression about a person of high society

There are examples that show how the common people refer to a person of high social rank—such as an emperor, a *shōgun*, or a god—with whom they have no personal connection. For example, Tamonten, a god, is treated as follows.

多聞天の仰せらるゝは、両人の者ども是へ月詣でをする事、神妙におぼしめすほどに、則これを下さるゝと仰せられて（連歌毘沙門）

tamonten *no* 'RPA' *ōseraruru* 'say (SRV)' ha, ryaunin no mono-domo koko he tsuki-maude o suru koto, shinmeu ni *ōboshimesu* 'think (SRV)' hodoni, sunahachi kore wo *kudasaruru* 'give (SRV)' to *ōserare* 'say (SRV)' te

'Tamonten (=God) said: it is praiseworthy that both of these men come to pray here every month, so this is given to them.'

A god is always treated with a supreme respectful expression, except in eight cases where *raru* is used and in two cases that use neutral verbs. The case particle *no* is commonly used and *no* is always used as the genitive case particle. In Table 14 there is no variation of honorific expression in accordance with an addressee. There is a tendency in modern honorifics to omit honorific expressions toward those with whom an addressee has no personal relation, but in *kyōgen* plays that depict feudal society, a person of high social rank is always treated with a supreme respectful expression. The following example shows how the messenger of a feudal lord treats his lord with a supreme respectful expression to a peasant.

仰出さるゝは、お笑ひ草のためと思召て仰出されたれば、なりにも似せず見事申上げた、前々はくだされね共、お通りを下さるゝ程に（松ゆつり葉）

ōse idasa ruru 'say (SRV)' ha, o-warahigusa no tame to *oboshimeshi* 'think (SRV)' te *ōse idasa re* 'say (SRV)' tare ba, nari ni mo nise zu migoto *maushiage* 'say (HVO)' ta, maemae ha *kudasare* 'give (ORV)' ne domo, otowori wo *kudasaru* 'give (ORV)' hodoni

'(Our feudal lord) said: I just said it for a joke. But you did it (=singing) quite well. He didn't give us a glass of wine before, but now he gives it, so...'

4.18 about a person of ordinary social rank with whom a speaker has no personal connection (Table 15)

shū(plural suffix)	4
no(genitive case)	35
no(noun clause)	49
no(nominative case)	17
ga(noun clause)	15
ga(nominative case)	84
seraru	18
raru	13
o-V-yaru	4
o-V-aru	1
ōseraru	35
mausu(ni)	23
mairu(ni)	5
itasu(ni)	1
shinzu(ni)	2
nasaru	10
sareru	5
oboshimesu	3
kudasaru	4
gozonji	2
mesaru	3
asobasu	1
gozaru	6
oshiyaru	5
mausaru	6
wasu	1
neutral verbs	9
mausu(ga)	1
itasu(ga)	3
mairu(ga)	1

Table 15 honorific expression about a person of common society

In Toraaki's plays, a master uses the supreme respectful expression *ōseraru* when talking to his servant.

今日はみな山一つあなたへ御ざあつて、お茶を比べさせられうと仰せらるゝが（したうはうがく）

kehu ha mina yama hitotsu anata he *gozaatsu* 'go (ORV)' te, ocha o kurabe saserare 'SRA' u to ōseraruru 'say (SRV)' ga

'Everybody invited me to go across the mountain to take part in a tea contest.'

And below, a servant uses *mausaru* for a group of young people.

みなみな若い衆の、初心講を結んで寄り合ひ申さるゝが、（ちぎりき）

mina-mina wakai-*shū* 'RS' *no* 'RPA' shiyoshinkau wo musun de yoriahi *mausaruru* 'do (ORV)' ga,

'These young fellows have a club and meet together.'

A farmer refers to his neighbor with the supreme respectful expression *ōseraru*.

皆の仰せらるゝは（水掛聟）

mina *no* 'RPA' ōseraruru 'say (SRV)' ha

'What everybody says,'

Here in Table 15 I list the honorific expression toward a referent that is of the same social rank as a speaker and with whom neither speaker nor addressee has a personal connection. The table shows that in most cases supreme respectful expressions are used, but there is the following exception.

何者やらん、かたのにて雉を射る者が有、にくひ事をいたす程に、（きんや）

nani mono ya ran, katano ni te kidi o iru mono *ga* 'HPA' aru, nikuhi koto o *itasu* 'do (HVN)' hodoni

'Who is he? There is a person that shoots pheasants in this preserve. He does a hateful deed.'

A thief is treated by the humble expression *itasu(ga)*. *No* is the genitive case particle and *ga* is the nominative case particle, but both *no* and *ga* are used as a nominative case particles in a noun clause.

In conclusion, an appropriate honorific expression is chosen according to the social status of a referent when he is an outsider to both a speaker and an addressee. The blind used to be ranked as *zatō*, *kōtō* and *kengyō* from the lowest to the highest. The following example illustrates how a man speaks about both a *kōtō* and a *zatō* when each goes to borrow his lute. In the first, the man is addressing the *kōtō* and therefore refers to the socially inferior *zatō* by the neutral expression *ihu*.

最前はくやうが来て、貸せと言ふ程に貸さうと言ふ約束をした（はくや

う)

saizen hakuyau *ga* 'HPA' ki te, kase to ihu hodoni, kasa u to ihu yakusoku o shi ta.

'Hakuyau (=*zatō*) came right now, and asked me to lend him a lute. So I promised to lend it.'

But in the next, the man is speaking to the *zatō* about the socially superior *kōtō* and so uses an ordinary respectful expression.

こうとうがわせて貸せと言はるる（はくやう）

kōtō *ga* 'HPA' *wase* 'come (ORV)' te kase to iha *ruru* 'RARU'.

'A *kōtō* came and asked me to lend it.'

From this, we can understand the importance of the social status of a referent when choosing a proper honorific expression. We can suppose that audiences were able to infer the social status of an unknown referent from the honorific expression used toward a character.

4.19 about a visitor (Table 16)

no(genitive case)	1
no(noun clause)	2
ga(noun clause)	4
ga(nominative case)	2
seraru	2
ōseraru	6
mausu(ni)	3
gozaru	6
shinzu	1
oide	1
mairu(ga)	3
mausu(ga)	1

Table 16   honorific expression about a visitor

Here we mean a visitor that has no connection, either by kinship or hierarchical relation, with a speaker. We see in Table 16 the variations of the honorific expression.

5. The honorific system toward a referent from the viewpoint of lexicon

So far I have analyzed honorific expressions that are based on concrete human relations, but hereafter I consider their use in abstract dual relations: between a referent and a speaker, and between a referent and an addressee. To avoid the associated complication of all vocabulary into consideration, I focus only on words that mean 'say', of which there are many words: *ōseraru, oshiyaru, iharu, mausaru, mausu, maushiagu, ōseagu, maushitsuku, maushitsukeraru, ōsetsukeraru, maushiiru, mukasu*. I shall focus on X of *X ga Y ni iu* (X says to Y). All of these words have their own honorific value and are switched according to different situations. In *kyōgen* scenes, the characters are stereotyped, and therefore it is easy to define the social status of each one. I try to assess the usage of honorific expression by taking into consideration the relation both between a referent and a speaker, on the one hand, and between a referent and an addressee, on the other. I divide these relationships into two categories: kinship relations based on blood ties and social status relations, which include both a hierarchical vertical order like master and servant, and a social vertical order like an emperor and a common person. The vertical order is further divided into three categories; superior, equal and inferior. In the tables I use the following abbreviations: K = kinship, S = social status of the first character. For the second character, S = superior, E = equal, and I = inferior. Therefore KS indicates that a referent is superior by kinship either to a speaker or an addressee. When a child refers to his parent, the referent is shown as KS. The relation between a referent and a speaker is shown on the vertical line, and the relation between a referent and an addressee is on the horizontal line.

Let me explain what each number means on Table 17. The number '14' at the intersection between E on the horizontal line and E on the vertical line indicates the frequency of usage of *ōseraru*. That is, *ōseraru* is used 14 times in order to refer to someone who is in an equal relation with both a speaker and an addressee. The first two numbers in parentheses show the percentage of each usage at vertical total in the first place, and that at horizontal line in the second place. The number '100.0' means that the word *ōseraru* is used for a referent that has an equal relationship with an addressee in 100.0 percent. The number '50.0' indicates the percentage that *ōseraru* is used for a referent that has an equal relationship with a speaker. The last two numbers in the parentheses show the percentage of each usage at the total usage in each table in the third place, and that at the total usage in the whole honorific expression. That is, the number '12.5' represent the percentage of all cases where the word '*ōsararu*' is used by referents of equal status, while '18.4' represents the percentage of all honorific expressions in which *ōsararu* is used. In the case of a monologue, the addressee is the audience, but because it is hard to discern the hierarchical relation between a character and an audience, monologues are omitted.

5.1 *ōseraru* (Table 17)

		ADDRESSEE'S					
		KI	SI	E	KS	SS	total
SPEAKER'S	KI	0	0	0	0	0	0
	SI	0	0	0	0	0	0
	E	0	0	14(100.0) (50.0) (12.5) (18.4)	0	14(15.9) (50.0) (12.5) (58.3)	28(25.0)
	KS	1(50.0) (25.0) (0.9) (50.0)	0	0	0	3(3.4) (75.0) (2.7) (75.0)	4(3.6)
	SS	1(50.0) (1.3) (0.9) (50.0)	0	0	8(100.0) (10.0) (7.1) (80.0)	71(80.7) (88.6) (63.4) (64.0)	80(71.4)
	total	2(1.8)	0	14(12.5)	8(7.1)	88(78.6)	112

Table 17 ōseraru

Ōse-idasa-ru and *ōse-tuke-raru* are included into this category with *ōseraru*. *Ōsu* is never used independently, but is always attached to *raru* (as *ōseraru*) except when it is used as the noun *ōse* (*ōse no gotoku* 'as you say'). Therefore we represent *ōseraru* in Table 17. *Ōseraru* is used to refer to a person who is superior or equal to both a speaker and an addressee, but it is never used to refer to someone who is inferior to either a speaker or an addressee. To be concrete, *ōseraru* is used for referents in the following contexts: for person who is high in social rank – such as a god, an emperor or a local lord; in a conversation between a monk and a parishioner, or between a *daimyō* and his visitor. A *daimyō* speaks to his servant in the following.

おのおの寄り合わせられて、ひとつ仰せられてはどつと笑ひ、笑ひさせらるゝが、あれはなに事ぞ（しうくがらかさ）

ono-ono yori-awa se-rare te, hitotsu *ōserare* te ha dotsu to warahi, warahi saseraruru ga, are ha nani goto zo

'Everybody is gathered here and somebody says something and then everyone roars with laughter. What is going on here?'

He refers by *ono-ono* 'each person', *hito* 'person' and *kata-gata* 'every body', but never mentions social status. But an audience can guess the referent's high social position by the usage of *ōseraru*. In such a context, the nominal case particle *no* is used 41 cases, genitive case particle *no* is used 11 cases, but *ga* is not used at all. According to Yamazaki's classification (1963), *ōseraru* belongs to the *konata* stage and is a supreme respectful expression. Rodriguez (1955) quotes *tono no ōseraruru ha* 'what our lord says' (*tono* is a respectful title for a lord.) as an example of a supreme respectful expression when a servant or a family member refers to his master or to the head of the family using a supreme respectful expression.

5.2 *mausu* (Table 18)

		ADDRESSEE'S					
		KI	SI	E	KS	SS	total
SPEAKER'S	KI	0	6(6.7) (75.0) (5.5) (85.7)	0	2(100.0) (25.0) (1.8) (100.0)	0	8(7.3)
	SI	0	7(7.9) (77.8) (6.4) (77.8)	2(12.5) (22.2) (1.8) (10.0)	0	0	9(8.3)
	E	0	73(82.0) (85.9) (67.0) (100.0)	11(68.8) (12.9) (10.1) (14.5)	0	1(100.0) (1.2) (0.9) (3.8)	85(78.0)
	KS	0	3(3.4) (100.0) (2.8) (42.9)	0	0	0	3(2.8)
	SS	1(100.0) (25.0) (0.9) (50.0)	0	3(18.9) (75.0) (2.8) (17.6)	0	0	4(3.7)
	total	1(0.9)	89(81.7)	16(14.7)	2(1.8)	1(0.9)	109

Table 18   mausu

Table 18 shows that *mausu* is used for a referent that is at the same time inferior to an addressee and inferior or equal to a speaker. Such a case is when, for example, a husband refers to his wife when speaking with a go-between.

いかやうにもあれが申すごとく致さう（はらきらず）

ikayau ni mo are ga *mausu* gotoku itasau

'I'll do anything that (=the wife) says.'

An example of a referent that is equal to a speaker and inferior to an addressee is when a servant speaks to his master about one of the other servants, also when a local tells a deputy official that he has been swindled.

あそこなものが参つて、むりにおしやう程にいな事じやと存じたれば、某がさげてゐる太刀をはひて、わがのじやと申す程に（ながみつ）

asoko na mono ga maitsu te, muri-ni oshiyau hodoni, ina koto ziya to zonzi tare ba, soregashi ga sage te wiru tachi o hahi te, wa-ga no ziya to *mausu* hodoni 'That man came and tried to do as he wanted. I thought it strange, but he took the sword from my waist on, put it on his waist, and said that it was his.'

Mausu is used when a referent is clearly inferior to an addressee, but even when a referent is superior to a speaker by kinship relation, *mausu* or *mausaru* is used if the referent is inferior to the addressee. *Mausaru* is usually used to refer to a superior kin, and as shown previously it can be used by a brother to express anger towards his elder brother when speaking with a teacher. *Ga* is used in 48 cases, but *no* is used in eight cases, as a nominal case particle; whilst *no* is used in two cases, and *ga* is in none as a genitive case particle. According to Yamazaki (1963), *mausu* is used for either the first or third person, but never for the second person. Yet, in Rodriguez (1955) there is an example of it being used for the second person —*Kisho no na ha nan to mausu zo* 'What is your name?'—as well as examples of it used for either the first or third person. As for the first person, Rodriguez (1955) writes, '*Mausu* should be used to respect an addressee or a third person who is present'. And as for the third person, he writes, 'It is common to use either a neutral verb with the humble auxiliary verb *marasuru,* or a humble verb in cases such as the following: a servant speaking of his master to a respectful person; a child referring to his parent; a wife referring to her husband, and a husband to his wife; or a man referring to his own kin'.

5.3 *ihu* (Table 19)

		ADDRESSEE'S					
		KI	SI	E	KS	SS	total
SPEAKER'S	KI	0	1(25.0) (20.0) (1.3) (14.3)	0	0	4(36.4) (80.0) (5.1) (100.0)	5(6.4)
	SI	0	2(50.0) (10.0) (2.6) (22.2)	18(29.5) (90.0) (50.0) (90.0)	0	0	20(25.6)
	E	0	0	39(63.9) (90.7) (50.0) (51.3)	2(100.0) (4.7) (2.6) (75.0)	2(18.2) (4.7) (2.6) (7.7)	43(55.1)
	KS	0	0	1(1.6) (100.0) (1.3) (14.3)	0	0	1(1.3)
	SS	0	1(25.0) (11.1) (1.3) (100.0)	3(4.9) (33.3) (3.8) (17.6)	0	5(45.5) (55.6) (6.4) (4.5)	9(11.5)
	total	0	4(5.1)	61(78.2)	2(2.6)	11(14.1)	78

Table 19 *ihu*

Table 19 shows that *ihu* is mainly used for a referent that is equal or inferior to a speaker. As in Table 18, for a referent that is inferior to a speaker, *mausu* is used when that referent is also inferior to the addressee; but when a referent is equal to an addressee, *ihu* is used As an example of a referent that is equal to an addressee and has no direct relation to a speaker, a virtuous man refers to such a referent when speaking to his servant.

身どもは律儀な者じやと、世間からも言ふと聞ひた程に（どんごむさう）
midomo ha richigi na mono ziya to seken kara mo *ihu* to kihi ta hodoni
'I heard that the world says that I am an honest person.'

Ihu is used to refer to a common person with whom a speaker has no direct relation, whereas *ōseraru* is used to refer to a person of high social status. In more than half the cases *ihu*, a neutral expression, is used to refer to a referent who is an equal of both a speaker and an addressee. *Ga* is used as a nominal case particle in 32 cases while *no* is used in twelve cases; and *ga* is used twice as a genitive case particle, but *no* is not used at all. According to Yamazaki (1963), *ihu* is a neutral expression and classified as belonging to the *wagoryo* or the *sochi* stage. Rodriguez (1955) writes, 'A neutral verb is used without any particle to refer to oneself or to someone of low social class when addressing a person of low social class, one's family or one's servant'.

5.4 *mausaru* (Table 20)

		ADDRESSEE'S					
		KI	SI	E	KS	SS	total
SPEAKER'S	KI	0	0	0	0	0	0
	SI	0	0	0	0	0	0
	E	0	0	7(38.9) (100.0) (15.9) (9.2)	0	0	7(15.9)
	KS	0	4(100.0) (57.1) (9.1) (57.1)	2(11.1) (28.6) (4.5) (28.6)	1(33.3) (14.3) (2.3) (11.1)	0	7(15.9)
	SS	0	0	9(50.0) (30.0) (20.5) (52.9)	2(66.6) (6.7) (4.5) (20.0)	19(100.0) (63.3) (43.2) (17.1)	30(68.2)
	total	0	4(9.1)	18(40.9)	3(6.8)	19(43.2)	44

Table 20   mausaru

Table 20 shows that *mausaru* is never used for a referent that is inferior to a speaker by either kinship or social status relation. A person is referred to using *mausaru* when he is superior to a speaker and has no kinship relation to an addressee. A wife or a child uses *mausaru* to an addressee who is superior to her husband or to his father. If an addressee is inferior to a husband or a father, the wife or the child will use *ōseraru*. A referent is also referred to using *mausaru* when he is superior to a speaker and equal to an addressee; so a servant uses it to a visitor that is equal to his master. Table 20 shows that *mausaru* is also used for a referent that is superior by social status, but as Table 14 shows that *mausaru* is never used, it is never used for a referent whose social status is far higher than one's own. *No* and *ga,* as nominal case particles, are used ten and five cases respectively; and *no* is used in nine cases as a genitive case particle.

A difficult question about the honorific character of *mausaru* still needs to be resolved. It can be either a dual honorific or an ordinary respectful expression. When *mausu* functions as a humble verb, *mausaru* should be interpreted as a dual honorific because *raru* is a respectful auxiliary verb. But when *mausu* has already made the transition to become the polite verb as used today, it should be interpreted as an ordinary respectful expression. As we saw in Table 18, *mausu* is only used for a referent that is inferior or equal to a speaker, so it is without doubt a humble verb. It is used to refer to a superior member of a speaker's in-group when addressing a superior who belongs to one's out-group. In this way a speaker makes an in-group referent humble to an out-group addressee, yet respects him because he is superior by kinship. But as Table 21 shows, *mausaru* has a similar distribution as *iharu,* – *mausu* having already made the transition to a polite verb – and is an ordinary respectful expression. Akita (1958) writes both that, '*Mausu* expresses humbleness and modesty toward an addressee who is superior', and that, '*Mausu* is used to convert the relation between an actor and a patient into the relation between an actor and an addressee and interprets its character as humble verb'. Rodriguez (1955) tells us how to interpret the phrase *bateren mo sayau ni mausare ta* 'A father also said so.' 'Only *raru* is appropriate to use when someone refers to a colleague, especially one who is also a member of his family'. It can be understood that *mausaru* is mainly used to refer to an in-group superior when speaking with an out-group addressee.

5.5 *iharu* (Table 21)

		ADDRESSEE'S					
		KI	SI	E	KS	SS	total
SPEAKER'S	KI	0	0	0	0	0	0
	SI	0	0	0	0	0	0
	E	0	0	1(20.0) (16.7) (4.3) (1.3)	0	5(35.7) (83.3) (21.7) (19.2)	6(26.1)
	KS	0	0	4(80.0) (44.4) (17.4) (57.1)	4(100.0) (44.4) (17.4) (44.4)	1(7.1) (11.1) (4.3) (25.0)	9(39.1)
	SS	0	0	0	0	8(57.1) (100.0) (34.8) (7.2)	8(34.8)
	total	0	0	5(21.7)	4(17.4)	14(60.9)	23

Table 21 iharu

Compound verbs such as *ihitukeraru, ihu* and *tukeru* are included in this category. There are only 23 cases. *Iharu* is never used toward a referent who is inferior to either a speaker or an addressee. It is used for a referent that is superior or equal to a speaker by kinship relation, predominantly for one who is at the same time equal to an addressee. *Iharu* is also used among relatives for a referent that is superior to a speaker by kinship relation. Among relatives, a superior is treated by *iharu, oshiyaru* or *mausaru*. A husband speaks about his father-in-law to his wife, in the following:

何とやら言はれたが忘れた、ろうろうしあらふゑんとやら、いふ物のうちに有といはれた（おか太夫）

nan to yara *ihare* ta ga wasure ta, rau-raushi ara hu wen to yara, ihu mono no uchi ni aru to *ihare* ta.

'(Father-in-law) said something, but I forgot. He said that is something inside something like that sounded "rau-raushi ara hu wen".'

Ga is used in five cases and *no* is used once as a nominal case particle; and while *ga* is not used as a genitive case particle, *no* is used once. Rodriguez (1955) cites an example for *ihare tare domo* '…said that…, though…', 'It is common to refer to someone that deserves some respect by using *iharu* when he is not present'. This tells us that *iharu* is an ordinary respectful expression.

5.6 *oshiyaru* (Table 22)

		ADDRESSEE'S					
		KI	SI	E	KS	SS	total
SPEAKER'S	KI	0	0	0	0	0	0
	SI	0	0	0	0	0	0
	E	0	0	3(60.0) (37.5) (13.6) (3.9)	1(25.0) (12.6) (4.5) (33.3)	4(33.3) (50.0) (18.2) (15.4)	8(36.4)
	KS	1(100.0) (25.0) (4.5) (50.0)	0	0	3(75.0) (75.0) (13.6) (37.5)	0	4(18.2)
	SS	0	0	2(40.0) (20.0) (9.1) (11.8)	0	8(66.7) (80.0) (36.4) (7.2)	10(45.5)
	total	1(4.5)	0	5(22.7)	4(18.2)	12(54.5)	22

Table 22 oshiyaru

Oshiyaru is mainly used for a referent that is superior to both a speaker and an addressee. In the next example of a superior being discussed among relatives, a wife speaks about her husband to her real father.

なふとゝさま、あれほどにおしやらは、こらへさせられい（こひ聟）

nau toto-sama, are hodo ni *oshiyara* ha, korahe sa serarei

'Well, my father. Please forgive him (=my husband) because he apologizes after all.'

No is used in ten cases and *ga* is used once as a nominal case particle, but there are no cases of genitive case particles. Yamazaki (1963) classifies *oshiyaru* as the belonging to *sonata* stage and is ordinary respectful expression.

5.7 *ihaseraru*

While *ōseraru* is a compound verb of the supreme respectful verb *ōsu* and the supreme respectful auxiliary verb *seraru*, *ihaseraru* is a compound of the neutral verb *ihu* and the supreme respectful auxiliary verb *seraru*. I have found one example of it used for a referent that is equal to both a speaker and to an addressee, and where *no* is used as the nominal case particle.

5.8 *ihasu*

The respectful auxiliary *su* is commonly used in compound words—much like *se* of *se-tamahu* or *seraru*—but it is also used independently. I can find only one example, and this is among relatives who refer to a superior relative.

5.9 *nukasu*

Nukasu is used five times as an insulting expression because it co-occurs with the insulting pronoun *yatsu*. *Ga* is used in two cases as a nominal case particle. These cases are used for a referent that is equal or inferior to a speaker. Yamazaki (1963) classifies *nukasu* as belonging to the *onore* stage and is insulting expression.

5.10 *ihiyaru*

There is only one example of *ihiyaru*, when a master is referred to among servants.

頼ふだ人の、それがしにわごりよをいひつきやつたらは、（ぶあく）

tanohu da hito no, soregashi ni wagoriyo o *ihi*-tsuki-*yatsu* tara ha

'If our master ordered me to punish you,'

Ihiyaru is used among equals to refer to a person that is superior, with *no* used as a nominal case particle. The origin of *yaru* is *aru* about which Rodriguez (1955) writes: '*Aru* is used on such occasions when a master talks with a respectful servant, a parent talks with a grown-up child, a padre talks with a younger padre, or a person talks with a humble stranger. But the honorific value is quite low'. In Toraaki's plays, *ihiyaru* is used among servants when they treat their master as an outsider. Yamazaki (1963) classifies *ihiyaru* as belonging to the *wagoriyo* stage and is rentral expression.

5.11 Flow chart (Table 23)

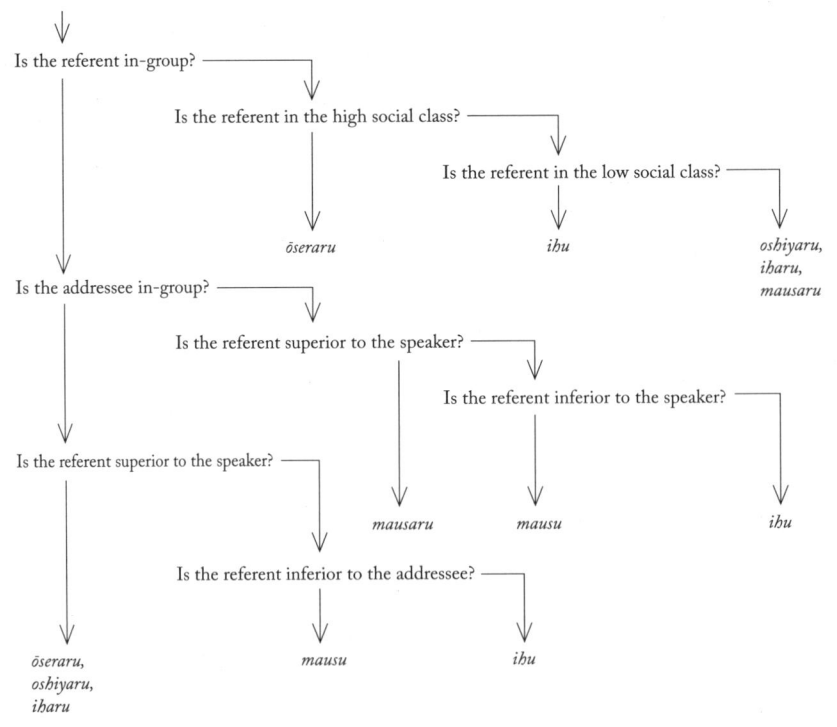

```
                    ↓
     Is the referent in-group? ─────────┐
            │                           ↓
            │              Is the referent in the high social class? ─────┐
            │                       │                                     ↓
            │                       │                    Is the referent in the low social class? ─┐
            │                       ↓                                     ↓                         ↓
            │                    ōseraru                                 ihu                    oshiyaru,
            ↓                                                                                   iharu,
     Is the addressee in-group? ──┐                                                             mausaru
            │                     ↓
            │        Is the referent superior to the speaker? ──┐
            │                  │                                ↓
            │                  │               Is the referent inferior to the speaker? ──┐
            │                  │                              │                           │
            ↓                  │                              │                           │
     Is the referent superior to the speaker? ─┐              │                           │
            │                                  ↓              ↓                           ↓
            │                               mausaru         mausu                        ihu
            │              Is the referent inferior to the addressee? ──┐
            ↓                     ↓                                     ↓
         ōseraru,              mausu                                   ihu
         oshiyaru,
         iharu
```

Table 23   flow chart

Table 23 is a flow chart that summarizes what has been covered so far. If the answer to each question is 'Yes', then move downward; if 'No', then move to the right. I show how each vocabulary is used in accordance with the attributes of both a referent and an addressee. The list is limited to words of high frequency such as *ōseraru*, *iharu*, *ihu*, *mausu*, *mausaru* and *oshiyaru*.

6. Conclusion

So far, we have seen how the honorific expression toward a referent is determined by, and changes in accordance with an addressee's relation vis-a-vis a referent and a speaker. We have also seen how words meaning 'say' *iu* are switched in accordance with the dual relation both between a referent and a speaker, on the one hand, and between a referent and an addressee, on the other. I conclude by itemizing the characteristics of the honorific expression toward a referent as found in Toraaki's plays concretely.

1. **An out-group referent that has no direct relation with a speaker is treated according to his social status.**

There are three types of honorific expressions used for a referent who has no direct relation with a speaker: supreme respectful expressions, ordinary respectful expressions and neutral expressions. The verb *iu*, *ōseraru* and *ihaseraru* for supreme respectful expressions, *mausaru* and *oshiyaru* for ordinary respectful expressions and *ihu* for neutral expressions are used according to the social status of a referent. *Mausu* is hardly used in humble expressions. Supreme respectful expressions like *ōseraru* and *ihaseraru* are used for gods, a ruling class of people like *shōgun*s (generals), local lords and deputy officials, and for the *samurai* class like *daimyō* and *shōmyō*. Ordinary respectful expressions are used for wealthy commoners, and neutral expressions are used for servants and the common class. It is not the relative relation between a referent and a speaker, but the absolute social order that determines the honorific expression toward a referent who has no direct relation with a speaker. Whilst one might expect that people in the lowest social class would be free to choose which respectful expression to apply to both rich commoners and the *samurai* class who are superior to them, it is in fact determined absolutely by social custom. And whilst the *samurai* class is superior to the common class, they don't use a humble expression. The common class is treated by the neutral expression *ihu*. *Mausu(ga)* is used only for insulting expressions.

2. **The honorific expression toward a referent who belongs to the speaker's in-group changes according to the addressee in addition to the referent's hierarchical relation to a speaker.**

The honorific expression toward a referent who is part of the in-group of a speaker can change in accordance with the position of an addressee. In modern honorifics, it is common for a speaker to treat an in-group member, whether he is superior or not, by humble expression when the addressee belongs to his out-group. That is, a speaker shows his deference to an addressee by humbling, or lowering, the status of the person in his in-group. This is the reason why modern honorifics are called addressee-oriented relative honorifics. But in Toraaki's plays the hierarchical relation between a referent and a speaker influences the honorific expression used toward the referent. In this sense, it has less in common with the addressee-oriented modern honorifics, and is instead referent-oriented. Let us look more closely at this.

2.1 An in-group inferior referent is treated by either humble or neutral expression.

An inferior by kinship relation, (e.g. a wife or a child), and an inferior by social status, (e.g. a servant), are commonly treated by humble expression. But a husband referring to his wife when speaking to his servant will use a neutral expression, and so it can be supposed that a referent is treated by neutral expression when the addressee is inferior to the referent. It is also supposed that an inferior referent is treated by either humble or neutral expression even when he or she belongs to the in-group of an addressee; therefore a teacher uses a humble expression to refer to his disciple when speaking to the disciple's wife. And below, when a go-between refers to the wife of the addressee, he uses the neutral expression *ihu*.

あれが言ふを聞くは、わごりよは、三界を家として、家の修理もせいで、女共にばかりかせがせて、所帯の事はこゝろがけもせぬが、腹がたつと言ふ（どもり）

are ga 'HPA' *ihu* o kiku ha, wagoryo ha sangai o iwe to shi te, iwe no shiyuri mo se i de, onna-domo ni bakari kasega se te, siyotai no koto ha kokoro-gake mo se nu ga, hara ga tatsu to *ihu*

'What I heard from your wife is that you always stray around the world, don't repair the house, make your wife work and never think of your household. She said she got angry with you.'

In contrast, an addressee-orientation is quite strong in modern honorifics, and to humble a referent who belongs to the in-group of an addressee means to make the addressee humble by association; therefore, it is rarely done.

2.2 An in-group equal referent is treated by either humble or neutral expression.

When an addressee is part of a speaker's in-group, the honorific expression used toward the referent is determined solely by the relationship between referent and addressee, as can be seen below when a grandson speaks to his grandfather about his other grandsons.

この者共は、この年になりまらすれ共（さいほう）

kono mono-*domo* 'HS' ha kono toshi ni nari marasure domo

'These fellows are very old enough to know better, though...'

And when a servant speaks of another servant to their master, he uses a humble expression because the referent is inferior to the addressee. That is, the position of an addressee influences the honorific expression toward the referent. In conversation with a person who does not belong to one's in-group, a neutral expression is commonly employed to refer to an in-group equal. In modern honorifics, with its addressee-orientation, an in-group referent—whether or not he is superior to a speaker—is commonly treated by humble expression because of his in-group-ness. The honorific system in Toraaki's plays is not so much addressee-oriented as modern honorifics.

2.3 An in-group superior referent is treated by either ordinary or supreme respectful expression.

The mistress of the house refers to her *daimyō* husband when addressing her servant. In this case, the addressee is an in-group inferior, therefore, a supreme respectful expression can be used for the in-group superior referent. But in other cases, it is common to refer to him by an ordinary respectful expression such as *raru*. When an addressee is an in-group person, *ōseraru, oshiyaru* and *iharu* are chosen according to a speaker's status; when an addressee is an out-group person, *mausaru* or *raru* is used. The honorific expression toward an in-group superior referent is determined by the relationship with an addressee; however, unlike in modern honorifics a humble expression is never used—either an ordinary or a supreme respectful expression is appropriate.

3. The proposal of the new term in/out-group honorifics.

The honorific expression toward an out-group referent who has no direct relationship with either speaker or addressee is fixed by the social status of the referent, whereas the honorific expression toward an in-group referent is determined by the relationship with the addressee. When an addressee belongs to a speaker's in-group, the honorific expression toward the referent is determined by the tripartite relations between referent, speaker and addressee, which is the hierarchical relation of either kinship or social status. The situation can be problematic when talking with an out-group person about a member of one's in-group. An inferior in-group member is treated by humble expression, but a superior in-group member is treated by ordinary respectful expression. In modern honorifics, an in-group member is treated by humble expression even if he is superior to a speaker, hence modern honorifics are called relative honorifics. Here I have coined a new term—in/out-group honorifics—because the term relative honorifics is used by many scholars with their own varied interpretations. I define in/out-group honorifics as a system in which the honorific expression toward a referent is determined by the criterion of whether the referent belongs to the in-group of either a speaker or an addressee. In *kyōgen*, instead of the humble expression, an ordinary respectful expression is used. In this sense, the honorific system in Toraaki's plays could be considered an intermediate system between hierarchical and in/out-group honorifics. When a wife refers to her husband, she uses a supreme respectful expression to her in-group servant, but she uses an ordinary respectful expression to an out-group visitor. In this sense, the honorific expression toward the in-group superior is based on the relation to an addressee. There still remains the problem of how to interpret a humble form + respectful form such as *mausaru*, which is often used to speak of an in-group superior to an out-group person. If I interpret this as dual honorifics, it is an intermediate form between the relative honorific *mausu* and the absolute honorific *raru*. If I interpret *mausu* as a polite form, it is an ordinary respectful expression. Rodriguez (1955) suggests that *raru* be used 'mainly when talking about an equal family member', and that *mausaru* be used 'when a priest talks about a superior priest to out-group person'. *Mausaru* is therefore supposed to be used to refer to an in-group superior when speaking to an out-group person. In the Muromachi period, whether a referent was an in-group or an out-group person was already an important criterion in determining the honorific expression to be used toward a referent. We can find similarities between the honorific expressions in *kyōgen* plays and the descriptions in *Arte da Lingoa de Iapam*, but the latter offers no clear description about the usage of *raru*. It states, 'A person in church should not use the honorific form to refer to elders and priests to an out-group person, but in exceptional cases *raru* can be used', but it can be difficult to know how to interpret this usage of *raru*. It can be interpreted that in/out-group honorifics have already been invented if we think that a speaker makes an in-group referent humble by using the lowest respectful expression, *raru*. But it is also possible to argue that absolute honorifics still prevail because no matter how low the respectful expression, it is nevertheless still used toward an in-group person. The best solution might be to view the honorific expression of this time as in a transitional stage toward in/out-group honorifics. Rodriguez (1955) writes, 'In conclusion, there are lots of special conditions for the usage of respectful and polite forms. It is better to learn by experience, by observing how learned people use them, than to try to learn the basic rules'. It can be surmised that multiple honorific systems co-existed and mixed according to social classes and situational factors, and that there was no conclusive and fixed rule.

And self-respectful expressions were still used.
抑是は、西の宮のゑびす三郎殿にて、おりやらします（ゑびす毘沙門）
somo-somo kore ha nishi-no-miya no webisu saburau-*dono* 'RS' ni te *oriyarashi* 'be (SRV)' masu

'I am Mr Webisu Saburau.'

Here, a god introduces himself with the self-respectful expression *dono* and *oriyarasu*.

4. Use of the honorific expression can be affected by the emotions.

It is the social custom for the proper honorific expression to be determined by social status and the relation with an addressee, but it may fluctuate for emotional reasons. In the following monologue, a wife, who would normally use an ordinary respectful expression for her husband, uses the insulting expression *aitsu-me* because she is angry with her husband.

なふ腹たちや、あいつめに食ひつかふかしらぬ（いなばだう）

nau hara tachi ya *aitsu-me* ni kuhituka hu ka shira nu

'I am very angry with him. I feel like biting him.'

5. The honorific expression can fluctuate due to debt.

A servant usually treats his master to out-group inferior by ordinary respectful expression, but may use the humble expression *mausu* when addressing a merchant to whom his master owes money. During the Muromachi period, the polite form started to develop, and this tendency supported the increase of an addressee-orientation in honorific expression. In addition to the hierarchical order by social status, mental debt to an addressee gradually became an influential factor in the use of honorific expression.

6. Because of scant materials, we cannot show variations of honorific expression based on the social status of the samurai and the common class, or by gender, but this problem should be solved.

It is quite possible that the honorific expression toward a referent branched into different systems according to the context of use; public or private situation. But the characters that appear in *kyōgen* plays are not the ruling class because *kyōgen* is a popular entertainment. I show how the honorific expression is used in a public situation in Chapter 5.

(Endnotes)

1   All the land was controlled by the nation until the latter half of the Heian period. When

people started to cultivate barren land and take possession, those who owned large tracks of land were called *daimyō* and those who owned small amounts of land were called *shōmyō* 小名. *Dai* means 'large', and *shō* means 'small'. *Myō* means *myōden* 名田 'registered land'.

2 In this time, diphthongs started to be pronounced as long vowels. As a consequence, [au] was pronounced as [ɔː] and [ou] was pronounced as [oː]. In modern Japanese, these distinctions merged into the same sound [oː]. In this chapter we transcribe [au] for [ɔː], and [ō] for [oː].

3 The quoted parts are shown within parentheses. The names of plays are shown.

4 Hachiya (1977) writes that in the play *Onigawara* in the *Kyōgen Rikugi-hon* a *daimyō* uses the ordinary respectful expression *raruru* when speaking of his wife to his servant. But in *Torahiro-hon*, published later, the respectful expression is not used. It is possible that this difference might reflect the historical shift of the honorific system. In chapter two there is an example from *Genji-Monogatari* of a husband referring his wife with a respectful expression when speaking to his servant from the standpoint that she is the wife of the master

5

REFERENT HONORIFIC EXPRESSION IN THE SHŌKAISHINGO

1. Introduction

In chapter four I examined *kyōgen* play as material for the Japanese language of the Muromachi period and I concluded that the honorific system was in a transitional stage between hierarchical and in/out-group honorifics. But the setting of *kyōgen* plays is mainly in the private rather than the public domain. Nowadays it is common to alternate between honorific registers in accordance with the domain. For example, in the Kansai region (Kyōto, Ōsaka, Kōbe), where the ancient capital was located, two different honorific expressions are code-switched by private and public domains; when speaking of one's father to an out-group person, in local dialect, a person says *otō-san soto ika hari mashi ta* 'My father has gone' (*san* is a respectful suffix, and *hari* is a respectful auxiliary), but in Standard Japanese, one says *chichi ha gaishutsu itashi te ori masu* (*chichi* is a humble noun, and *itashi* is a humble auxiliary). It is believed that in the Muromachi and Edo periods different honorific expressions were also code-switched in accordance with the context. There is no extant material written by Japanese of the colloquial public Japanese of this time; therefore, we utilize the *Shōkaishingo* 捷解新語, a Japanese textbook edited in Korea. Consisting of Japanese conversations in official settings, it was used to train Korean interpreters as official intermediaries in commercial transactions with Japanese officials and as interpreters between Korean and Japanese directors.

Let us look at diplomatic relation between Japan and Korea at that time. Hideyoshi, who had unified the whole country and brought it under his control, tried to spread his influence to foreign countries. He invaded Korea twice, in 1592 and 1597, both times in vain. Tokugawa established diplomatic relations in 1607 and, even after the closed-door policy was implemented in the early seventeenth century, the government maintained peaceful relations with Korea. The kings of Korea sent twelve missions to Japan between 1607 and 1811.

2. Data

There is no doubt that the *Shōkaishingo* was edited by Kang Woosung 康遇聖, as a textbook of Japanese language for Korean interpreters, but it is less clear when this textbook was published. Ogura (1964) proposes that it was published in 1618, but it is more commonly believed that it was after 1625 since this book consists of ten volumes (cf., Ōtomo 1957; Nakamura 1961; and Lee 1984). Kang Woosung was captured as a prisoner of war and was sent to Japan in 1592 when he was twelve years old. He spent ten years in Japan, became an interpreter after he was sent back to Korea, then visited Japan several times as an officer. The *Shōkaishingo* was written by an author that was fluent in Japanese and was a native Korean speaker. But we need more language in order to trust that the *Shōkaishingo* is a reliable source of the Japanese. First of all, as Hamada (1970) suggests, there is the possibility that because the Korean language is grammatically similar to Japanese the text reflects Korean bias. There is also no proof about which kind of Japanese was written in the *Shōkaishingo*. According to Morita (1973), 'It seems that the *Shōkaishingo* reflects a colloquial dialect, a rather vulgar one, spoken in the Kyoto area in the Muromachi period or at the beginning of the Edo period and retaining some influence of Kyūshū dialect'. It is said that the Japanese contemporary honorific system is relative honorifics, but, on the contrary, the Korean contemporary honorific system is absolute honorifics. In fact, the criterion that determines honorific expressions for Korean is not the same as that used for Japanese, so it might be misleading to state that the Korean contemporary honorific system is absolute honorifics.[1] There are not many remaining materials, and there is no certainty about the past Korean honorific system (cf., Aan, 1981). A comparative study was done of the Korean and

Japanese content in the *Shōkaishingo*, and it can be seen that the Japanese text doesn't always correspond to the Korean translation. If the native knowledge of the Korean interpreter interferes in the Japanese text, there must be correspondence at all times between the Japanese text and the Korean translation. As a result, the author, Kang Woosung, recognized the differences between the Japanese and Korean honorific systems. We need to bear this in mind when studying the *Shōkaishingo*. *Shōkaishingo* went through several editions. I begin with the first edition and show the revisions made in later editions. I use the Japanese linguistic department of Kyoto University (ed. 1972, 1973) as a resource.

3. Analysis

In the first edition of the *Shōkaishingo*, when each character starts a conversation on a new line, we can understand that a new character is introduced; however, there is no clear information about who is speaking. In a revised version, we are told that there is a host or a guest, and this makes it easier to guess whose conversation follows. A host indicates that a Korean is speaking, while a guest tells us that it is a Japanese. It is also possible to assume to whom a conversation belongs by its content and honorific expression. I analyze the honorific expression toward referents from both the Korean (K) and Japanese (J) side.

3.1 Honorific expression in the first edition of the *Shōkaishingo*
A. Lee Dynasty

There are only examples of exchanges between the Korean side and the Tsushima clan side.

official(K)→official(J)[2]
朝廷よりも書契毎に御覧じられて（三12オ）[3]
teutei yori mo shokei goto ni *goranji rare* 'look (SRV)' te[4]
'The palace checked each letter.'

Supreme respectful expressions like the two cases of *goranjiraru* and the three cases of *oboshimesu* are used. After the Japanese government officially closed the door to foreign countries, the Tsushima clan, from a small island close to the Korean peninsula, was permitted to trade with Korea with the proviso that the clan paid tribute to the Lee Dynasty. It is to be expected that a Korean official would use supreme respectful expressions when speaking of his king. There are two kinds of auxiliary verb—*(sa)shiraru*[5] and *raru*—suffixed to a verb; *(sa)shiraru* is used for a referent that should be paid higher respect, and is used for the Lee Dynasty. The people who are treated by *(sa)shiraru* are the head officials of Tonegi 東莱 and Pusan 釜山, the head of a mission, the lord of Chikuzen and the heads of department. The ablative case particle *yori* is used to refer to the Lee Dynasty and, in the Korean translation, the respectful particle 긔셔 is assigned (cf., Tsuji, 1997). In contemporary Japanese also, in stead of making an actor explicit, an honorific expression by locative case—such as *ni oka re mashi te wa* 'in one's place (literally)'—can be used to refer to a person who is worthy of respect. The people who are treated by *yori* are the *shōgun*, the head officials of Tonegi and Pusan, and the heads of missions.

B. *shōgun*

Foreign countries dealing with Japan must have wondered whether it was the *shōgun* or *tennō*, who had sovereign power. It was after 1635 that equal diplomatic relations were established between the Lee Dynasty and the shōgunate. According to an official statement from the Edo government, the *shōgun* was not an emperor, but used the title *taikun* 大君 which in return was used by the Korean contingent. In the first version, there were various names used, amongst them *kanpaku* 関白, *taikun*, *kubō* 公方, *uesama* 上様, and *kōgi* 公儀. In one situation, the head of the Korean mission was granted an audience with the *taikun*, and the Japanese magistrate speaks to him on behalf of the *taikun*.

magistrate(J)→head of the Korean mission(K)

上様仰しらる所は、海上遥々の道に、御無事にお越しの由、大慶に存じられて（七13オーウ）

uesama *oshiraru* 'say (SRV)' tokoro wa, kaijō haru-baru no michi ni, go-buji ni o-koshi no yue, taikei ni *zonji rare* 'think (ORV)' te

'The shōgun is delighted that you could cross safely all the way by sea.'

magistrate(J)→head of the Korean mission(K)

大君も殊の外喜び斜めならず（七21ウ）

taikun mo koto-no-hoka yorokobi nanome nara zu

'The shōgun's happiness was not ordinary.'

The magistrate calls the *shōgun uesama* and *taikun,* and refers to him by *oshiraru, mausaru, zonjiraru* and *zonzu*. *Mausu* and *zonzu* became polite forms during this time and they are used toward an addressee.[6] Although *oboshimesu* and *oshiraru* exist as supreme respectful expressions the ordinary respectful expressions *zonjiraru* and *mausaru* are used. The head of the Korean mission replies as follows, using a respectful expression for *shōgun:*

head of the Korean mission(K)→magistrate(J)

さてさて早々御懇懃なる御尋ね、忝き仕合せを、申す様も御座らん。（七16ウ）

sate-sate go 'RP'-ingin naru o 'RP'-tazune, katajikenaki shiawase o, mausu sama mo gozara n

'Words cannot describe my gratitude for your kindness in visiting us so soon.'

C. the head officials of Tonegi and Pusan

There were Japanese offices in Sampo and Seoul that, like today's embassies, dealt with diplomacy and trade between Japan and Korea. The head officials of Tonegi and Pusan directly controlled these offices and were treated respectfully by both Korean and Japanese officials.

official(J)→official(K)

東莱聞かしらりてもかど病とは思し召すまい程に（一31オ）

tonegi kika *shirari* 'ORA' te mo kado-yamai to ha *oboshimesu* 'think (SRV)' mai hodoni

'Even when Tonegi hears about you, he never thinks that you feign illness.'

official(K)→official(J)

東莱仰しらるは（二1オ）

tonegi *oshiraru* 'say (SRV)' ha

'What Tonegi says is…'

They use supreme respectful expressions such as *oboshimesu* and *sashiraru*. There are many words to mean 'say' but, other than for the head officials of Tonegi and Pusan, it is only for the *shōgun*, the lord of Tsushima, and the heads of the Korean missions that the exalted verb *oshiraru* is used.

D. the head of the Korean mission

The head of the Korean mission was the head of a goodwill mission sent by the Lee Dynasty in order to celebrate the succeession of the new Japanese *shōgun*, or to negotiate the return of war prisoners who had been captured during the fight against Hideyoshi's invasion. There were twelve missions sent between 1607 and 1811, and the author of the *Shōkaishingo*, Kang Woosung, came to Japan three times as an interpreter. When a Japanese official refers to the head of the Korean mission he uses *sashiraru*.

official(J)→official(K)

都はいつころ立しられて、ここもとへはいつころ着かしらると申すか。（五11オ－11ウ）

miyako wa itsu koro tata *shirare* 'ORA' te, koko-moto we wa itsu koro tsuka *shiraru* 'ORA' to mausu ka

'When do you say (the head of the Korean mission) leaves the capital and arrives here?'

And the Korean official refers to the same person in the following way:

official(K)→official(J)

都は何月何日立たしられて、釜山浦には何月何日に着かわしられ、御逗留は二十四五日程なされて、

miyako wa nan-gwachi nan-ka tata *shirare* 'ORA' te, pusan-kai ni wa nan-gwachi nan-ka ni tsukawa *shirare* 'ORA', *go* 'RP'-touriu wa nijiu-shi-gonichi hodo *nasare* 'do (ORV)' te

'(The head of the Korean mission) leaves the capital on such a day in such a month, arrives at Pusan on such a day in such a month, and stays twenty four or five days…'

He uses a supreme respectful expression like *sashiraru* in four cases, *nasaru* and *oshiraru*. This honorific expression seems appropriate because the head of the Korean mission is the representative of the Lee Dynasty. The referents for whom one uses the verb *nasaru* are the *shōgun*, the head of the Japanese mission, the lord of Tsushima, the lord of Chikuzen, and head officials of Pusan other than the head of the Korean mission.

E. the lord of Tsushima

The honorific expression toward the lord of Tsushima required delicacy. As Kang Woosung writes in the narrative sections:

信使より呼び掛けて仰しらるは、……好う御座ろうと仰しられたれば、太守申すは（八30オ－32オ）

shinsu yori yobikake te *oshiraru* 'say (SRV)' wa, …you gozarou to *oshirare* 'say (SRV)' tare ba, taishu[7] *mausu* 'say (HVN)' wa

'The head of the Korean mission says, "…it is nice", then the lord of Tsushima answers …'

For the head of the Korean mission he uses *oshiraru* and, in contrast, for the lord of Tsushima *mausu* is used. In the Japanese conversational part, they each use the polite form to refer to the other and no difference is apparent. But in the Korean translation, there exist various degrees of polite forms so that the head of the Korean mission talks to the lord of Tsushima using a less polite form, and the lord of Tsushima talks to the head of the Korean mission using a more polite form. The lord of Tsushima is only the head of local government and is ranked below the head of the Korean mission who belongs to the central government, and Kang Woosung reflects this difference in status between them.

A Japanese official who is subordinate to the lord of Tsushima refers to him when talking to a Korean official who is of the same rank:

official(J)→official(K)

対馬の守仰しらる所は、信使渡らしらる様には聞かれども、……我等両人を俄に差し渡された程に（五2ウ－3オ）

tushima no kami *oshiraru* 'say (SRV)' tokoro wa, shinshi watara *shiraru* 'ORA' you ni wa kika *re* 'RARU' domo, …ware-ra riyaunin wo niwaka-ni sashi-watasa *re* 'RARU' ta hodoni

'The lord of Tsushima told us that he heard the mission would come…he sent both of us,'

He uses *oshiraru* and *raru*, but to an addressee who is supposed to be the head of the

Korean mission, he uses the humble expressions *mausu* and *maushiaguru*:

    official(J)→head of the Korean mission(K)

    太守申す所は、……門安こそ申し上げまるすれ（五19ウ－20オ）

    taishu *mausu* 'say (HVN)' tokoro wa, …mon'an koso *maushiage* 'say (HVN)' marusure

    'What the lord of Tsushima said to you, …sends his greeting.'

This might be because the lord of Tsushima is a subject of the Lee Dynasty that sends the Korean mission.

F. the mother of the lord of Tsushima

    There is only one case where a referent is a superior by kinship relation, and that is when the lord of Tsushima speaks of his mother to the head of the Korean mission:

    lord of Tsushima(J)→head of the Korean mission(K)

    年寄った母を持ちまるしたに、朝鮮の楽を壁越しながら聞きたいと望みで御座る程に（八23ウ－24オ）

    toshiyot ta *haha* o mochi marushi ta ni, teusen no gaku wo kabe-goshi nagara kiki-tai to nozomi de gozaru hodo ni

    'I have an old mother, and she would like to hear Korean music, even if it's from a distance.'

    lord of Tsushima(J) →head of the Korean mission(K)

    彼の珍しい囃子をも母ぢや者聞かれて（八27オ－ウ）

    kano medurashii hayashi wo mo *haha-diya-mono* kika re 'ORA' te

    'My mother heard some remarkable music.'

The former contains a neutral expression and the kinship term *haha*,[8] and the latter uses the ordinary respectful expression *raru* and the kinship term *haha-diya-mono*. These examples fluctuate between neutral and ordinary respectful expression. It is written in the *Shakkanki* (collected in Zoku-Gunshoruijū-kankōkai, 1958) that 'It is better to use *oya-diya-mono* rather than use one's name in front of a master or a noble person, for to mention one's name is a respectful gesture'. *Haha-diya-mono* is the official way to mention one's mother.

G. the lord of Chikuzen

There is a situation in which the lord of Chikuzen is mentioned by the lord of Tsushima when addressing the head of a mission. The lord of Tsushima is subordinate to the Lee Dynasty, but the lord of Chikuzen has no direct hierarchical relation with them, therefore, the supreme respectful expression *shiraru* is used to refer to him.

lord of Tsushima(J)→head of the Korean mission(K)

筑前の守より、是まで無事着しられ他と有って、祝いに下人を遣わしらる為と（七1オ）

chikuzen-no-kami yori, kore made buji tsuka shirare ta to at te, iwai ni genin wo tsukawa *shiraru* 'SRA' tame to

'As you have arrived here safely, the lord of Chikuzen has sent his servants to celebrate your safe arrival.'

And the messenger of the lord of Tsushima refers to his lord.

messenger of the lord of Tsushima(J)→head of the Korean mission(K)

筑前の守申し置きまるする所は、……堅く申されたれども、……太守聞かれても、……旦那が面目なう存じまるせう程に（七4ウ－5オ）

chikuzen-no-kami *maushi-oki* 'say (HVN)' masuru tokoro wa,…kataku *mausare* 'say (ORV)' tare domo, …taishu kika *re* 'RARU' te mo, …danna *ga* 'HPA' menmoku nau *zonjirare* 'think (ORV)' maruse u hodoni,

'What the lord of Chikuzen ordered us to do is…, …he was definite that…, …*taishu* heard that…,…because our master might feel ashamed….'

He refers to his master by using the ordinary respectful expression *raru* in *mausaru*, *kikaru* and *zonjiraru*. Rodriguez (1955) writes about *raru*, 'It is common to use *raru* for people to whom it is worth paying some amount of awe and respect, mainly when they are not present'. *Raru* seems to be an auxiliary to show a low level of respect. And the nominal case particle *ga* is used as a humble expression. In the first version of the textbook, there is a clear distinction made about the use of nominal case particles *ga* and *no*. That is, *ga* is used for a speaker or a speaker's in-group, and *no* is used for an addressee or an addressee's in-group (cf., Han, 1998). Here is how the Korean side refers to the lord of Chikuzen when addressing the lord of Tsushima.

head of the Korean mission(K) →lord of Tsushima(J)

筑前殿地界二泊まで、おびただし賄いなされたに（七2オ）

chikuzen-*dono* 'RP' chikei huta-tomari made obitadashi makanai *nasare* 'do (SRV)' ta ni

'The lord of Chikuzen entertained us in two harbors at countless expense.'

The respectful expression includes the title *dono* and the verbs *nasaru* and *mausu(ni)*. As Rodriguez (1955) writes about respectful titles, '*Sama* is the highest, *kou* is the second highest, *dono* is the third highest and *rou* is the lowest for monks to whom we need to show some respect'.

H. *makanai-bugyō* who entertains the Korean mission

When a Korean mission that consisted of more than four hundred people traveled to Edo through the feudal provinces, each clan selected a *makanai-bugyō* in order to share the great expense of entertaining the Korean mission[9].

The lord of Tsushima speaks of a *makanai-bugyō* to the head of the Korean mission:

lord of Tsushima(J)→head of the Korean mission(K)

奉行衆の断りには、……仔細を申して、わざと三日路を一日に参ったに（八4ウ－5ウ）

bugiyau-*shū* no kotowari ni wa, …shisai wo *maushi* 'say (HVN)' te, wazato mikadi o ichi-nichi ni *mait* 'come (HVN)' ta ni

'What the *makanai-bugyō* refused to do is, …they explained in detail their reason, and took the trouble to come all the way in one day rather than take the usual three days.'

Whilst he uses the humble expressions *mausu* and *mairu*, the head of the Korean mission uses a neutral expression:

head of the Korean mission(K)→lord of Tsushima(J)

奉行衆へ懇ろに言うて（八4オ－ウ）

bugiyau-*shū* he omomuro ni yuu te

'I will report to the *makanai-bugyō* politely.'

The plural suffix *shū* is used. According to Rodriguez (1955), '*Shū* is used for respect toward an ordinary or inferior person, and its honorific value seems neutral'. The *makanai-bugyō* who entertain the Korean mission are important people to the Tsushima clan, and it is appropriate that the lord of Tsushima treats him as an inferior to the head of the Korean mission, since his duty is to entertain the mission.

I. a *samurai* who entertains the Korean mission

In the textbook there is a *samurai* who works under the *makanai-bugyō*, and he is treated by humble expression like *mausu* and the plural suffix *ra* by the Japanese.

lord of Tsushima(J)→head of the Korean mission(K)

此の賄衆申す所は（六17ウ）

kono makanai-*shū mausu* 'say (HVN)' tokoro wa

'What the *samurai* says is,'

lord of Tsushima(J)→head of the Korean mission(K)

あれらが雑作を無に成すも由無く（六19オ）

are-*ra ga* 'HPA' zausa wo mu ni nasu mo

'Bringing their effort to naught.'

Rodriguez (1955) writes, '*Ra* is used to humble the first person or to disdain greatly the second and third person'. Here the lord of Tsushima once again treats the entertainer as an inferior person but, in the following, the head of the Korean mission treats the subordinate of an addressee by respectful expression.

head of the Korean mission(K)→lord of Tsushima(J)

賄衆よりも御懇ろな事で御座る（六15ウ）

makanai-*shū* yori mo *on* 'RP'-nengoro na koto de gozaru

'It is very kind of the *makanai-shū*.'

J. young people

When a group of young Japanese looks after the Korean mission at a welcome party, the Korean official treats them as follows:

official(K)→official(J)

御歌唄わしらりた若衆達（九5オ）

on 'RP' -uta utawa *shirari* 'SRA' ta waka-*shū-tachi* 'RS'

'The young people who sang a song'

The Korean official treats the young people by the respectful expression *shiraru*, and the Japanese official replies using a neutral expression, which shows that the determinant of an honorific expression toward a referent, in addition to the social status, is whether or not the referent belongs to an addressee's in-group.

K. a maid

The lord of Tsushima treats his maids with the humble expression *domo*.

lord of Tsushima(J)→head of the Korean mission(K)

我等腰元の若い者どもを踊りをさせて、御目に懸けたうこそ御座れ（六6ウ）

ware-ra koshimoto no wakai mono-*domo* 'HS' o odori wo sa se te, o-me ni kake tau koso gozare

'I would like to make our young maids dance for you.'

In contrast, the head of the Korean mission treats the maids, who are part of the addressee's in-group, with the respectful expressions *on* and *shū*.

head of the Korean mission(K)→lord of Tsushima(J)

御腰元衆の芸を見せうと仰しらる程に（六7ウ）

on 'RP' -koshimoto-*shū* no gei o mise u to oshiraru hodoni

'You said that you would show us the dance of your maids.'

This example shows that regard for an addressee makes a speaker use respectful language even for a low status person who belongs to an addressee's side. According to Rodriguez (1955), '*Domo* is used for the first person, and when it is used for the second or the third person, the referent should be a person of low status otherwise the speaker offends the referent. And *domo* is used for inanimate objects or animals'.

L. *shiyaugwan* 正官

The Tsushima clan sent a ship for Japan-Korean trade, and the head of the Japanese mission was called a *shiyaugwan*, and his assistant a *tousenshiyu* 都船主. Addressing Tonegi the *tousenshiyu* refers to his senior to using a humble expression.

tousenshiyu(J)→Tonegi(K)

正官人に申したらば、御目に懸らんを、いかう悲しお存じまるして（二4ウ－5オ）

shiyaugwan ni maushi tara ba, *o-me ni kakara* 'meet (HVN)' n o, ikau kanashio *zonji* 'think (HVN)' marushi te

'If I tell the head of the Japanese mission (that you would like to meet him), he will feel very sorry that he can't meet you.'

Whereas a Korean official refers to the head of the Japanese mission using a respectful expression:

official(K)→*tousenshiyu*(J)

正官人出でられずば、……たとゑ正官人御気相に御座るとも、……出でさしられて実に堪えられずんば、先に御立ちなさるとも、（一29オ－30オ）

shiyaugwan ide *rare* 'RARU' zu ba,...tatowe shiyaugwan-ji *on* 'RP'-kiai ni gozaru tomo,...ide *sashirare* 'SRA' te, zitsu ni taerare zu n ba, saki ni *o*-tachi-*nasaru* 'ORA' tomo

'If the head of the Japanese mission doesn't come..., ...but even if he is not feeling well, ...come and he can leave early if he cannot stay.'

M. Japanese *sosa* 送使

Trade between Japan and Korea is divided into two categories: a public trade that is transacted through the Tsushima clan directly and a private trade that is transacted between the common people in Tsushima and the merchants in Korea. Japanese merchants or *sosa* may belong to the Japanese side but they have no direct hierarchical relation with a Japanese official, who in the next exchange with a Korean official treats them by ordinary respectful expression *raru*.

official(J)→official(K)

送使方も対面ならば、奇特に思わるるは存ぢ前ぢや程に（一7オ－ウ）

sosa-*gata* mo taimen nara ba, kitoku ni omowa *ruru* 'RARU' wa zonjimawe diya

'If you come all the way to meet (*sosa*), they will feel honored.'

And in return a Korean official refers to the *sosa* by the supreme respectful expressions *oboshiaru* and *mesaru*:

official(K)→official(J)

送使方へは如何思しあるやら心に懸かる程に（一5オ）

sosa-*gata* he wa ikaga *oboshiaru* 'think (SRV)' yara kokoro ni kakaru hodoni

'I am worried about what the *sosa* thinks about it.'

The plural prefix *gata* 方 that shows direction is used only to mention *sosa*, though its honorific value is not certain.

N. *daikanwa* 代官倭

Officials of the Japanese commission, whether *buke* or *chōnin*, were called *daikanwa* and were assigned to the trading section. The *buke*'s salary reflected their position: 230 *koku* for the chief, 150 *koku* for the next level and the rest are vassal, and the honorific expression used toward them reflects their low social status. Korean officials treat them by a neutral expression and with the plural suffix *shiyu*.

official(K)→official(J)

代官衆に余り選るなと仰しられ（三25ウ）

daikan-*shū* ni amari yoru na to oshirare

'Please tell the *daikan* not to choose very much.'

The head of the Japanese mission uses the plural suffix *domo* for them:

head of the Japanese mission (J)→official (K)

其れは判事衆と代官どもが如才御座るまい。（三26オ）

sore wa hansu-*shū* to daikan-*domo* 'HS' ga diyosai gozaru mai

'About that, the *hansu* and *daikan* would not make a mistake.'

Of the plural suffixes used to mention them, there are three examples of *domo* and one of *shū* used by the Japanese, and four examples of *shū* used by the Koreans.

O. *genin* 下人

The word *genin* is not a specific title but the generic term for people of low caste, and the term itself is a humble expression. The Korean contingent refers to Japanese *genin* by adding the suffix *domo*.

head of the Korean mission(K)→lord of Tsushima clan(K)

久々苦労した下人どもに、別に印し致す事も無し（八3オ－ウ）

hisa-hisa kurau shi ta genin-*domo* 'HS' ni betsuni shirusi itasu koto mo nashi

'We have nothing to leave to the *genin* who have worked hard for us for a long time.'

Those on an addressee's side who are of low social status are treated by a neutral or humble expression and this shows how important social status is in determining the honorific expression toward a referent at this time.

P. a boatman

A Korean official treats his own boatman in the following manner:

official(K)→official(J)

朝鮮の船頭達（五14オ）

teusen no sendou-*tachi*

'Boatmen of Korea.'

A plural suffix *tachi* is used, but its usage might be a mistake. *Tuur*, a humble expression, is used in a Korean translation. Rodriguez (1955) writes that, '*Tachi* is used for the most respectful person as the second and third person suffix. But it is often used to mention the not so noble person'. When *tachi* is used correctly, it can be considered a neutral suffix. And in return, a Japanese official refers to his own boatman by neutral expression.

Q. a musical band

The Korean missions would travel to the capital in the form of a procession lead by a musical band that must have become quite fashionable among both the ruling and the common classes. A dance called *tōjin odori* that emulates this band is still performed as a traditional entertainment in various parts of Japan. *Tōjin* means Chinese, but for the common Japanese all foreigners, even Europeans, were called *tōjin* and were treated with a neutral expression.

lord of Tsushima(J)→head of the Korean mission(K)

楽仕る者（八24オ）

gaku *tsukamatsuru* 'do (HVN)' mono

'The people who play music'

In return, the Korean also uses a neutral expression.

3.2. Summary of honorific expression in the first version of the *Shōkaishingo*

1. A speaker utilizes a lower honorific expression toward a superior referent on his side in order to show regard to an addressee.

   Honorific expressions used toward a superior referent who belongs to a speaker's side can fluctuate, and the choice of a respectful, dual or neutral expression can apply even to the same addressee. A speaker treats his superior using a respectful expression when an addressee is low in his status, but refrains from doing so when an addressee is higher in status. And humble expression is used when a speaker's superior referent is inferior to an addressee. In chapter three, I concluded that the honorific expression used in *Heike-Monogatari* was hierarchical honorifics, which was defined as the honorific system in which the honorific expression toward a referent is determined not by the relationship between a speaker and an addressee, but by the hierarchical order in which they are placed. In the first version of the *Shōkaishingo*, hierarchical honorifics are used and the regard toward an addressee can be found there. But the regard is not like that of today's in/out-group honorifics that is based on the criterion of whether or not a referent is part of one's in-group; rather, it is based on the position that addressee and referent occupy in the hierarchical order. In today's in/out-group honorifics, a speaker refrains from using a respectful expression when a referent is part of the speaker's in-group, but in the first version of the *Shōkaishingo*, a respectful expression is used when an addressee is inferior to a referent, and the criterion of in-group is less important. A respectful expression is used, however, when a referent belongs to an addressee even if he is inferior to a speaker. In that sense, the honorific system in the first version of the *Shōkaishingo* shows more regard to an addressee and draws closer to in/out-group honorifics. The examples of the variety of honorific expressions that can apply when a person speaks of his superior to a much higher addressee show the fluctuating nature of this transitive stage.

2. A speaker chooses a higher honorific expression toward a referent belonging to an addressee to show regard to the addressee.

When a referent belongs to an addressee's in-group, a speaker often adjusts the honorific expression choosing one that is higher than his status might warrant. The head of the Korean mission uses respectful language toward the lord of Tsushima who is in an inferior position within the Korean Dynasty not only as an addressee but also as a referent. A referent that belongs to an addressee is sometimes referred to by a higher respectful expression even if he is low in status. This shows that the respect one has for an addressee influences the honorific expression used toward a referent.

3. A referent of low status is treated by neutral or humble expression.

The social status of a referent cannot be ignored as a determinant of honorific expression. People of low social status, like boatman and *genin*, are treated by neutral or humble expression not only when part of a speaker's in-group but also when they belong to the in-group of an addressee. In today's in/out-group honorific system, an in-group referent of an addressee is treated by respectful expression even when he is inferior to both speaker and addressee. But this attitude cannot be found in the first version of the *Shōkaishingo*, where social status is an important factor.

3.3. Revisions in the last edition

Many revisions were made before the last edition, *jyūkan-bon*, was supposedly published by Choi Hagryngu 崔鶴齡 in 1781. There may be two reasons for the revisions: to correct errors, and to adjust the linguistic changes that had taken place during the 150 years since the first version was published. Yasuda (1973) points out that the colloquial expression based on the Kyūshū dialect[10] in the first edition was subsequently replaced by the Kyōto dialect that was the common speech at that time, and the vulgar terms became official Chinese words or elegant words. The last edition was revised to reflect both the shift to the standard Japanese spoken at that time and the adaptation to these linguistic changes.

A. *shōgun*

The honorific expression toward a *shōgun* in the narrative part was drastically changed by Choi Hagryngu, and the various terms that had been used to refer to the *shōgun* were replaced with *kubō-sama*.

公方様より御執政方を以（七13ウ）

kubō-*sama* 'RS' yori *go* 'RP' -shitsusei-gata wo motsu te

'From the shōgun through to the administrators…'

There is now a clear distinction made between those who are referred to with either of the honorific suffixes *sama* or *dono*. The higher suffix *sama* is used only for the *shōgun*, the head of the Korean mission and Tonegi. Below, a Japanese official refers to the *shōgun*:

bugyō(J)→head of the Korean mission(K)

信使無事故、是迄御着成されまして、目出度思召されまする。近日内御逢成されませう程に（七13オ−14オ）

shinshi kotoyuwe naku kore made o-tsuki-nasare mashi te medetau *oboshi-mesa-re* 'feel (SRV)' masuru. kinjitsu-uchi *o-ai-nasare* 'SRA' mase

'The shōgun feels happy that you have arrived here without any problem. He might see you soon.'

In the first edition, the *shōgun* is treated by the ordinary respectful expression *raru*, but in the last edition this has been replaced by supreme respectful expressions *oboshi-mesa-ru* and *o-V-nasaru*. The reason for this change is that the *shōgun* has since been instated as the sovereign ruler of all Japan and his status is therefore elevated.

B. the lord of the Tsushima clan

In the narrative parts, the actions of the lord toward the head of the Korean mission are referred to using *mausaru*, whereas *mausu* was used in the first edition.

対馬の守申されまするは（八6オ）

tsushima-no-kami *mausare* 'say (ORV)' masuru wa

'What the lord of the Tsushima clan says…'

The messenger always refers to his lord using *mausaru* when speaking to the Korean side.

messenger of Tsushima(J)→official(K)

対馬の守申されまするは（五3オ）

tsushima-no-kami *mausare* 'say (ORV)' masuru wa

'What the lord of the Tsushima clan says…'

messenger of Tsushima(J)→head of the Korean mission(K)

太守申されまするは（五20オ）

taishu *mausare* 'say (ORV)' masuru wa

'What the lord says…'

In the first edition, *oshiraru* is used for the former and *mausu* for the latter, whereas in the last edition the honorific expression toward the lord of the Tsushima clan is fixed.

C. a *makanai-bugyō* who entertains the Korean mission

In the narrative parts, the actions of the *makanai-bugyō* toward the head of the Korean mission are referred to by using *mausaru*, whereas *mausu* was used in the first edition.

賄奉行衆より態と人を遣わして申さるるは（ハ1ウ）

makanai-bugyō-*shū* yori waza-to hito wo tsukawashi te, *mausa-ruru* 'say (ORV)' wa

'What the *makanai-bugyō* kindly tells you through the messenger is…'

In the next example, the lord of the Tsushima clan uses *mausaru* as well as *mausu* and *mairu*.

lord of Tsushima(J)→head of the Korean mission(K)

奉行衆より断り申されまするは（ハ6オ）

bugyō-*shū* yori kotowari *mausare* 'say (ORV)' masuru wa

'What the *makanai-bugyō* refuses to do is…'

D. *shiyaugwan*

The Japanese side treats the head of the Japanese mission by the ordinary respectful expression *raru* whereas a neutral expression is used in the first edition.

tousenshiyu(J)→official(K)

正官は舟に酔われまして草臥て寝て居られまする。（一20ウ－21オ）

shiyaugwan wa hune ni yowa *re* 'RARU' mashi te, kutabire te, ne te, ora *re* 'RARU' masuru.

'Shiyaugwan was sea-sick and became tired, so he is sleeping.'

tousenshiyu(J)→Tonegi(K)

御目に懸からぬ事を残念に存じられて（ニ13オ）

o-me ni kakara nu koto o zannen ni *zonji* 'feel (HVN)' *rare* 'RARU' te

'(Shiyaugwan) feels very sorry that he can't meet you.'

E. the head Korean officials Tonegi and Pusan

As in the first edition, in the narrative part, Tonegi is treated by the supreme respectful expressions *otsushiyaru* and *ōseraru*.

東莱様よりおつしやれまするは（ニ7オ）

> tonegi-*sama* 'RS' yori *otsushiyare* 'say (SRV)' masuru wa.
>
> 'What Tonegi says is…'

In three examples Korean officials refer to their head, who is an in-group member, to the Japanese side by using *mausaru*, whereas the supreme respectful expression *oshiraru* is used in the first edition.

> **Korean official(K)→messenger of Tsushima(J)**
>
> 東萊様申されまするは（五7ウ）
>
> tonegi-*sama* 'RS' *mausare* 'say (ORV)' masuru wa
>
> 'What Tonegi says is…'

The top official, Tonegi, is treated by *sama*, but the next in charge, Pusan, is treated by *dono*. This usage of the suffix reflects the difference in their social status.

> **Korean official(K)→tousenshū(J)**
>
> 東萊様釜山殿に申して（一18ウ）
>
> tonegi-*sama* 'RS' pusan-*dono* 'RS' ni *maushi* 'say (HVO)' te
>
> 'I'll talk to Tonegi and Pusan.'

3.4. Conclusion about the revisions in the last edition

1. **In the last edition a speaker uses a lower honorific expression towards his superior when addressing a person who does not belong to his in-group and to whom he wants to show respect than in the first edition.**

   Whereas in the first edition the honorific expression is determined by the hierarchical order between an addressee and a referent, a speaker deliberately keeps the honorific expression lower even when an in-group referent is superior to the addressee. This linguistic device to demonstrate one's regard to an addressee is more firmly fixed in the last edition. For example, Korean officials treat the head Korean officer Tonegi to the lord of the Tsushima clan by the supreme respectful expression *oshiraru* in the first edition because Tonegi is superior to their lord, but *mausaru* is used in the last edition to keep the honorific expression toward an in-group referent lower. That means that the criteria that determine the honorific expression at this time is closer to that of the present-day in/out-group honorifics. However, the humble expression is not yet used to denigrate an in-group referent as it is in present-day in/out-group honorifics. Rodriguez (1955) writes, 'Only *raru* is appropriate to use when someone refers to his colleague, especially a member of his family, for it sounds queer to talk about one's colleague, family or religion to an out-group person using extremely polite language. So, only *raru* should be used when for example a priest talks about his colleague to an out-group person'. That is, a speaker should lower the honorific tone when he talks about an in-group person to an out-group person. The principle of this honorific expression is quite similar to that of today's system, in which the humble expression is used, but still the respectful expression co-exists even though it is kept as low as possible. This reflects the importance of the hierarchical status of this time.

4. Conclusion

The honorific expression of the first edition is based on hierarchical honorifics. That is, the honorific expression toward a referent is determined by the relative status in the hierarchical order between an addressee and a referent: when a referent is superior to an addressee, a respectful expression is used, and when a referent is inferior to an addressee, a humble expression is used. But when a referent belongs to the in-group of an addressee, a more respectful expression is preferred even if the referent is inferior to the speaker. This is the criterion of in/out-group honorifics. A respectful expression is sometimes used when a speaker refers to his in-group superior to an out-group addressee, but the respectful expression is kept as low as possible by using the least respectful auxiliary *raru*—a usage that was not part of the original hierarchical honorifics. There exist some inconsistencies in the first edition, where the following two criteria contradict each other: that of hierarchical honorifics where a respectful expression should be used when the in-group referent is superior to an addressee; and that of in/out-group honorifics, where a humble expression should be used in order to refer to an in-group referent when speaking to an out-group addressee. But honorific expression becomes unified in the last edition, and leans toward in/out-group honorifics where respect for an addressee is the prime criterion of the honorific expression. The *Shōkaishingo* also indicates that the honorific system was still in a transitional stage from hierarchical to in/out-group honorifics, and this process can be traced through the revisions made from the first to the last edition.

(Endnotes)

1. Shin (1986) reports the following honorific usage in Korean: when a wife refers to her husband to an out-group person, she uses a respectful expression if the out-group person is inferior to her husband, but not if the out-group person is superior to her husband. And when a wife refers to her husband to a superior out-group person, she doesn't use a respectful expression, but when she refers to her father-in-law, she does. In conclusion, it seems that the criteria for speaking of in-group referents to out-group addressees are fluctuating in modern Korean.
Seo (1984) reports that the traditional *apjonpeop* 圧尊法, a relative honorific system that uses a humble expression to treat in-group referents, will die out among the younger generation.
2. This means a Korean official speaks to a Japanese official.
3. The original text consists of ten volumes, and the first digit is the number of the volume. Each volume consists of bound papers folded into two. The second digit shows the number of pages. The third number オ means the front page and ウ means the back page.
4. The original text is written in *hiragana*, and *hangeul* is attached on the right hand-side in small letters. *Hiragana* in the ordinary Japanese orthographic system doesn't necessarily reflect pronunciation, because the traditional orthographic system was formed in accordance with the pronunciation of the Heian period when *hiragana* was invented. It is supposed that the *hiragana* description in this text shows the pronunciation of this time, and *hangeul* is annotated in order to show the pronunciation. *Hangeul* is the Korean orthographic system. But it is not clearly known which sound each *hangeul* character represents, because there were dialectal varieties and historical diversions from the modern Korean. Rather the *hangeul* characters are used as data for the Korean pronunciation at that time. I, therefore, use the *hiragana* description.
5. *Shiraru* derives from *seraru* as the result of a phonological change, [e]>[i].
6. Tsujimura (1992b) and Han (1995) both say *mausu* was used as a polite form at this time. The former argues that the Korean corresponding to *mausu* is a neutral expression, while the latter shows examples of *mausu* being used not only for the inferior of a speaker's in-group but also for the addressee. In Chapter 4, we concluded that *mausu* has two characters: a humble form and a polite form. It might be reasonable to suggest that *mausu* moved closer to a polite form.
7. *Taishu* 太守 is the reference term for 'lord'.
8. In Chapter 7 of this book, we show *haha* as the reference term used among the *buke* classes.

9   As an example from Osaka, the following were assigned the responsibility of entertaining the Korean mission: in the year 1617 Saemon Fujihiro Hasegawa, the *daimyo* of Sakai, and Magozaemon Sueyoshi and Kiyouemon Ogawa, rich merchants and local administrators; from 1619 local magistrates; and from 1682 Okabe, the lord of Mino.
10 Kyūshū is the place where most of the Japanese traders came from, and its dialect might have been used not only for private conversation but also for public transactions between Japanese and Korean.

6

REFERENT HONORIFIC EXPRESSION IN THE KAMIGATA DIALECT OF THE EARLY EDO PERIOD: IN KYŌGEN AND JŌRURI DOMESTIC PLAYS

1. Introduction

Kamigata 上方 was the central area bounded by Kyoto, Nara, and Osaka geographically. The big cities of western Japan, such as Kyoto, Nara, and Osaka, had been the centre of the country since the eighth century, with the capital located in Nara and then Kyoto before moving to Edo in 1603. The small town of Edo (now Tokyo) became the seat of power of the Tokugawa family and gave its name to the 250 year period during which they ruled. First of all, let us consider why we need to study the honorific system of a dialect which had lost its position as the tongue of the capital. We lack material of the dialect spoken in the early Edo period, but what is important is that its honorific system was borrowed from the *kamigata* dialect. In the late Edo period, the Edo dialect established its own honorific system but it still owes much to that of the *kamigata* dialect. Edo was cultivated by Ieyasu Tokugawa, the first *shōgun* of the Tokugawa family, when he moved his administration there. Although it was the new capital, it had been a rough town of soldiers where a vulgar tongue was spoken in comparison with the *kamigata* area, where the high and refined imperial cultures had richly flourished. Therefore, Edo borrowed heavily from *kamigata*, especially its honorific system and the refined cultural heritage. In today's standard Japanese—created on the basis of the Tokyo dialect—*u-onbin*[1], the feature of *kamigata* dialect, is still very influential—most notably when followed by *gozaimasu* (the polite form of 'to be'). So we say, *ureshū-gozaimasu* not *ureshiku-gozaimasu*, and *arigatō-gozaimasu* not *arigataku-gozaimasu*. In the Edo period, Japan was divided into about three hundred feudal clans, each controlled by a *daimyō*, or head of the *samurai*. The central government (*bakufu* 幕府) in Edo controlled all of the clans. In each feudal clan people spoke their own regional dialects that were mutually unintelligible to outsider. So, in order for members of the ruling class (*buke* 武家) to communicate, it was necessary to employ a common language, called *buke-kotoba* 武家言葉 (*kotoba* is language). Later, *buke-kotoba* was based on the Edo dialect, but in the early Edo period, it owed much to the *kamigata* dialect that had been for so long the language of the centre of power. In *kamigata* also, the *buke* lived and spoke a kind of language that reflected their social class. Komatsu (1975) finds that there are common linguistic features between *buke-kotoba* in *kamigata* and in Edo. Both *buke* and common people appear in *kyōgen* domestic plays and *jōruri* 浄瑠璃. In this chapter I focus on the honorific expression toward two kinds of superior referent: a kinship superior such as a father, and a hierarchical superior such as a master.

2. Data

Jōruri domestic plays[2] by Chikamatsu Monzaemon 近松門左衛門, which number 24, are utilized more than any other source as reliable data for the *kamigata* dialect of the early Edo period, and here I use them as my text (cf., Chikamatsu zenshu kankōkai, (ed.) 1986), together with *jōruri* domestic plays other than Chikamatsu (cf., Otoha, 1960 and Kaion kenkyūkai, (ed.) 1977). The world that is depicted in *kyōgen* domestic plays by Chikamatsu Monzaemon is mostly that inhabited by common society, and although *buke* are also included, these are mainly lower-class *buke* who live together with the common people. Therefore, as a source for the language of the *buke* class, I use the *kabuki* domestic plays by Monzaemon Chikamatsu (cf., Takano, (ed.) 1927). Many scholars have utilized *jōruri* and *kabuki* plays to evaluate how reliably they reflect the words used in daily life. First, comparative studies on grammatical phenomena in *jōruri* and *kabuki* scenarios made clear that different words were used and that the words of *jōruri* were more traditional than that of *kabuki* (cf., Kobayashi, 1972, Yamagata, 1982 and 1989; and

Sakanashi, 1970). Komatsu's (1985) research focused on how accurately the words of the *buke* class in *jōruri* plays by Chikamatsu reflect the colloquial language of that time. He concluded that the literary and classical language of the *buke* class reflected in these plays was not used simply for dramatic effect, but was due to the conservatism of the *buke* class who maintained the use of classical words, in contrast to the common people. *Jōruri* plays are divided into three parts: narrative, conversational and monologue; but it is sometimes difficult to impose a clear demarcation between the narrative and conversational parts, so I use only the latter as follows. The name of the scene is listed by such order as Japanese title, its pronunciation, its English title if it is translated and the year of publication.

近松世話浄瑠璃 (*jōruri* domestic plays by Chikamatsu Monzaemon)

 曽根崎心中（曽根崎）'Sonezaki shinjū', 'The love suicides at Sonezaki', 1703

 薩摩歌（薩摩）'Satsumauta', 1704

 心中二枚絵草紙（絵草紙）'Shinjū nimai ezōshi', 1706

 卯月の紅葉（紅葉）'Uzuki no momiji', 1706

 堀川波鼓（堀川）'Horikawa nami no tsuzumi', 'The drum of the waves of Horikawa', 1707

 卯月の潤色（潤色）'Uzuki no iroage', 1707

 重井筒（重井筒）'Kasanuizutsu', 1707

 心中万年草（万年草）'Shinjū mannensō', 'The love suicides of the stonecrop', 1708

 丹波与作待夜の小室節（小室節）'Tanba yosaku matsuyo no komuro uta', 'Yosaku from Tamba', 1708

 淀鯉出世滝徳（滝徳）'Yodogoi shusse no takinobori', 1708

 五十年忌歌念仏（歌念仏）'Gojūnenki uta nebutsu', 1709

 心中刃は氷の朔日（朔日）'Shinjū yaiba wa kōri no tsuitachi', 1709

 今宮の心中（今宮）'Imamiya no shinjū', 1710

 冥土の飛脚（飛脚）'Meido no hikyaku', 'The courier to hell', 1711

 夕霧阿波鳴渡（夕霧）'Yūgiri awa no naruto', 1712

 長町女腹切（女腹切）'Nagamachi onna no harakiri', 1712

大経師昔暦（昔暦）'Daikyōshi mukashi-goyomi', 'The almanac of love', 1715

生玉心中（生玉）'Ikudama shinjū', 'Double suicide at Ikutama', 1715

鑓の権三重帷子（鑓の権三）'Yari no gonza kasane katabira', 'Gonza the lancer', 1717

山崎与次兵衛寿の門松（門松）'Nebiki no kadomatsu', 'The uprooted pine', 1718

博多小女郎波枕（博多）'Hakata kojorō namimakura', 'The girl from Hakata, or love at sea', 1718

心中天の網島（網島）'Shinjū ten no amijima', 'The love suicides at Amijima', 1720

女殺油地獄（油地獄）'Onnagoroshi abura jigoku', 'The woman-killer and the hell of oil', 1722

心中宵庚申（庚申）'Shinjū yoi gōshin', 'The love suicides on the eve of the kōshin festival', 1722

歌舞伎狂言 (*kabuki* plays)

夕霧七年忌（七年忌）'Yūgiri nananenki', 1684

傾城阿波の鳴門（鳴門）'Keisei awa no naruto', 1695

傾城江戸桜（江戸桜）'Keisei edo zakura', 1698

傾城壬生大念仏（壬生）'Keisei mibu dainenbutsu', 1702

浄瑠璃集 (*jōruri* plays)

八百屋お七（お七）'Yaoya ohichi', 1704

夏祭浪花鑑（夏祭）'Natsumatsuri naniwakagami', 1745

紀海音集 (*jōruri* domestic plays by Ki no Kaion)

心中涙の玉井（玉井）'Shinjū namida no tamanoi', 1703

椀久末松山（松山）'Wankyū sue no matsuyama', 1710

袂の白しぼり（白しぼり）'Tamoto no shiroshibori', 1710

なんば橋心中（なんば）'Nanbabashi shinjū', 1710

今宮心中丸腰連理松（連理松）'Imamiya shinjū marugoshi renri no matsu', 1711

梅田心中（梅田）'Umeda no shinjū', 1712

傾城三度笠（三度笠）'Keisei sandogasa', 1713

傾城思升屋（思升屋）'Keisei omoimasuya', 1715

I try to quote as faithfully as possible the original text, but orthography and Chinese characters are adjusted for easier legibility. I phonetically transcribe into the alphabet according to the pronunciation of the period.

The best way to determine which honorific system – absolute or relative – is used in *jōruri* and *kabuki* plays is to look at how an in-group superior of a speaker is treated, in terms of either respectful or humble expression. If it is with a respectful expression, then absolute honorifics was the honorific system of this time; and if a humble expression is chosen, then it is relative honorifics. But it is necessary to divide in-group superiors into two groups: kinship superiors, such as parents and husbands; and hierarchical superiors, such as masters. In the early Edo period, the social class system of *shinōkōshō* 士農工商 was strictly enforced, so we need to analyse the data bearing in mind the social class distinctions of *buke* and *chōnin* 町人. *Shinōkōshō* classified people into four classes: military *shi* 士, agricultural *nō* 農, industrial *kō* 工 and mercantile *shō* 商, from the highest to the lowest in that order. The three lowest classes are *chōnin* or town people in social class laws promulgated by Hideyoshi Toyotomi in 1591, the servants in *buke* households were counted as *buke*, but in reality the honorific expression toward them was different from that used toward real *buke*, and I classify them also as *chōnin*.

Honorific expression can be divided into two parts: a term of reference and a predicate. As for terms of reference, honorific suffixes such as *dono* and *sama*, the humble suffix *domo*, and address terms without titles are listed as words of honorific value. *Ki* 貴—as in *ani-ki* 兄貴—is used as a neutral expression in present-day Japanese, but there is no definite criterion to judge its honorific value at that time so I categorize *ki* as a neutral expression. Also *chichi* 父 and *haha* 母 are today considered humble expressions, but I categorize them as neutral expressions, for the same reason. As for the predicate, honorific auxiliary verbs such as *shiyaru* and *yaru*, and humble verbs such as *mairu* and *itasu*, are listed as words of honorific value. Here I classify honorific expressions into the following four categories.

1. respectful expressions (RE)

2. respectful title expressions (RTE)
3. neutral expressions (NE)
4. humble expressions (HE)

A respectful expression uses the respectful form in the predicate, and doesn't exclude the use of a respectful title. A respectful title expression uses the respectful form for a title but not in the predicate. One can often find such utterance as *totosama wo yoroshiku* 'please take good care of my father', where there is no room for the predicate to express an honorific attitude. Therefore, I have set up the special category of respectful title expression. A neutral expression is one that is used for both title and predicate, and a humble expression is used for either title or predicate. To make it more complicated, dual expressions like *itasaru* and *mōsaru* is commonly found in those days. Yamazaki (1963) conducted a detailed investigation of the honorific expression in the *kamigata* dialect of the early Edo period, and his interpretation of a dual expression such as *itasaru* is that a speaker pays respect to an addressee by denigrating his in-group superior by using *itasu*, but at the same time shows his respect to his superior by using *raru*. Here I analyse dual expressions as a kind of humble expression and note them if necessary. An example such as *tsureai jingorō* 'FN' *nobora ruru* 'RARU' *hadu nare domo*, 'my husband, Jingorō, might come here', has no respectful title, but the respectful auxiliary *raru* is used as the predicate, and the sentence is treated as a respectful expression focusing on the predicate.

The honorific expression toward a referent can fluctuate according to the relation a speaker has to an addressee. For example, both respectful and humble expressions can be used to refer to a speaker's father, depending on the addressee. Yamazaki (1963) classifies honorific expressions in the *kamigata* dialect of the early Edo period into five categories for male language and six categories for female language (Table 1). Each category is named after the second person pronoun – a speaker talks to a supreme respectful addressee by using *omahe*; to an ordinary respectful addressee by *konata*; to an equal by *sonata*; to an inferior addressee by *sochi*; and an addressee to be insulted by *onore*. There is an additional category for female language where a speaker talks to a supreme respectful addressee by *konasan*.

male language	female language	
omae	omae	
		konasan
konata		
	konata	
sonata		
	sonata	
sochi		
	sochi	
onore	onore	

Table 1 classification of honorific expression

3. An analysis

I analyze the data applying the method explained in section two. I can list up the following rules.

3.1 self-introduction

① **A kinship superior is called by his first name when a speaker introduces himself by referring to their relationship.**

　私は此度お願ひ申しあげし御領内助作がいとこ。京大経師以春手代助右衛門と申す者（昔暦、551）[3]

　watashi wa kono tabi *o-negai-mōshiage* 'HAN' shi goryōnai *sukesaku* 'FN' ga itoko kyō daikyōji koreharu tedai ukeemon to mōsu mono

　'I am a cousin of Sukesaku, who asked your favour, and I work as a clerk for the artisan Koreharu.'

A wife calls her husband by his first name when she introduces herself:

　私は備中の玉嶋におりまする辰と申して。徳兵衛女房でござんする。（夏祭、253）

watashi wa bicchū no tamashima ni ori masuru tatsu to mōshi te, *tokubē* 'FN' nyōbō de gozansuru

'My name is Tatsu, living at Tamashima in Bicchū, and I'm the wife of Tokubē.'

But next she uses the respectful suffix *dono* and the auxiliary verb *raru* after her self-introduction is over:

まあ連合徳兵衛殿事は。僅な科で。国を立ち退かれまして。和泉とやらに居られましたを（夏祭、253）

maa tsureai tokubē-*dono* 'RS' koto wa, wazukana toga de, kuni o tachi-noka *re* 'RARU' mashi te, izumi to yara ni ora *re* 'RARU' mashi ta o

'My husband, Mr Tokubē, was convicted of a petty crime, and remains in Izumi.'

There are fourteen cases where formulaic humble expressions are used to refer to a kinship superior when greeting someone and introducing oneself. The only exception is the following:

おとに聞くあづま殿か。今のふみも見ました。わしや与次兵衛殿の女房きくといふ者（門松、357）

oto ni kiku aduma-dono ka. Ima no humi mo mi mash ita. washā yojirobē-*dono* 'RS' no nyōbō kiku to jū mono

'Are you Miss Azuma? I heard about you. I have read your letter. I am Kiku, the wife of Mr Yojirobē.'

In this case, the wife uses the respectful title *dono* to address her husband's lover, Azuma.

3.2 a wife about her husband (Table 2)

	buke	chōnin	total
RE	12(63.2)	27(54.0)	39(56.5)
RTE	4(21.1)	15(30.0)	19(27.5)
NE	1(5.3)	7(14.0)	8(11.6)
HE	2(10.5)	1(2.0)	3(4.3)
	19	50	69

Table 2   honorific expression
          from a wife about her husband
          by social class

② **To any addressee it is usual for a wife to refer to her husband using a respectful expression.**

69 examples of how a wife refers to her husband were found, and Table 2 analyses these according to the social class of the speaker. There is not much difference between the classes, except that wives of the *buke* class appear to use more humble expressions than do those of the common class. We also find that a humble expression is only used when an addressee fits into either the *omae* or *konasan* categories, but again there is little difference. We see that an honorific expression is not determined by the status of an addressee whether or not he is an in-group. Three interactions that utilize humble expressions follow:

もつたいなやおそろしや彦九郎といふ男を持ち（堀川、511）

mottaina ya osoroshi ya *hikokurō* 'FN' to yuu otoko o mochi

'I don't deserve my husband, Hikokurō.'

わたしがおとこの新七においとまをくだされ。お出入さへとめられたれど。真実お為になる者はお家で新七ばつかり（滝徳、532）

watashi ga otoko no *shinhichi* 'FN' ni o-itoma o kudasare, o-deiri sae tomerare tare do, shinjitsu o-tame ni naru mono wa o-ie de *shinhichi* 'FN' bakkari

'My husband, Shinhichi, was dismissed and forbidden to visit the house, but it is only Shinhichi who is of any use to the house.'

何がわるふて新七が御意見は御意にいらぬぞ（滝徳、533）

nani ga waruu te *shinhichi* 'FN' ga *go* 'RP' -iken wa gyo-i ni ira nu zo

'What is wrong with the suggestion Shinhichi gave?'

Only the husbands' first names are used and no humble verbs are used. In fact, the wife in the last example uses the respectful prefix *go* (*go-iken*) to refer to her husband's suggestion. Amongst the examples of neutral expressions, *kochi no hito* 'a man of this side, literally' is used twice as a term of reference:

よいよいこちの人が京からの帰りを待つてつめひらかせ。たいていでいとまは取らぬ（庚申、558）

yoi-yoi *kochi-no-hito* ga kyō kara no kaeri wo mat-te tsume-hiraka se, taitei de itoma wa tora nu

'It is all right. Let's wait until my husband returns from the capital and ask him to negotiate. We won't concede so easily.'

And *nushi* 'a master, literally', is also used twice as a term of reference:

なる程ぬしは伊勢の留守。けぶたい者も他にない大じの事じや（白しぼり、40）

naru-hodo *nushi* wa ise no rusu. kebutai mono mo hoka ni nai daiji no koto ja

'My husband is away in Ise. There is nobody to interrupt us.'

The following respectful verbs are used: *raru* (23 examples), *gozaru* (3), *nasaru* (3), *yaru* (2), *shiyaru* (2), *tamau* (2), *o-V-nasaru* (2), *mesaru* (1), *yansu* (1)

All of these are used for all categories, from *omae* to *sochi*, and respectful verbs are still employed for husbands even when a speaker needs to be respectful to an addressee. Verbs of considerably high honorific value – *tamau*, *o-V-nasaru*, *shiyaru* and *gozaru* – are also used. Because *raru* is used for more than half the examples, it is quite important to examine its honorific value. Yamazaki (1963) tells us that *raru* is used for referents in all categories, from *omae* to *sochi*, and that its honorific value

	omae	konasan	konata	sonata	sochi	onore	total
sama+raru	0	1	2	0	0	0	3
dono+raru	0	1	0	1	0	0	2
NE+raru	3	8	2	0	0	0	13
FN+raru	1	1	3	0	0	0	5

Table 3   the usage of 'raru' by the combination of title toward an addressee

is quite vague. Rodriguez (1955) states, '*Raru* should be added to show a slight respect. …it is ordinarily used for a person to whom it is worth paying some respect when he is not present'. That is, *raru* is an honorific auxiliary of low honorific value. Table 3 shows how *raru* is used in combination with an honorific title. There are examples where *raru* is used but the referent is mentioned by first name:

つれあひの新兵衛おくに待ちうけゐられます（薩摩、683）

tsureai no *shinbē* 'FN' oku ni machi-uke ira *re* 'RARU' masu

'My partner, Shinbē, is waiting for you inside.'

つれあひ甚五郎のぼらるるはづなれ共（女腹切、12）

tsureai *jingorō* 'FN' nobora *ruru* 'RARU' hazu nare do

'My partner, Jingorō, is coming here.'

A combination of *raru* and neutral expressions *kochi*, *tsureai*, and *nushi* are used in the following:

これのはけさから庄屋殿へつめられ。今はるすでござる（飛脚、322）

kore no wa kesa kara shōya-dono he tume *rare* 'RARU', ima wa rusu de gozaru

'My husband has been in the master's house since this morning. He is absent now.'

こちのはまだしまはず。天満のはて迄いかれます（女殺、174）

kochi no wa mada shimawazu, tenma no hate made ika *re* 'RARU' masu

'My husband is not off yet. He will go to Tenma.'

These examples show that *raru* has a wide range of honorific values.

As for honorific titles, *dono* is used in 22 examples, and *sama* in thirteen examples. Other historical documents show that *sama* has a higher honorific value than *dono*. Table 4 shows how *dono* and *sama* are used in relation to an addressee, but there is no clear distinction between them.

	omae	konasan	konata	sonata	sochi	onore	total
sama	1	6	2	4	0	0	13
dono	5	6	2	4	4	1	22

Table 4　the usage of 'dono' and 'sama'
　　　　by honorific expression toward an addressee

3.3 a son about his parents (Table 5)

	buke→buke	buke→chōnin	chōnin→buke	chōnin→chōnin	total
RE	1(12.5)	3(27.3)	1(16.7)	17(35.4)	22(30.1)
RTE	0	1(9.1)	3(50.0)	1(2.1)	5(6.8)
NE	3(37.5)	3(27.3)	2(33.3)	26(54.2)	34(46.6)
HE	4(50.0)	4(36.4)	0	4(8.3)	12(16.4)
total	8	11	6	48	73

Table 5   the honorific expression from a son about his parent by social class
(buke→buke) means buke talks to buke

③ **Generally the son of a *buke* family uses either a neutral or a humble expression for his parents, whereas the son of a *chōnin* family uses a respectful or a neutral expression.**

Table 5 shows how a son treats his parents to an out-group person, and is divided by social class of both a speaker and an addressee. I then show how an honorific expression can change based on a speaker's honorific expression toward an addressee; *buke* in Table 6 and *chōnin* in Table 7. In the case of the *buke*, the more a

	omae	konata	sonata	sochi	onore	total
RE	1(14.3)	0	0	3(50.0)	0	4(21.1)
RTE	0	0	0	0	1(100.0)	1(5.3)
NE	3(42.9)	1(50.0)	0	2(33.3)	0	6(31.6)
HE	3(42.9)	1(50.0)	3(100.0)	1(16.7)	0	8(42.1)
total	7	2	3	6	1	19

Table 6   the honorific expression from a son about his parent
by honorific expression toward an addressee
buke

	omae	konata	sonata	sochi	onore	total
RE	1(16.7)	5(62.5)	0	9(33.3)	3(42.9)	18(33.3)
RTE	0	1(12.5)	0	3(11.1)	0	4(7.4)
NE	2(33.3)	2(25.0)	5(83.3)	15(55.6)	4(57.1)	28(51.9)
HE	3(50.0)	0	1(16.7)	0	0	4(7.4)
total	6	8	6	27	7	54

Table 7   the honorific expression from a son about his parent
by honorific expression toward an addressee
chōnin

speaker wishes to pay respect to an addressee, the more an honorific expression shifts from respectful, to neutral and then to a humble one. As for the *chōnin*, it shifts from neutral, to respectful and then to a humble expression. I can interpret these tables in the following way: the more a *buke* speaker wishes to enhance an addressee's esteem, the lower he makes the honorific expression used toward an in-group superior. On the contrary, a *chōnin* chooses a neutral expression when he feels he can be relaxed with an addressee, and he shifts the honorific register from respectful to humble in proportion with his regard for an addressee.

	buke	chōnin	total
oyaji	1(5.0)	21(33.3)	22(26.5)
oyaji-sama	0	3(4.8)	3(3.6)
chichi/haha	8(40.0)	15(23.8)	23(27.7)
oya	6(30.0)	7(11.1)	13(15.7)
oya-domo	2(10.0)	4(6.3)	6(7.2)
oya-tachi	0	3(4.8)	3(3.6)
oyaja-hito	1(5.0)	7(11.1)	8(9.6)
toto-sama	1(5.0)	3(4.8)	4(4.8)
chichi-ue	1(5.0)	0	1(1.2)
total	20	63	83

Table 8   the terms of reference from a son about his parent by social class

In Table 8 I show the terms of reference used. In contemporary Japanese, *chichi* and *haha* are used as humble terms of reference, but in those days they could co-occur with a respectful predicate:

たつた今母が出られた道であひはせなんだか（庚申、581）
tatta ima *haha* ga de *rare* 'RARU' ta michi de ai wa se nanda ka
'My mother has just left. Didn't you meet her on your way?'
某が父は斑鳩左衛門。……父左衛門はお果てなさるる。（鳴門、250-251）
soregashi ga *chichi* wa ikaruga *zaemon* 'FN'…*chichi zaemon* 'FN' *o*-hate-*nasaruru* 'RA'
"My father is Ikaruga Zaemon…. He will pass away.'

And *oyaji*, a neutral expression today, can co-occur with a respectful and a dual expression:

それでもおやぢが女房ども女房どもといはれました（壬生、131）

sore de mo *oyaji* ga nyō bo domo nyōbo domo to iwa *re* 'RARU' mashi ta

'My father said, "My wife".'

Oyaji is mainly used among the *chōnin*, and *chichi* and *haha* among *buke*. Children commonly use *totsu-sama*, *toto-sama* and *kaka-sama*, regardless of their social class.

Of the following respectful predicates, *raru* is used in eleven cases, *yaru* is used in three cases, and *waseru* is used only once.

二親たちが自慢して武士のやうしにやられたが（白しぼり、61）

huta-oya-*tachi* ga jiman shi te bushi no yōshi ni ya *rare* 'RARU' ta ga

'My parents adopted him out to a *buke* family.'

Oya means parent and the plural suffix *tachi* is used here.

親仁が目玉むかるるだけはむきやつても往ぬ事ならぬ（夏祭、203）

ojaji ga medama muka ruru dake wa muki *yat* 'RA' te mo inu koto nara nu

'I can't concede even that my father got angry about that.'

Yamazaki (1963) writes that *yaru* used for the third person referent has a respectful connotation, but when it is used for the second person addressee it has no such meaning.

親仁がここへいつわせたことがある（生玉、611）

ojaji ga koko he itsu *wase* 'come (RV)' ta koto ga aru

'My father had come here.'

According to Yamazaki (1963), *waseru* is used only for the second person addressee and has a low respectful register. The following predicates are used: *oshiyaru* in two cases; and *o-V-nasaru*, *tamau* and *mashimasu*, once each.

3.4 a daughter about her parents (Table 9)

	buke	chōnin	total
RE	8(57.1)	33(57.9)	41(57.7)
RTE	4(28.6)	20(35.1)	24(33.8)
NE	1(7.1)	4(7.0)	5(7.0)
HE	1(7.1)	0	1(1.4)
total	14	57	71

Table 9   honorific expression from a daughter about her parent by social class

raru	10
nasaru	5
osshiyaru	5
tamau	3
V-te	2
kudasaru	2
gozaru	2
kudasansu	1
shiyaru	1
nsu	1
mieru	1

Table 10   respectful predicate from a daughter about her parent

④ **Generally speaking, a daughter treats her parents with a respectful expression.**

We see in Table 9 that how it is common for a daughter to speak of her parents using a respectful expression, regardless of their social class. *Totsu-sama* and *kaka-sama* are used 72 times.

とつさまもるすなり（紅葉、467）

totsu-sama 'RS' mo rusu nari

'My father is out now'

わたしが母は京の六条。……ま一度京の母さまにも一目あふて死にたいぞ
（飛脚、324）

watashi ga *haha* wa kyō no rokujō….ma ichi-do kyō no *haha-sama* 'RS' ni mo hitome ō te shini tai zo

'My mother lives at Rokujō in Kyōto. I would like to meet her once more before I die.'

Other examples include three cases of *oya-tachi* 'parents', two cases of *tete-oya* 'father', and one case of *haha* 'mother'.

Table 10 lists the kind of words used in the predicative part. Below are examples of the use of *raru*.

外に出られましたが追っ付け帰られませう（鳴門、287）

soto ni de *rare* 'RARU' mash ita ga, ottsuke kae *rare* 'RARU' mashō

'He is out now, but will be back soon.'

Her father is mentioned by first name, and below *gozaru* is used.

奥にはとと様すやすやと寝てござる（庚申、559）

oku ni wa *toto-sama* 'RS' suya-suya to ne te *gozaru* 'RA'

'He is sound asleep in an inner room.'

The respectful expressions *tamau* and *osshiyaru* are used in the following.

父様はかのやうに腹立て給へば、最早母様に逢ひ給ふまい（鳴門、291）

toto-sama 'RS' wa kano yō ni, hara tate *tamae* 'RA' ba, mohaya *kaka-sama* 'RS' ni ai *tamau* 'RA' mai

'My father has become so angry that he might not meet my mother.'

おれが思ふはとと様のきのふのやうにおつしやつても（白しぼり、55）

ore ga omō wa *toto-sama* 'RS' no kinō no yō ni *osshiyat* 'say (RV)' te mo

'I always think well of my father even though he spoke like that yesterday.'

There is a big difference between the honorific expressions used by sons and daughters.

3.5 a younger brother about his elder brother or sister

⑤ **Generally speaking, the younger brother of a *buke* family treats his elder sibling either with a neutral or a humble expression, whereas in a *chōnin* family a younger brother treats his elder siblings either with a respectful or a neutral expression.**

I have found 22 cases of a younger brother speaking of his elder siblings. Of these, eight use respectful expressions (36.4%), four use respectful title expressions

(4.5%), nine use neutral expressions (40.9%), and four use humble expressions (18.2%). The respectful predicate *teja* is used twice, as follows.

そなたも姉の知つてじやげな（生玉、577）

sonata mo ane no shit *teja* 'RA' ge na

'My elder sister seems to know you quite well.'

Te, combined with various illocutionary articles as in *teja, tezo, teka* and *tenara*, is mainly used as a respectful expression toward an addressee. In present-day Kansai dialect, this *te* remains as a respectful expression in the form *teya*.[4] *Tamau* is used in three cases.

身が兄に大蔵殿とてあつたが、これは幼少より他門へ養子に行き給へば、面体とても知らぬ（鳴門、271）

mi ga *ani* ni daizō-*dono* 'RS' to te at ta ga, kore wa yōshō yori tamon e yōshi ni iki *tamae* 'RA' ba, mentei to te mo shira nu

'I had one elder brother named Mr Daizō, but he was adopted when he was a child, so I don't remember what he was like.'

O-V-*nasaru* is used twice.

誠の兄が御出なされても、この意見より外はない（鳴門、273）

makoto no *ani* ga *o*-ide-*nasare* 'RA' te mo, kono iken yori hoka wa nai

'Even though my elder brother comes to persuade me, I can't change my opinion.'

And *raru* (2 cases), *nasaru* (2), *waseru* (1), *mashimasu* (1), and *gozaru* (1) are also used as respectful predicates.

As for terms of reference, *ani-ki* and *ane-ki* are used six times.

兄きへ渡せ（網島、720）

ani-ki e watase

'Give that to my elder brother.'

Ani and *ane* are used three times, as are *ani-ja* and *ane-ja* ; while the following are all used once: *ani-ue* and *ane-ue*, first name together with *sama*, first name together with *dono; ani-sama* and *ane-sama*.

There follows a good example to show how honorific expression fluctuates according to the situation.

某が父は斑鳩左衛門殿、総領に大蔵、中兄十介……総領は親左衛門殿と相性が悪いとあつて、幼少より他門へ養子に参つたれば他人同然。中兄十介は……邸を出て行方が知れず（鳴門、250-251）

soregashi ga *chichi* wa ikaruga zaemon-*dono* 'RS' sōryō ni *daizō* 'FN', chūkē *jūsuke* 'FN'…, sōryō wa oya zaemon-*dono* 'RS' to aishō ga warui to at te, yōshō yori tamon e yōshi ni *mait* 'go (HVN)' ta reba tannin dōzen, chūkē *jūsuke* 'FN' wa…yashiki o de te ikukata ga shire zu

'My father is Mr Ikaruga Zaemon, the eldest brother is Daizō, and another brother is Jūsuke…. Daizō did not get along with Mr Zaemon and was adopted when he was a child, therefore, he is not one of our family. Jūsuke left home and disappeared.'

The respectful title *dono* is used for the father but the elder brother is referred to by his first name and with the humble verb *mairu*. The addressee in this passage is treated according to the supreme *omae* stage, and the same elder brother Daizō was in another context treated by *dono* and *tamau*, as shown in a previous example. *Ani* and *ane* are used only by the *buke* class:

とうりう致せし兄半兵衛。……幸と今日のお献立を致させし不調法は私（庚申、539）

tōryū *itase* 'do (HVN)' shi *ani hanbei* 'FN'…saiwai to kyō no o-kondate o *itasa* 'do (HVN)' se shi bu-chōhō wa watashi

'My brother, Hanbei, stayed here. …I should be blamed for having made him cook.'

3.6 a younger sister about her elder brother or sister

⑥ **A younger sister generally uses a respectful expression for her elder siblings.**

There are only eleven cases: three of respectful expressions (27.3%), four of respectful title expressions (36.4%), three of neutral expressions (27.3%), and one of a humble expression (9.1%). *Raru* and *gozaru* are used as respectful expressions and *sama* is used as a respectful title in the following:

わしは江戸に姉様がござんすが（江戸桜、341）

washi wa edo ni *ane-sama* 'RS' ga *gozan* 'be (RV)' su ga

'I have one elder sister in Edo.'

兄様は夕べからまだかへられず（絵草紙、188）

ani-sama 'RS' wa yūbe kara mada kaera *re* 'RARU' zu

'My elder brother hasn't come back yet since last evening.'

Ani and *ane* are used as neutral expressions:

知つての通り種腹一つの兄も有り。いもともあれど（朔日、497）

shit te no tōri tane-hara hitotsu no *ani* mo ari. *imōto* mo are do.

'As you know, I have one real elder brother and one real sister, though…'

Next is the only case of a humble expression.

兄兵庫に十介殿を呼び返し、家を渡して下されと申せば、却つて私も殺そうと致せし故（鳴門、296）

ani hyōgo 'FN' ni jūsuke-dono o yobi-kaeshi, ie o watashi te *kudasare* 'HAO' to *mōse* 'say (HVO)' ba, kaet te watashi mo koros ō to *itase* 'do (HVN)' shi yue

'When I asked my elder brother, Hyōgo, to call Mr Jūsuke and give him his house back, he tried to kill me.'

The sister refers to her brother by his first name and the humble verb *itasu*, but at the same time she uses the humble verbs *kudasaru* and *mōsu* for her own action. In this way she enhances his position and treats him respectfully.

3.7 a servant about his master (Table 11)

	buke	chōnin	total
RE	18(58.1)	21(42.9)	39(48.8)
RTE	6(19.4)	10(20.4)	16(20.0)
NE	2(6.5)	14(28.6)	16(20.0)
HE	5(16.1)	4(8.2)	9(11.3)
total	31	49	80

Table 11   honorific expression from a servant about his master by social class

	omae	konata	sonata	sochi	onore	total
RE	9(39.1)	6(37.5)	7(43.8)	12(63.2)	5(83.3)	39(48.8)
RTE	5(21.7)	5(31.3)	5(31.3)	1(5.3)	0	16(20.0)
NE	3(13.0)	4(25.0)	3(18.8)	5(26.3)	1(16.7)	16(20.0)
HE	6(26.1)	1(6.3)	1(6.3)	1(5.3)	0	9(11.3)
total	23	16	16	19	6	80

Table 12   honorific expression from a servant about his master by honorific expression toward an addressee

	buke→buke	buke→chōnin	chōnin→buke	chōnin→chōnin	total
RE	6(35.3)	12(85.7)	4(44.4)	17(42.5)	39(48.8)
RTE	5(29.4)	1(7.1)	1(11.1)	9(22.5)	16(20.0)
NE	2(11.8)	0	3(33.3)	11(27.5)	16(20.0)
HE	4(23.5)	1(7.1)	1(11.1)	3(7.5)	9(11.3)
total	17	14	9	40	80

Table 13   the honorific expression from a servant about his master by social class

⑦ **The honorific expression that a servant uses toward his master fluctuates depending on factors like an addressee's social position and the conversational context.**

Table 11 shows how a servant treats his master to an out-group person according to a speaker's social status, as either *buke* or *chōnin*. Table 12 shows how a servant treats his master to an out-group person, based on his own attitude toward an addressee. Table 12 testifies that the lower the speaker's attitude toward an addressee, the more a respectful expression is used. In contrast, the higher the speaker's regard toward an addressee, the more a humble expression is adopted. When a servant needs to elevate an addressee, a humble expression serves to lower his master's status. And when a servant doesn't need to elevate an addressee, a respectful expression to refer to his master is appropriate. Table 11 classifies honorific expressions only by a speaker's social status, but Table 13 also takes into consideration an addressee's social status. When a servant in a *buke* household speaks of his master in conversation with a *buke*, a humble or neutral expression is preferred, but when addressing a *chōnin*, a respectful expression is preferable. This is because his *buke* master is necessarily higher in social status than a *chōnin* addressee. Among *chōnin*, masters are commonly treated with respectful expressions. The following conversations set in a messenger's shop demonstrate the use of honorific expressions toward masters at this time. A servant interacts with a customer who is a servant in a *buke* household.

> 忠兵衛は留守なればお下し物の御用ならば。私に仰聞られませ（飛脚、280)
>
> *chūbē* 'FN' wa rusu nare-ba o-kudashimono no goyō nara-ba watashi ni ōse kikaserare mase
>
> 'Chūbē is out now, so if you have something to order, please tell me.'

He refers to his master (the shop-owner) by first name thereby performing a humiliating speech act. But in reply the customer refers to his own master using a respectful expression.

> ゑどの若だんなより御状が来た。……是此通り仰せ下された（飛脚、281)
>
> edo no wakadanna yori *go* 'RP'- jō ga kita….. kore konotōri *ōse-kudasare* 'order (RV)' ta
>
> 'A letter came from my young master in Edo. …he ordered this.

Another customer, this time from a *chōnin* household, comes in and refers to his own master using *mausaru:*

> 此者に渡して人をつけて下され。手形もどそと申さるる（飛脚、282)
>
> kono-mono ni watashite hito o tsukete kudasare. Tegata modoso to *mōsaruru* 'say (RV)'
>
> 'Please give this to him and get somebody to help him. My master says to return the cheque.'

Although a *chōnin* servant uses a humble expression to subordinate his master to a *buke* customer, he uses *raru* when speaking of his master to a *chōnin* customer.

> 今でも旦那かへられたらば此方から返事せう（飛脚、282)
>
> imademo danna kahe *rare* 'RARU' ta raba konohou kara henji shō
>
> 'When our master comes back, we will tell you.'

Among each other *chōnin* treat their masters with the respectful expressions.

> 是々扇屋殿。我らは藤屋伊左衛門さまの御老母。藤屋妙順さまよりのお使

い。伊左衛門さまはてゝごの御勘当今は此世になきお人なれば。お袋さまの我まゝに勘当御免はなりがたし（夕霧、578）

kore-kore ōgiya dono. warera wa hujiya izaemon-*sama* 'RS' no *go* 'RP'-rōbo hujiya myōjun-*sama* 'RS' yori no o tsukai. Izaemon-*sama* 'RS' wa tetegono *go* 'RP'-kandō ima wa konoyo ni naki *o*-'RP'hito nareba ohukuro-*sama* 'RS' no wagamama ni kandō *go* -'RP' men wa narigatashi

'How are you, Mr Ōgiya ? We are messengers from Mrs Fujiya Myoujyun, the mother of Mr Izaemon. Mr Izaemon was disinherited by his father, who passed away, so his mother cannot dispel it by her will.'

頼みましたい事あるとておふくろ様やおそめさま。けさから待つてでござんした（白しぼり、43）

tanomi mashi tai koto aru to te ohukuro-*sama* 'RS' ya osome-*sama* 'RS'. kesa kara matsu *te* 'RA' de gozanshi ta

'Our mistress and Miss Osome waited for you since this morning because they had something to ask you.'

Below, the servant of a *buke* is addressing a monk and uses *itasaru* to refer to his master.

旦那が悲母第七年にあたりし故。御当山に石碑を立て日牌をそなへ申すに付。しだう銀五百枚奉納致され候（万年草、694）

danna ga hibo dai-hichinen ni Atari shi yuhe. go-tōzan ni sekihi o ta te hihai wo sonahe *mōsu* 'HA' ni tsuke. shidō-gin go-hyaku mai hōnō *itasare* 'do (RV)' sōrō

'This year is the seventh anniversary of the death of our master's mother, so he donated five hundred silver coins in order to construct a monument.'

He also uses his master's first name:

主人郷左衛門さぞ満足（庚申、536）

shujin *gōzaemon* 'FN' sazo manzoku

'Our master Gōzaemon will be satisfied.'

⑧ A male servant modifies the honorific expression used toward his master according to the addressee, but a female servant always uses a respectful expression.

	buke→buke	buke→chōnin	chōnin→buke	chōnin→chōnin	total
RE	4(44.4)	10(83.3)	3(50.0)	12(42.9)	29(52.7)
RTE	0	1(8.3)	0	2(7.1)	3(5.5)
NE	2(22.2)	0	2(33.3)	11(39.3)	15(27.3)
HE	3(33.3)	1(8.3)	1(16.7)	3(10.7)	8(14.5)
total	9	12	6	28	55

Table 14 the honorific expression from a servant about his master by social class male servant

	buke→buke	buke→chōnin	chōnin→buke	chōnin→chōnin	total
RE	2(25.0)	2(100.0)	1(33.3)	5(41.7)	10(40.0)
RTE	5(62.5)	0	1(33.3)	7(58.3)	13(52.0)
NE	0	0	1(33.3)	0	1(4.0)
HE	1(12.5)	0	0	0	1(4.0)
total	8	2	3	12	25

Table 15 the honorific expression from a servant about her master by social class female servant

As we saw hereto, only men use humble expressions to treat kinship superiority. By looking at Tables 14 and 15 we can see the different patterns of honorific expression used by male and female servants respectively. Whereas male servants alter honorific expressions relative to the context, female servants use respectful expressions, though the examples are not many. Table 16 shows the respectful forms used to refer to a master. There are various forms used, from those with low respectful value such as *raru*, to those of high respectful value such as *tamau*, *oboshimesu* and *o-V-nasaru*. Dual expressions such as *itasaru* and *mōsaru* are also used.

raruru	10
o-V-nasaru	6
itasaru	5
ōsu	3
mōsaru	2
tamau	2
oboshimesu	1
sassharu	1
sensu	1
sharu	1
ossharu	1
agaru 'eat'	1

Table 16   respectful predicate from a servant about her master

4. Conclusion

1. Women usually treat their superior, whether of kinship or hierarchical relation, with a respectful expression.

While men make choices about which honorific expression they will employ based on situation and their social relation to an addressee, women predominantly use a respectful expression. Mashita (1966) and Abe (1990) write that during times such as the Edo period when men were predominant, women usually talked to their husbands and elder brother using polite and respectful forms, and it was also reasonable for them to refer to their male superiors using a respectful form. But an analysis of present day Japanese honorific usage shows a similar result. This gender difference in honorific expressions might derive not from any characteristic of the Edo period but from the disposition of women, who, at any time, have a tendency to prefer more polite forms of address than men.

2. Men of the *buke* class usually use hierarchical or in/out-group honorifics, but men of the *chōnin* class tend to use absolute honorifics.

When men of the *buke* class refer to an in-group superior they alter their honorific register according to the social position of the addressee. A humble expression is used to *buke* whose status they need to raise; a respectful expression is used to *chōnin* or *buke* with whom they feel intimacy. As well, a dual expression like *itasaru*—an intermediate expression combining the humble verb *itasu* and the respectful *raru*—and sometimes a neutral expression are also used. It is reasonable to conclude that two discrete honorific systems co-exist and are used by the *buke* class: a formal system—hierarchical or in/out-group honorifics—that treats in-group superiors by humble expression when the conversational act is between members of the *buke* class; and an informal system—absolute honorifics—that treats in-group superiors by respectful expression when the addressees are member of the *chōnin* class. Only absolute honorifics are used among the *chōnin* class.

3. Hierarchical or in/out-group honorifics are used as a formal standard language, whilst absolute honorifics are used as an informal private language.

Hierarchical or in/out-group honorifics are used among men of the *buke* class in a formal situation when one's speech act must be carefully constructed, and absolute honoifics are used among men of the *chōnin* class and women regardless of their social class. It is only men of the *buke* class who take part in formal activities and, consequently, hierarchical or in/out-group honorifics can be considered a formal standard language. Using only these data it is quite hard to come to a conclusion about whether the formal honorific system has reached the stage of in/out-group honorifics or remains at the stage of hierarchical honorifics. Given the existence of dual expressions that combine the humble and respectful forms, it is more likely to be in the intermediate stage between hierarchical and in/out-group honorifics

4. The *buke* class may have inherited its honorific system from the *kuge* class.

In this chapter, I conclude that hierarchical or in/out-group honorifics were used among men of the *buke* class, and that absolute honorifics were used among men of the *chōnin* class. But where did the honorific system of the *buke* class come from? The only possible source is the *kuge*, aristocracy who created and maintained the manners and tastes of the imperial court. The *buke* were originally soldiers who protected the *kuge*'s territory. With no culture of their own to preserve, the *buke* were parvenus who borrowed many customs from the *kuge* tradition, including its formal speech and manners[5]. It can also be surmised that *jochū-kotoba* 女中言葉 — a female formal language of the Edo period—might have succeeded *nyōbō-kotoba* 女房言葉—a female formal language of the royal court. *Onnachōhōki* 女重宝記 is one of the remaining records of *jochū-kotoba* of the early Edo period. The frequent usage of *yamato-kotoba* 大和詞, original Japanese words, and the honorific prefix *o*—both characteristics of *nyōbō-kotoba*—shown therein proves that *jochū-kotoba* owe much to *nyōbō-kotoba* (cf., Sugimoto, 1985). And the honorific system of *jochū-kotoba* would be different from *buke-kotoba*.

(Endnotes)

1 *Onbin* 音便 is certain regular phonetic change in inflected forms, depending on usage. There are four types of *onbin*: *i-onbin*, *u-onbin*, *hatsu-onbin* and *soku-onbin*. In the case of *u-onbin* for adjective, *ku*-conjugation becomes *u* like *ureshiku-gozaimasu* changes into *ureshiu-gozaimasu*.
2 *Jōruri* and *kabuki* plays can be categorized into domestic plays and historical plays. Domestic plays are called *sewa-mono* 世話物 and depict contemporary events.
3 The quoted parts are shown within parentheses. The names of plays are shown by the abbreviation which is noted for each text and the number indicates the quoted pages of each text.
4 Kotani (1989) reports the decline of the *teja* honorific form among the young generation in Kobe, Kansai.
5 Matsui (1974) mentions that the *buke* incorporated *kuge* customs and usages into their manners.

7

REFERENT HONORIFIC EXPRESSION IN THE EDO DIALECT OF THE LATE EDO PERIOD: IN NANBOKU'S KI-ZEWA-MONO

1. Introduction

Scholars of Japanese linguistics commonly agree that the Edo dialect was formed in the late Edo period. Previously, the language spoken in the city of Edo had been an admixture of the varied dialects of the people who had migrated to Edo from different regions of Japan. In the early seventeenth century, Edo became the capital, but it was remote from *kamigata* where the refined language from the ancient period was spoken as the approved standard. The Edo dialect could not take its place; furthermore Edo was greatly influenced by *kamigata* culturally, and the Edo dialect owed its official honorific expression to the *kamigata* dialect. It was after the late Edo period that the Edo dialect formed its own linguistic system and got rid of *kamigata* influence. At this time honorific forms such as *o-V-da* and *o-V-nasaru*—unique to the Edo dialect—were created. The divergence of speeches according to social class, the social dialects, also occurred in the late Edo period. Here I will look at the honorific expression toward an in-group person that belongs to a speaker.

2. Data

I use the *ki-zewa-mono* 生世話物 of Tsuruya Nanboku 鶴屋南北 (1755-1829) as the source for colloquial material of the late Edo period. There are pros and cons about the value of using *kabuki* plays as reliable language data, hence they are not utilized actively by many scholars. Hattori (1973) cautions that care must be taken. First of all, it is very hard to approve of such texts as reliable indications of the language as it was first performed because most of what is left has passed through many revisions through the centuries. Secondly, *kabuki* plays are the collaborative efforts of many writers, hence it is hard to find unity throughout whole play. Thirdly, there is a tendency to rigidly maintain the traditional pattern of *kabuki*, and this raises doubts about whether the dialogues of the plays reflect the daily conversation of the time when they were written on scenarios. Despite these misgivings, Hattori uses the play *Tōkaidō Yotsuya kaidan* as the source for honorific expressions. Yamagata (1980), having compared *kabuki* plays with the popular *share-hon* genre of literature that is widely regarded as reliable, believes that *kabuki* dialogue scenario with its conservative language, differs from the colloquial expression of the Edo town folk.

There are several reasons why we chose the *ki-zewa-mono* of Tsuruya Nanboku. Born in Edo, and living there until his death, Nanboku was a native speaker of the Edo dialect. His complete works are still reproduced in print and fine bibliographical studies on Nanboku have been produced from the view point of theatre. *Kabuki* plays can be categorized into three genres: *jidai-mono* 時代物 'historical dramas', *sewa-mono* 世話物 'domestic dramas', and *o-ie-mono* お家物 '*buke* family dramas'. During the Genroku period, *kabuki* developed into multiple dramatic structures —such as *jidai-sewa* 時代世話 or *o-ie-sewa* お家世話—which merged the characteristics of each genre. That is, the first part of a play started as a *jidai-mono* or *o-ie-mono*, and in the second part it became a *sewa-mono*. The latter evolved into an independent genre called *ki-zewa-mono* established by Nanboku. Kawatake (1959) writes that *ki-zewa-mono* was 'a new term that proclaimed to depict the life of the common people realistically, using innovative methods unbound by tradition' and 'a social drama that glorified the dark side of society and developed into an independent art'. I have chosen *ki-zewa-mono* because living words should be shown in the words of plays, and I exclude stereo-typed words because these are transmitted as traditional words. The reason I do not utilize *share-bon*, *kokkei-bon* or *ninjō-bon*, which are trusted as reliable source of the colloquial language is that the world depicted in these is limited only to the *chōnin* or the red-light district, whereas *kabuki* plays also cover the world of the *buke*. Also the former are fictional works —the creation of authors who may have distorted the colloquial language—whilst the words in *kabuki* are those spoken by the actors. Hachiya (1982) states, 'It is important to compare colloquialisms from one scene to another in order to use *kabuki* plays as linguistic data'. Here I limit our interest only to the honorific expression toward referents, and I try to evaluate the *ki-zewa-mono* as linguistic data by comparing the first and second person pronouns used in *share-bon*, *kokkei-bon* or *ninjō-bon*.

I use *Tsuruya nanboku zenshū* as the text (cf., Gunji, Hirosue, Urayama, et al., (eds.) 1971-1974). The quoted examples are represented by the name of the scene —listed hereunder—and the number of pages of the text, within parenthesis. The name of the scene is listed by such order as Japanese title, its pronunciation, its English title if it is translated and the year of publication.

彩入御伽草 'Iroeiri otogizōshi', 1808

心謎解毛絲 'Kokoro no nazotoketa iroito', 1810

勝相撲浮名花觸 'Kachizumō ukina no hanabure', 1810

絵本合法衢 'Ehon gappō ga tsuji', 1810

当穐八幡祭 'Dekiaki yawata no matsuri', 1810

謎帯一寸徳兵衛 'Nazo no obi chotto no tokubē', 1811

色一座梅椿 'Iroichiza mume to shiratama', 1812

解脱衣楓累 'Gedatsu no kinu momijigasane', 1812

於染久松色読販 'Osome hisamatsu ukina no yomiuri', 1813

杜若艶色紫 'Kakitsubata iromoedozome', 1815

桜姫東文章 'Sakurahime azumabunshō', 1817

四天王産湯玉川 'Shitennō ubuyu no tamagawa', 1818

浮世柄比翼稲妻 'Ukiyozuka hiyoku no inazuma', 1823

法懸松成田利劒 'Kesakakematsu narita no riken', 1823

東海道四谷怪談 'Tōkaidōchū yotsuya kaidan', 'The Ghost of Yotsuya', 1825

盟三五大切 'Kamikakete sango taisetsu', 1825

紋盡五人男 'Monzukushi gonin otoko', 1825

3. Analysis

In order to discover the prevalent honorific system, we need to analyse the honorific expression used toward the in-group superior referent of a speaker, who can be divided into two groups: a kinship superior such as a parent, elder brother, or husband; and an hierarchical superior such as a master. In the late Edo period, the caste system of *shinōkōshō* 士農工商, although on the verge of collapse, still prevailed and so we need to view the data in accordance with the social castes of *buke* and *chōnin* 町人. In the caste law proclaimed by Hideyoshi Toyotomi in 1591, the servants in a *buke* family counted as *buke*, but in reality the honorific expression used toward them differed from that used for real *buke*, and therefore we have classified them as *chōnin*.

Honorific expressions can be divided into two parts: a term of reference and a predicate. Let us take the example of honorific expressions toward a father. Respectful expressions contain either a respectful term of reference such as *oyaji-sama*, *oyaji-dono* or *chichi-ue* 父上[1], or a respectful predicate such as *irassharu* or *oide-ninaru*. And humble expressions contain either a humble term of reference, such as *oya-domo*, or a humble predicate such as *mairu* or *itasu*. We categorize honorific expressions into the following three groups.[2]

1. respectful expressions (RE)
2. neutral expressions (NE)
3. humble expressions (HE)

A respectful expression includes a respectful form used in either the term of reference or the predicate, while a humble expression is one that contains a humble form in either a term of reference or a predicate. A neutral expression is one that contains neither a respectful nor a humble expression. I found no contradictory patterns such as use of respectful expressions in terms of reference and humble expressions in predicates of the same sentence.

The results of my analysis are listed numerically with the number in each table indicating token frequency.

There are cases where a humble expression is always used regardless of the attributes of either a speaker or an addressee; when making a self-introduction is one such instance:

萩井の庄司が娘（法懸松成田利劔、285）[3]

ogii no *shōji* 'FN' ga musume

'I am the daughter of Ogii no Shōji.'

高橋瀬左衛門が弟同苗弥十郎（絵本合法衢、407）

takahashi *sezaemon* 'FN' ga otōto dō nayazirō

'I am Takahashi Nayazirō, the younger brother of Takahashi Sezaemon.'

A speaker Y introduces himself with reference to an elder kin X—father, elder brother or husband—by using the ritualized and formulaic pattern X *ga kinship term*, Y (e.g. 'the son of X, Y'). There are 25 such cases and I exclude them from our analysis.

3.1 about parents

We need to take into account not only the social attribute of a speaker—whether they are *buke* or *chōnin*—but also their gender.

3.1.1 about his parents

The most common terms of address for one's parents are *oyaji* and *ofukuro* or *chichi* and *haha*; Table 1 shows how these terms are used according to a speaker's social status.

	buke	chōnin	total
oyaji-ofukuro	3(12.0)	24(100.0)	27(55.1)
chichi-haha	22(88.0)	0(0.0)	22(44.9)
total	25	24	49

Table 1   the terms of reference from a son to his parents by social class

Komatsu (1985) defined all utterances of the *buke* class as *buke no kotoba* 'the language of the *buke*', and labelled its characteristic utterance features as *buke-kotoba* '*buke* language'. Buke-kotoba is defined as the double-faced social language of the *buke*, the language of a ruling class that stands against the *chōnin*, as well as a common language that unites *buke* from all parts of Japan. Table 1 demonstrates that *chichi* and *haha* are *buke-kotoba*. The usage of *oyaji* and *ohukuro* by *buke* is restricted to *buke* who have been financially or socially ruined. Other examples are *oya*, *totsu-san*, *kaka-sama* or a first name like *Genbē*. In present-day usage *chichi* and *haha* are humble forms used only for a speaker's parent, but in late Edo dialect we can find cases where *chichi* and *haha* are used with the respectful form *raru*:

母の横死をとげられ（絵本合法衢、380）

haha no ōshi o toge *rare* 'RARU'

'My mother died an unnatural death.'

It is therefore not appropriate to define *chichi* and *haha* as a humble form according to the context of present-day usage. And *oyaji* and *ofukuro* do not have any respectful connotation in contemporary usage, although in the late Edo dialect we can find them used with the respectful suffix *dono* in the following *chōnin-kotoba*.

親父どののりんしよくは兎も角も（当穐八幡祭、119）

oyaji-dono 'RS' no rinshoku wa tomokakumo

'Apart from the jealousy of my father.'

Table 2 shows how the honorific expression varies according to the social status of both speaker and addressee. Humble expressions are used among the *buke* and by *chōnin* when they are addressing a *buke*. The only exception is the case of a *buke* child using respectful language, and I can dismiss this because a child has not yet mastered the honorific system of *buke* society that forms part of his social education.

	buke→buke	buke→chōnin	chōnin→buke	chōnin→chōnin	total
RE	1(3.3)	4(40.0)	2(15.3)	15(53.6)	22(27.2)
NE	15(50.0)	6(60.0)	5(38.5)	13(46.4)	39(48.1)
HE	14(46.7)	0(0.0)	6(46.2)	0(0.0)	20(24.7)
total	30	10	13	28	81

Table 2 honorific expression from a son to his parents
by social class
(buke→buke) means *buke* talks to *buke*

Many studies have been done on the honorific expression used by a speaker to an addressee (Kojima, 1974; Tsujimura, 1968; Ikegami, 1963a, 1963b, 1967, 1968; and Yamazaki, 1990), which I can divide into four categories:

1. superior expressions (SE)
2. equal expressions (EE)
3. inferior expressions (IE)
4. insulting expressions (ISE)

I will check how the honorific expression toward a referent varies in accordance with the honorific expression used toward an addressee. From Table 3 to Table 6, I will examine the honorific expression from the perspective of the social status of both speaker and addressee. In the following, a humble expression is used by *chōnin* addressing a *buke*.

	SE	EE	IE	ISE	total
RE	1(7.7)	0(0.0)	0(0.0)	0(0.0)	1(3.3)
NE	2(15.4)	5(62.5)	7(87.5)	1(100.0)	15(50.0)
HE	10(76.9)	3(37.5)	1(12.5)	0(0.0)	14(46.7)
total	13	8	8	1	30

Table 3 honorific expression from a son to his parents
by honorific expression toward addressee
buke→buke

	SE	EE	IE	ISE	total
RE	0(0.0)	1(100.0)	3(42.9)	0(0.0)	4(40.0)
NE	1(100.0)	0(0.0)	4(57.1)	1(100.0)	6(60.0)
HE	0(0.0)	0(0.0)	0(0.0)	0(0.0)	0(0.0)
total	1	1	7	1	10

Table 4 honorific expression from a son to his parents
by honorific expression toward addressee
buke→chōnin

	SE	EE	IE	ISE	total
RE	2(16.7)	0(0.0)	0(0.0)	0(0.0)	2(15.4)
NE	4(33.3)	0(0.0)	1(100.0)	0(0.0)	5(38.5)
HE	6(50.0)	0(0.0)	0(0.0)	0(0.0)	6(46.2)
total	12	0	1	0	13

Table 5   honorific expression from a son to his parents by honorific expression toward addressee chōnin→buke

	SE	EE	IE	ISE	total
RE	3(50.0)	0(0.0)	10(58.8)	2(66.7)	15(53.6)
NE	3(50.0)	2(100.0)	7(41.2)	1(33.3)	13(46.4)
HE	0(0.0)	0(0.0)	0(0.0)	0(0.0)	0(0.0)
total	6	2	17	3	28

Table 6   honorific expression from a son to his parents by honorific expression toward addressee chōnin→chōnin

左様なら親父も参つて帰りましたか（東海道四谷怪談、182）

sayō nara *oyaji* mo *mait* 'come (HVN)' te kaeri mashi ta ka

'Well, did my father go back?'

A respectful expression is used by a *chōnin* addressing a *chōnin*:

殊に、おれが親の源次郎殿の、恩になつた、石浜の御家中主水さまの弟、……こんな相談も、お袋が聞かれて（勝相撲浮名花触、242）

kotoni ore ga oya no genjirō-*dono* 'RP' no on ni nat ta ishihama no go-kachū mondo-sama no otōto …konna sōdan mo ohukuro ga kika *re* 'RARU' te

'He is a brother of Mr Mondo in Ishihama, to whom my father, Mr Genjirō, is in debt …if my mother listens to this agreement.'

We can interpret the numbers on each table as follows: humble expressions are used for polite conversation among the *buke*, or as polite speech acts by *chōnin* to *buke*. The humble expression can be viewed as the public common language of the *buke* because it is used mainly when a *buke* talks to another *buke* using a superior expression. Similarly, *chōnin* use humble expressions to *buke* because *chōnin* inhabiting the same public domain as the *buke* need to use the same public common language of the *buke* on official occasions. It is said that a *buke* speaks with the same speech style as a *chōnin* when he is relaxed, and this can be understood when we see in Tables 3 and 4 that *buke* also use respectful expressions toward an inferior addressee. But it must also be understood that the humble expression is not part of the honorific system of the *chōnin*, who do not use the humble expression among themselves. When a humble expression is used by *chōnin* to addressing *buke*, the honorific form is either *gozarimasuru* or *zonjimasuru*, and these supreme polite forms show that the speech situation is highly formal.

3.1.2 a daughter about her parents

	buke→buke	buke→chōnin	chōnin→buke	chōnin→chōnin	total
RE	15(88.2)	12(100.0)	2(100.0)	14(93.3)	43(93.5)
NE	2(11.8)	0(0.0)	0(0.0)	1(6.7)	3(6.5)
HE	0(0.0)	0(0.0)	0(0.0)	0(0.0)	0(0.0)
total	17	12	2	15	46

Table 7   honorific expression from a daughter to her parents by social class

Table 7 shows the honorific expression in accordance with the social status of both speaker and addressee. There is a case of humble expressions being used when a daughter introduces herself:

そりやわたしが親たちの御かゐ名。昔思へばなつかしき、その過去帳はわたしが御先祖と。……塚本与太夫が娘おさん（杜若艶色紫、313）

soryā watashi ga oya-*tachi* 'RS' no *go* 'RP'-kaimyō. Mukashi omoe ba natsukashiki, sono kakochō wa watashi ga *go* 'RP'-senzo to. ...tsukamoto *yodayū* 'FN' ga musume osan

'These are the posthumous Buddhist names of my parents. How well I recall the good old days! My ancestors are listed in the register of the dead. I am Osan, the daughter of Tsukamoto Yodayū.'

In all the other 43 situations, respectful forms are used. A daughter addresses her parents as *toto-san* or *kaka-san*, and uses respectful verb forms like *shiyansu*, *reru* or *o-V-nasaru*. Because of the historical shift of inflectional patterns, *raru* or *ru* started to move to *rareru* or *reru* in this period. For example, *ikaru* 'go' changed to *ikareru*. There has not been much research on *buke* women's language, but as far as I can interpret, a *buke* daughter uses a respectful expression for her parents whereas a *buke* son uses a humble expression. Table 8 shows how honorific expressions are used in accordance with the honorific expression toward an addressee.

	SE	EE	IE	ISE	total
RE	14(87.5)	24(100.0)	3(100.0)	2(66.7)	43(93.5)
NE	2(12.5)	0(0.0)	0(0.0)	1(33.3)	3(6.5)
HE	0(0.0)	0(0.0)	0(0.0)	0(0.0)	0(0.0)
total	16	24	3	3	46

Table 8 honorific expression from a daughter to her parents
by honorific expression toward addressee

3.2 a wife about her husband

	SE	EE	IE	ISE	total
RE	16(61.5)	21(87.5)	12(100.0)	0(0.0)	49(79.0)
NE	6(23.1)	3(12.5)	0(0.0)	0(0.0)	9(14.5)
HE	4(15.4)	0(0.0)	0(0.0)	0(0.0)	4(6.5)
total	26	24	12	0	62

Table 9 honorific expression from a wife to her husband
by honorific expression toward addressee

Table 9 shows how the honorific expression changes according to the relation with an addressee. There are a few cases of a humble expression being used when a superior expression is used toward an addressee, but it is not common at all.

	SE	EE	IE	ISE	total
RE	4(57.1)	3(100.0)	1(100.0)	0(0.0)	8(72.7)
NE	3(42.9)	0(0.0)	0(0.0)	0(0.0)	3(27.3)
HE	0(0.0)	0(0.0)	0(0.0)	0(0.0)	0(0.0)
total	7	3	1	0	11

Table 10 honorific expression from a wife to her husband
by honorific expression toward addressee
buke→buke

	SE	EE	IE	ISE	total
RE	3(100.0)	4(80.0)	1(100.0)	0(0.0)	8(88.9)
NE	0(0.0)	1(20.0)	0(0.0)	0(0.0)	1(11.1)
HE	0(0.0)	0(0.0)	0(0.0)	0(0.0)	0(0.0)
total	3	5	1	0	9

Table 11 honorific expression from a wife to her husband
by honorific expression toward addressee
buke→chōnin

	SE	EE	IE	ISE	total
RE	3(42.9)	1(100.0)	0(0.0)	0(0.0)	4(50.0)
NE	2(28.6)	0(0.0)	0(0.0)	0(0.0)	2(25.0)
HE	2(28.6)	0(0.0)	0(0.0)	0(0.0)	2(25.0)
total	7	1	0	0	8

Table 12 honorific expression from a wife to her husband
by honorific expression toward addressee
chōnin→buke

	SE	EE	IE	ISE	total
RE	6(66.7)	13(86.7)	10(100.0)	0(0.0)	29(85.3)
NE	1(11.1)	2(13.3)	0(0.0)	0(0.0)	3(8.8)
HE	2(22.2)	0(0.0)	0(0.0)	0(0.0)	2(5.9)
total	9	15	10	0	34

Table 13 honorific expression from a wife to her husband
by honorific expression toward addressee
chōnin→chōnin

I will verify this by taking the social status into consideration from Table 10 to Table 13. While a male adult introduces himself by the first person pronoun—*sessha wa X* 'I am X'—a female adult introduces herself with reference to her husband's first name:

わたくしは……三之助と申す者の女房。（杜若艶色紫、313）

watashi wa...*sannosuke* 'FN' to mōsu mono no nyōbō.

'I am the wife of Sannosuke.'

But once the self-introduction is over, she treats her husband with a respectful expression. The following number of terms of address can be found: *-dono* (26), *-san* (8), *tēshu* (5), *nushi* (4), *otto* (3), *kochi-no-hito, kono-hito, ano-hito* (4), first name (15).

As for the honorific predicate, *shiyansu* and *reru* are used mainly. And *teja* or *te* is used by a *chōnin* wife.

3.3 about an elder brother or sister

3.3.1 about his elder brother or sister

	buke→buke	buke→chōnin	chōnin→buke	chōnin→chōnin	total
RE	5(22.7)	8(36.4)	0(0.0)	6(46.2)	19(33.3)
NE	9(40.9)	14(63.6)	0(0.0)	6(46.2)	29(50.9)
HE	8(36.4)	0(0.0)	0(0.0)	1(7.7)	9(15.8)
total	22	22	0	13	57

Table 14 honorific expression from youger brother to elder sibling by social class

Table 14 shows how a young brother's attitude towards his elder siblings is similar to how a son treats his parents. Remember that when *buke* talk to each other they mainly use humble expressions and this form, then, is the public common language of a society where *buke* are the ruling class. *Buke* will also use a respectful expression to *chōnin*.

	SE	EE	IE	ISE	total
RE	0(0.0)	0(0.0)	4(57.1)	1(20.0)	5(22.7)
NE	5(62.5)	0(0.0)	3(42.9)	1(20.0)	9(40.9)
HE	3(37.5)	2(100.0)	0(0.0)	3(60.0)	8(36.4)
total	8	2	7	5	22

Table 15 honorific expression from youger brother to elder sibling by honorific expression toward addressee buke→buke

	SE	EE	IE	ISE	total
RE	3(100.0)	0(0.0)	5(29.4)	0(0.0)	8(36.4)
NE	0(0.0)	2(13.3)	12(70.6)	0(0.0)	14(63.6)
HE	0(0.0)	0(0.0)	0(0.0)	0(0.0)	0(0.0)
total	3	2	17	0	22

Table 16 honorific expression from youger brother to elder sibling
by honorific expression toward addressee
buke→chōnin

	SE	EE	IE	ISE	total
RE	2(66.7)	2(50.0)	2(40.0)	0(0.0)	6(46.2)
NE	0(0.0)	2(50.0)	3(60.0)	1(100.0)	6(46.2)
HE	1(33.3)	0(0.0)	0(0.0)	0(0.0)	1(7.7)
total	3	4	5	1	13

Table 17 honorific expression from youger brother to elder sibling
by honorific expression toward addressee
chōnin→chōnin

We can see more precisely from Table 15 to Table 17 how the honorific expression toward an addressee is formulated. In the examples that follow, the honorific expression toward the same person, an elder brother in this case, alters from one addressee to another. When the addressee is also a *buke*, a humble expression is employed to refer to one's elder brother.

兄の主水が難儀となつているといふ咄しを聞きましたが、貴殿にはその様な事は御ぞんじないか（勝相撲浮名花触、250）

ani no *mondo* 'FN' ga nangi to nat te iru to iu hanasi o kiki mashi ta ga, kiden ni wa sono yōna koto wa go-zonji nai ka

'I heard that my elder brother, Mondo, is in trouble. Do you know anything about it?'

But when the addressee is a *chōnin*, a neutral expression is used.

さつき兄貴のところから、使をよこした五十両は、どふしてくれる（勝相撲浮名花触、256）

sakki *ani-ki* no tokoro kara tukai o yokoshi ta gojū-ryō wa, dō shi te kureru

'How can you compensate me the fifty-ryō that my elder brother sent me to collect?'

And respectful expression is also used such as follows.

兄主水どのが尋ねに歩くと聞いて、白藤に相談せふと、来懸かる広小路で、兄貴のすつ影（勝相撲浮名花触、273）

ani mondo-*dono* 'RS' ga tazune ni aruku to kii te, shirahuji ni sōdan-shō to, ki-kakaru hiro-kōji de, *ani-ki* no sutu-kage

'I heard that my elder brother, Mr. Mondo, hangs around here, so I came to ask Shirahuji about him. On the way, I found his table.'

The humble expression is mainly used when a *buke* talks to a *buke* to whom he should use a superior or equal expression. As for terms of address, *buke* use *ani* and *ane*, and *chōnin* use *ani-ki* and *ane-ki*. Here I interpret *ani-ki* and *ane-ki* as neutral expressions, but there are examples where they are used with the respectful title *dono*:

聞けば兄貴の十右衛門どのが、万八にいられるといふ事、一寸あつていかふと思つて道よりしましたのさ（色一座梅椿、81）

kike ba *ani-ki* no zyūemon-*dono* 'RS' ga, manpachi ni ira *reru* 'RARU' to ihu koto, chotto at te ikō to omot te michiyori si mash ita no sa

'I heard that my elder brother, Mr Zyūemon, was in Manpachi, so I dropped by to meet him.'

When I define *ani-ki* and *ane-ki* as respectful expressions, when *buke* address *chōnin*, respectful expressions are used in fifteen cases whereas neutral expressions are used in seven cases; and among *chōnin*, respectful expressions are used in twelve cases whereas neutral expressions are not used. As a result, humble expressions are used among *buke* and respectful expressions are used among *chōnin*. *Reru* is used as the respectful form in the predicate part.

3.3.2. about her elder brother or sister

	buke→buke	buke→chōnin	chōnin→buke	chōnin→chōnin	total
RE	12(70.6)	9(100.0)	4(66.7)	18(100.0)	43(86.0)
NE	2(11.8)	0(0.0)	1(16.7)	0(0.0)	3(6.0)
HE	3(17.6)	0(0.0)	1(16.7)	0(0.0)	4(8.0)
total	17	9	6	18	50

Table 18   honorific expression from youger sister to elder sibling by social class

Let us look at how a young sister treats her elder siblings. First of all, Table 18 shows the results based on social status, which shows the same pattern as when a daughter speaks of her parents. That is, the honorific expression is used in most cases and humble expressions are used only in four cases out of 50. The daughter of a *buke* family talks to the lord of the clan. In this case, a very official situation, *ani* is used.

わたしが身は兄次第、兄さへおとり立て下さりますれば（絵本合法衢、347）

watashi ga mi wa *ani* sidai, *ani* sae o-toritate kudasari masure ba

'I don't care what happens to me, as long as you take good care of my elder brother.'

	SE	EE	IE	ISE	total
RE	24(80.0)	12(100.0)	6(100.0)	1(50.0)	43(86.0)
NE	3(10.0)	0(0.0)	0(0.0)	0(0.0)	3(6.0)
HE	3(10.0)	0(0.0)	0(0.0)	1(50.0)	4(8.0)
total	30	12	6	2	50

Table 19   honorific expression from youger sister to elder sibling by honorific expression toward addressee

Table 19 shows the results based on the honorific expression used toward an addressee.

A humble expression is used when a superior expression is appropriate toward an addressee. In the late Edo period, a younger sister used the following respectful expressions to refer to her elder brother or sister: *ani-san* or *ane-san* as address terms; and *sansu, shiyansu, o-V-nansu* or *reru* as predicates.

3.4 a servant about his master

	buke→buke	buke→chōnin	chōnin→buke	chōnin→chōnin	total
RE	14(63.6)	28(100.0)	22(68.8)	45(84.9)	109(80.7)
NE	5(22.7)	0(0.0)	2(6.3)	7(13.2)	14(10.4)
HE	3(13.6)	0(0.0)	8(25.0)	1(1.9)	12(8.9)
total	22	28	32	53	135

Table 20 honorific expression from a servant to the master
by social class

Table 20 shows how a servant treats his master with the results based on the social status of both speaker and addressee. In all 28 cases where the servant of a *buke* family speaks of his master to a *chōnin*, a respectful expression is used. The reason for this is that social hierarchy places the *buke* above the *chōnin* class.

	buke→buke	buke→chōnin	chōnin→buke	chōnin→chōnin	total
RE	9(52.9)	20(100.0)	19(70.4)	39(84.8)	87(79.1)
NE	5(29.4)	0(0.0)	2(7.4)	6(13.0)	13(11.8)
HE	3(17.7)	0(0.0)	6(22.2)	1(2.2)	10(9.1)
total	17	20	27	46	110

Table 21 honorific expression from a servant to the master
by social class
male servant

	buke→buke	buke→chōnin	chōnin→buke	chōnin→chōnin	total
RE	5(100.0)	8(100.0)	3(60.0)	6(85.7)	22(88.0)
NE	0(0.0)	0(0.0)	0(0.0)	1(14.3)	1(4.0)
HE	0(0.0)	0(0.0)	2(40.0)	0(0.0)	2(8.0)
total	5	8	5	7	25

Table 22 honorific expression from a servant to the master
by social class
female servant

Let us check whether there also exists any difference based on gender. Table 21 shows male speakers, and Table 22 shows female speakers. When a man from a *buke* family speaks of his elder kin to another *buke*, he uses a humble expression in 46.7 percent of cases in Table 2, but in 17.7 percent of classes in Table 21. Let us check examples of the use of humble expressions.

屋形の主、三国の太夫、お出迎ひ仕るべき筈の所（法懸松成田利劔、229）

yakata no nushi, mikuni no *taihu o*-demukae-*tukamatsuru* 'HAN' beki hazu no tokoro

'The lord Mikuni no Taihu should come to welcome you.'

主人伊東三郎右衛門（法懸松成田利劔、250）

shujin *itō-saburō-uemon* 'LN+FN'

'My master, Itō Saburō Uemon.'

	chōnin→buke	chōnin→chōnin	total
RE	16(66.7)	21(91.3)	37(78.7)
NE	2(8.3)	2(8.7)	4(8.5)
HE	6(25.0)	0(0.0)	6(12.8)
total	24	23	47

Table 23　honorific expression from a servant to the master
　　　　　by social class
　　　　　the master is buke

	chōnin→buke	chōnin→chōnin	total
RE	6(75.0)	24(80.0)	30(78.9)
NE	0(0.0)	5(16.7)	5(13.2)
HE	2(25.0)	1(3.3)	3(7.9)
total	8	30	38

Table 24　honorific expression from a servant to the master
　　　　　by social class
　　　　　the master is chōnin

I counted servants of *buke* families as *chōnin* because their speech is much closer to that of *chōnin*, but I re-classify them by dividing the social status of their masters. Table 23 shows cases where the master is a *buke*, and Table 24 is for *chōnin*.

	SE	EE	IE	ISE	total
RE	7(53.8)	4(66.7)	2(100.0)	1(100.0)	14(63.6)
NE	4(30.8)	1(16.7)	0(0.0)	0(0.0)	5(22.7)
HE	2(15.4)	1(16.7)	0(0.0)	0(0.0)	3(13.6)
total	13	6	2	1	22

Table 25　honorific expression from a servant to the master
　　　　　 by honorific expression toward addressee
　　　　　 buke→buke

	SE	EE	IE	ISE	total
RE	17(63.0)	2(100.0)	0(0.0)	3(100.0)	22(68.8)
NE	2(7.4)	0(0.0)	0(0.0)	0(0.0)	2(6.3)
HE	8(29.6)	0(0.0)	0(0.0)	0(0.0)	8(25.0)
total	27	2	0	3	32

Table 26　honorific expression from a servant to the master
　　　　　 by honorific expression toward addressee
　　　　　 chōnin→buke

Let us see how an honorific expression toward a master varies according to the expression used to an addressee—from *buke* to *buke* in Table 25, and *chōnin* to *buke* in Table 26. A *chōnin* refers to his master with a humble expression when addressing a *buke* by using a superior expression.

There are some examples of fluctuations between humble and respectful expressions:

御願申せと、親方が申付けましてござりまする（杜若艶色紫、308）

o-negai-mōse to oyakata ga *mōshitsuke* mashi te gozari masuru

'My master ordered me to ask your favour.'

私と御一処にと申付けましてござりまする（於染久松色読販、43）

watakushi to go-issho ni to *mōshitsuke* mashi te gozari masuru

'He asked you to come with me.'

X *mōshitsukeru* Y to Z expresses that X asks Y to ask or order Z. In these cases, X is a master, Y is a servant and Z is a referent. This kind of expression doesn't need to show the hierarchical relation between X and Z directly, but shows only X and Y. This kind of expression is appropriate when Y needs to show respect to both X (master) and Z (referent). There are also cases where the honorific expression varies according to an addressee:

親方が、かたがた言付けて行かれました（四天王産湯玉川、229）

oyakata ga katagata ii-tsuke te ika *re* 'RARU' mashi ta

'My master left leaving some messages.'

団十郎は、則私の師匠にござります（四天王産湯玉川、240）

danjūrō 'FN' wa sunawachi watakushi no shishō ni gozarimasu

'Danjūrō is my master.'

In the former, an actor is addressing a monk and refers to his master using a respectful expression; in the latter, he refers to his master only by first name when addressing the high commissioner.

3.5 synthetic analysis

When analysing the data, I divided each factor into the following criteria: when a speaker is male or female, and *chōnin* or *buke*; when an honorific expression toward an addressee is superior, or equal, and so on. I try to analyse synthetically which factor is functioning most effectively. As part of multiple linear regression analysis, *suryōka riron I-rui* 'Qualification I' is cultivated in Japan[4]. This statistical method evaluates the dependent variables that are quality factors. That is, an honorific expression is determined by a combination of multiple —in this case, five— factors. For example, how did male A of *buke* B treat his master C to *buke* addressee D, to whom a superior expression E was used? That is, factor A is the gender of a speaker, factor B is the social status of a speaker, factor C is the social factor of a referent, factor D is the social factor of an addressee, and factor E is the honorific expression used toward the addressee. In order to statistically analyse the honorific expression toward a referent, the total frequency of humble expressions is divided by the total frequency of all expressions. That is, the ratio to be expressed, of humble expression to all expression, is used as a dependent variable. Table 27 shows the result. The wider the difference between the two numbers within each factor category, the more effectively it functions as a determining factor. That reflects also in the coefficient of partial correlation. We can interpret from Table 27 that a humble expression is apt to be used when an addressee belongs to the *buke* class, the speaker is male, the honorific expression toward the addressee is superior, and the referent is a kin relation. The social status of a speaker is not working so efficiently because *buke* also use respectful expressions to *chōnin* addressee.

variables	quality	CSC	CPC
gender of a speaker			
male	8.86381	0.25245	0.32548
female	−6.31211		
social class of a speaker			
buke	−1.33271	−0.10003	0.03351
chōnin	1.13618		
social class of an addressee			
buke	9.0617	0.33366	0.37925
chōnin	−8.59299		
social class of a referent			
buke	2.15541	0.07195	0.07331
chōnin	−3.25706		
social relation to a referent			
kinship	5.25915	0.1778	0.24122
hierarchy	−7.12176		
honorific expression to an addressee			
SE	8.49609		
EE	−1.51441	0.22021	0.25251
IE	−6.64434		
ISE	−1.54312		
constant term	9.39027		
MCC	0.53365		
AEP	2.14528+01		

Table 27 Qualification I
CSC means Coefficient of Simple Correlation
CPC means Coefficient of Partial Correlation
MCC means Multiple Correlation Coefficient
AEP means Average Error of Predication

3.6 analysis of respectful predicates

There are 97 examples of predicates used for respectful expressions and I list them in detail: *Reru* or *ru* (51 examples, 52.6%), *nsu* as in *sansu, nansu, yansu* or *gozansu* (32 examples, 33.0%); *te* (5 examples, 5.2%); *osshiyaru* (3 examples, 3.1%); *shiyaru* (2 examples, 2.1%); *nasaru* (2 examples, 2.1%); *gozaru* (1 example, 1.0%); *o–V-asobasu* (1 example, 1.0%). What is characteristic is that all the examples of *nsu* are used by female speakers. There are some questions about the honorific value of these *nsu* and *reru* or *ru* forms, which make up more than 85% of examples. The *nsu* form emerged in the *kamigata* dialect of the early Edo period as a female word or a word used in the *yūri*[5]. It was also used in male *kamigata* dialect of the late Edo period, but in Edo *nsu* was used exclusively by the women of the *yūri*. As for the *reru* or *ru* forms, which are known to have a low honorific value, Rodriguez (1955) writes, 'An in-group superior should not be treated by a more respectful form than *raru* or *ru* when he is mentioned to an out-group person'. And we cannot ignore that these forms originated in *kamigata* dialect. What can we make of this kind of usage in relation to the honorific system in general? Is it appropriate to think that the notion of the humble expression is combined with the notion of the respectful expression when an in-group superior is referred to in a conversation with an out-group person? That is, a superior should be shown respect with a respectful expression that should however be kept as low as possible when the addressee is an out-group person.

4. Comparison with other kinds of data

'*Kuaiwa Hen: Twenty-five Exercises in the Yedo Colloquial, for the use of students, with Notes*' (1873) by Ernest Satow is the source used for the colloquial language of the *buke* at the end of the Edo period, especially that of the well-educated upper class *buke*. When I compare *ki-zewa-mono* with the '*Kuaiwa Hen*', I find in the latter eight examples that refer to members of a speaker's in-group. Below are some examples by the page from the revised version published by *Tōyōbunko*. A servant speaks to his master about his father and uses a humble expression:

おやじが急病だと申し田舎から手紙が参りました（59）

oyaji ga kyūbyō da to *mōshi* 'say (HVN)' inaka kara tegami ga *mairi* 'come (HVN)' mashi ta

'A letter came from my house saying that my father was suddenly taken ill.'

Next, a servant in a *buke* household addresses a guest.

主人へ申し聞けますから（68）

shujin e *mōshi* 'say (HVO)'-kike masu kara

'I will talk to my master.'

In *ki-zewa-mono* also a *buke* uses the same kind of expression to another *buke*:

私めが、親人にとくと申し聞けまして（紋盡五人男、389）

watashi me ga oya-hito ni tokuni *mōshi* 'say (HVO)'-kike mashi te

'I will talk to my parents.'

X *mōshi-kike* Y is used in the same way as X *mōshi-tsuke* Y. Speaker X lowers himself to his in-group superior Y, but gives no indication of Y's direct relationship with the addressee. A servant from a *buke* household addresses an employee of a hotel.

ただ今伺ったらすぐに（風呂を）めすそうだから（78）

tadaima *ukagat* 'ask (HVO)' tara suguni *mesu* 'take (RV)' sō da kara

'I asked my master, and he is going to take a bath now.'

ねえさん、旦那、お中食をあそばすから（86）

nēsan, danna, o-chūshoku o *asobasu* 'eat (RV)' kara

'Miss, my master wants to eat lunch now.'

As in *ki-zewa-mono*, servants of *buke* speak of their masters to *chōnin* by using respectful expressions. Also, the honorific system of the *chōnin* depicted in *share-bon*, *kokkē-bon* and *ninjō-bon* is quite similar to that in *ki-zewa-mono*, therefore, we can trust *ki-zewa-mono* as sources for data of the late Edo.

5. Summary

1. In/out-group honorifics are rooted in the ruling social class, the *buke* class. They are mainly used in exchanges between *buke*, but are also used by *chōnin* addressing *buke* when they use a superior expression. We can interpret in/out-group

honorifics as an honorific system supported by the *buke* class that is the common language in official situations. Consequently in/out-group honorifics are used by men who daily perform in an official capacity. Women, even those of the *buke* class, do not use in/out-group honorifics as often. There is an honorific system developed among the *chōnin* class, but it is based on expressions of respect rather than humble speech acts.

2. In/out-group honorifics are predicated on the notion of the in-group rather than on hierarchical order. On the contrary, in absolute honorifics the honorific expression is determined solely by the social status of a referent. It is understood that absolute honorifics held an important position in the Edo period, when hierarchical order was strictly maintained. A *buke*, in conversation with a peer, may use a humble expression, but when a *buke* speaks to a *chōnin*, who is lower in social status, he uses a respectful expression which is used more often for one's master than for one's kinship superior.

3. In/out-group honorifics are used in ritualized exchanges such as self-introductions or relaying messages. These are the official contexts where sanctioned patterns of verbal conduct are employed socially, and in such a situation a humble expression is used. This fact shows us that in/out-group honorifics are part of a formal honorific system.

(Endnotes)

1   *Ue* means 'a higher place' and is suffixed to a kinship term like *chichi-ue* in honorific usage.
2   In Chapter 6, respectful expressions are subdivided into respectful expressions and respectful title expressions.
3   The quoted parts are shown within parentheses. The names of plays are shown and the number indicates the quoted pages of each text.
4   This statistical method was developed by Japanese statistician, Chikio Hayashi. The analysis is processed by personal computer using the multi-valiant analysis program HALBAU.
5   *Yūri* 遊里 was an isolated quarter of prostitution approved by the Edo government, quite different from today's red-light districts. In the Edo period, with its strictly observed social hierarchy, the *yūri* was a place where people could be free from the hierarchical distinctions of the outer world. *Buke* were not allowed to carry the swords that were the status symbol of their

class, and various cultures flourished in the *yūri*. There also existed a hierarchy among prostitutes, or *yūjo* 遊女. High-class *yūjo* trained as musicians, dancers or poets, and men came to dip themselves in the highly-sophisticated atmosphere of the *yūri*. *Yūjo* were trained to speak a social-dialect that was unique to the yūri and in some cases this spread outside its confines and into the ordinary world.

8

REFERENT HONORIFIC EXPRESSION IN CHŌNIN-KOTOBA OF THE LATER EDO PERIOD: IN SHARE-BON, KOKKEI-BON AND NINJŌ-BON

1. Introduction

In chapter 7, I reached to the conclusion that in the later Edo period *buke* class uses an honorific system that humble expression is used to mention in-group superior, whereas *chōnin* class uses an honorific system that respectful expression is used to mention in-group superior. And *buke* class also treats his in-group superior by respectful expression when he doesn't need to show regards to an addressee. As a conclusion, I think that an honorific system that humble expression is used to mention in-group superior is official honorific system and that *chōnin* class especially high *chōnin* class switches two types of honorific systems: humble expression in official situation and respectful expression in private situation. I still have some question to be solved about private language among *chōnin* class. In this chapter, I focus on the private language among *chōnin* class. As a famous phrase by Fukuzawa Yukichi, 'When we listen somebody speaking over wall, we can clearly guess which social class he belongs to: high *buke*, low *buke*, farmer or merchant', we can find out that the great diversity of social dialect was created in this period. *Chōnin-kotoba* I say here covers the language of *chōnin* and *yūjo*.

2. Data

Share-bon, *kokkei-bon* and *ninjō-bon* are commonly used as data for *chōnin kotoba* in the later Edo period. These books are written from Meiwa, An'ei (1764) to

Bunka, Bunsei (1830) and the colloquial style is used. I use the following books as data. The name of the scene is listed by such order as Japanese title, its pronunciation and the year of publication.

遊子方言 'Yūshi hōgen', 1770
辰巳之園 'Tatsumi no sono', 1770
金々先生栄花夢 'Kinkinsensei eiga no yume', 1775
甲駅新話 'Kōekishinwa', 1775
道中粋語録 'Dōchūsugoroku', 1779
卯地臭意 'Ujishūi', 1783
総籬 'Sōmagaki', 1787
傾城買四十八手 'Keiseikai shijūhatte', 1790
錦之裏 'Nishiki no ura', 1791
仕懸文庫 'Shikake bunko', 1791
傾城買二筋道 'Keiseikai futasujimichi', 1798
辰巳婦言 'Tatsumifugen', 1798
東海道中膝栗毛 'Tōkaidōchū hizakurige', 1802
戯場粋言幕の外 'Gekijō suigen maku no soto', 1806
浮世風呂 'Ukiyoburo', 1809
早変胸機 'Hayagawari mune no karakuri', 1810
客者評判記 'Kyakusha hyōbanki', 1811
狂言田舎繰 'Kyōgen inaka ayatsuri', 1811
四十八癖 'Shijūhachi kuse', 1812
一杯奇言 'Ippaikigen', 1813
浮世床 'Ukiyodoko', 1813
人間万事嘘誕計 'Ningen banji usobakari', 1813
古今百馬鹿 'Kokon hyakubaka', 1814
人心覗機関 'Hito no kokoro nozoki karakuri', 1814
春色梅児誉美 'Shunshoku ume goyomi', 1832
春色辰巳之園 'Shunshoku tatsumi no sono', 1833
風月花情春告鳥 'Fūgetsu kajō harutsugedori', 1836

3. Analysis

We need to analyse the honorific expression toward the in-group superior referent of a speaker in order to find out the honorific system. And the in-group superior referent of a speaker can be divided into two groups: kinship superior like parent, elder brother, husband and etc. and hierarchical superior like master. In present day's Japanese, in/out-group honorifics are used commonly that in-group referent even if he is superior to a speaker should be treated by humble expression when an addressee is an out-group person. Let us check the honorific expression among *chōnin* class. Honorific expression can be divided into two parts: a term of reference and a predicate. As for the term of reference, respectful suffix like *dono* and *sama*, humble suffix *domo* and address term without title are listed as the words of honorific value. As for predicate, respectful auxiliary verbs like *shiyaru* and *yaru*, humble verb like *mairu* and *itasu* and etc are listed as the words of honorific value. These two parts, a term of reference and predicate, are combined and compose honorific expression. Here I classify honorific expressions into such four categories as follows.

1. respectful expression (RE)
2. respectful title expression (RTE)
3. neutral expression (NE)
4. humble expression (HE)

Respectful expression means an expression that respectful form is used for predicate, and this doesn't exclude the use of respectful title. Respectful title expression means an expression that respectful form is used for title but not for predicate. The case that a speaker makes himself humble to an in-group superior like *ani-sama ni sashiage* 'give(HVO)' *mashi ta* 'I gave to my brother.' is counted as respectful expression toward the brother. It is quite often that we can find out such utterance as *totosama wo yoroshiku* 'please take good care of my father', that there is no room for predicate to express honorific expression. Therefore, I set up special category, respectful title expression. Neutral expression is an expression that neutral expression is used for both title and predicate. Humble expression is an expression that humble expression is used for either title or predicate. I check the honorific expression dividing in-group superior into two groups: kinship superior and hierarchical superior.

3.1 about a kinship superior

3.1.1 about her husband

There are 21 examples that a wife refers her husband to out-group person, and within 21 examples, six examples are respectful expression, three examples are humble expression and others are respectful title expression that neutral expression is used for predicate but *san*, *sama* or *dono* are used for terms of address. There are lots of cases that a wife treats her husband in *share-bon* and *kokkei-bon* by Shikitei Sanba 式亭三馬. Respectful expression is used such as follows.

1. 旦那があゝおつしやるから一寸おあがりなせへ（浮世床、58）[1]
danna ga ā *ossharu* 'say(RV)' kara chotto o-agari-nasē
'My husband says so. Please come in.'

2. 宿でも一寸お見舞に参りたがつてゞございましたが、……御用が追々重なりまして、……お飯さへろくろく落着いてはくださいません程でございますのさ。……草臥れますから主もおまへさん、ほつほつと云つてでございます。……主が申されますには（浮世床、183-184）
yado de mo chotto o-mimai ni *mairi* 'come(HVN)' ta gat *te* 'RA' de gozaimashi ta ga…*go* 'RP'-yō gat sui-tsui kasanari mashi te,…o-manma sae roku-roku ochitsui te wa kudasai masen hodo de gozaimasu no sa….kutabire masu kara nushi mo omae-san, hotsu-hotsu to it *te* 'RA' de gozaimasu….nushi ga *mōsare* 'say(RV)' masu ni wa
'My husband wanted to pay a visit,…was busy,…had no time to take meals at ease…he gets tired…as he says.'

In Example 2, humble expression like *mairu* is used on one hand, but respectful expression *te* is used on the other hand. And *mōsareru* is used also. There is a controversy about the grammaticality of the word *mōsareru*. Some think that *mōsareru* is ungrammatical because humble verb *mōsu* cannot co-occur with respectful auxiliary *reru*, but other think that *mōsareru* is grammatical because *mōsu* already obtained a function as polite form. According to Yamazaki (1963), *mōsaru* is used mainly by *buke* in early Edo along with *itasaru* and *mairaru*, and taking an example from a sentence *watakushi shujin Anekawa Ukon…iede o itasaruru* 'my master Anekawa Ukon ran away from home', it explains, 'A speaker provides a referent humble applying the relation between a speaker and an addressee on the background by using *itasu*, and provide a referent superior applying the relation between a speaker and a referent on the background by using *raruru*. In this case, a speaker doesn't treat his kinship superior or master inferior to an addressee, but grasps a referent that should be treated with the special recognition as in-group superior'. This expression is a keyword in order to understand the shift of honorific system. In present-day Japanese, it is common within a family that a father refers himself to his child as *otō-san* putting him in his child place. Both Sugimoto (1988) and Komatsu (1985) refer that this usage is widely used in *chōnin-kotoba* of the later Edo period also. A wife also mentions her husband by *totsut-tsama* or *oyaji-dono* putting her in his child place such as follows.

    3.あれがお蔭で、私が不断とつざまにしかられます（浮世風呂、58）

    are ga o-kage de watashi ga hudan *totsut-tsama* 'RS' ni shika rare masu

    'Owing to him, I will be scolded by my husband.'

    4.親仁どのはわたしにばかり食つてかゝる（浮世風呂、200）

    oyaji-*dono* 'RS' wa watashi ni bakari kut te kakaru

    'My husband falls upon me always.'

Respectful suffix *dono* like danna-*dono* is used such as follows.

    5.旦那殿は胸がやけると言つてお雑煮をタッタ二切れだが（浮世風呂、183）

    danna-*dono* 'RS' wa mune ga yakeru to it te o-zōni o tatta huta-kire da ga

    'My husband complains stomach upset and eats only two pieces of race cakes.'

Humble expression is used for official occasion like greeting such as follows.

    6.宿でも、おうわさ申しておりました（人間万事嘘誕計、869）

    yado demo, o-uwasa *mōshi* 'say (HVN)' te *ori* 'HA' mashi ta

    'My husband always speaks of you.'

At the official occasion like greeting including self-introduction in Chapter 7, humble expression is commonly used for any social class, and it is so in the case of *chōnin* class.

3.1.2 a younger brotehr or sister about his or her elder siblings

There are three examples that mention elder siblings. A younger sister treats her elder brother by respectful expression and respectful suffix *san* such as follows.

7. お兄イさんは何処にどふして御在なさるか。こんなに私がつらい思ひをするとはちつとも知らずにおいでだらふ（春色梅児誉美、67）

o 'RP'-anii-*san* 'RS' wa doko ni dōshi te *oide* 'be(RV)' *nasaru* 'RA' ka. Konna ni watashi ga turai omoi wo suru to wa chittomo sirazu ni *oide* 'be(RV)' da rō

'Where is my elder brother? He doesn't know how much painful situation I find myself in.'

8. 兄さんが来て居てネ（春色辰巳之園、330）

ani-*san* 'RS' ga kit e ite ne

'My elder brother came to visit me.'

And a younger brother treats his elder sister by respectful title such as follows.

9. 姉さんの宿下の時に行たア（浮世風呂、40）

ane-*san* 'RS' no yado-sagari no toki ni it ta a

'I visited my elder sister when she came back as her holiday.'

3.1.3 a son about his parents

There are 20 cases, and respectful expression is used for seven examples such as follows.

10. その壱分母者に進ぜたら、どないに悦ばしやろうぞい（浮世床、69）

sono ichibu haha-ja[2] ni *shinze* 'give(HVO)' tara, donai-ni yorokoba *shiyarō* 'RA' zoi

'How much would my mother be delighted if I give her this money.'

11. それはおほかた、寺参にでもいかれた時でござりませう。おめへ御ぞんじとあれば、さだめて何とか、詞をかけられたでござりやせう（東海道中膝栗毛、91）

sore wa ōkata, tera-mairi ni de mo ika *re* 'RARU' ta toki de gozarimashō. Omē *go-zonji* 'know'(RV) to are ba, sadame te nan to ka, kotoba o kake *rare* 'RARU' ta de gozariyashō.

'That might be the time when my mother visited a temple. She might have called you if she had known you.'

An addressee in Example 10 is an intimate of a speaker and that in Example 11 is a stranger, but in both cases, respectful expression like *shiyaru*, *reru* and *go-zonji* is used. There are other cases that neutral expression is used such as follows.

12. お袋の病気も、おれが事を苦労にしての事だ（傾城買四十八手、412）

o-hukuro no byōki mo, ore ga koto o kurō ni shi te no koto da

'My mother got sick owing to worry on me.'

Example 12 is a case that a young man talks to *yūjo* in a familiar way. *O-hukuro* is used for the term of reference to one's mother. There is a description about *o-hukuro* in Toraaki's *kyōgen* scenario such as follows.

てゝおや（父親）はしんぶと言ひ、はゝおやはおふくろ（舎弟）

tete-oya wa shinbu to ī, haha-oya wa ohukuro

'a father is called "shinbu" and a mother "ohukuro".'

and also in *Vocabvlario da lingoa de Iapam*[3] such as follows.

フクロ：母。普通はヲフクロと言い、これは女性達の間でも、また、他の人々の間でも用いる

hukuro: haha. Hutū wa o-hukuro to ī, kore wa josē-tachi no aida de mo, mata, ta no hito-bito no aida de mo mochiiru

'hukuro: mother. "O-hukuro" is usually called even among females and out-group people.'

O-hukuro is used commonly among lower class *chōnin*, but upper class *chōnin* uses the same kind of terms of reference as *buke* like *oji*, *oba* and *haha* such as follows.

13. 母親ばかりであまやかされ、……大事の伯父の病死。……叔母といふは家付の娘で母の姉（春色梅児誉美、166-167）

hahaoya bakari de amayakasa re,…daiji no *oji* no byōshi….*oba* wa to iu wa ietsuki no musume de *haha* no ane

'I was indulged by my mother…my uncle died of a disease…my aunt is the eldest child and sister of my mother.'

3.1.4. a daughter about her parents

There are 18 cases, and respectful expression is used for three cases such as follows.

14. わたしのおツかさんはきついからむせうとお叱りだよ。……おつかさんがさらへさらへお言ひだと（浮世風呂、162）

watashi no okka-*san* 'RS' wa kitsui kara mushō to *o*-shikari-*da* 'RA' yo….
okka-*san* 'RS' ga sarahe-sarahe to *o*-ii-*da* 'RA' to

'My mum is so strict that she always gets angry with me….She ordered me to train.'

15. おとつさんがおいひだもの（客者評判記、465）

otot-*tsan* 'RS' ga *o*-ii-*da* 'RA' mono

'My dad says so.'

These are uttered by children and *o*-V-*da* is used. Totally it is common to treat by neutral expression and the term of referent like *totsu-tsan*, *kaka-san* and *okkā*. About the term *okkā*, there is a description such as follows.

16. 子のおかげで母御母御と、他人にいはれるのを有りがたいと思はねへで（春色辰巳之園、406）

ko no okage de *okkā okkā* to hito ni iwa reru no o arigatai to omowanē de

'She doesn't feel grateful to be respected being called '*okkā, okkā*' owing to her child.'

3.2. a servant about his master

There are eleven cases that a servant refers his master to a guest, humble or neutral expression is used for nine cases such as follows.

17. ただ今お座敷へ、参りました（総籬、371）

tada-ima o-zashiki e, *mairi* 'come (HVN)' mashi ta

'My master has just gone to a drawing room.'

18. ゑんさんに七右ェ門申します。こんばんはよふお出でなされました。……それへ参ります。まつぴら御免なすつてくださりましと、申し付けました。（総籬、377）

en-san ni *hichizaemon* 'FN' *mōshi* 'say(HVN)' masu. konban wa yō o-ide-nasare mash ita....sore e mairi masu. mappira go-men-nasut te kudasati mashi to, *mōshitsuke* mash ita.

'Hichizaemon, my master, left a message to you, En-tsan, saying, 'Welcome all the way to here today. ...Excuse me for a moment. I'll be with you shortly.

Example 18 is a situation that a servant gives a message of his master, and the same pattern of expression is used for other data such as follows: first of all he mentions his master by first name and say, *X-san ni Y mōshi masu Z to, mōshitsuke mash ita* (X is the name of the addressee, Y is the name of his master and Z is the content of message). Regional dialect is used for the other two examples and there respectful expression is used such as follows.

19. 聟様もよい男、嫁御様もゑらい器量よしでおざります。おきのどくなことは、あちらの座敷に、寝やしやりますから、睦言が聞へましよ（東海道中膝栗毛、204）

muko-*sama* 'RS' mo yoi otoko, yome-*go* 'RS'-*sama* 'RS' mo erai kiryō yoshi de ozarimasu. kinodokuna took wa, achira no zashiki ni, ne *yashiyari* 'RA' masu kara, mutsugoto ga kikoe mashō

'A bridegroom is handsome and bride is also very beautiful. I am sorry that you may hear soft whispering because they sleep at drawing room over there.'

It is common for a servant to treat his master to an addressee who is superior to his master by humble expression, but other cases by respectful expression. Eleven cases out of fifteen cases are respectful expressions such as follows.

20. いへもう私の旦那をお誉め申すもいかがでございますが、惣別お気立てのよいおかたでネおまえさん（浮世風呂、123）

ie mō watakushi no danna wo *o-home-mōsu* 'HAO' mo ikaga de gozaimasu ga, sōbetsu *o* 'RP'-kidate no yoi *o-kata* 'RN' de ne omae-san

'I should mind praising my master, but he is good natured.'

21. ソシテ奥様の御意に入りまして、名をばお呼び遊ばさずに、おちやツぴいヤ、於茶ヤ於茶ヤとお召し遊ばして、（浮世風呂、101）

soshite *oku-sama* 'RN' no *gyo* 'RP' -i ni iri mashi te, na wo ba *o-yobi-asobasa* 'RA' zu ni, ochappī ya ocha ya ocha ya to *o-meshi* 'call(RV)'-*asobashi* 'RA' te

'The mistress took a fancy to my daughter, and she never call her by first name, but by nickname, ochappī or ocha.'

Example 21 is in the situation when a woman talks about her daughter who works as domestic service in *buke*'s family. In Edo period, a young girl is trained the official way of speaking *asobase-kotoba* when she works as domestic service in *buke*'s family. There is a description of *asobase-kotoba* such as follows, and in *asobase-kotoba* a master is treated by respectful expression to any addressee.

22. おしつけ御奉公にお上がり遊ばすと、それこそもう大和詞でお人柄におなり遊ばすだ（浮世風呂、203）

oshitsuke go-hōkō ni o-agari-asobasu to, sore koso mō yamato-kotoba de o-hitogara ni o-nari-asobasu da

'When your daughter starts to work as domestic service, she speaks in refined manners.'

3.3 about a *yūjo*

In *yūri*, a special social dialect is used among *yūjo* that is different from other *chōnin* speech. This social dialect is named *yūri-kotoba*, *sato-kotoba* or *kuruwa-kotoba*. In this time each regional dialect kept its own characteristic clearly, and people could guess the birthplace of the speaker only from its voice. But in *yūri*, *yūjo* is trained to speak *kuruwa-kotoba* that has no trace of the regional dialect of outer world. The honorific system is also different from that of ordinary *chōnin*. A mistress of *cha-ya*[4] refers her husband, the master, to a customer by humble expression such as follows.

23. 今日のはきふな御用のお文そふで、御座りましたによつて、外の者では、間違うと申して、自身に持つて参りました（遊子方言、283）

konnichi no wa kyūna go-yō no o-humi sō de, gozarimashi ta niyotte, hoka no mono de wa, machigau to *mōshi* 'say (HVN)' te, jishin ni mot te *mairi* 'go(HVN)' mashi ta

'A letter came to summon my husband in a hurry. And he said that other people couldn't take my place, so he left by himself.'

But she refers *yūjo* by respectful expression such as follows.

24. はい、染之介さんは、おわるう御座ります。さつき、むかふの内にお出なんし

た（遊子方言、284）

hai somenosuke-*san* 'RS' wa *o* 'RP'-warū gozarimasu. sakki mukō no uchi ni o-de-*nanshi* 'RA' ta.

'Miss. Somenosuke is out now. She left for the house over there right now.'

She doesn't treat *yūjo* as in-group person like her husband to a customer. *nansu* is tipical *yūri-kotoba* that derived from *nasare-masu*. And *yūjo* treats her colleague *yūjo* to a customer by respectful expression such as follows.

25. そふ申しんしたなれば、主や、そんなお方は知らんと、言いなんした（遊子方言、292）

sō *mōshi* 'say(HVO)' nshi ta nare ba, nushi ya, sonna o-kata wa shira n to, ī *nanshi* 'RA' ta

'I talked to her like that, you know, and she said she was not acquainted with that man.'

26. 今に来さりませう（道中粋語録、331）

ima ni ki *sari* 'RA' mashō

'She might come soon.'

A young *yūjo* in apprenticeship refers her elder *yūjo* to merchants by respectful expression such as follows.

27. 八十兵衛さんへ、おいらんがちよつとお出なんしツサ（錦之裏、428）

yasobei-san e, oiran ga chotto *o-de-nanshi* 'RA' ssa

'Hi, Mr. Yasobei. Oiran migh be coming soon.'

And a *yūjo* refers her master to a customer by neutral expression such as follows.

28. 中の間でも、わつちにはあきれけへつて居ンすとさ。もしせいて上ゲねヘ時は、ふてて鞍替と覚悟して居ンす。（傾城買四十八手、411）

naka no ma de mo, wacchi ni wa akirekēt te i *nsu* to sa. moshi sei te age nē toki wa, hute te kuragae to kakugō shi te i *nsu*.

'Anyone in my family is shocked. If I don't do it in a hurry, I am resigned to be sold to another place.'

Nsu is a polite form that developed only in *yūri* of Yoshiwara in Edo city.

To summarize, an absolute honorifics are used among *yūjo*. Yamazaki (1990) states that there exists a rigid hierarchical stratum among *yūjo* with *oiran* at the top and this hierarchical relation reflects in the usage of honorifics. And *yūri* exists independent from the outer world where social status determines everything, and among *yūjo* the absolute honorifics based on the hierarchical stratum is used irrelevant to customers. In present-day's in/out group honorifics, humble expression is used to refer the in-group superior to out-group person, but among *yūjo* a superior is mentioned by respectful expression even to customers. A mistress of *cha-ya* refers her husband by humble expression, but refers *yūjo* by respectful expression to customers. And a *yūjo* treats her master by neutral expression, but her superior *yūjo* by respectful expression to customers. It might be right to think that there exists a rigid hierarchical stratum among *yūjo*, and a superior is treated by respectful expression applying absolute honorifics.

3.4. about a superior in social stratum

A superior in social stratum is treated by respectful expression such as follows.

29. 御役人さまがお出があればさぞ怖かろう（春色梅児誉美、111）

o 'RP'-yakunin-*sama* 'RS' ga *o* 'RP'-de ga are ba sazo kowak arō

'You might be scared if an officer comes here.'

30. 地主さまへ往つて来ねへきやアならねへ（浮世床、83）

jinushi-*sama* 'RS' e it te kone kyā nara nē

'I should go to see my landlord.'

These referents have no direct relation to the speakers, and an intimate superior to both a speaker and an addressee is also treated by respectful expression such as follows.

31. 親方がとうとう今朝がた御臨終なされた（東海道中膝栗毛、41）

oyakata ga tōtō kesa-gata *go*-rinjū-*nasare* 'RA' ta

'My master has passed away early in the morning.'

In present day a respectful expression is omitted toward a referent to whom an addressee doesn't have direct relation even if he is superior to a speaker, but in the later Edo period, we can understand that the social status functions importantly to determine the honorific expression because a superior by social status like official or landowner is treated by respectful expression.

3.5. total analysis

I try to analyse the honorific expression toward an in-group superior of a speaker in relation with an addressee. In present day Japanese honorifics, an honorific expression toward a referent varies in accordance with situation. In traditional Japanese honorific studies *ba* 場 or *bamen* 場面 is used as the technical term for speech situation. *Ba* is apprehended as a total unity of various factors that consists of honorific expression. That is, individual attribute like the age, gender, profession, education and etc. of both a speaker and an addressee, such mutual relation between a speaker and an addressee as intimacy, superiority and etc., external circumstance of speech event like private or public situation and topic and so on. But it is too complicated to take all of these factors into consideration, so I scrutinize the honorific system on the basis of the honorific expression of a speaker toward an addressee. It is easily understood that honorific expression toward a referent varies in accordance with the relation between a speaker and an addressee. For example, in present day's Japanese, there are several expressions possible to mention that his own father is coming such as follows; A: *chichi* 'HP' *ga mairi* 'come'(HV) *masu* 'polite form', B: *chichi* 'HP' *ga ki* 'come'(neutral verb) *masu* 'polite form', C: *oyaji* 'neutral form' *ga kuru* 'come'(neutral verb) *zo* 'non-polite form', D: *o-tō-san* 'RN' *ga ki* 'come'(neutral verb) *masu* 'polite form', E: *o-tō-san* 'RN' *ga kuru* 'come'(neutral verb) *yo* 'non-polite form'. Cases A and B are humble expression, C is neutral expression and D and E are respectful title expression. But D and E are considered to be erroneous expressions because in-group person should not be treated by respectful title like *san* to out-group person. According to Shibata & Suzuki (1959, 1961), these kinds of expressions are commonly used by children, but are erased before they graduate from junior high school, sixteen years old, by school education. But this kind of honorific expression is a correct and traditional usage in many regional dialects. And *chichi* 'HP' *ga mairu* 'come'(HV) *zo* sounds queer because *zo* that is only used to a friendly addressee as neutral expression co-occurs with humble expression toward a referent *chichi* and *mairu*. In conclusion, in present day's Japanese, humble expression toward a referent can co-occur with polite expression *masu* like A and B, and neutral expression toward a referent can co-occur with non-polite expression *zo* or *yo* like C. We can understand how the honorific expression toward a referent is determined by the relation to an addressee like this. Lots of studies were done upon the honorific expression between a speaker and an addressee by Kojima (1973, 1974), Tsujimura (1968), Ikegami (1963a, 1963b, 1967, 1968) and Yamazaki (1990), so I use the result of these studies. The honorific expression toward an addressee can be categorized into five such as follows.

1. supreme superior expression (SSE)
2. ordinary superior expression (OSE)
3. equal expression (EE)
4. inferior expression (IE)
5. insulting expression (ISE)

And the honorific expression toward a referent can be categorized into four such as follows.

1. respectful expression (RE)
2. respectful title expression (RTE)
3. neutral expression (NE)
4. humble expression (HE)

	SSE	OSE	EE	IE	ISE	total
RE	4(23.5)	2(66.7)	5(19.2)	6(66.7)	0(0.0)	17(30.9)
RTE	4(23.5)	0(0.0)	14(53.8)	2(22.2)	0(0.0)	20(36.4)
NE	6(35.3)	1(33.3)	7(26.9)	1(11.1)	0(0.0)	15(27.3)
HE	3(17.6)	0(0.0)	0(0.0)	0(0.0)	0(0.0)	3(5.5)
total	17	3	26	9	0	55

Table 1 honorific expression to a superior by kinship
by honorific expression toward addressee

	SSE	OSE	EE	IE	ISE	total
RE	10(58.8)	2(100.0)	4(44.4)	0(0.0)	2(50.0)	17(30.9)
RTE	1(5.9)	0(0.0)	2(22.2)	0(0.0)	0(0.0)	18(56.3)
NE	1(5.9)	0(0.0)	3(33.3)	0(0.0)	2(50.0)	3(9.4)
HE	5(29.4)	0(0.0)	0(0.0)	0(0.0)	0(0.0)	5(15.6)
total	17	2	9	0	4	32

Table 2 honorific expression from a servant to the master
by honorific expression toward addressee

8. REFERENT HONORIFIC EXPRESSION IN CHŌNIN DIALECT OF THE LATER EDO PERIOD

	SSE	OSE	EE	IE	ISE	total
RE	10(55.6)	3(50.0)	4(44.4)	0(0.0)	0(0.0)	17(53.1)
RTE	6(33.3)	3(50.0)	4(44.4)	0(0.0)	0(0.0)	13(40.6)
NE	1(5.6)	0(0.0)	0(0.0)	0(0.0)	0(0.0)	1(3.1)
HE	1(5.6)	0(0.0)	0(0.0)	0(0.0)	0(0.0)	1(3.1)
total	18	6	8	0	0	32

Table 3   honorific expression to a superior in yūri
by honorific expression toward addressee

And I try to show a referent into three groups: a superior by kinship relation (Table. 1), from a servant to a master (Table. 2) and a superior in *yūri* (Table. 3). I show the honorific expression toward an addressee on the line, and that toward a referent on the column. The number shown on each cell means the frequency by type. That is, the honorific expression by the same speaker to the same addressee is counted one case however many times the utterance occurred by token. The percentage for line is shown within the round bracket. Neutral expression means the honorific expression without either respectful or humble expression. What is common for these three tables is that humble expression is used only when the supreme superior expression is used. That is, humble expression is used only when a speaker need to show the best regard to an addressee. Humble expression is used only 7.5 percent in total. We can find out that respectful expression is used for any honorific expression toward an addressee. That is to say, absolute honorifics are the common honorific system among *chōnin* in the later Edo period.

	kinship	servant	yūri
o-V-nasaru	2	4	4
go-N	2	5	2
0-V-da	6	0	2
shiyaru	4	1	1
reru/rareru	3	2	0
o-V-asobasu	1	3	0
nansu	0	0	4
ossharu	1	1	1
V-te	2	1	0
osseisu	0	0	2
oboshimesu	1	0	0
kudasaru	1	0	0
total	23	17	16

Table 4   respectful forms

	kinship	servant	yūri
san	15	5	13
sama	6	9	2
dono	5	1	0
X-go(oji-go)	6	0	0
don	2	0	0
X-ki(ani-ki)	2	0	0
go-X(go-danna)	1	0	0
total	37	15	15

Table 5   respectful suffix

Let us check which kinds of respectful verbs and auxiliaries are used on Table. 4. Here I list the frequency by token. *Go*-N is the respectful prefix such as follows.

32. ソシテ奥様の御意に入りまして（浮世風呂、101）

sosite *oku-sama* 'RN' no *gyo* 'RP'-i ni iri mashi te

'The mistress took a fancy to my daughter.'

And, according to Komatsu (1971) and Yamazaki (1990), the following *shi* and *shit* are considered as a conjugated form of *shiyaru*.

33. 先だたした唐琴やの義理ある両親（春色辰巳之園、366）

sakidata *shi* 'RA' ta karakoto-ya no giri aru ryōshin

'My deceased parents at Karakoto-ya, whom I owe too much.'

34. おいらんがさう言はしつた（錦之裏、424）

oiran ga sō iwa *shit* 'RA' ta

'Oiran said so.'

V-te is used such as follows.

35. わしが親方の知てじや（東海道中膝栗毛、332）

washi ga oyakata no shit *teja* 'RA'

'My master knows well.'

Osseisu and *nansu* are used only among *yūjo*, and, therefore, they are *yūri-kotoba*. And Table.5 is a list to show respectful suffixes. Tsujimura (1968) says that the honorific value goes lower from *sama, san, dono* to *don*.

Now I think about the honorific words in relation with the question of honorific system, absolute or relative honorifics. Rodriguez (1955) writes, 'Only *raru* is appropriate to use when someone refers his colleague, especially a member of his family. It sounds queer to talk about his colleague, family or religion to out-group person by the extremely polite way. That is to say, only *raru* should be used when a priest talks about his colleague to out-group person'. This description may show that in/out-group honorifics are norms of honorific system at the time, but the data we analysed here doesn't support Rodriguez's description that the respectful expression toward in-group superior should be kept as low as possible. This problem comes back to a question which kind of speech level or the speech of which social class Rodriguez tried to describe. It might be reasonable to think that there was a diversity of honorific system according to social class.

Another question is how honorific system was created in Edo language. Originally Edo dialect was rooted in *kantō* dialect that was very poor for the honorific expression, imported the honorific expression from *kamigata* dialect, adopted the loan honorifics to Edo style and created its own honorifics finally. Tsuchiya (1986) says that honorific word originated from *kamigata* dialect was spoken as refined speech among *chōnin* class, and Furuta (1988) states that *kamigata* dialect was spoken among *buke* class in *kabuki* scenario. The question comes out whether the distinction was kept between honorific expression that came from *kamigata* dialect like *reru*[5], *te*, and *shiyaru* and honorific expression that was developed in Edo like *o-V-da* or not. It looks like that *reru*, *te*, and *shiyaru* are used for an addressee to whom supreme superior expression is used, and that *o-V-nasaru* is used for an addressee to whom equal expression is used, but I can not say anything further because of the limitation of data.

4. Conclusion

1. The honorific system among *chōnin* class in the later Edo period is based upon absolute honorifics. In the later Edo period when social hierarchical system is very strictly kept, absolute honorifics exist that respectful expression should be used for the superior to a speaker irrelevant to the addressee. Especially, that is clearly kept in the world of both *yūjo* that is isolated from outer world and from a servant to his master that hierarchical order is strongly maintained. We still find out the

feature of absolute honorifics when a superior in kinship relation is mentioned. But we can not ignore the fact that in/out-group honorifics also exist. In/out-group honorifics are used when a supreme superior expression is used toward an addressee. It is less common to treat a master by respectful expression toward a customer. How should we conclude the fact that two different honorific systems co-exist? In Chapter 7, I could reach a conclusion that in/out-group honorifics are the official common language of *buke* class, and that absolute honorifics are the honorific system of *chōnin* class. And some of upper *chōnin* class follow the honorific system of *buke* and in/out-group honorifics invade into *chōnin* class. It can be supposed that in/out-group honorifics invade into *chōnin* class when they should pay a good regard to an addressee in an official occasion. And one question is left unsolved. How should we think of neutral expression? That is to say, should the honorific system shift from neutral expression, and respectful and humble expression follow in that order according to the degree of regard that should be paid to an addressee? Neutral expression is used when the least regard is paid to an addressee, then respectful expression is used when a speaker should pay a bit more regard, and humble expression is used in official situation when a speaker should pay the most regard to an addressee. Or neutral expression can be used when a speaker doesn't need to pay regard so much as humble expression. That is, should the honorific system shift from respectful expression, and neutral and humble expression follow in that order according to the degree of regard that should be paid to an addressee?

    2. It is important to find out the difference of honorific value between the honorific words borrowed from *kamigata* dialect and the honorific words cultivated in Edo.

    3. Gender also functions as a factor to determine the honorific usage. Male uses in/out-group honorifics more often than female. Here I didn't analyse data by gender statistically because of the lack of data, but in Chapter 7, I have shown that female treats her superior, either by kinship or hierarchical relation, by respectful expression. This shows that in/out-group honorifics are used as a official common language by male, but that absolute honorifics are used as a norm in *o-yashiki-kotoba* or *jochū-kotoba* by female.

(Endnotes)

1 The quoted parts are shown within parentheses. The names of plays are shown and the number indicates the quoted pages of each text.

2 Cf. we mention about the term of reference *haha-ja* in Page 158 in Chapter 5. But its pronunciation is supposed to have changed from *haha-diya* to *haha-ja* because [di] sound merged phonetically with [ji].

3 This is a Japanese Portuguese dictionary published in 1603 in Nagasaki of Japan. In the Muromachi period, lots of Christian mission came to Japan for propagation and published grammar books, dictionaries and textbook in Portuguese for the study of Japanese language. These bibliographies are studied by Japanese linguists as data for the Japanese of the Muromachi period. This dictionary is translated into Japanese, and we use the Japanese version translated by Doi, T. , Morita. T. & Chonan (1980).

4 *Cha-ya* means tea shop literally, but a brothel in fact.

5 Kaneda (1952) says that *reru* was not used in colloquial expression and it still had the characteristics of literal expression in the later Edo period.

9

REFERENT HONORIFIC EXPRESSION IN THE FORMAR MEIJI PERIOD: IN ZANGIRI-MONO OF MOKUAMI

1. Introduction

How do we consider the position of the former Meiji period in the whole history of honorific expression? Before Meiji period, *buke-kotoba* is used as a common language all over Japan only in the official situation only among *buke* class, but within each feudal clan regional dialects are spoken among common people, and honorific expression of each regional dialect is spoken also. And after Meiji Restoration, each clan is abolished and prefecture is established instead. The social hierarchical order is also collapsed and all the Japanese people are announced to be equal regardless of their birth. Even in Edo period, each clan is controlled by Edo government but still got independent from central government. Meiji government pursued the establishment of a democratic country. It was urgent need for Meiji government to set up the common language that can be communicable to any Japanese from any region and of any social status. As a result, a common Japanese is established on the basis of the speech in Tokyo, and also that of *yamanote* 山の手 'uptown' where most of the inhabitants are middle class people. In Tokyo once called Edo, there are mainly two varieties of languages spoken: *buke-kotoba* as an official language among *buke* and *Edo* dialect as a language among *chōnin*. And a new language called *Tokyō* dialect is created on the basis of *Edo* dialect. There are a few factors that promote the development of *Tokyō* dialect: the change of honorific expression other than the mixture of other regional dialects and the influence of foreign loan words. Under the social upheaval that the social hierarchical order was broken and the equality of all Japanese was proclaimed, new type of honorific system became necessary and polite form *desu* and *masu* became spread out for common people. The former Meiji period is considered to be the germination or formation period. The role of *Tōkyō* dialect as a common language all over Japan and *Tōkyō* dialect takes a major role as common Japanese language afterward. Here I focus on the honorific expression of *Tōkyō* dialect in the former Meiji period.

2. Data

I use *zangiri-mono* 散切物 by Kawatake Mokuami 河竹黙阿弥 as data. *Zangiri-mono* is *kabuki* scenario setting in the manners and customs of the former Meiji period. In Edo period people wore topknot that has fixed style according to their social status. But Meiji government banned topknot and people started to cut their hair in European way. This hair-style is named *zangiri-atama*, a crop-haired head. Kawatake (1966) says that Mokuami went out to city to observe the daily events in the street in order to depict the manners and customs realistically. The characters cover various types of people from merchant, student, *geisha* and so on. I use Kawatake (1924-1925) the following *zangiri-mono* as data. The name of the scene is listed by such order as Japanese title, its pronunciation and the year of publication.

東京日新聞（鳥越甚内）'Tōkyō nichinichi shinbun', 1873

繰返開花婦美月（三人片輪）'Kurikaesu kaika no fumizuki', 1874

富士額男女繁山（女書生繁）'Fujibitai tsukuba no shigeyama', 1877

勧善懲悪孝子誉（孝子善吉）'Kanzen chōaku kōshi no homare', 1877

人間万事金世中（リットンの翻案劇）'Ningen banji kane no yononaka', 1879

綴合於伝仮名書（高橋お伝）'Tojiawase oden no kanabumi', 1879

霜夜鐘十字辻筮（六浦正三郎、杉田薫）'Shimoyo no kanejūji no tsujiura', 1880

木間星箱根鹿笛（神経病の幽霊）'Konoma no hoshi hakone no shikabue', 1880

島衞月白浪（島蔵と千太、引退狂言）'Shimachidori tsuki no shiramami', 1881

水天宮利生深川（筆屋幸兵衛）'Suitengū megumi no fukagawa', 1885

恋闇鵜飼燎（娼妓小松）'Koiyami ukai no kagaribi', 1886

月梅薫朧夜（花井お梅）'Tsuki to ume kaoru oboroyo', 1888

3. Analysis

3.1 a servant about his master

It is the addressee that determines the honorific expression of a servant toward his master. I can find out some rules, so itemize them up one by one.

① **A servant doesn't treat his master by respectful expression to an addressee that is equal or superior to his master.**

The term superior is quite abstract, but concretely a servant doesn't treat his master by respectful expression to a judge, an official like policeman, a customer, and to an addressee whom his master is indebted.

   1. (a male servant → a customer)

ただ今主人がお目にかかりますれば、しばらくお待ちくださいまし（水天宮、126）[1]

tadaima shujin ga *o-me ni kakari* 'see(HVN)' masure ba, shibaraku o-machi kudasai mashi

'My master will meet you soon, so please wait for a moment.'

   2. (a male servant → a judge)

主人半左衛門を殺害なし、金札七十円を奪い取りたるは（東京日新聞、278）

shujin *hanzaemon* 'FN' o satsugai nashi, kinsatsu o ubai-tori taru wa

'who killed my master, Hanzaemon, and took seventy yen from him.'

A male servant treats his master by his first name without title and humble expression like *o-me ni kakaru*.

② **A servant treat his master by respectful expression to an addressee that is inferior** to his master.

First of all, a servant treats his master by respectful expression to an addressee that is inferior to his master.

3. (a male servant → a rickshaw-man)

さあ、旦那様から二人へ御褒美、これで一杯飲まつしやい（富士額、487）

sā, danna-*sama* 'RS' kara hutari e go-houbi, kore de ip-pai nomas shai

'Well, this is the reward from my master to both of you, so drink over there with this money.'

4. (a female servant → a person who is indebted to her master)

御新造が御覧なすつて様子を聞き、さぞお困りなさんせうから一杯上げようと仰る故、お呼び申しに来ましたわいな（水天宮、36）

go 'RP'-shinzō ga *go-ran-nasut* 'look(RV)' te yōsu o kiki, sazo o-komari-nasan shō kara ip-pai age yō to *ossharu* 'say(RV)' yue, o-yobi-mōshi ni ki mashi ta waina

'The mistress understood the situation and said to give you a drink. So I came to call you.'

Respectful expression like respectful suffix *sama*, respectful prefix *go*, respectful verb *go-ran-nasaru* and *ossharu* and etc. is used to addressees who are clearly inferior to his master.

Respectful expression is commonly used to an addressee that has no direct hierarchical relation with his master such as follows.

5. (a male servant → a visitor)

いや旦那様は御存じないこと、私がでかしたことゆゑに、分署へ一緒にござらしやい（霜夜鐘、583）

iya danna-*sama* 'RS' wa *go-zonji* 'know(RV)' nai koto, watakushi ga dekashi ta koto yueni, bunsho e issho-ni gozara shiyai

'My master has nothing to with this trouble. It's my own business, so come to the police with me.'

6. (a female servant → a visitor)

あゝもしもし、姉さんはお参りにいつて、内にはおいでなさいませんよ（月梅薫、578）

ā moshi-moshi, ane-*san* 'RS' wa o-mairi ni it te, uchi ni wa *o-ide-nasai* 'RA' mase n yo

'Hallo, the mistress is gone to a temple, and not here.'

There is a good example that shows the difference of honorific expression between a speaker's father and master such as follows.

7. (a female servant → a stranger)

元値で親父が旦那様へお上げ申したあのかんざし（霜夜鐘、589）

motone de oyaji ga danna-*sama* 'RS' e *o-age-mōshi* 'HAN' ta ano kanzashi

'The ornamental hairpin that my father sold at cost to my master.'

This example shows that a speaker makes her father humble to her master using humble auxiliary *o-V-mōsu*, and, as a result, the speaker treats her master by respectful expression.

In total, I can conclude that a speaker determines the honorific expression toward his master taking the hierarchical relation between his master and an addressee into consideration. That is, when an addressee is superior to his master, the master is treated by humble expression, and, in other situations, the master is treated by respectful expression. It is the norm of present day's in/out-group honorifics to treat a speaker's in-group master not by respectful expression to out-group addressee regardless of the hierarchical relation between his master and an addressee. When we take the situation into consideration, in/out-group honorifics are common in official situation and absolute honorifics are used in private situation. That is, when an addressee is a person that a speaker should show his regard, the speech level should become official, and, on the contrary, when an addressee is a person that a speaker can feel relaxed, the speech level should become private.

3.2 a wife about her husband

③ **A wife doesn't treat her husband by respectful expression to an addressee who is superior to her husband, but this may fluctuate by situation.**

8. (a wife → a customer)

奥の三畳に寝て居ります（繰返、452）

okuno sanjō ni ne te *ori* 'be(HVN)' masu

'My husband is sleeping at a back room.'

9. (a wife → a teacher of her husband)

毎度丹次郎が上がりまして、御厄介になると申すこと。不器用ものでござりますれば、さぞ御迷惑でござりませうが、好きな道とてお稽古をお願ひ申しておまえ様に御迷惑をかけまする（月梅薫、737）

maido *tanjirō* 'FN' ga *agari* 'come(HVN)' mashi te, go-yakkai ni naru to mōsu koto. bukiyō-mono de gozarimasure ba, sazo go-meiwaku de gozarimashō ga, sukina michi to te o-keiko o *o-negai-mōshi* 'HAN' te omae-sama ni go-meiwaku o kake masuru

'I am sorry that my husband, Tanjirō, comes here so often to cause you trouble. He is so clumsy that you have a lot of trouble with him. But he is very eager to study under you.'

The addressees whom humble expression are used are the customer, a person to whom her husband is indebted, the landlord and etc. Highly polite form like *gozarimasu* is used toward an addressee. But a wife who was born in *buke* family treats her husband to the same addressee by humble expression in Example 10 and by respectful suffix *dono* in Example 11 such as follows.

10. (a wife → a person to whom her husband is indebted)

九郎兵衛もよろしく申しました（木間星、709）

kurobē 'FN' mo yoroshiku *mōshi* 'say(HVN)' mashi ta

'Kurobē sends his regards to you.'

11. (a wife → a person to whom her husband is indebted)

九郎兵衛殿と馴合つて、あの様な事を申しまして（木間星、723）

kurobē-dono 'RS' to nare-at te, ano yōna koto o mōshi mashi te

'I am sorry to have said you like that in league with Mr. Kurobē.'

④ **A wife treats her husband by respectful expression to an addressee who is not superior to her husband.**

First of all, a wife treats her husband by respectful expression within either her parents' family or her husband's parents' family such as follows.

12. (a wife → a father-in-law)

お話申して見ませうが、……今お書物をなすつてだから、後まで待つて下

さいまし（島衛、221）

o-hanasi-*mōshi* 'HAO' te mi mashō ga…ima *o* 'RP'-kakimono o *nasut* 'do(RV)' te dakara, ato made mat te kudasai mashi

'I'll talk with my husband about you….but he is writing something now, so please wait for a moment.'

13. (a wife → a husband of her sister)

浪之助さんが、外ならぬ病気ゆゑ、人様の前へでますのがお気の毒でなりません（綴合、588）

naminosuke-*san* 'RS' ga hoka-naranu byōki yue, hito-sama no mae e de masu no ga *o* 'HP'-ki-no-doku de nari mase nu

'I am very sorry that Mr. Naminosuke needs to come out in public in spite of disease.'

O-V-*mōshi* in Example 12 is the humble expression of the speaker to the referent and *o* in Example 13 is the humble prefix of the speaker to the referent, and, consequently, these expressions become respectful expressions toward the referent. In present day's honorific system, a wife doesn't refer her husband by respectful expression to her parents' family because her husband is in-group person of the wife and out-group person from her parents. But to the parents of her husband, she might refer her husband either by respectful expression as in-group person of her husband's parents or by humble expression as in-group person of herself. But it is common for a wife to treat her husband to any family members by respectful expression in the former Meiji.

To a servant, a wife refers her husband by respectful expression such as follows.

14. (a wife → a servant)

旦那はどこへもおいでぢやないかえ（木間星、669）

danna wa doko e mo *oide* 'go(RV)' ja nai ka e

'Is my husband not here?'

15. (a wife → a servant)

旦那どのゝ言はれる通り……一生懸命働くがよい（人間万事、22）

danna-*dono* 'RS' no iwa *reru* 'RARU' tōri…isshō-kenmei hataraku ga yoi

'You should work as hard as possible as my husband ordered you.'

To an addressee whom the husband has direct relation with, a wife treats her husband by respectful expression such as follows.

> 16. (a wife → a neighbour)
>
> 畳へ書いていやしやんす、早よう読んで見やしやんせ（繰返、506)
>
> tatami e kai te iya *shiyansu* 'RA', hayō yonde miya shiyanse
>
> 'My husband is writing something on a mat, so read it right now.'
>
> 17. (a wife → a friend)
>
> どこへもおいでになされません（霜夜鐘、470)
>
> doko e mo *o*-ideni-*nasare* 'RA' masen
>
> 'My husband is not here anywhere.'

In Example 16, *shiyansu* is used. Yamazaki (1959) writes that *shiyansu* is used in the former Edo as a female language to an intimate addressee, and continues to be used in the former Meiji. And respectful suffix like *dono* and *san* are commonly used such as follows.

> 18. (a wife → a friend of her husband)
>
> 五郎七どの（繰返、548)
>
> gorohichi-*dono* 'RS'
>
> 'Mr. Gorohichi.'
>
> 19. (a wife → a landlord)
>
> 新三郎さん（木間星、659)
>
> shinzaburō-*san* 'RS'
>
> 'Mr. Shinzaburō.'

In conclusion, a wife usually treats her husband by respectful expression to her intimate addressee like her family, a servant and her friend. But to an addressee that is superior to her husband in an official situation to whom highly polite form like *masu* and *gozaimasu* is used, respectful expression is not used.

3.3 a daughter about her parents

⑤ A daughter doesn't treat her parents by respectful expression when she talks to an addressee who is superior to her parents.

> 20. (a daughter → a person to whom her parents are indebted)

母もお案じ申し上げます（霜夜鐘、621）

haha mo *o-anji-mōshi-age* 'HAN' masu

'My mother also worries about you.'

21. (a daughter → a customer)

お袋が参つて居れば相談して、明日御返事いたしませう（島衙、453）

o-hukuro ga *mait* 'come(HVN)' te *ore* 'HAN' ba sōdan-shi te, asu go-henji-itashi mashō

'I'll give you an answer tomorrow after I talk with my mother because she is now here by chance.'

22. (a daughter → a person to whom her parents are indebted)

先日内を出ました時まで、達者でおりましてございまする（恋闇、746）

senjitsu uchi o de mashi ta toki made, tassha de *ori* 'HAN' mashi te gozaimasuru

'My father was quite sound when he left home a few days ago.'

Humble expression are used in the above three cases. And a term of reference *chichi* and *haha* is used only in very official occasion in Example 21. *O-hukuro* is used by a female as we saw in Chapter 8[2]. So is *o-tot-tsan* also.

⑥ **A daughter treats her parents by respectful expression to any addressee other than the superior to her parents.**

First of all, a daughter treats her parents by respectful expression to a servant such as follows.

23. (a daughter → a servant)

おつか様はお変わりはなかつたか（木間星、770）

o-kka-sama 'RS' wa *o* 'RP' -kawari wa nakat ta ka

'Was mum well?'

24. (a daughter → a servant)

お父さんがおこりなさるにや及ばない（月梅薫、799）

o-tot-tsan 'RS' ga okori *nasaru* 'RA' nya oyoba nai

'There is no need for dad to get angry.'

It is common for a daughter to treat her parents to her intimates by respectful expression such as follows.

25. (a daughter → her colleague)

余計な御苦労父様に掛け申さにやならぬゆゑ、早く死にたうございました わいな（富士額、532）

yokēna go 'RP'-kurō toto-sama 'RS' ni kake mōsa 'HAO' nya naranu yue, hayaku shini tō gozarimashi ta waina

'I may put my father to unnecessary trouble, so I wanted to die as soon as possible.'

26. (a daughter → her lover)

小さい時に親父に別れ、跡に残つた母さんが長煩いに当人より傍で私が痩せる程苦しむ中で死なれた故（恋闇、616）

chīsai toki ni oyaji ni wakare, ato ni nokot ta kaka-san 'RS' ga naga-wazurai ni hata de watashi ga yaseru hodo kurushimu naka de shina re 'RARU' ta yue

'I left my father when I was still infant, and my mother who was left behind died after a lingering illness worrying that she had been giving me so much trouble as made me thin.'

Parents are sometimes treated without respectful verb but respectful suffix *san* is used such as follows.

27. (a daughter → a passer-by)

おつかさんが亡くなりまして、……おとつさんが帰るまでは、お夜食も食べませんが（水天宮、57）

okka-san 'RS' ga nakunari mashi te,…o-tot-tsan 'RS' ga kaeru made wa, o-yashoku mo tabe mase n ga

'Mum died, …I don't eat my dinner before dad comes back.'

3.4 a son about his parents

⑦ A son treats his parents by humble expression when he talks to an addressee who is superior to her parents.

28. (a son → a person whom his father is indebted)

親父がお借り申した一万円のあの金は（人間万事、83）

oyaji ga o-kari-mōshi 'HAN' ta ano kane wa

'Ten thousand yen that my father borrowed from you.'

9. REFERENT HONORIFIC EXPRESSION IN THE FORMAR MEIJI PERIOD

29. (a son → a person whom his father is indebted)

父がお噂をいたしますのでお名前は承知致してをりまする（霜夜鐘、499）

chichi ga o-uwasa o *itashi* 'do(HVN)' masu node o-namae wa shōchi itashi te ori masuru

'I remember your name because my father always mentions about you.'

30. (a son → his master)

母が御礼に上がりたいと申します（月梅薫、619）

haha ga o-rei ni *agari* 'come(HVN)' tai to *mōshi* 'say(HVN)' masu

'My mother wants to come to express her thanks.'

Parents are referred by *chichi* or *haha* and treated by humble verbs *mōsu*, *itasu* and *agaru*. And an addressee is treated by very polite form like *masu* and *gozarimasu*.

⑧ **A son treats his parents by respectful expression to his servant and family.**

31. (a son → his wife)

お伝、洗つて上げたかな（綴合、577）

o-den, arat te *age* 'HAO' ta ka na

'O-den, did you wash my father?'

32. (a son → his servant)

親父様が表向きお梅を貰つてくださると、そちにお話されたとか（勧善懲悪、190）

oyaji-*sama* 'RS' ga omotemuki o-ume o morat te *kudasaru* 'RA' to, sochi ni *o* 'RP'-hanashi *sare* 'do(RV)' ta to ka

'I heard that my father talked to you that he would permit me to marry O-ume.'

Kudasaru is used.

⑨ **A son treats his parents either by respectful, neutral or humble expression to an addressee whom he is familiar to.**

33. (a son → his friend)

親父様には欲に迷い……御病死なされしゆえ（人間万事、12）

oyaji-*sama* 'RS' ni wa yoku ni mayoi... *go* 'RP'-byōshi *nasare* 'do(RV)' shi yue

'My father became blinded by avarice,...and died of illness.'

A father is treated by supreme respectful expression *go*-V-*nasaru* in Example 33, but I can find the cases that a father is treated both by humble and respectful expression to the same addressee such as follows.

    34. (a son → his relative)

父林左衛門が、……悦びまして居りませう（人間万事、67）

chichi hayashi *zaemon* 'FN' ga,…yorokobi mashi te *ori* 'be(HVN)' mashō

'My father, Hayashi Zaemon, …may be delighted.'

    35. (a son → his relative)

親父様へお目に懸けとうございます。お悦びなされませう（人間万事、94）

oyaji-*sama* 'RS' e *o-me ni kake* 'show(HVO)' tō gozaimasu. O-yorokobi-*nasare* 'RA' mashō

'I would like to show this to my father. He will be delighted.'

In Example 34 humble expression like first name and *oru*, but in Example 35 respectful expression like *sama*, *o-V-nasaru* and speaker's humble expression to his father *o-me ni kakeru* are used. And as the example of neutral expression we can list the following examples.

    36. (a son → his lover)

なにお袋が来て居るとか（木間星、744）

nani o-hukuro ga ki te iru to ka

'What! My mother is here!'

    37. (a son → his lover)

兄貴に別れてお袋と居馴れた土地の神奈川から…… 深川へ碇を下ろすと言ひてえが（勧善懲悪、138）

aniki ni wakare te o-hukuro to i-nare ta tochi no kanagawa kara…hukagawa e ikari o orosu to ītē ga

'I left familiar Kanagawa with my mother leaving my brother behind …may settle down in Fukagawa.'

A son treats his parents by respectful expression when he uses respectful expression to an addressee, and, on the contrary, he treats his parents by neutral expression when he uses impolite expression to an addressee. This shows that a son is expected to treat his parents by respectful expression to a friendly addressee but need to show

9. REFERENT HONORIFIC EXPRESSION IN THE FORMAR MEIJI PERIOD 257

some regards still.

⑩ **The speech style of the men born in *buke* family or students is quite similar to present day's in/out-group honorifics.**

Many of people born in *buke* family could not adapt their life style to newly-born social system and were ruined and their speech style is different from that of ordinary people such as follows.

38. (a son → his ex-servant)
母人が御大病とな。父が譲りの千寿院村正の刀（東京日新聞、267）
haha-bito ga *go* 'RP'-taibyō to na. chichi ga yuzuri no senjuin muramasa no katana
'My mother is in serious illness. Senjyuin Muramasa's sword that my father assigned to me.'

A ruined *buke* uses *chichi* and *haha* to his ex-servant, and *chichi* and *haha* might be *buke-kotoba*.[3] The speech style of policemen and students is also very distinctive such as follows.

39. (a son → a person who is indebted to the son)
母も会ひたく申してをれば尋ねてくりやれ（霜夜鐘、543）
haha mo ai taku *mōshi* 'say(HVN)' te *ore* 'HA' ba tazune te kuryare
'My mother always says to me that she wants to meet you, so please visit her.'

40. (a son → a person who is indebted to the son)
僕が父死去せし折は旅行中にて、母は……寓居致して居りました……昨今立居も不自由にて床に就かれし故（霜夜鐘、539）
boku ga chichi shikyo se shi ori wa ryokō-chū ni te, haha wa …gūkyo *itasi* 'do(HVN)' te *ori* 'HAN' mashi ta. …sakkon tachi-i mo hu-jiyū ni te toko ni tsuka *re* 'RARU' shi yue
'I was on a journey when my father died, and my mother lived in anoother place,…she is in so serious illness that she can't move by herself and stays in bed all the time.'

These addressees are the people who are indebted to the speaker, a police, and treated by friendly form like *kuryare,* but a police treats his mother by humble expression like *itasu, oru* or *mōsu*. The first person pronoun *boku* is distinctively use like a symbol of student. But respective auxiliary *re* is used at the same time mixed with humble expression and this sentence shows the situation that honorific expression is still fluctuating. Students of that time are called *shosei* and they are sons of *buke* family. Sons of *buke* family are sent to Tokyo to study, and worked sometimes as apprentice. Sugimoto (1967), Hida (1981) and Matsui (1988) testify that *shosei-kotoba* left a great amount of influence upon the creation of Standard Japanese. And many of the policemen in Tokyo are from the family of *buke*.

3.5 a young sister about elder brother or sister

⑪ A young sister doesn't treat her elder brother or sister by respectful expression to an addressee that is superior her elder brother or sister. But respectful suffix *san* like *ani-san* is used even when respectful expression is omitted, and, as a result, *ani* or *ane* is known to be very official term of reference.

41. (a young sister → a customer)
兄さんが売先へ、出所を聞きに参りました（繰返、473）
ani-*san* 'RS' ga urisaki e, shussho o kiki ni *mairi* 'go(HVN)' mashi ta
'My elder brother has left for a shop to inquire where they got it from.'

42. (a young sister → a judge)
父の記念に姉の所持致し居りましたるを……私が持ち帰りましてござります（繰返、822）
chichi no kinen ni ane no shoji *itashi* 'do(HVN)' *ori* 'HA' mashi taru o,… watakushi ga mochi-kaeri mashi te gozari masu
'My elder sister possessed that in memory of our father…but I took it back.'

⑫ A young sister commonly treats her elder brother or sister by respectful expression.

43. (a young sister → a neighbour)
兄さんを、尋ねたその日に死なしやんして、……持つて帰らしやんしたわいなあ（綴合、709）
ani-*san* 'RS' o, tazune ta sono hi ni shina *shiyanshi* 'RA' te,…mot te kaera *shiyanshi* 'RA' ta wainā
'My elder brother died on the day when I visited him,…somebody took it

back.'

44. (a young sister → her lover)

朝日山の兄さんが、守りに入れて居やしやんす（勧善懲悪、369）

asahiyama no ani-*san* 'RS' ga, mamori ni ire te iya *shiyansu* 'RA'

'My brother, Asahiyama, keeps it in his charm.'

We can notice that *shiyansu* is mainly used as respectful auxiliary.

3.6 about a colleague

⑬ A judge treats his colleague by respectful expression to the common people. This may reflect the social hierarchy or the trend of the times that puts the government above people.

45. (a judge → the common people)

浜崎氏がお調べあるを分からぬ詮議とは、何ごとなるぞ（勧善懲悪、257）

hanasaki-*shi* 'RS' ga *o* 'RP' -sirabe aru o wakara nu sengi to wa, nani-goto naru zo

'Why do you complain that you don't agree with that? Mr. Hanasaki examined that all the way.'

4. Conclusion

1. Humble expression toward in-group superior is used when a referent is inferior to such addressee as an officer like a judge or policeman, to whom a referent is indebted like creditor, employer, landlord or a customer. The honorific expression toward an addressee is quite polite. It is reasonable to think that in/out-group honorifics are popular in official situation even among common people.

2. The honorific expression doesn't fluctuate when the hierarchical relation between an addressee and in-group superior is clearly fixed. That is, in-group superior is never treated by respectful expression when an addressee is superior to him. But, on the contrary, he is always treated by respectful expression when an addressee is inferior to him. And within a family an in-group superior is treated by respectful expression to an addressee who is superior to him. For example, a wife

treats her husband by respectful expression to her own father. It is when the hierarchical relation between an addressee and in-group superior is not clearly fixed that the honorific expression fluctuates.

Basil Hall Chamberlain, an English man who came to Japan to give lectures on Japanese linguistics and linguistics in general at Tokyo University in the sixth year of Meiji, left a passage on Japanese honorific usage in the book titled 'A Handbook of Colloquial Japanese' (1888) such as follows.

> In speaking of others (what we should call the third person), honorifics are used only if the person spoken of is superior in rank to the person spoken to, or if he is present and, though not a superior, at least an equal, or assumed to be such for courtesy's sake.

He explains the importance of the relative hierarchical order between an addressee and the referent as a factor to determine the honorific expression.

3. The speech style of *shosei-kotoba* and people who were born in *buke* family is quite similar to the present day's honorific usage. It is well-known that *shosei-kotoba* left a great influence upon the establishment of Standard Japanese. That is also true for honorific expression. *Shosei-kotoba* is supposed to succeed *buke-kotoba*, and, therefore, present day's in-group honorifics succeed *buke-kotoba*.

4. The standard of in/out-group of Meiji period is different from that of present day. Especially that in family is quite different. In present day, the smallest group, family, consists of a married couple and a children born between them, and a wife never treats her husband by respectful expression to her own parents because her husband is in-group and her parents are out-group from her. But a wife treats her husband to her husband parents sometimes by respectful expression as an in-group of husband's parents, and sometimes by humble expression as an in-group of herself. But in Meiji period, a married couple is not considered as an independent group but as a member of big family system. Both respectful and humble expression are used to refer ones own parents to relatives in Meiji period, but in present day's honorifics in-group parents are never treated by respectful expression to out-group relatives.

5. I can insist the importance of situation as a factor to determine the honorific expression. Yamazaki (1964) states that two different honorific systems co-existed:

public and private honorifics. My data also show that in/out-group honorifics are used in official situation and absolute honorifics are used in private situation. When I investigate the honorific system of regional dialects, that is reminiscence of the past languages, I can conclude that in/out-group honorifics are not the honorific system of common people. Let us check the following facts: that in regional dialects either absolute honorifics or non-honorifics exist, that the surrounding dialects of Edo is the area of non-honorifics, and that *kamigata* dialect that left a great influence upon Edo dialect is absolute honorifics.

(Endnotes)

1. The quoted parts are shown within parentheses. The names of plays are shown and the number indicates the quoted pages of each text.
2. Cf. Chapter 8. p.231.
3. Cf. Chapter 7. p.206.

10

REFERENT HONORIFIC EXPRESSION IN THE PRESENT DAY

1. Introduction

In this chapter I focus on the honorific expression toward in-group superior of both hierarchical and kinship relation between the twenties of Meiji period and the thirties of Shōwa. But in the regional society like western Japan the absolute honorifics are still maintained, being diminishing though, and I describe the honorific expression toward a referent in regional dialects on the next chapter and focus on that of central Japan, Tokyo. I limit our focus on the honorific expression used in Tokyo after the twenties of Meiji because of the following reason. That is to say, it is Tokyo dialect that became the base of Standard Japanese that was established as a norm and the period from the twenties to the end of Meiji is considered as the latter Meiji and the term for the establishment of Tokyo dialect according to the division by Matsumura (1957). And Tokyo dialect once established as a norm gained the position of Standard Japanese, spread all over Japan through school education and mass-communication and was approved as the common language communicable all over Japan. I can trace the development of the honorific expression toward a referent by studying the honorific expression used in Tokyo dialect after the twenties of Meiji. I limit my interest upon Tokyo dialect, but we cannot ignore the social dialectal difference between *yamanote-kotoba* 山の手ことば and *shitamachi-kotoba* 下町ことば. *Yamanote-kotoba*, the tongue of uptown literally, succeeds the tradition of *buke-kotoba* and spreads all over Japan gaining the position of Standard Japanese as mentioned such as follows, Standard Japanese is 'the language spoken among the educated people in *yamanote* of Tokyo' by Jinbō (1941). On the contrary, *shitamachi-kotoba*, the tongue of downtown literally, also succeeds the tradition of the tongue of common people in Edo period, but lost its home place of speakers by tragedies of both the big earthquake of *Kantō* and the air raid upon Tokyo during The World War Two. Its diminution in present day is testified by some studies (cf., Nagata (1986) and Kokugakuin daigaku nihon bunka kenkyū-sho. (ed.) (1996)). In this chapter I treat both *yamanote-kotoba* and *shitamachi-kotoba* as the same language and take the difference into consideration if needed.

2. Data

I use scenarios, novels and movies made public after the twenties of Meiji such data as follows. The name of the data is listed by such order; the name of author, its pronunciation, Japanese title, its pronunciation and the year of publication.

Novels

夏目漱石 (Natsume Sōseki),「吾輩は猫である」'Wagahai wa neko de aru', 1906

夏目漱石 (Natsume Sōseki),「三四郎」'Sanshirō', 1907

夏目漱石 (Natsume Sōseki),「道草」'Michikusa', 1915

石川達三 (Ishikawa Tatsuzō),「生きている兵隊」'Ikiteiru heitai', 1939

石川達三 (Ishikawa Tatsuzō),「武漢作戦」'Bukan sakusen', 1939

丹羽文雄 (Niwa Fumio),「海戦」'Kaisen', 1942

岩田豊雄 (Iwata Tomio),「海軍」'Kaigun', 1942

梅崎春生 (Umezaki Haruo),「桜島」'Sakurajima', 1946

梅崎春生 (Umezaki Haruo),「日の果て」'Hi no hate', 1947

中山義秀 (Nakayama Gishū),「テニヤンの末日」'Teniyan no matsujitsu', 1948

井伏鱒二 (Ibuse Masuji),「遥拝隊長」'Yōhai taichō', 1949

大岡昇平 (Ōoka Shōhei),「女中の子」'Jochū no ko', 1950

大岡昇平 (Ōoka Shōhei),「俘虜記」'Furyoki', 1951

大岡昇平 (Ōoka Shōhei),「野火」'Nobi', 1952

野間宏 (Noma Hiroshi),「真空地帯」'Shinkū chitai', 1952

阿川弘之 (Agawa Hiroyuki),「春の城」'Haru no shiro', 1952

川端康成 (Kawabata Yasunari),「山の音」'Yama no oto', 1952

源氏鶏太 (Genji Keita),「三等重役」'Santōjūyaku', 1952

五味川純平 (Gomikawa Junpei),「人間の条件」'Ningen no jōken', 1955

獅子文六 (Shishi Bunroku),「娘と私」'Musume to watashi', 1956

源氏鶏太 (Genji Keita),「実は熟したり」'Mi wa zyukushitari', 1959

三浦哲郎 (Miura Tetsuo),「忍ぶ川」'Shinobu kawa', 1962

源氏鶏太 (Genji Keita),「定年退職」'Teinen taishoku', 1962

阿川弘之 (Agawa Hiroyuki),「暗い波濤」'Kuroi hatō', 1974

Scenario

依田学海 (Yoda Gakkai),「政党美談淑女の操」'Seitō bidan shukujo no misao', 1888

尾崎紅葉 (Ozaki Kōyō),「恋の病」'Koi no yamai', 1892

小栗風葉 (Oguri Fūyō),「予備兵」'Yobihei', 1904

小山内薫 (Osanai Kaoru),「非戦闘員」'Hi sentōin', 1904

岡田八千代 (Okada Yachiyo),「灰燼」'Haijin', 1906

島村泡鳴 (Shimamura Hōmei),「焰の舌」'Honō no shita', 1906

佐藤紅緑 (Satō Kōryoku),「雲のひびき」'Kumo no hibiki', 1907

佐野天声 (Sano Tensei),「意志」'Ishi', 1907

真山青果 (Mayama Seika),「暴風雨」'Bōfūu', 1909

吉井勇 (Yoshii Isamu),「偶像」'Gūzō', 1910

長田秀雄 (Nagata Hideo),「歓楽の鬼」'Kanraku no oni', 1910

木下杢太郎 (Kinoshita Mokutarō),「和泉屋染物店」'Izumiya somemonoten', 1911

佐藤紅緑 (Satō Kōryoku),「廃馬」'Haiba', 1911

中村吉蔵 (Nakamura Kichizō),「老後」'Rōgo', 1912

長谷川時雨 (Hasegawa Shigure),「ある日の午後」'Aruhi no gogo', 1912

中村吉蔵 (Nakamura Kichizō),「剃刀」'Kamisori', 1914

中村吉蔵 (Nakamura Kichizō),「飯」'Meshi', 1915

武者小路実篤 (Mushanokōji Saneatsu),「その妹」'Sono imōto', 1915
有島武郎 (Arishima Takeo),「死と其の前後」'Shi to sono zengo', 1917
山本有三 (Yamamoto Yūzō),「嬰児ごろし」'Eijigoroshi', 1920
関口次郎 (Sekiguchi Jirō),「母親」'Hahaoya', 1921
小山内薫 (Osanai Kaoru),「第一の世界」'Daiichi no sekai', 1921
谷崎潤一郎 (Tanizaki Junichirō),「愛すればこそ」'Aisureba koso', 1921
正宗白鳥 (Masamune Hakuchō),「人生の幸福」'Jinsei no kōfuku', 1924
久保田万太郎 (Kubota Mantarō),「不幸」'Fukō', 1924
久保田万太郎 (Kubota Mantarō),「短夜」'Tan'ya', 1925
武者小路実篤 (Mushanokōji Saneatsu),「愛欲」'Aiyoku', 1926
藤森成吉 (Fujimori Seikichi),「犠牲」'Gisei', 1926
藤森成吉 (Fujimori Seikichii),「何が彼女をさうさせたか」'Nani ga kanojo o sō sasetaka', 1927
里見弴 (Satomi Ton)「たのむ」'Tanomu', 1928
三好十郎 (Miyoshi Jūrō),「傷だらけのお秋」'Kizu darake no oaki', 1930
川口一郎 (Kawaguchi Ichirō),「二十六番館」'Nijūrokubankan', 1932
佐藤春夫 (Satō Haruo),「暮春挿話」'Boshun sōwa', 1932
里見弴 (Satomi Ton),「小暴君」'Shōbōkun', 1932
小山祐士 (Koyama Yūshi),「瀬戸内海の子供ら」'Setonaikai no kora', 1934
水上瀧太郎 (Minakami Takitarō),「律子と瑞枝」'Ritsuko to Mizue', 1934
三宅由岐子 (Miyake Yukiko),「春愁記」'Shun'yūki', 1934
岸田国士 (Kishida Kokushi),「沢氏の二人娘」'Sawashi no futari musume' 1935
森本薫 (Morimoto Kaoru),「華々しき一族」'Hanabanashiki ichizoku', 1935
内村直也(Uchida Naoya),「秋水嶺」'Shūsuirei', 1935
真船豊 (Mafune Yutaka),「遁走譜」'Tonsōfu', 1937
久板栄二郎 (Hisaita Eizirō),「北東の風」'Hokutō no kaze', 1937
伊賀山昌三 (Igayama Shōji),「むささび」'Musasabi', 1939
三好十郎 (Miyoshi Jūrō),「浮標」'Fuhyō', 1940
久保田万太郎 (Kubota Mantarō),「波しぶき」'Namishibuki', 1942
久保田万太郎 (Kubota Mantarō),「あきくさばなし」'Akikusa banashi', 1946

鈴木政男 (Suzuki Masao),「落日」'Rakujitsu', 1947
三好十郎 (Miyoshi Jūrō),「廃墟」'Haikyo', 1947
川口一郎 (Kawaguchi Ichirō),「田宮のイメヱジ」'Tamiya no imēji', 1947
森本薫 (Morimoto Kaoru),「女の一生」'Onna no isshō', 1948
三好十郎 (Miyoshi Jūrō),「その人を知らず」'Sono hito o shirazu', 1948
三島由紀夫 (Mishima Yukio),「火宅」'Kataku', 1948
菊田一夫 (Kikuta Kazuo),「堕胎医」'Dataii', 1948
山田時子 (Yamada Tokiko),「女子寮記」'Joshiryōki', 1949
岸田国士 (Kishida Kokushi),「女人渇仰」'Nyonin kakkō', 1949
真船豊 (Mafune Yutaka),「たつのおとしご」'Tatsu no otoshigo', 1949
田中澄江 (Tanaka Sumie),「ほたるの歌」'Hotaru no uta', 1949
堀田清美 (Hotta Kiyomi),「子ねずみ」'Konezumi', 1949
永井荷風 (Nagai Kafū),「春情鳩の街」'Shunjō hato no machi', 1949
三好十郎 (Miyoshi Jūrō),「胎内」'Tainai', 1949
鈴木政男 (Suzuki Masao),「人間製本」'Ningen seihon', 1949
岸田国士 (Kishida Kokushi),「椎茸と雄弁」'Shiitake to yūben', 1950
福田恆存 (Fukuda Tsuneari),「キティ颱風」'Kitī taifū', 1950
久板栄二郎 (Hisaita Eizirō),「巌頭の女」'Gantō no onna', 1952
三好十郎 (Miyoshi Jūrō),「冒した男」'Okashita otoko', 1952
矢代静一 (Yashiro Seiichi),「城舘」'Yakatajiro', 1954
田中澄江 (Tanaka Sumie),「鋏」'Hasami', 1955
小幡欣治 (Obata Kinji),「畸形児」'Kikeiji', 1956
加藤衛 (Katō Mamoru),「秋」'Aki', 1956
小山祐士 (Koyama Yūshi),「二人だけの舞踏会」'Futari dake no butōkai', 1956
大橋喜一 (Ōhashi Kiichi),「楠三吉の青春」'Kusunoki sankichi no seishun', 1956
風見鶏介 (Kazami Keisuke),「薯の煮えるまで」'Imo no nieru made', 1957
鈴木元一 (Suzuki Gen'ichi),「御料車物語」'Goryōsha monogatari', 1957
堀内茂男 (Horiuchi Shigeo),「市場」'Ichiba', 1958
松木ひろし (Matsuki Hiroshi),「娑婆に脱帽」'Shaba ni datsubō', 1958

広田雅之 (Hirota Masayuki), 「友情舞踏会」 'Yūjō butōkai', 1959

西島大 (Nishijima Ōki), 「昭和の子供」 'Shōwa no kodomo', 1960

椎名麟三 (Shiina Rinzō), 「第三の証言」 'Daisan no shōgen', 1960

寺村修司 (Teramura Shūji), 「血は立ったまま眠っている」 'Chi wa tatta mama nemutte iru', 1960

大橋喜一 (Ōhashi Kiichi), 「消えた人」 'Kieta hito', 1964

movies

小津安二郎 (Ozu Yasuzirō), 「一人息子」 'Hitori musuko', 1936

佐々木康 (Sasaki Yasushi), 「少年航空兵」 'Shōnen kōkūhei', 1936

小津安二郎 (Ozu Yasuzirō), 「淑女は何を忘れたか」 'Shukujo wa nani o wasuretaka', 1937

田坂具隆 (Tasaka Tomotaka), 「五人の斥候兵」 'Gonin no sekkōhei', 1938

小津安二郎 (Ozu Yasuzirō), 「戸田家の兄妹」 'Todake no ani imōto', 1941

小津安二郎 (Ozu Yasuzirō), 「父ありき」 'Chichi ariki', 1942

黒沢明 (Kurosawa Akira), 「一番美しく」 'Ichiban utsukusiku', 1944

原研吉 (Hara Kenkichi), 「水兵さん」 'Suihei san', 1944

黒沢明 (Kurosawa Akira), 「わが青春に悔いなし」 'Waga seishun ni kui nashi', 1946

黒沢明 (Kurosawa Akira), 「素晴らしき日曜日」 'Subarashiki nichiyōbi', 1947

小津安二郎 (Ozu Yasuzirō), 「長屋紳士録」 'Nagaya shinshiroku', 1947

小津安二郎 (Ozu Yasuzirō), 「風の中の牝鶏」 'Kaze no naka no mendori', 1948

小津安二郎 (Ozu Yasuzirō), 「晩春」 'Banshun', 1949

黒沢明 (Kurosawa Akira), 「野良犬」 'Norainu', 1949

黒沢明 (Kurosawa Akira), 「醜聞（スキャンダル）」 'Shūbun', 1950

黒沢明 (Kurosawa Akira), 「白痴」 'Hakuchi', 1951

小津安二郎 (Ozu Yasuzirō), 「麦秋」 'Bakushū', 1951

小津安二郎 (Ozu Yasuzirō), 「お茶漬けの味」 'Ochazuke no aji', 1952

黒沢明 (Kurosawa Akira), 「生きる」 'Ikiru', 1952

瑞穂春海 (Mizuho Shunkai), 「悲しき瞳」 'Kanashiki hitomi', 1953

小津安二郎 (Ozu Yasuzirō), 「東京物語」 'Tōkyō monogatari', 1953

福田晴一 (Fukuda Seiichi), 「二等兵物語」 'Nitōhei monogatari', 1955

黒沢明 (Kurosawa Akira), 「いきものの記録」 'Ikimono no kiroku', 1955

木下恵介 (Kinoshita Keisuke), 「喜びも悲しみも幾年月」 'Yorokobimo kanashimimo iku toshitsuki', 1956

小津安二郎 (Ozu Yasuzirō), 「東京暮色」 'Tōkyō boshoku', 1957

小津安二郎 (Ozu Yasuzirō), 「彼岸花」 'Higanbana', 1958

小津安二郎 (Ozu Yasuzirō), 「お早う」 'Ohayō', 1959

小津安二郎 (Ozu Yasuzirō), 「秋日和」 'Aki biyori', 1960

小津安二郎 (Ozu Yasuzirō), 「秋刀魚の味」 'Sanma no aji', 1962

古沢憲吾 (Kurosawa Kengo), 「ニッポン無責任時代」 'Nippon musekinin jidai', 1962

黒沢明 (Kurosawa Akira), 「天国と地獄」 'Tengoku to jigoku', 1963

I limit my data only to narrative parts and analyse the honorific expression toward in-group superior referent taking the relation between a speaker and an addresser into consideration.

Honorific expression can be divided into two parts: a term of reference and a predicate. Here we classify honorific expressions into such five categories as follows.

1. respectful expression (RE)
2. respectful title expression (RTE)
3. neutral expression (NE)
4. humble title expression (HTE)
5. humble expression (HE)

Respectful expression means an expression that respectful form is used for predicate like *otō-san* 'RN' *ga oideninat* 'come(RV)' *ta* 'my father came', and this doesn't exclude the use of respectful title. Respectful title expression means an expression that respectful form is used for title but not for predicate. The case that a speaker makes himself humble to an in-group superior like *otō-san* 'RN' *ni sashiage* 'give(HVO)' *mashi ta* 'I gave to my brother.' is counted as respectful expression toward the brother. It is quite often that we can find out such utterance as *otō-san* 'RN' *wo yoroshiku* 'please take good care of my father', that there is no room for predicate to express honorific expression. Therefore, we set up special category, respectful title expression. Neutral expression is an expression that neutral expression is used for both title and predicate. Humble title expression is an expression that humble title is used and either neutral or null expression is used for predicate like *chichi* 'HT' *ga kita*. Humble expression is an expression that humble expression is used for predicate like *chichi* 'HT' *ga mairi* 'come(HVN)' *mashi ta*. There was no such contradictory example as respectful title and humble predicate like *otō-san* 'RN' *ga mairi* 'come(HVN)' *mashi ta*, and all examples come into any of the five categories.

3. Analysis

3.1. about a superior by kinship relation

Let us check how a superior by kinship relation is treated. First of all, a term of referent for one's father or mother is classified such as follows; *toto-sama* and *haha-sama*, *o-tot-tsan* and *o-kka-san*, *o-tō-sama* and *o-kā-sama*, *o-tō-san* and *o-kā-san*, *oyaji* and *o-hukuro*. I classify *oyaji* and *o-hukuro* as neutral expression and others respectful titles. In Meiji period, *o-X-sama* pattern like *o-tō-sama* and *o-kā-sama*, *X-san* pattern like *ani-san* and *ane-san*, *o-X-san* pattern like *o-tot-san* and *o-kka-san* and neutral title like *oyaji* and *o-hukuro* are used. There is clear difference of a term of reference used by the social classes. Kojima (1974) mentions that *o-X-sama* pattern is used among newly-risen officials and educated citizens and *o-X-san* pattern is used among common people. Let us quote a description about the term of address or referent upon one's parents from a journal.

> We cannot find any child who calls his parents *chan* and *o-kkā* even in lower class of people. This might be the result of school education. It was common to call *o-tot-tsan* and *o-kka-san* in Edo, but there are lots of so-called snobbish gentlemen who make their children call them *o-tō-sama* and *o-kā-sama* nowadays. (*Tōkyō keizai zasshi*, 21 Aug. 1897)

The term, *o-tō-sama* and *o-kā-sama*, become very popular in the latter Meiji and a newly-made term, *o-tō-san* and *o-kā-san*, is adopted in *junjō shōgaku dokuhon* 尋常

小学読本, that is an authorized textbook for primary school published in 1904. Eight years primary education is enacted as a compulsory education for all Japanese in 1886 and the same textbook edited by the nation is taught in all primary schools. A newly-made term, *o-tō-san* and *o-kā-san*, is adopted in an authorized textbook, spreads all over Japan in company with the education in primary school through Taishō and Shōwa period. But even after the Second World War, *o-tō-san* and *o-kā-san* are not used exclusively but co-exist with other terms. Especially in lower class society, *o-tot-tsan* and *o-kka-san* are still used. It is understood that *oyaji* and *o-hukuro* are used irrelevant of the gender of speakers in Meiji such as follows.

おやじや母がただいま住んで居りますところは川越でございます（意志）[1]
oyaji ya haha ga tadaima sun de ori masu tokoro wa kawagoe de gozai masu
'It is Kawasaki where my father and mother are living now.'

This is the utterance by female while *oyaji* and *o-hukuro* are used only by male in unofficial manners in present-day Japanese. In Edo period, *oyaji* and *o-hukuro* can be attached by respectful suffix *dono* and *sama* like *oyaji-dono* and *oyaji-sama*, and therefore we can understand that they are not humble expression at all. But in Japanese-English dictionary, *Waeigorinshūsei* 和英語林集成 the third version, that is published in 1886, there is a description such as follows.

OYAZI オヤヂ　親父 n. Father (one's own)
OFUKURO オフクロ　阿母 n. Mother—one's own

Oyaji and *o-hukuro* are used only for speaker's own parents as humble expression, and we can guess *oyaji* and *o-hukuro* have shifted their honorific value.

Let us study how the school textbook taught on the honorific expression toward family member. It is well-known by the studies of many scholars that Standard Japanese spreads all over Japan and is established as a norm through school education. It is an authorized textbook published by nation that is used at the time of school education. The importance of the authorized textbook can be easily understood because almost all Japanese children studied under compulsory primary school. *Shōgakkō sahō shidō yōkō* 小学校作法指導要項, that is a guidance book for school teachers published in 1910, instructs such as follows.

An appropriate respectful expression should be used to refer the name of other people. But it is customary not to use any respectful expression to refer the name of own family or kin to out-group people.

The term 'appropriate' used here can be interpreted to the appropriateness to the social status of a referent. And *chōgakkō sahō shidō yōkō* 中学校作法指導要項, that is published by Imperial educational committee in 1933, instructs such as follows.

An appropriate respectful expression should be used to refer the name of the third person other than a addressee. But it is customary not to use any respectful expression to refer the name of own family or kin to out-group people.

And the comment on this instruction is added such as follows.

It depends on the social status of an addressee how to treat ones own family or kin. That is, if an addressee is superior, *chichi, haha, sohu, ani, ane, otōto* and *imōto* should be used and if an addressee is inferior, *o-tō-sama, o-kā-sama* and *o-anī-sama*.

That is to say, when an addressee is superior, humble expression like *chichi* and *haha* is a norm, but when an addressee is inferior, respectful expression like *o-tō-sama* and *o-kā-sama* is preferred even when a referent is in-group of a speaker.

Then let us check an actual example in the authorized textbooks. Lots of revision were done for the authorized textbooks. The following is an example from the textbook published in 1904.

私の家には、お父さんとお母さんがおいでです。おぢいさんも、おばあさんもおいでです。

watashi no ie ni wa, *o-tō-san* 'RN' to *o-kā-san* 'RN' ga *oide* 'be(RV)' desu. *o-jī-san* 'RN' mo, *o-bāsan* 'RN' mo *oide* 'be(RV)' desu.

'In my house, my father and mother are living. And my grandfather and grandmother are living as well.'

Respectful expression is used to refer superior by kinship in the textbook for lower grades. The textbook published in 1910 is such as follows.

オトウサン ヤ ニイサン ハ マイアサ ハヤク カラ タンボ ヘ イキマス。……オバアサン ガ オルスヰヲ シマス。……オヂイサン ハ イロイロナ オモシロイハナシ ヲ キカセテ クダサイマス。

o-tō-san 'RN' ya *nī-san* 'RN' wa maiasa hayaku kara tanbo e iki masu. …*o-bā-*

san 'RN' ga o-rusui o shi masu....*o-jī-san* 'RN' wa iro-iro-na omoshiroi hanashi o kika se te *kudasai* 'RA' masu.

'My father and elder brother go to a paddy field from early in the morning....My grandmother stays at house....My grandfather tells me many interesting stories.'

Respectful form for predicate is only used for grandfather here. But the revision was done in the next year 1911 from *o-bā-san ga o-rusui o shi masu* to *o-bā-san ga o-rusui o nasai masu* because predicate *shi* 'do' is impolite for grandmother and its respectful form *nasai* took place. And we can guess that the norm for the appropriate honorific usage had been still fluctuating in this time from the following passage.

おばさんからいただいたおとしだま……母がいいました

o-ba-san 'RN' kara *itadai* 'receive(HVO)' ta o-toshidama...*haha* 'HN' ga ī mashi ta

'A New Year's present that I received from my aunt...My mother said,'

Respectful expression is used for aunt while humble expression is used for mother. There is a description in the text published in 1918 such as follows.

いつかうちの　おとうさんが　道で「……」と、おつしやつたら、五一ぢいさんは「……」といつて

itsu-ka uchi no *o-tō-san* 'RN' ga, michi de ... to *osshat* 'say(RV)' tara, goichi jī-san wa ... to it te

'Someday my father called to Goichi jī-san on the way, and he replied,'

In this passage, an old man, *goichi jī-san*, who is supposed to be low in social status, is treated by neutral expression while in-group father, who is supposed to be high in social status, is treated by respectful expression. These examples shown up to here are textbooks for lower classes, and we show the literal expression for upper classes. The following example is shown how to write a letter in the text published in 1904,

父に話しましたら、……いただけと申しました

chichi 'HN' ni hanashi mashi tara,...itadake to *mōshi* 'say(HVN)' mashi ta

'When I talked to my father, he said...,'

And in the text published in 1910 also,

父は……申しております

chichi 'HN' wa ... *mōshi* 'say(HVN)' te *ori* 'HAN' masu

'My father said...,'

Humble expressions are used for the in-group superior. But the boundary for in-group-ness of this time is different from that of present-days. That is, parents are treated by respectful expression to the letter for ones uncle and aunt such as follows.

お父さんにうかがいますと

o-tō-san 'RN' ni *ukagai* 'ask(HVO)' masu to

'I asked to my father...'

おかあさんにるすをしていただいて

o-kā-san 'RN' ni rusu o shi te *itadai* 'ask (HVO)' te

'I asked to my mother to keep a house.'

Uncles and aunt might be considered to be the same group member under the big family system, but in present-days it is usual to treat ones own in-group father by humble expression to out-group uncle. In the textbook published in 1933, the honorific expression moves from *osshiyaru* 'say(RV)', *iwa-reru* 'RARU' to neutral expression as the classes become higher. We can find out the fluctuation for the norm of honorific expression toward superior by kinship relation. Yanagita (1938) criticises such as follows.

> The passage written in the school textbook like *uchi no o-kā-san* 'RN' ga nani-nani to *osshai* 'say(RV)' *mashi ta* 'my mother said such and such' doesn't conform to the rule of honorifics. We cannot find anybody who addresses in-group superior with respectful title *sama* in front of the superior other than primary schools.

And textbook for primary Japanese 7 published in 1942 explains in the chapter 'how to use honorifics properly' such as follows.

> We should treat our in-group superior by humble expression in front of the out-group person just like we make humble ourselves in front of the out-group person. Therefore, the courteous way of saying is such as follows.
>
> 父がよろしく申しました。

chichi 'HN' ga yoroshiku *mōshi* 'say(HVN)' mashi ta.

'Father sends his regards to you.'

母は、今日はまゐりません。

haha 'HN' wa kyō wa *mairi* 'come(HVN)' mase n

'Mother doesn't come today.'

私のをぢは、大阪にをります。

watashi no *oji* 'HN' wa ōsaka ni *ori* 'be(HVN)' masu.

'My uncle is in Osaka now.'

The speech above is preferable to the speech such as follows.

おとうさんがよろしくおつしやいました。

o-tō-san 'RN' ga yoroshiku *osshai* 'say(RV)' mashi ta.

'Father sends his regards to you.'

おかあさんは、今日おいでになりません。

o-kā-san 'RN' ha kyō *oide-ni-nari* 'come(RV)' mase n

'Mother doesn't come today.'

私のをぢさんは、大阪にをられます。

watashi no *oji-san* 'RN' wa ōsaka ni *orare* 'be(RV)' masu

'My uncle is in Osaka now.'

ねえさんは、お仕事をしておいでです。

nē-san 'RN' wa o-shigoto wo shi te *oide* 'do(RV)' desu.

'Sister is working now.'

	family hood	parents' home	servant	friend	superior	stranger	inferior	total
RE	8(80.0)	0(0.0)	11(91.7)	1(5.9)	0(0.0)	0(0.0)	0(0.0)	20(32.3)
RTE	2(20.0)	3(75.0)	1(8.3)	4(23.5)	1(11.1)	0(0.0)	2(50.0)	13(21.0)
NE	0(0.0)	0(0.0)	0(0.0)	0(0.0)	2(22.2)	0(0.0)	1(25.0)	3(4.8)
THE	0(0.0)	1(25.0)	0(0.0)	11(64.7)	4(44.4)	3(50.0)	1(25.0)	20(32.3)
HE	0(0.0)	0(0.0)	0(0.0)	1(5.9)	2(22.2)	3(50.0)	0(0.0)	6(9.7)

Table 1 honorific expression to a superior by kinship
Meiji period (1888–1912)

	family hood	parents' home	servant	friend	superior	stranger	inferior	total
RE	9(39.1)	2(25.0)	4(80.0)	2(12.5)	0(0.0)	0(0.0)	0(0.0)	17(28.3)
RTE	8(34.8)	0(0.0)	1(20.0)	0(0.0)	0(0.0)	0(0.0)	0(0.0)	9(15.0)
NE	5(21.7)	0(0.0)	0(0.0)	3(18.8)	2(100.0)	0(0.0)	0(0.0)	10(16.7)
THE	1(4.4)	4(50.0)	0(0.0)	8(50.0)	0(0.0)	5(83.3)	0(0.0)	18(30.0)
HE	0(0.0)	2(25.0)	0(0.0)	3(18.8)	0(0.0)	1(16.7)	0(0.0)	6(10.0)

Table 2   honorific expression to a superior by kinship
Taishō period (1912–1926)

	family hood	parents' home	servant	friend	superior	stranger	inferior	total
RE	9(42.9)	3(50.0)	3(50.0)	3(5.6)	0(0.0)	0(0.0)	0(0.0)	18(14.5)
RTE	9(42.9)	2(33.3)	0(0.0)	13(24.1)	4(28.6)	1(9.1)	4(33.3)	33(26.6)
NE	3(14.3)	0(0.0)	3(50.0)	19(35.2)	4(28.6)	2(18.2)	2(16.7)	33(26.6)
THE	0(0.0)	1(16.7)	0(0.0)	18(33.3)	3(21.4)	3(27.3)	6(50.0)	31(25.0)
HE	0(0.0)	0(0.0)	0(0.0)	1(1.9)	3(21.4)	5(45.5)	0(0.0)	9(7.3)

Table 3   honorific expression to a superior by kinship
Shōwa period before WW2 (1926–1945)

	family hood	parents' home	servant	friend	superior	stranger	inferior	total
RE	19(33.3)	1(8.3)	0(0.0)	6(3.8)	0(0.0)	0(0.0)	0(0.0)	26(8.1)
RTE	25(43.9)	5(41.7)	2(40.0)	55(35.0)	11(55.0)	20(35.1)	4(33.3)	122(38.1)
NE	11(19.3)	3(25.0)	3(60.0)	52(33.1)	5(25.0)	11(19.3)	0(0.0)	85(26.6)
THE	2(3.5)	3(25.0)	0(0.0)	43(27.4)	4(20.0)	26(45.6)	8(66.7)	86(26.9)
HE	0(0.0)	0(0.0)	0(0.0)	1(0.6)	0(0.0)	0(0.0)	0(0.0)	1(0.3)

Table 4   honorific expression to a superior by kinship
Shōwa period after WW2 (1945–1972)

I show the examples appeared in data in accordance with the period from Table 1 to Table 4. The personal relation of a speaker to an addressee is shown on the horizontal line. 'Family hood' means a case that a speaker refers to his family member, 'parents' home' means how a husband or wife treats his superior in his parents' home to his spouse family, 'servant' to his servant, 'friend' to his friend, 'superior' to his superior addressee, 'stranger' to an addressee whom a speaker doesn't have any personal relation, and 'inferior' to his inferior addressee. Uncles, aunts and a bride are included into a family hood. First of all, children treat their parents to their uncles and aunts by respectful expression in Meiji such as follows.

亡くなつたお母さまが末期の水を呉れとおツしやつた時（焔の舌）

nakunat ta *o-kā-sama* 'RN' ga matsugo no mizu o kure to *osshat* 'say(RV)' ta toki

'When my deceased mother asked to the last earthly drink,'

And respectful expression is still maintained until Taishō, before and just after the World War Two such as follows.

おかあさまがおっしゃる（お茶漬けの味）

o-kā-sama 'RN' ga *ossharu* 'say(RV)'

'Mother said so.'

But it is common for children to treat their parents to their uncles and aunts by either neutral or humble expression in present days. Uncles and aunts are considered as an out-group on the basis of nuclear family in present days while a big family hood includes uncles and aunts within in-group until just after the World War Two. The numbers on each table represent how to treat superior by kinship relation, and the more respectful expression is supposed to be used to address them. We make sure that respectful expression is used in almost all cases in Meiji and Kokuritsu Kokugo Kenkyūsho (1964) shows how many people feel the respectful expression toward an elder in a family appropriate. As a result, 50 percents of informants older than 51 years old answered that respectful expression was appropriate, but the number fell into 18.8 percents for the informants below 30 years old. And an interview done by Nagata (1988) after twenty three years gets an answer that its number fell into only 3.8 percents of the informants from 10 to 19 years old[2]. We can understand that the honorific usage within a family diminishes after the thirties of Shōwa.

There are some examples when an addressee is a servant. In Meiji period, it was common among upper class family to employ servants and superiors by kinship relation are treated by respectful expression. But this tendency declines as the time goes by. A servant was supposed to be treated as the lowest member of a family and we can find the examples to the thirties of Shōwa that a wife treated her husband by the respectful expression like *danna-sama* 'RN' *wa irassharu* 'be(RV)' 'Dear husband is here', or that a husband treated his wife by the respectful expression like *oku-sama* 'RN' *irassharu* 'be(RV)' 'Dear wife is here' to their servant. But it is quite rare to use respectful expression present days because a servant is treated out-group person.

'Parents' home' means how a bride treats her superior in her parents' home to her husband family. There is no fixed honorific expression but it fluctuates in each period. There are examples that respectful expressions are used such as follows.

お父さんやお母さん、キツト心のなかぢや思つていらつしやると思うわ（瀬戸内海の子供ら）

o-tō-san 'RN' ya *o-kā-san* 'RN', kitto kokoro no naka ja omot te *irassharu* 'RA' to omou wa

'I think your father and mother are always thinking of you.'

お母さまが「どうしたの」とおたづねになつたことよ（暮春挿話）

o-kā-sama 'RN' ga 'dō shi ta no' to *o-tazune-ni-nat* 'RA' ta koto yo

'Mother asked what happened to me.'

Humble expression is also used by a husband to mention his mother to a father of his wife such as follows.

この間のこと、ぼくは承知なんですが、母に話したら、そればっかりはというもんですから（娘と私）

kono aida no koto, boku wa shōchi nan desu ga, *haha* 'HN' ni hanashi tara, sore bakkari wa to iu mon desu kara

'I don't care about that matter at all, but when I talked with my mother, she didn't agree with that.'

	Male		Female	
	PE	NPE	PE	NPE
RE	0(0.0)	1(20.0)	0(0.0)	0(0.0)
RTE	0(0.0)	0(0.0)	0(0.0)	4(57.1)
NE	0(0.0)	0(0.0)	0(0.0)	0(0.0)
THE	2(100.0)	4(80.0)	2(66.7)	3(42.9)
HE	0(0.0)	0(0.0)	1(33.3)	0(0.0)

Table 5 honorific expression to a superior by kinship to friends
Meiji period (1888–1912)

10. REFERENT HONORIFIC EXPRESSION IN THE PRESENT DAY

	Male		Female	
	PE	NPE	PE	NPE
RE	0(0.0)	0(0.0)	2(22.2)	0(0.0)
RTE	0(0.0)	0(0.0)	0(0.0)	0(0.0)
NE	0(0.0)	1(16.7)	1(11.1)	0(0.0)
THE	1(100.0)	5(83.3)	4(44.4)	0(0.0)
HE	0(0.0)	0(0.0)	2(22.2)	0(0.0)

Table 6   honorific expression to a superior by kinship to friends
Taishō period (1912–1926)

	Male		Female	
	PE	NPE	PE	NPE
RE	0(0.0)	0(0.0)	0(0.0)	1(5.9)
RTE	1(20.0)	2(8.7)	0(0.0)	10(58.8)
NE	3(60.0)	17(73.9)	0(0.0)	1(5.9)
THE	1(20.0)	4(17.4)	4(80.0)	5(29.4)
HE	0(0.0)	0(0.0)	1(20.0)	0(0.0)

Table 7   honorific expression to a superior by kinship to friends
Shōwa period before WW2 (1926-1945)

	Male		Female	
	PE	NPE	PE	NPE
RE	0(0.0)	0(0.0)	1(3.0)	9(15.3)
RTE	3(13.0)	9(25.7)	10(30.3)	29(49.2)
NE	14(60.9)	24(68.6)	1(3.0)	12(20.3)
THE	6(26.1)	2(5.7)	21(63.6)	9(15.3)
HE	0(0.0)	0(0.0)	0(0.0)	0(0.0)

Table 8   honorific expression to a superior by kinship to friends
Shōwa period after WW2 (1945–1972)

Then let us check how a speaker treats his superior by kinship relation to his friend. We can see it from Table 1 to Table 4, but let us check it more in precise in accordance with gender of a speaker and the honorific expression toward an addressee from Table 5 to Table 8. The honorific expression toward an addressee is divided into two categories: polite expression (PE) and non-polite expression (NPE). Polite expression includes superior expression and non-polite expression includes equal, inferior and insulting expression. We can survey through all period that female uses *chichi* and *haha* when she treats an addressee by respectful expression and *o-tō-san* and *o-kā-san* when she treats an addressee by neutral expression while man uses neutral expression *oyaji* and *o-hukuro* irrelevant of an addressee.

	Male		Female	
	PE	NPE	PE	NPE
RE	0(0.0)	0(0.0)	0(0.0)	0(0.0)
RTE	3(15.0)	0(0.0)	1(6.7)	8(100.0)
NE	7(35.0)	1(33.3)	1(6.7)	0(0.0)
THE	10(50.0)	2(66.6)	13(86.7)	0(0.0)
HE	0(0.0)	0(0.0)	0(0.0)	0(0.0)

Table 9   honorific expression to a superior by kinship to a stranger
Shōwa period after WW2 (1945–1972)

There also exists fluctuation for the honorific expression in Shōwa period after World War Two when an addressee is a stranger, so we list it on Table 9. Female speaker switches two kind of terms; *chichi* and *haha* when she uses polite form to an addressee and *o-tō-san* and *o-kā-san* when she uses non-polite form. Male speaker uses *oyaji* and *o-hukuro* as well other than *o-tō-san* and *o-kā-san* or *chichi* and *haha*. *Oyaji* and *o-hukuro* become male language in this period while female also used them in Meiji period.

	Male	Female
RE	0(0.0)	0(0.0)
RTE	2(18.2)	4(80.0)
NE	2(18.2)	0(0.0)
THE	3(27.3)	1(20.0)
HE	4(36.4)	0(0.0)

Table 10   honorific expression to a superior by kinship to a superior
Shōwa period before WW2 (1926–1945)

	Male	Female
RE	0(0.0)	0(0.0)
RTE	0(0.0)	9(42.9)
NE	4(66.7)	2(9.5)
THE	2(33.3)	9(42.9)
HE	4(36.4)	1(4.8)

Table 11 honorific expression to a superior by kinship to a superior
Shōwa period after WW2(1945–1972)

Table 10 and Table 11 show how a speaker treats his superior to a superior addressee. Female uses *o-tō-san* and *o-kā-san* 80.0 percents before the war and 42.9 percents even after the war while male uses *oyaji* and *o-hukuro* mainly. But *chichi* and *haha* is used only 20.0 percents before the war but 47.6 percents after the war[3].

3.2. about a husband

	family hood	parents' home	friend	superior	stranger	inferior	total
RE	0(0.0)	0(0.0)	0(0.0)	0(0.0)	0(0.0)	1(100.0)	1(14.3)
RTE	1(50.0)	0(0.0)	0(0.0)	0(0.0)	0(0.0)	0(0.0)	1(14.3)
NE	1(50.0)	0(0.0)	1(100.0)	1(100.0)	0(0.0)	0(0.0)	3(42.9)
THE	0(0.0)	0(0.0)	0(0.0)	0(0.0)	0(0.0)	0(0.0)	0(0.0)
HE	0(0.0)	1(100.0)	0(0.0)	0(0.0)	1(100.0)	0(0.0)	2(28.6)

Table 12 honorific expression to a husband
Meiji period (1888–1912)

	family hood	parents' home	friend	superior	stranger	inferior	total
RE	0(0.0)	0(0.0)	0(0.0)	0(0.0)	0(0.0)	0(0.0)	0(0.0)
RTE	0(0.0)	0(0.0)	1(25.0)	0(0.0)	0(0.0)	1(100.0)	2(15.4)
NE	0(0.0)	0(0.0)	2(50.0)	1(100.0)	3(75.0)	0(0.0)	6(46.2)
THE	0(0.0)	1(100.0)	1(25.0)	0(0.0)	0(0.0)	0(0.0)	2(15.4)
HE	2(100.0)	0(0.0)	0(0.0)	0(0.0)	1(25.0)	0(0.0)	3(23.1)

Table 13 honorific expression to a husband
Taishō period (1912–1926)

	family hood	parents' home	friend	superior	stranger	inferior	total
RE	1(12.5)	0(0.0)	0(0.0)	0(0.0)	1(16.7)	1(25.0)	3(7.5)
RTE	3(37.5)	1(50.0)	1(6.3)	0(0.0)	0(0.0)	1(25.0)	6(15.0)
NE	2(25.0)	1(50.0)	7(43.8)	0(0.0)	2(33.3)	1(25.0)	13(32.5)
THE	1(12.5)	0(0.0)	2(12.5)	3(75.0)	1(16.7)	1(25.0)	8(20.0)
HE	1(12.5)	0(0.0)	6(37.5)	1(25.0)	2(33.3)	0(0.0)	10(25.0)

Table 14   honorific expression to a husband
Shōwa period before WW2 (1926–1945)

	family hood	parents' home	friend	superior	stranger	inferior	total
RE	1(14.2)	0(0.0)	0(0.0)	0(0.0)	0(0.0)	1(11.1)	2(2.1)
RTE	1(14.2)	1(16.7)	3(6.5)	1(12.5)	1(4.8)	0(0.0)	7(7.2)
NE	4(57.1)	3(50.0)	27(58.7)	6(75.0)	13(61.9)	3(27.3)	56(57.7)
THE	1(14.2)	2(33.3)	16(34.8)	1(12.5)	6(28.6)	3(27.3)	29(29.9)
HE	0(0.0)	0(0.0)	0(0.0)	0(0.0)	1(4.8)	2(18.2)	3(3.1)

Table 15   honorific expression to a husband
Shōwa period after WW2 (1945–1972)

Table 12 to Table 15 show how a wife treats her husband in accordance with an addressee. First of all, let us check how a wife treats her husband to the family of her husband. Kinship terms are usually used when an addressee is inferior by kinship relation. For example, a wife refers her husband *oji-san* 'uncle' to her nephew or niece by husband's position within kinship from the view point of her nephew or niece. In English also, a wife sometimes refers her husband to his child 'your father'. But in Japanese this kind of usage developed even when the out-group person is an addressee. For example, a wife refers her husband to a strange child *oji-san* because her husband looks like uncle from the side of the child when both her husband and the child were counted in a family chart. But this kind of usage is only applicable to inferior addressee, and terms like *shujin* 主人 'master', *uchi-no-hito* 内の人 'a person in my home' or first name added with respectful suffix *san* is usually used to a superior. In present days when a wife refers her husband to the family of her husband, all kind of honorific expression are used: for example, if the first name of her husband is *Tarō*, neutral expression like *Tarō* 'FN' *ga it ta* 'Taro said.', humble expression like *Tarō* 'FN' *ga mōshi* 'say(HVN)' *mashi ta*, or respectful expression

Tarō-san 'RS' *ga osshai* 'say(RV)' *mashi ta*. Hayashi (1973) reports that each family has its way of manners how a wife should call her husband to the family of her husband, and our data cannot find any historical change either.

A wife refers her husband to her parents' family either by his family name or *ano hito* 'that person'. We can find out the tendency that a wife has been diminishing to talk to her husband by polite form by such ratio as follows: 100% in Meiji, 72.7% in Taishō, 42.1% before the war and 43.1% after the war. This may be the result of the equal rights for both sexes.

A wife refers her husband to her friends or inferior by respectful expression in the former Meiji, and refers to her servant even in the latter Meiji such as follows.

さう、お帰りになつたの（歓楽の鬼）

sō, o-kaeri-*ni-nat* 'RA' ta no

'So, my husband left already.'

Yanagita, who was born in 1875, mentions that a wife used to refer her husband to out-group person by respectful verb *osshai* 'say(RV)' *mashi ta* in Tokyo when he was a child (cf., Yanagita (1938)). Absolute honorifics are considered to exist only in western Japan, but his description testifies that they also remained in Tokyo. But as times go by after the former Meiji in Tokyo, respectful expression shifts to neutral or humble expression. Terms of reference *taku* 宅 'house' or *uchi no hito* is commonly used in Meiji, but *shujin* took the place from Taishō. Miyake (1944) writes such as follows.

> *Shujin* is commonly recommended to use when a wife refers her husband to out-group person. But if an addressee is a friend of her husband, she should refer only by his last name without any title (however, this way of usage is quite new). It is also same to the superior of her husband like teacher.

The way to refer only by the last name without any title spreads from Taishō.

3.3. about a superior within a military

Now we study how a superior by hierarchical relation is treated by a speaker. The language used in a military will give us an important data for the norm of official language because strict training was done for not only a military practice but also a proper language usage. We can find out that different honorific expression was recommended between an army and a navy such as follows.

Respectful title *dono* is not used in our navy （少年航空兵）

	Superior	Equal	Inferior	total
RE	15(36.6)	2(50.0)	5(38.5)	22(37.9)
RTE	18(43.9)	0(0.0)	2(15.4)	20(34.5)
NE	0(0.0)	1(25.0)	2(15.4)	3(5.2)
THE	8(19.5)	1(25.0)	4(30.8)	13(22.4)
HE	0(0.0)	0(0.0)	0(0.0)	0(0.0)

Table 16　honorific expression to a superior army

	Superior	Equal	Inferior	total
RE	12(63.2)	7(87.5)	5(41.7)	24(61.5)
RTE	0(0.0)	0(0.0)	0(0.0)	0(0.0)
NE	3(15.8)	1(12.5)	6(50.0)	10(25.6)
THE	4(21.1)	0(0.0)	1(8.3)	5(12.8)
HE	0(0.0)	0(0.0)	0(0.0)	0(0.0)

Table 17　honorific expression to a superior navy

Table 16 shows the usage in an army, and Table 17 in a navy. The relationship between an addressee and superior of a speaker is shown on horizontal line. That is, superior means a referent that is superior to an addressee. Dual expression includes *mōsareru*, *orareru* and etc[4].

As for army, we need to add respectful title expression because *dono* is used. Private conversation is excluded from our data, and a report to the superior by military rank is done by fixed style with official honorific expression. There are cases that title reflecting the position in an army like *gunsō* 'sergeant' and *sekkōchō* 'scout' is used when a speaker refers his superior to much higher superior. And a soldier refers his direct superior to much higher commander by dual expression such as follows.

副官殿がおいで下さるように申されました（生きている兵隊）

hukukan-*dono* 'RS' ga oide kudasaru yōni *mōsare* mashi ta

'The adjutant asked you to come.'

Even among private conversation among soldiers *dono* is used to refer to their superior, and the importance of hierarchical order in an army can be understood. But there are eight cases that neutral expression is used to refer one's superior to one's men, and all of these cases are the case that a military officer refers other military officer to soldiers. There might be big demarcation among officer, sergeant and soldier. That is, an officer might refer his superior officer to a soldier by neutral expression, but a sergeant always refers his superior officer by respectful expression.[5]

As for navy, there is no respectful title expression because *dono* is not used. Dual expression is used 50.0 percents of cases that a speaker treats his superior to much superior. For example, *mōsareru* is preferred to *ossharu* for these cases. And there are some cases that neutral expression is used to refer one's superior, but this case is limited to the case when an officer refers his superior officers. There is a data on the honorific usage in an office, the same hierarchical society as a military society. Yoshizawa & Hayashi (1973) is a result of an interview study done for workers in some enterprise in 1962. Mere workers refer their superior chief to much superior head 39.8% by respectful expression *irasshai mase n* and 56.6% by humble expression *ori mase n*. Kokuritsu kokugo kenkyūsho (ed.) (1982) also shows the result of the same kind of interview done in 1972. An informant is asked to guess the hierarchical order between the two referents in questionnaire in this interview. For a question *kachō ga watashi o heya ni yobi mashi ta* 'A chief called me to his office' that neutral expression is used for 'a chief', an informant is asked to guess the hierarchical order between the chief and an addressee. 27.3% answered that an addressee is superior to a chief while 41.1% answered that a chief is superior to an addressee. The question presupposes that respectful expression should be used like *yoba re* 'RARU' *mashi ta* or *o-yobi-ni-nari* 'RA' *mashi ta* in the traditional manners of honorifics.

What is common for both an army and a navy is that humble expression is not used at all. It may derive from the concept that all the members within military organization belong to the same community. That is to say, even when a soldier refers his superior of his corps to other superior of other corps, all the members of military organization are conceived as the same member of community not his corps as in-group and other corps as out-group. And the hierarchical grouping like officer, sergeant and soldier is strongly working within military community.[6]

3.4 about a master from a servant or about a one's superior official

	family hood	friend	superior	stranger	inferior	total
RE	0(0.0)	2(100.0)	0(0.0)	8(80.0)	1(100.0)	11(68.8)
RTE	0(0.0)	0(0.0)	0(0.0)	0(0.0)	0(0.0)	0(0.0)
NE	0(0.0)	0(0.0)	0(0.0)	2(20.0)	0(0.0)	2(12.5)
THE	0(0.0)	0(0.0)	0(0.0)	0(0.0)	0(0.0)	0(0.0)
HE	0(0.0)	0(0.0)	3(100.0)	0(0.0)	0(0.0)	3(18.8)

Table 18   honorific expression to a master
Meiji period (1888–1912)

	family hood	friend	superior	stranger	inferior	total
RE	3(75.0)	0(0.0)	0(0.0)	3(60.0)	0(0.0)	6(66.7)
RTE	1(25.0)	0(0.0)	0(0.0)	2(40.0)	0(0.0)	3(33.3)
NE	0(0.0)	0(0.0)	0(0.0)	0(0.0)	0(0.0)	0(0.0)
THE	0(0.0)	0(0.0)	0(0.0)	0(0.0)	0(0.0)	0(0.0)
HE	0(0.0)	0(0.0)	0(0.0)	0(0.0)	0(0.0)	0(0.0)

Table 19   honorific expression to a master
Taishō period (1912–1926)

	family hood	friend	superior	stranger	inferior	total
RE	3(100.0)	0(0.0)	0(0.0)	3(33.3)	1(100.0)	7(53.8)
RTE	0(0.0)	0(0.0)	0(0.0)	2(22.2)	0(0.0)	2(15.4)
NE	0(0.0)	0(0.0)	0(0.0)	3(33.3)	0(0.0)	3(23.1)
THE	0(0.0)	0(0.0)	0(0.0)	1(11.1)	0(0.0)	1(7.7)
HE	0(0.0)	0(0.0)	0(0.0)	0(0.0)	0(0.0)	0(0.0)

Table 20   honorific expression to a master
Shōwa period befor WW2 (1926–1945)

	family hood	friend	superior	stranger	inferior	total
RE	3(75.0)	1(11.1)	0(0.0)	8(29.6)	3(50.0)	15(31.3)
RTE	1(25.0)	0(0.0)	1(50.0)	0(0.0)	0(0.0)	2(4.2)
NE	0(0.0)	3(33.3)	1(50.0)	17(63.0)	3(50.0)	24(50.0)
THE	0(0.0)	5(55.5)	0(0.0)	0(0.0)	0(0.0)	5(10.4)
HE	0(0.0)	0(0.0)	0(0.0)	2(7.4)	0(0.0)	2(4.2)

Table 21 honorific expression to a master
Shōwa period after WW2 (1945–1972)

Table 18 to Table 21 show how a servant treats his master or an office worker treats his superior official. Items on the horizontal line mean the relationship between a referent and an addressee. That is, if it is superior, it means an addressee who is superior to a referent. Concretely, such case as a servant treats his master to a customer or visitor, an office worker treats his boss to a customer or etc.

Three cases that a master is treated by humble expression in Meiji are the cases that a servant treats his master to a customer, and an office worker treats his boss to a customer or out-group visitor by humble expression after the war. It was common that maidservant and house boy worked in middle or upper class family before the war, and they treated their master toward out-group person by respectful expression. It is characteristic shift that a speaker treats his superior to his friends by respectful expression in Meiji, but by neutral or humble expression after the war.

It is common for an office worker to treat his superior official toward out-group person by humble expression nowadays. When and how was this linguistic custom established? Ikegami (1973) mentions such as follows.

It might be possible to find out the concrete period when such rule in an office as not to use respectful expression for in-group superior toward out-group person is established because this rule is a symptom of a group of movement that was promoted and became fashionable somewhere. …It might be reasonable to guess this rule is coincidental with the economic movement of the last stage of Taishō that each company has shift from a small scale organization like family partnership or limited partnership to a large scale one like a joint-stock company.

And there are some opinions why this linguistic custom was supported among common people. Mr. Toshiki Tsujimura insists that the criterion of honorific usage shift from the hierarchical order to the regards toward benefit or profit in Meiji, and Mr. Etsutarō Iwabuchi states that commercialism had given a fresh impetus for the conceptual change of honorifics among people. But our data shows that a servant of merchant treats his master to a customer by humble expression in the latter Meiji such as follows.

主人も早速参上仕りますのですが、色々用向きが取り込みまして参上いたしかねますにつき（政党美談淑女の操）

shujin mo sassoku *sanjō* 'come(HVN)' *tsukamatsuri* 'HAN' masu no desu ga, ito-iro yōmuki ga tori-komi mashi te *sanjō* 'come(HVN)' *itashi* 'HAN' -kane masu ni tsuki

'My master also wants to come as soon as possible, but he is too busy to come.' Neutral or humble expression is usually used in this case even in the former Meiji as shown in Chapter 9, and consequently it is easy to suppose that the custom to treat in-group superior to out-group by humble expression was widely supported in merchant society and that this custom spread all over Japan nowadays. According to my interview data for the young people from ten to twenty-nine years old done in 1987 (cf. Nagata (1988)), the number who supports the rule that an office worker should not use respectful expression for in-group superior toward out-group person is 90.1% for the youth working in the world but only 48.1% for the youth still studying at school. We understand this rule is gained by social education in the world. Tanaka (1969) that summarised the interview data done by the National Institute for Japanese Language in 1964 shows that the number who supports this rule varies according to the education and occupation of informants. That is, the number is 55.7% among the graduates of universities, 17.9% among workers who only finished compulsory education by the education, and 56.2% among office workers, 11.8% among workers in agriculture, forestry and fishing by occupation. Among companies that gain profits only through the customers' service like restaurant, hotels, shop and so on, some companies set up the training of manner of speech to newcomers, and each company prepares each manual for the manner of speech. To summarize these data, more people are started to get higher education where Standard Japanese is taught that supports in/out-group honorifics as norm, and more people are started to work for office-work that trains to treat in-group superior to out-group by humble expression.

4. Summary

It might be reasonable to conclude that in/out-group honorifics are established. And it might be also reasonable to conclude that in/out-group honorifics once were the official language of *buke* class spread all over Japan when we consider the fact that in/out-group honorifics existed only among *buke* class and absolute honorifics were used among common people. When new society was created in Meiji, we can easily guess that hierarchical order still functioned rigidly even after the declaration that all Japanese were equal for their rights. The idea of absolute honorifics, that a superior by both kinship and hierarchical relation should be treated by respectful expression even to out-group people, was commonly maintained. For example, in rural community villages are independent community of their own, and whole members of village are like members of one big family hood. And in villages each member finds his position not as a member of each family but as a member of whole village. There was no in/out-group idea developed within a village like that a family member is in-group and other member in a village is out-group.

What social change brought in/out-group honorifics to the position of norm? Some think that commercialism gave a great influence upon the spread of in/out-group honorifics. The regard for the out-group customer who gives profits was a motive for the humble expression toward a superior of in-group person. But we cannot neglect the big influence of Standard Japanese that was taught through compulsory school education. It is sure that there is very strong custom among merchants to treat a master to a customer by humble expression in the latter Meiji, and it is originated from the official language of *buke* class. But it is mainly through the school education that in/out-group honorifics spread all over Japan. Social change may be a big factor for the spread of in/out-group honorifics also. In/out-group honorifics that are based upon Standard Japanese came into rural community because the concept that whole village is one independent community has been destroyed. And the tendency of addressee-oriented-ness has been stronger and stronger in present day honorifics, and the shift from absolute to in/out-group honorifics is one of the symptoms of addressee-oriented-ness. The tendency is reported that the respectful expression is going to be diminished toward a referent that doesn't belong to an addressee. In the past it was common sense to respect any superior because all the member of community should find his relative position within a society in relation with other members. And the tendency that the respectful expression is going to be diminished toward a referent that doesn't belong to an addressee may reinforce the rule of in/out-group honorifics that in-group of the speaker side should be humiliated and that out-group of the addressee side should be respected.

I limited my interest only for the speech in Tokyo, but try to study the honorific system in rural community in the next chapter. Lots of information is reported for the decay of absolute honorifics that still remain in wester Japan, and if this tendency goes on, it means that only in/out-group honorifics will be used in Japan.

(Endnotes)

1   The quoted parts are shown within parentheses by the names of plays.
2   Nagata (1988) reports the result of an interview done on the same questionnaire as the kokuritsu kokugo kenkyūsho (1964) after twenty three years among young generations.
3   Shibata & Suzuki (1959) reports children start to use *haha* instead of *o-kā-san* from fourteen years old and have shifted to *haha* completely until sixteen. But our result is different from this report that is based on the interview done in 1959. This report says that the training to make shift from *o-kā-san* to *haha* starts from twelve years old, so our result should reflect the linguistic life before this kind of training become popular in school education.
4   Such problematic usage as that humble expression is combined with respectful expression is used in present days like *mōsa* 'say' *reru* 'RARU'. Uno (1977) discusses how to interpret this problem. That is to say, some scholar denies it as erroneous usage because *mōsu* still functions as humble verb, but other scholar justifies it because *mōsu* has changed its function into polite form.
5   Mikami (1953) writes a rule within an army that a lieutenant should refer his superior marshal to general by neutral expression. Officers might have recognised general as a rank above

themselves.

6 Kang (1997) reports that a senior of a speaker is treated by respectful expression in a cheering party of universities as well as military regardless of an hierarchical superiority between an addressee and a referent.

11

REFERENT HONORIFIC EXPRESSION IN REGIONAL DIALECTS

1. Survey of the honorific expression toward a referent in regional dialects

Fujiwara (1978) made it possible to survey honorific expressions in regional dialects all over Japan. Honorific expressions toward a referent are divided into two parts: subject and predicate. The parts of the subject that have an honorific function are the terms of kinship, prefixes, and case particles. Terms of kinship are used both to address and refer to superior kin and non-kin. It is quite common within a regional community for people to call each other by kinship terms[1]. Respectful suffixes such as *san*, *tsan*, *yan*, and *tsa* are used quite extensively. Case particles *no* and *ga* are still used with an honorific functional load, except in central Japanese where these particles have lost this functional aspect. As for the predicate, respectful verbs, such as *gozaru* and *ossharu*, and respectful auxiliaries are used to express honorific value. We can list respectful auxiliaries such as *reru*, *sharu*, *nsu*, *nasaru*, *sai*, *o*-V-*ru*, *o*-V-*aru*, *yaru* or *yansu*, all of which, according to Okumura (1966), were found in historical documents in central Japan where they were once used and still survive in the regional dialects. Compared with other basic vocabularies, the distribution of these honorific vocabularies is too complicated to help us trace their process of transmission, because these honorific vocabularies passed quickly through the cycle of transmission, expansion, loss of honorific value due to over-use, and finally replacement by newly transmitted vocabularies.

2. History of the honorific expression toward a referent based on the distribution of regional forms

Dialect geography, or geographical dialectology, which started in Europe at the end of the nineteenth century, was introduced into Japan by Kunio Yanagita who studied its methodology in Europe and applied it to the Japanese dialect. To trace the language's historical change through the geographical distribution of its regional forms, he collected dialect forms of the word 'snail' from all over Japan and charted its distribution on a map. His work justified the applicability of its methodology to Japanese dialects as well. The basic concept of dialect geography is the principle of continuity of an area. That is, if dialect form A is distributed around form B, A is expected to be older than B. In the previous stage, the old form A was used all over an area, but a new form B is created in the central area and seeps into the area where previously occupied by the old form A. The old form A is pushed outwards around the new form B in the present stage of regional dialect. Having collected data from the reports of many linguists, Katō (1977) provides a linguistic map, Chart 1, that makes it possible to survey the honorific expressions used all over Japan. Japanese dialects are categorized into four groups: A. dialect without any honorific expressions; B. dialect with only polite expressions; C. dialect with respectful expressions only for out-group members, as well as polite expressions; and D. dialect with respectful expressions for both out-group and in-group members, as well as polite expressions. The honorific system becomes increasingly more complicated as it moves from A to D. The distribution in Chart 1 is as follows: A is located in north Kantō and south Tōhoku; B surrounds A; C surrounds B; and D surrounds C. When we divide Japan into two areas, east and west, first of all, D exists in the western area and stretches to the end of the country, Okinawa; while A is located in north Kantō and south Tōhoku, B surrounds A, and C surrounds B in the eastern area. Such an interpretation seems reasonable when we apply the methodology of dialect geography—the principle of continuity of an area—as follows. First of all, C (=dialect with respectful expressions only for out-group members, as well as polite expressions) is transmitted from the central area, Kyōto, and D (=dialect with respectful expressions for both out-group and in-group members, as well as polite expressions) is transmitted afterwards. D is deemed the newest dialect only through an analysis of its geographical distribution, but philologists conclude that D is reminiscent of the old honorific system because it can be found in the old literature. There is no question that a dialect without an honorific system is older than one with an honorific system. This historical fact also testifies to the correctness of the hypothesis that all the honorific forms used in the dialect had existed in the literature of the central area. But it is still not easy to determine which is older, C or D. There is no humble form in the dialect vocabulary, and, therefore, in/out-group honorifics has developed in the central society as the official language but has never existed in regional dialects. As for the honorific system in the Tokyo dialect that was the basis for Standard Japanese, Kindaichi (1977) writes:

> The vast area that includes not only the Kantō but also Shizuoka, Yamanashi, Nagano, Fukushima, Yamagata and Miyagi lacks any honorific system and is designated a non-honorific area, according to the term by Kyōsuke Kindaichi[2]. The area where polite expressions do not exist is wider, and covers not only the area we have listed here but also Aichi, Gifu and Hokuriku. Tokyo speech is now rich in honorific expressions, but these were imported from the Kansai, for Tokyo was originally a non-honorific area. There is evidence of this in the mixture of the Tokyo dialect with forms of western Japanese such as *orareru*, *arimasen* or *yōgozaimasu*.

Dialectologists believe that the honorific system of Standard Japanese is not based upon the Tokyo dialect.

▧ dialect with respectful expressions for both out-group and in-group members, as well as polite expressions

▨ dialect with respectful expressions for both out-group and in-group members, as well as polite expressions, but the respectful expressions are not developed well

☰ dialect with respectful expressions only for out-group members, as well as polite expressions

☷ dialect with respectful expressions only for out-group members, as well as polite expressions, but the respectful expressions are not developed well

▒ dialect with only polite expressions

☐ dialect without any honorific expressions

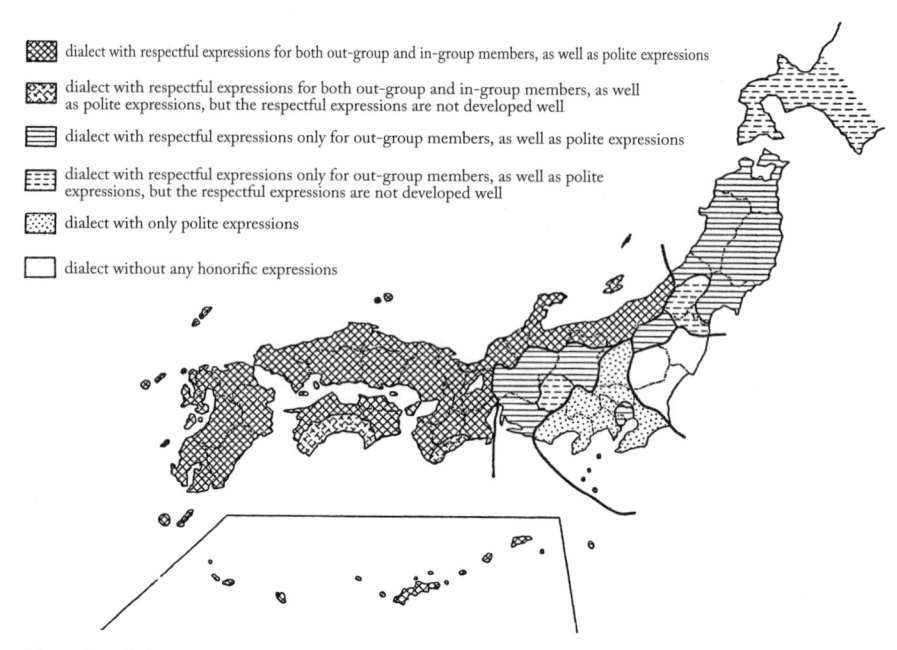

Chart 1   dialect division in accordance with honorific expressions

We can see that in regional dialects respectful expressions are reserved for awe-inspiring natural phenomena. Chart 2 shows that many dialects have respectful expressions for thunder, according to the dialect geographical study in Kokuritsu Kokugo Kenkyūsho (1967). The area of the study covers Tōhoku, north-Kantō, Tōkai and western-Kyūshū, and we can apply to it the principle of continuity of an area. The theory of dialect geography proves that respectful expressions for the natural world reflect the old sphere of Japanese language. Varieties of respectful verbs are used: *ochirasu* in Kumamoto, *oteras* in Kagoshima, *amarassharu* in Ōita, *amarasseru* in Nagoya, *osagarininaru* in Ibaragi and Miyagi, and *odokairu* in Tōhoku. The theory that honorifics originated from the taboo towards awe-inspiring beings (cf. Kindaichi 1941) also demonstrates that respectful expression for the supernatural world is a reflection of the quite old sphere of Japanese language.

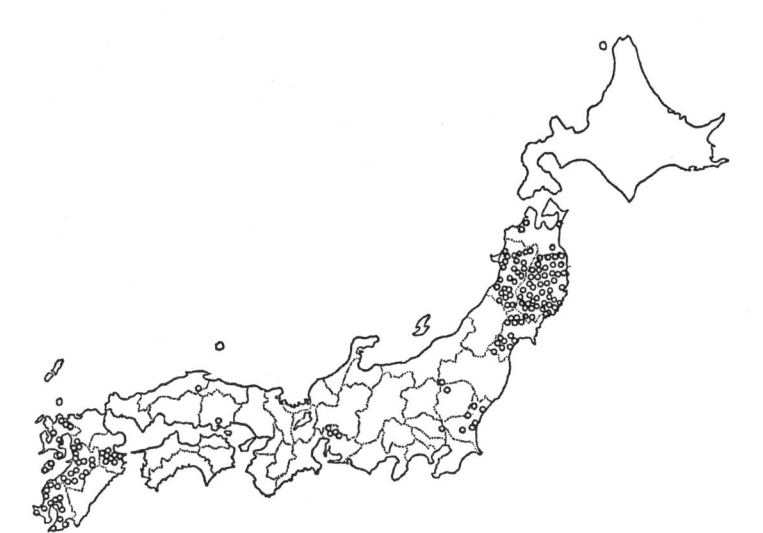

Chart 2   dialects that have respectful expressions for the natural world *e.g.* thunder

3. Respectful expression toward in-group members

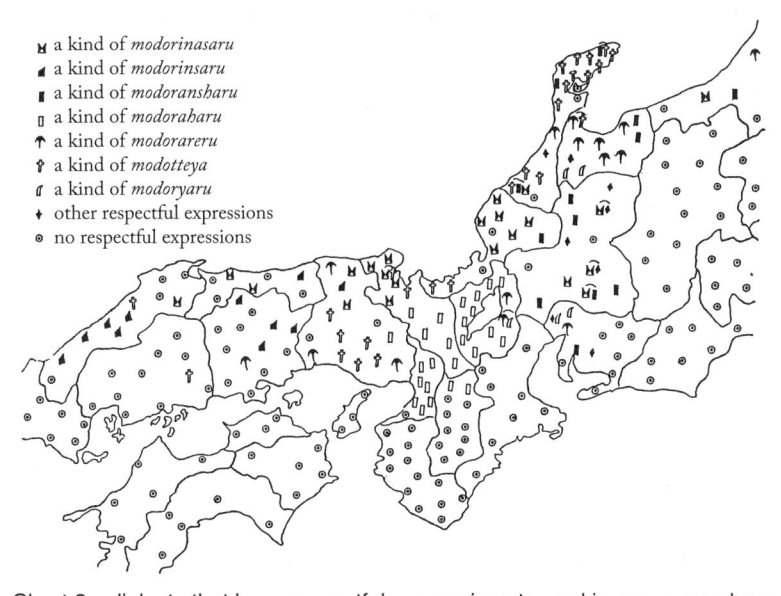

- ⋈ a kind of *modorinasaru*
- ◀ a kind of *modorinsaru*
- ▮ a kind of *modoransharu*
- ◻ a kind of *modoraharu*
- ↑ a kind of *modorareru*
- ⸷ a kind of *modotteya*
- ₫ a kind of *modoryaru*
- ✦ other respectful expressions
- ⊙ no respectful expressions

Chart 3   dialects that have respectful expressions toward in-group members

Chart 3, based on Ītoyo (1987), shows that dialects that have respectful expressions toward in-group members cover a vast area, from the Japan Sea coast to all of the Kinki region, and stretching across to Kyūshū and Okinawa. Various forms are used, but the main concern is whether the degree of respect is regulated according to whether or not a referent belongs to one's in-group; that is, whether the form to express respect for in-group members is kept lower than that used to express respect for out-group members? The range of the people that are considered part of an in-group varies from one dialect to another. For example, some dialects show respect to grandparents but not to parents; others respect those who belong to one's hierarchical in-group, like teachers. Ītoyo (1987) states that 'it may be worth noticing that considerably low respectful forms are used' on the one hand, but he also mentions that 'a respectful expression is used even for one's husband in Kansai or Hokuriku, and it is not necessarily limited to a low one. High respectful forms such as *nasaru, naharu, sharu* are also used'. According to the Naganokenshi kankōkai (1992), areas of dialects without any honorifics and those with respectful expressions toward in-group members are located side by side in Nagano prefecture. In the Hokushin dialect, the respectful auxiliary *ru*, which, according to Yoshio Mase who wrote the report, shows a low degree of respect, is used toward one's in-group and a respectful auxiliary, like *nasaru*, that shows a higher degree of respect for out-group members. But *ru* is also used to refer to an out-group person, and so we cannot judge whether or not the form to express respect for an in-group is kept lower. Kurosaki (1997) writes, 'we often find that a wife refers to her husband or to her father-in-law with a respectful expression, but in most cases *teya*, which shows not a very high degree of respect, is used'. He also states that the respectful expressions of Standard Japanese are used for referents that should be paid higher respect. *Haru* is commonly used as a respectful auxiliary for in-group superiors. Maeda (1977) believes that *haru* has already become a polite form, and Kishie (1998) finds that *haru* has more recently changed into an affectionate expression. Nakai (1997) writes, 'in Nara prefecture, *haru* or *yaharu* doesn't serve to show respect toward a referent but functions as a kind of beautified form, because an expression without *haru* or *yaharu* sounds abrupt'. Yet contrary to his statement, *haru* and *yaharu* are used as respectful language toward out-group superiors. According to Fujiwara (1978), *haru* or *yaharu* is considerably low in its honorific value and is used for in-group superiors, while *naharu* is used to a higher status referent. I analysed each form mentioned in Fujiwara (1978), but could find no evidence in any regional dialect that respectful expressions are kept lower because of in-group-ness.

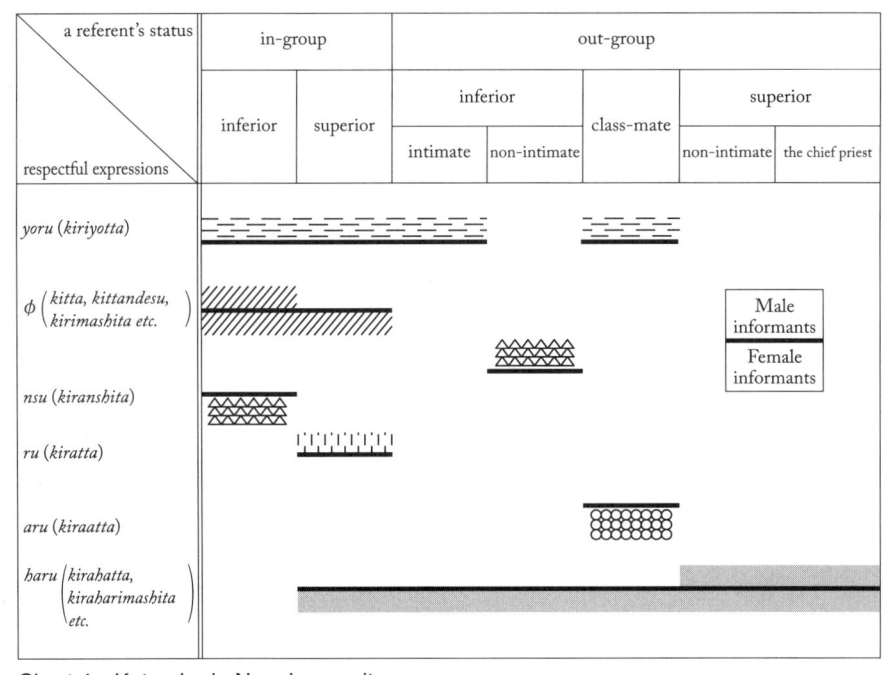

Chart 4   Kata-cho in Nagahama city

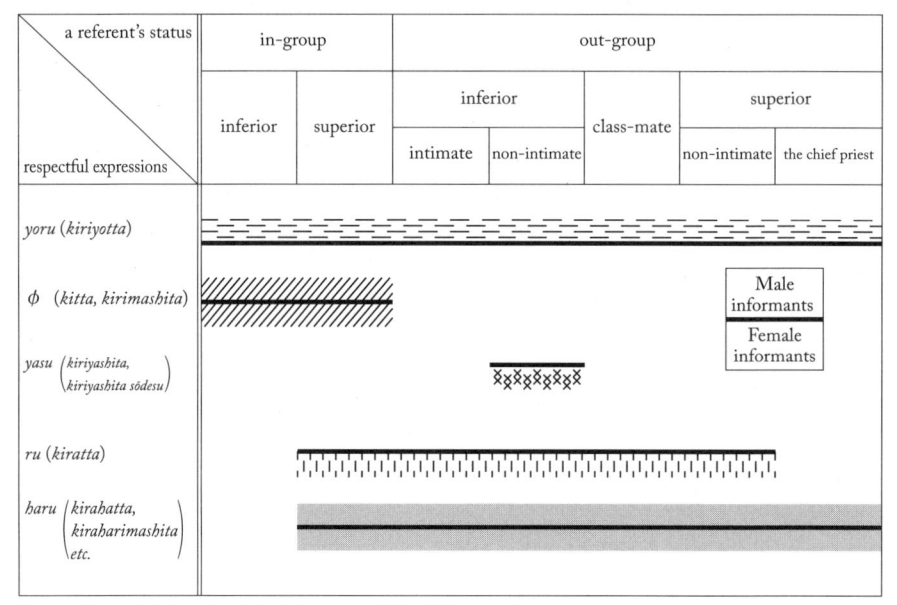

a referent's status	in-group		out-group				
	inferior	superior	inferior		class-mate	superior	
respectful expressions			intimate	non-intimate		non-intimate	the chief priest
yoru (*kiriyotta*)							
ϕ (*kitta, kirimashita*)						Male informants	
yasu (*kiriyashita, kiriyashita sôdesu*)						Female informants	
ru (*kiratta*)							
haru (*kirahatta, kiraharimashita etc.*)							

Chart 5　neighbouring Torii honmachi in Hikone city

There are, however, differences from one region to another in regard to respectful expressions toward one's in-group. According to a survey in the Lake Biwa region (Shimono, 1995), there still exist variations by region and gender among the elder generation who have maintained the traditional honorific system. Chart 4 and 5 show a variation of verbal form of 'cut' in the expression 'A referent cut his finger with a knife' according to the referent's status. That is, in Chart 4 (Kata-cho in Nagahama city), men differentiate their respectful expressions according to a referent's status: *ru* to in-group superiors, *haru* to out-group superiors, and *yoru* to inferiors; while women use *haru* to refer to many referents. In Chart 5 (neighbouring Torii honmachi in Hikone city), men treat in-group superiors with *haru* within the family, but adopt neutral expressions to out-group addressees. Women present a different usage of the honorific expression: *ru* is used to any intimate addressee, whether in-group or out-group, while *haru* is used to an unfamiliar out-group addressee. *Haru*'s honorific value shifts to the polite form because it is used to speak of an in-group superior to someone that a speaker needs to address politely.

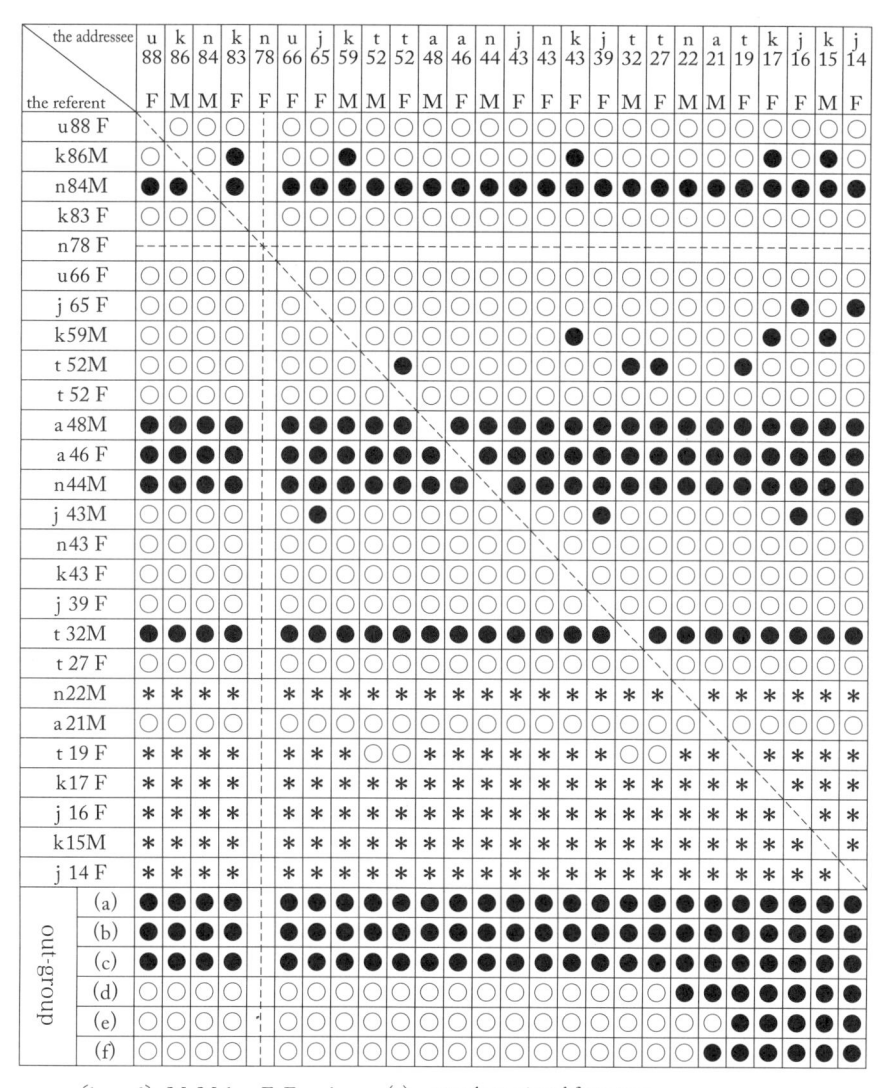

11. REFERENT HONORIFIC EXPRESSION IN REGIONAL DIALECTS   301

[legend] M Male   F Female
● *ikas · sat · ta*
○ *ik · kya · ta*
* *it · ϕ · ta*

(a) a teacher assigned from town
(b) a priest coming from neighboring village
(c) a priest coming from town
(d) a tofu seller coming from neighboring village
(e) a peddler of medicine coming from town
(f) a bill collector coming from neighboring village

Chart 6   Maki Gokagō Ecchū in Hokuriku

Sanada (1973) is a report of an interview done in Maki Gokagō Ecchū in Hokuriku where the respectful expression toward one's in-group remains. Chart 6 shows how a 78 year old woman (n78F in Chart 6) expresses the behaviour 'go' of each member of her village to the other members. Maki is a small village with only six families of 27 people, who we will name all the villagers X1, X2, ... X27. The 78 years old woman talks about their behaviour as 'X1 goes' to X2, X3, ... X27, and 'X2 goes' to X1, X3, ... X27. The verb 'go' has three honorific gradations, from the highest *ikas-saru*, *ika-reru* and *iku*. Chart 6 shows that the honorific expression toward each villager does not change according to the addressee. The code for each villager shows the family name, age and gender respectively. The respondent belongs to family 'n', and uses respectful expressions to speak of her family members to other villagers. In Maki village the honorific expression toward a village member is determined by the rank of each family-hood. The head family, 'n', is ranked the highest, and its branch families, 'a', 't' and 'u', are ranked next, with independent families, 'j' and 'k', ranked the lowest. Consequently, any person who belongs to a family that ought to be treated by the highest honorific *ikas-saru* is so treated by any villager—whether in-group or out-group—speaking with any other villager.

Next, we will look at the results of interviews conducted in Ōsato in Okinawa (cf. Nagata, 1996), another area where a respectful expression toward an in-group member is used. Chart 7 shows the results focused on 'come' of 'my father comes' in accordance with the situation. In Okinawa nowadays, Standard Japanese is taking the place of regional dialect. That is, the old and middle-aged villagers are bilingual between Standard Japanese and regional dialect, but the young villagers turned to a monolingual of Standard Japanese as a result of language contact. In regional dialect, the verb 'come' has the following variations based on the degree of respect to be accorded: the highest is *mensēn*, next is *mēn*, and last is the neutral *chūn*. The polite form is expressed by adding *bin*. The following variants are used as Standard Japanese forms: the highest respectful verb is *irassharu*, the next is *mieru*, the neutral form is *kuru*, and the humble form is *mairu*. The polite form is expressed by adding *masu*. In the gender column, M and F means male and female respectively. Chart 7 shows that *mensēn* is commonly used among those in their eighties, and still used by those in their seventies and late sixties. But use of *mensēn* starts to fluctuate in one's early sixties, and is used only when an addressee is superior and on an official occasion. Some informants in their sixties report, '*mensēn* is a polite form to be used only to superior addressees' and we can understand that this polite form begins to be used in middle age. There is no informant under forty who uses *mensēn*, and some indicate that it is erroneous to use it. 37F uses the humble form *mairi-masu*, which is a humble form of Standard Japanese. The chart shows the declining use of respectful expressions toward members of an in-group. Sanada (1973) also demonstrates that respectful expressions toward one's in-group remain till middle age, but the younger generation treats their in-group with the neutral expression *it-ta*. According to Sanada (1983), the results of interviews repeated after ten years using the same methodology show that the honorific system based upon family rank has already collapsed.

304

11. REFERENT HONORIFIC EXPRESSION IN REGIONAL DIALECTS   305

[situation]
A–1 To a tourist from mainland
B–1 To a native-born old officer at a local office
B–2 To a native-born middle-aged officer at a local office
B–3 To a native-born young officer at a local office
C–1 To a native-born old villager who is not familiar
C–2 To a native-born middle-aged villager who is not familiar
C–3 To a native-born young male villager who is not familiar
C–4 To a native-born young female villager who is not familiar
D–1 To an intimate old villager at an official local meeting
D–2 To an intimate middle-aged villager at an official local meeting
D–3 To an intimate young male villager at an official local meeting
D–4 To an intimate young female villager at an official local meeting
D–5 To an intimate elder villager of the same generation at an official local meeting
D–6 To an intimate younger villager of the same generation at an official local meeting
E–1 To a parent (for a middle-aged informant) or a grandparent (for a young informant) at home
E–2 To a child (for an old informant) or a parent (for a young informant) at home
E–3 To a grandchild (for an old informant) or a child (for a middle-aged informant) at home
E–4 To a elder brother or sister at home
E–5 To a younger brother or sister at home
F–1 To an intimate friend in a relaxing situation

[legend]
M   Male   F   Female
●   mensebin
○   mensēn
◐   mēbin
✚   irassbaimasu
✛   mieru / trassbaru
∨   ujbyn / chabin
✕   kimasu
□   kuru
·
✹   mairimasu

Chart 7 Ōsato in Okinawa

Where should we locate the respectful expression toward an in-group in regional dialects, in the context of the whole Japanese honorific system? In most cases, the use of respectful expressions toward one's in-group is reminiscent of the absolute honorifics that existed in ancient Japanese, and is a distinctive feature of regional dialects, unlike the in/out-group honorific system of Standard Japanese where an in-group referent is treated with a humble expression. It is the reason why the term "respectful expression toward in-group" draws attention, but essentially the honorific expression in regional dialects is determined by the status of a referent within a regional community. In urban society, a family is a group composed of family members, and the community other than one's own family stands as an out-group. But in rural society, a community is composed of all the villagers, who are all members of one group. Consequently, any member of a rural community is an in-group member of village society; therefore, all in-group members of a family should be treated according to their position within the rural community. In the village of Ōsato, hierarchy by seniority is strongly maintained, and any old person should be treated with a respectful expression. In-group elders are also elders from the viewpoint of the other members in the same village, and it is a matter of course that they are referred to with respectful expressions to any of the villagers.

According to Shibata (1978), all the residents of Machino-chō in Ishikawa prefecture call each other by terms of kin, according to their positions in their own family. For example, the head of a family is addressed by the kinship term for father not only by his family but also by other members in his village, because a father is expected to play the role of the head of a family in traditional Japanese rural society. This rule applies not only to the head of a family but also to all member of this village; for example, a wife or the parents of the head of a family. In urban society also, people are called by kinship terms like *oji-san* or *o-nī-san*, according to their seniority and level of intimacy. In Machino-chō the distinction of kinship terms is determined by the rank of each family as well. Still using as an example the head of a family, five categories are listed from the lowest family's rank to the highest: A. *pappa, chāchā* and *chā*; B. *tōto* and *tot-tsama*; C. *o-toto*; D. *o-toto-sama* and *oyas-sama*; E. *danna-sama*. This classification can also be considered as an honorific system in which the term of address or reference is determined by a family's rank within the village. These are absolute honorifics in which the honorific expression is determined by age in Ōsato and by a family's rank in Machino-chō.

What to think about the phenomena that respectful expressions toward in-group superiors are kept lower than those for out-group superiors or addressees? Miyaji (1987) tells us about the existence of words in Kansai dialects that are only used for a referent; for example, in Shiga prefecture *ru* and *raru* are mainly used to refer to a third person. We can explain why words that are only used to refer to a referent can exist on the base of historical data in the following way. By examining the historical data, we can see that words to express respect have been quite quick to shift. That is, when a new word is first introduced, it is used to show a high degree of respect, but once it becomes popular, it loses its original nuance, and is replaced by a new word. The old word is still used, but only to refer to a person who is not present, because people hesitate to use a word with a spent meaning to an addressee who participates in a conversation. Similarly, words used to refer only to status inferiors should not be used to refer to any addressee who is present but remain to be used to refer to a person who is not present. According to Miyaji (1987), *ru* and *raru* are used to refer to superiors, and *yoru* is used to refer to inferiors. It is quite interesting that *ru* and *raru* are mainly used to refer to the father of a speaker.

When we survey some regional dialects, we find that both kinds of dialects co-exist: those with words to express a lower degree of respect toward in-group than out-group referents or addressees; and dialects that don't show that kind of tendency. We also find that dialects in urban areas exhibit lower-key respectful expressions toward in-group members than toward out-group referents or addressees, unlike dialects in rural areas where tight-knit communities maintain conservative values. This may reflect the difference in consciousness between in-group and out-group. All villagers belong to one in-group and so it is appropriate to treat superiors within one's 'family' with a respectful expression. But in urban areas where community cohesion is already lost, a speaker keeps the respectful expression toward in-group members lower than toward out-group referents or addressees. This compromise lessens the conflict between two contradictory systems: one in which superiors must be treated with respectful expressions, and one in which in-group referents should not be treated with respectful expressions to out-group addressees. This tendency has been gathering power, and it is reported from various regions that respectful expressions toward those belonging to one's in-group will disappear. This phenomenon should be interpreted as the decline of the rural community. As the wave of standardized Japanese spreads all over Japan, one also finds that in many parts of the country the honorific system of Standard Japanese is used in circumstances where one needs to show the highest respect, displacing the regional colloquial honorific system. As a consequence, in some areas where respectful expression toward an in-group still co-exists with Standard Japanese, it is kept lower than that toward out-group referent or an addressee.

(Endnotes)

1 Nihon Hōgen Kenkyū-kai (1978) summarizes the terms of kinship used all over Japan and Kokuritsu Kokugo Kenkyūsho (1979) describes them in detail.

2 Kindaichi (1959) believes the honorific system may have initiated in any one of the ancient Japanese dialects, but shifted into a non-honorific situation in these areas. Kōyō Yamaguchi taught me that, in non-honorific areas, every member talks with each other equally, regardless of the difference in gender and age.

12

CONCLUSION

1. The shift in the honorific system used toward a referent

Surveying the history of the use of honorific expressions toward a referent, there is no definite way of knowing about any honorific system of prehistoric times; however, by interpreting the distribution of honorific expression through dialect geography, we can conclude that there were no honorifics in the oldest stage—at least not in the language spoken by the common people. Kindaichi (1941) argues that the origin of honorific expression toward a referent is predicated on the taboos and superstitions associated with the supernatural and beings of the spirit world. The following may substantiate this hypothesis: in peripheral areas respectful expressions for supernatural beings still survive in present day dialects, and many still believe that word is itself a spirit. Euphemisms for awesome or frightening existence are also extant in either historical literature or in some dialects. Context is the determining factor for the usage of honorifics. According to Tsujimura (1989), honorifics were originally humble prayers to a god or an emperor—in a formal setting like the imperial court—which subsequently developed and became part of official usage in common society. Kindaichi (1941) further states that absolute honorifics were the next evolutionary stage after the period of taboo.

I chose *Genji-Monogatari* as the oldest possible source of colloquial expression, and defined the honorific system functioning therein as status honorifics, whereby an honorific expression toward a referent is determined by the status of the referent. A speaker determines the honorific expression toward a referent based on their relationship, but the position of the addressee is also an important factor. That is, an honorific expression toward a referent is determined by the complex relationship that comprises speaker, addressee and referent. If all three members are part of one family, the honorific expression toward the referent is determined by his position within the family. If, on the other hand, all three members constitute an hierarchical society, the honorific expression is determined by the referent's position within that society. For example, the honorific expression that a father uses to speak of his son changes according to the status of the person he is addressing. If the addressee is his wife—that is, the mother of his son—their son is treated with a humble expression on the basis that the son is inferior within the family-hood. But if the addressee is their servant, the son is treated with a respectful expression because the son's hierarchical status places him above the addressee, his servant. Social status, too, plays an important function in the triad of speaker, addressee and referent. For example, when a son becomes a noble person such as an emperor, he is treated with a respectful expression even by his father. As emperor, the son's social status overrides his kinship position as son. In this case, the term 'status' includes kinship, hierarchical and social status. The honorific system in *Genji-Monogatari* is not absolute honorifics because we cannot ignore the role that an addressee plays in determining honorific expression. But the honorific system used by commoners of that time is absolute honorifics, and so there must have existed two types of honorific systems: public and private honorifics.

Heike-Monogatari was used as a source for the Kamakura period and I have defined the honorific system functioning therein as hierarchical honorifics, whereby an honorific expression toward a referent is determined by the hierarchical order between a referent and an addressee. That is, a speaker may moderate his use of a respectful expression toward his superior referent if the addressee is superior to the referent. In *Genji-Monogatari*, a servant always treats his master with a respectful expression to all addressees, but in *Heike-Monogatari* a servant refrains from using a respectful expression for his master if an addressee is superior to his master. In this sense, the position of an addressee plays a more important role in hierarchical than in status honorifics. Matsui (1974) presents the following example of hierarchical honorifics from an historical document that reveals the etiquette of the *buke* class. In *Shakkanki*, one is advised to treat one's parents with a humble expression: 'in front of noble people, it is better to refer to parents as *oyaja-mono*, instead of calling them by name'. *Buzakki* recommends treating one's master by his title and the humble verb *mōsu*, instead of using a respectful expression containing words of Chinese origin: 'Don't mention your master by his Chinese name when you are sent to another house as a messenger. To make your master humble to your addressee use a humiliative form such as *jibushō* 'TN' *mōse* 'say (HV)' *to mōshi* 'say (HV)' *sōrō* — '*jibushō* ordered me to tell you'. But in *Heike-Monogatari* also, when a referent's social status is extremely high, he is treated with a respectful expression by his kinship superiors. We find many examples where a retired emperor treats his son, the present emperor, with exalting speech. In this sense, the honorific system of an earlier time, status honorifics, still endures during the period depicted in *Heike-Monogatari*. But when we consider that, even today, the empress treats the emperor with a respectful expression in official situations, honorific usage by the imperial family should be counted as an exception to the norms of society at large. The official honorific system of hierarchical honorifics, used by the *buke* in *Heike-Monogatari*, succeeded the language of the *kuge*. It should be noted that the *buke*'s language was a vulgar one, before they rose from their lowly position as military guards of the *kuge*. In *Heike-Monogatari*, we saw how the *buke* Yoshinaka Kiso was laughed at by aristocrats because of his vulgar speech and behaviour. But the *buke* created their own manners based on the ancient practices and customs of the aristocratic *kuge*, and we can reasonably hypothesize that after they gained power and succeeded the *kuge*, their official language was that which had belonged to the *kuge*. As the warrior Kiyomori married his daughter into the imperial family after he took the reigns of power, the *buke* owed much to the *kuge* for their manners and customs

In examining *Toraaki's kyōgen* plays set in the Muromachi period, it appears that respect for an addressee had gained more prominence and the addressee had greater importance. When addressing someone superior to a superior referent a speaker uses either a mixed expression , such as *mōsaru*, which falls between the humble and the respectful or the lowly respectful expression *raru*. But the hierarchical order between a speaker and a referent is still important. There were some examples of an inferior referent being treated with a humble expression even to the wife of the referent, and also of a wife treating her husband with a respectful expression of low honorific register. *Toraaki's* plays are good sources for the language of the common people, but for examples of the official language I examined the *Shōkaishingo*, a Japanese textbook published for Korean learners. Continually revised over a period of more than one hundred and fifty years, through it we can therefore trace the changes in the honorific expressions used in official Japanese. Not only do we find that regard for an addressee continued to rise in importance, but also that the incipient stage of in/out-group honorifics can be detected. An inferior referent is now treated with a respectful expression of low degree if he belongs to an addressee's in-group, as is a superior referent who belongs to a speaker's in-group. The criterion of whether or not a referent belongs to one's in-group has become an important determinant of the honorific expression. The concept of in/out-groupness would never have taken hold without the social organisational concept of *uchi* 家, 'household', which unites its members in solidarity against an out-group. The smallest unit of *uchi* is the family, whose members all live in the same house, and the largest unit is the feudal clan of the *buke* class, whose members all earn their living under one feudal lord. *Uchi* can assert its existence only in opposition to an out-group. The term 家 was originally pronounced *ie*—meaning physical existence—but gradually came to be pronounced *uchi*, and later developed to indicate abstract existence, such as a household or family. It was in the early Edo period that the social organization of *uchi* was created. Sakakura & Asami (1996) show that there was a term called *uchi* even in the Nara period, but that its meaning was 'inside the house', and it was not until after the Kamakura period that the meaning changed to social organization.

Looking at *kyōgen* and *jōruri* of domestic plays in the *kamigata* dialect as sources for the early Edo period, a great deal of variation in the honorific expression was found, based on social factors like class or gender. Men of *buke* class treat their in-group superiors by humble expression in official situations, while *chōnin* or women of *buke* class treat their in-group superiors by respectful expression. A humble expression would also be used by a *chōnin* when speaking of his master to an addressee who belongs to the *buke* class, hence the *chōnin* also mastered the official honorific system of the *buke* class. Summarizing these cases, in/out-group honorifics were used on official occasions, but only by men of *buke* class. Women always used a respectful expression to refer to superiors, and absolute honorifics were used in a private setting regardless of social class and gender.

In the late Edo period, there is a decrease in sources of the *kamigata* dialect and a proliferation of material containing the dialect of the city of Edo. Plays, such as the *ki-zewa-mono* of Nanboku, and the literary genres of *share-bon, kokkei-bon and ninjō-bon*—all show that in/out-group honorifics were established as the official language of the *buke* class. Men of this class treat members of their in-group, whether a superior by kinship or hierarchy, with a neutral or humble expression when talking to an out-group member in an official situation. However, when addressing a *chōnin*, they use a respectful expression. This tells us that in/out-group honorifics were part of an official honorific system only used for an addressee to whom a speaker needed to pay the highest respect. *Chōnin* or *buke* women treated in-group superiors by respectful expression in any circumstances. Honorific words did not exist in the Edo dialect originally and were mostly borrowed from the *kamigata* dialect. In/out-group honorifics spread into the *chōnin* class and were also used by them only in an official context such as when talking to *buke*. In surveying the history of women's official language, we find it within the inner chambers of the shogunal palace as *nyōbō-kotoba*, which had been the elegant speech of noble women at the royal court; as *o-yashiki-kotoba*, it spread among female servants who worked in *buke* families; and as *jochū-kotoba*, it also became the province of *chōnin* class women.

At the beginning of the Meiji period, the social hierarchical system by birth collapsed and all Japanese became equal by law. In the plays, or *zangiri-mono* by Kawatake Mokuami, I find that in/out-group honorifics were used among students and officers who were ex-*buke*. We also find that the criterion of the honorific system shifts from social hierarchical order to monetary debt or psychological favour. For example, a merchant speaks of his master to a customer using a humble expression. But among commoners absolute honorifics are still prevalent. I examined films, novels and plays in order to trace the shifting honorific system up to the present day. There were significant changes after the defeat of World War Two. Through the occupation policy of the U.S.A. equal rights for both sexes, and democracy, were brought into Japan. In/out-group honorifics spread all over Japan through the education system. If we follow the trajectory of the revisions made to authorized school textbooks, we can see the controversies and debates that took place over proper honorific usage. Once in/out-group honorifics were adopted as the norm in school textbooks, they spread all over Japan because the percentage of school attendance was remarkably high. In 1925, radio broadcasting commenced and all Japanese had the opportunity to listen to the same language. Ten years later, Standard Japanese, based on the Tokyo dialect, was approved as the appropriate language for broadcasting by the NHK committee (the national broadcaster), and its honorific system spread all over Japan through the new medium. If we look at the research on dialects, we can ascertain that absolute honorifics are still used in many regional dialects. However, the tendency since World War Two has been for regional Japanese dialects to disappear, with the increasing popularity of the in/out-group honorifics of Standard Japanese. After the Meiji period, this honorific system became popular among merchants as a proper way to speak to a customer. With a large number of the population engaged in commercial activities we cannot ignore that in/out-group honorifics has spread in tandem with its continued growth. In summary, the official honorific system prevalent today spread in the following process. First of all, *buke* speech succeeded the language of the aristocratic *kuge*, and it was adopted as the norm during the Meiji period when Standard Japanese spread throughout Japan through school education and broadcasting. As an honorific system, the historical development of addressee-oriented-ness follows the shift from status, to hierarchical, and finally to in/out-group honorifics. Absolute honorifics were commonly used in private language, and the common people used absolute honorifics in private situations. There are many areas where honorifics do not exist in the regional dialect, but where they do exist, they are absolute honorifics, for in/out-group honorifics did not extend from central society to the peripheral world of regional dialects.

There are many studies on contemporary honorific expression because it is possible to conduct interviews without needing to rely on philological study, which is always limited by a lack of data. In general, the tendency has been for addressee-oriented-ness to become more eminent and for the honorific expression toward a superior who doesn't belong to either speaker or addressee to be omitted. Research was conducted on the employment of honorific expression toward teachers—traditionally to be respected—by different generations. Ōishi (1989) reports that the older generation uses respectful expressions, but Nagata (1988) finds that the younger generation uses neutral expressions. Honorific usage that treated a superior with a respectful expression within a family-hood has become obsolete, and Watanabe (1977) states that special honorific expressions only applicable to the royal family have also become obsolete. Honorific expression toward a superior who does not belong to either a speaker or an addressee will eventually disappear. According to the Bunkachō Bunkabu Kokugoka (1999), 64 percent of those interviewed support that an office worker speaking of his superior to a colleague use a neutral expression; while more than 75 percent support a respectful expression being used by a nurse speaking of the driver to a car accident victim, or by a television host speaking to a guest on TV. It appears, then, that there is support for respectful expressions toward a third person who does not belong to either speaker or addressee to be used in public situations, but not in private settings. The situational aspect of speech is a determining factor for the use of an honorific expression toward a third person, and it is significant that the criterion for honorific expression is shifting from superiority to intimacy. According to Bunkachō Bunkabu Kokugoka (1998), to the question of whether a shopkeeper should address an intimate customer using an honorific form, all interviewees answered positively—23.0 and 47.3 in the case of a retail shop and department store respectively. As for whether or not an office worker should use the honorific form to a superior in his office, 85.9 percent responded positively for when it is in working hours, whilst 36.2 percent responded positively for after working hours. Even when dealing with the same referent, the necessity to use an honorific expression varies according to the situational factor, with intimacy being the more important criterion. People tend to dispense with using an honorific expression toward an addressee that is intimate though superior, but, on the contrary, one needs to use an honorific expression toward an addressee that is unfamiliar though inferior. We find the same tendency for the use of honorific expression toward a referent: a speaker may dispense with an honorific expression toward an intimate referent, but uses it for an unfamiliar referent. But it is too hasty to conclude that honorific expressions toward referents are moving toward simplification. Inoue (1981) states that, at the same time, use of a respectful expression toward a referent has been increasing—as a polite gesture toward an addressee to whom a speaker wishes to pay high regard. The honorific expression toward a referent is, therefore, determined by the regard one has for the addressee, and the character of the honorific expression toward the referent—conveyed through refined speech—is an extension of the polite attitude toward the addressee, and is not used out of respect for the referent. Honorific expression toward a referent is determined solely by the relationship that exists between a speaker and an addressee.

2. Words to be used for the honorific expression toward a referent

In the Heian period, various kinds of respectful words, such as the following, were utilized according to the degree of respect one wished to convey: *se-tamahu* as a supreme respectful auxiliary; *tamahu* as an ordinary respectful auxiliary; and *raru* as the lowest respectful auxiliary. In the honorific system of the Heian period, social status was an absolute criterion with great influential power. In today's honorific system, regard for an addressee is expressed by using a neutral or humble expression toward a referent that is inferior to the addressee. But in the Heian period, an addressee was not offended if an inferior referent was treated by respectful language, as long as the addressee was accorded a higher respectful word. There existed at that time a peculiar honorific form, dual honorifics, that does not exist in modern honorifics. As previously mentioned, an honorific form incorporating both humble and respectful expressions, such as *mōshitamahu* or *kikoetamahu*, was quite often used in *Genji-Monogatari*. For Watanabe (1973), this kind of honorifics belongs to a transitional stage: 'the honorific form of humble expression plus respectful expression would only have existed at a time of change in honorific characteristics, when the object of the respectful expression shifted from referent to speaker'. As time passes, in *Heike-Monogatari*, only *raru* is combined with humble forms like *mōsaru* or *itasaru*, while *tamahu* also exists. In *Genji-Monogatari*, *raru* is classified as the lowest degree of respectful expression. Taking into consideration that dual honorifics still existed later on in the Muromachi period, but only combined with *raru*, we might conclude that the honorific system had by then shifted and it was now possible to respect a referent who previously would have been humiliated, but only with the least degree of respect. According to Watanabe (1973), the tendency toward speaker-oriented-ness became more prominent in the Muromachi period.

It is difficult to judge the honorific value of *raru*, given that its main use since the Muromachi period was when speaking of in-group superiors to out-group members. In present day honorifics, it is becoming the norm to treat in-group superiors to out-group members by humble expression, whereas *raru* had been mainly used before in/out-group honorifics were established by the implementation of Standard Japanese. Rodriguez (1955) made an objective observation of the Japanese language of the Muromachi period, and gives us a clue to this question: 'Only *raru* is appropriate to use when someone refers to his colleague, especially a member of his family, for it sounds peculiar to talk in an extremely polite way about colleagues, family or religion to an out-group person.' We can understand from this passage that the honorific value of *raru* is not high. From the viewpoint of absolute or relative honorifics in the Muromachi period, the usage of *raru* can be understood as a compromise between the criterion of in/out-group honorifics that an in-group referent should be humbled, and the requirement of absolute honorifics that any superior should be respected. The modern period is therefore a transitional stage from absolute to relative honorifics, and the low respectful expression *raru* is a suitable compromise between the two antagonistic criteria.

Today, three different types of honorific forms co-exist: the *shiyaru* type, such as *irassharu* or *ossharu*, that originated in the Edo period; the *o-V-ni-naru* type that came from the Edo dialect; and the *raru* type that has a long tradition from *kamigata* origins. There is an astonishing number and a rich variety of humble forms — *o-V-suru, o-V-itasu, o-V-sasete-itadaku* — that might derive from the criterion of in/out-group honorifics that self lowering forms be used for an in-group person. While the honorific system of the past mainly focused on raising the status of a referent, in the present honorific system use of the humble form is more complicated because addressee-oriented-ness means that an in-group referent, or a referent inferior to an addressee, should be treated by humble expression.

3. The provenance of relative honorifics

Where do relative honorifics come from? There are only two alternatives: imported or domestic, based on internal or external change. Here I have classified what is called relative honorifics into three systems: status, hierarchical or in/out-group honorifics. The term 'relative honorifics' was invented by Kyōsuke Kindaichi as an oppositional system to absolute honorifics, but there is no consensus among scholars about the nature of relative honorifics. Some include what I have termed 'status honorifics', but only because it is different from absolute honorifics, while other researchers limit the boundary of relative honorifics to in/out-group honorifics. There is no help for it, because there were only two alternative choices, absolute or relative honorifics.

Nishida (1998) argues that the idea of relative honorifics came from the courteous manners in the royal courts of the Nara and Heian periods:

> It is certain that relative honorifics and its concept were established among the highest ranked echelons of the royal court. It is reasonable to suppose that its origin was based on the control of respectful language—toward a speaker, or a referent who belongs to speaker—in the presence of a noble addressee. But what motivated the aristocracy to control their respectful expression toward a speaker or a referent? I believe that the humble manners at the royal court were transferred into the speech. The etiquette at royal court required that one

remains one step lower than usual in order to show respect to a noble attendant. For example, a rule book of court ceremonies states: 'In the presence of a prince or prime minister, get up from your seat. When you encounter ministers of the right or the left, or chiefs, move your seat. Otherwise, there is no need to move'. These etiquettes, established in the Nara period, prescribe how to show respect in accordance with the rank or status of an addressee. Such a level of courtesy shows humility.

And the influence from Chinese custom is also acknowledged:

> We cannot ignore the influence of Chinese honorifics. Without an awareness of humility—seeing himself as 'a small fellow'—an emperor could not have referred to himself in the first person pronoun as 'the slave of the three noble treasures'.

'The slave of the three noble treasures' is a description in the *shoku-nihon-gi* 続日本紀 of an emperor who humbles himself before an image of the Buddha: 'I serve Buddha as the slave of the three noble treasures'. But this theory reflects just one side of honorific usage in the Heian period, for in Chapter two there are examples of the honorific expression used toward a referent in *Genji-Monogatari*. There are humble expressions used to show respect toward a noble person, but respectful expressions are also used. The essence of status honorifics is that the honorific expression is determined by the status relation among the triad of speaker, addressee and referent.

The Korean language has common features with Japanese, and its honorific system developed from the contact with the culture and language of China. Before the invention of Hangeul characters in the fifteenth century, there were no orthographic devices to express the colloquial language, so the Chinese language was used. Therefore, Korean offers us scant data. Aan (1989) writes:

> Absolute honorifics were used in the middle ages to express the hierarchical relation between a master and a servant. ... A master was treated by respectful expression even to an addressee who was superior to him. It is common in present day honorifics for an office superior to be treated by respectful expression to an addressee who is of the same, or lower, rank to the referent, but not in

other cases. … Even in the middle ages the characteristic of relative honorifics that expresses the kinship relation between a father and a child can be found. And today's honorifics sometimes omit the respectful expression toward a speaker's parent because of a regard for the speech situation.

In contemporary Korean honorifics, there is a system called *apjonpeop* 圧尊法, in which a humble or neutral expression should be used to speak of a superior referent to an addressee who is superior to that referent. But this system is more complicated than that of Japanese. Seo (1984) shows instances where *apjonpeop* is applied to an elder brother, but not to parents, in the case of an out-group superior addressee; but it is applied to parents when the addressee is a grandparent. In conclusion, it seems that the Korean honorific system, like the Japanese, is moving from absolute to relative honorifics. But the question still left unsolved is why that shift occurred. Perhaps the answer lies in the autonomous inner changes of Korean society, or in the imported influence of the Chinese language. Some scholars doubt the origin of *apjonpeop*, and assume that it was introduced from Japanese honorifics during the Japanese occupation.

There is still much that is unclear about Chinese honorifics. Under the present socialist regime that banned social hierarchy, traditional Chinese honorifics that had been part of old China are not in use, although they still remain in literature. Koshimizu (1977) states that in/out-group-ness functions as the standard for honorific expression. The respectful prefix *ling* 令 is used only to mention a referent who belongs to an addressee (as in *ling-zun* 令尊 and *ling-tang* 令堂); and the humble prefixes *she* 舎 and *jia* 家 are used only to refer to someone who belongs to a speaker (as in *she-di* 舎弟 and *jia-fu* 家父). Peng (1999) writes:

> Relative honorifics might have been discovered in a document of the *Chunqiu Zhanguo* 春秋戦国 period (770 B.C.~222 B.C.) and the basic structure was completed at this time. Various new expressions were added, and expressive content has since enriched the language. Relative honorifics, as a complete system, was established in modern times (*Yuan* 元, *Ming* 明 and *Qing* 清).

But honorific expression in Chinese covers only the relation between a speaker and an addressee, and it is unacceptable that its domain extended to an hierarchical relation like servant and master. In Chinese also, there exists a system that lowers one's family member and respects an addressee's family member, but this can be interpreted as deriving from the relation between a speaker and an addressee. And Peng (2000) also mentions the following:

> In Chinese, when a speaker refers to his parents to an out-group person, terms like *jia-zun* 家尊, *jia-fu* 家父 and *jia-mu* 家母 are used in order to express both humility toward the addressee and respect toward the parents. Strong negative prefixes like *yu* 愚 or *zhuo* 拙 cannot be used to mention one's parents, and are only appropriate to speak of oneself, a comrade or an inferior belonging to one's in-group.

According to Tōdō (1974), the Chinese honorific system developed only among bureaucrats, as a formal male language only, its main function being for a speaker or an addressee to save face. Hamada (1970) argues that the most popular respectful prefix in Japanese, *oho* 御, was introduced from Chinese during the Nara or Heian periods, while most scholars commonly believe that *oho* derives from the Japanese word *ohoshi* 'much'. In conclusion, we can concur that some words, or rules of word formation, may have been introduced from Chinese, but it is still unclear whether the Chinese honorific system had any influence on Japanese honorifics. Kindaichi (1988) suggests that the Chinese language influenced Japanese honorifics during the Edo period, and that in/out-group honorifics might have been introduced from Chinese.

I believe it is not clear whether the courteous manners of the royal court were influenced by the Chinese model, but the progressive change from status to hierarchical and then in/out-group honorifics is certainly due to the internal changes within Japanese society. Especially, the birth of in/out-group honorifics could only be possible coincidental with the creation of the social organization of *uchi*.

4. The honorific system—in literary Japanese

In literary language, the relation toward a referent is fixed because a writer is a particular person and in most cases readers are non-particular majorities. The honorific expression toward a referent is determined by the two-dimensional relations between a speaker and a referent, and between an addressee and a referent; but in literature it is determined by the one-dimensional relation between a speaker and a referent. The addressee is a non-particular majority and there is no direct relation between an addressee and a referent. Therefore, in this book I have limited the scope of interest to colloquial Japanese. Literary language is more traditional and conservative than the colloquial language; this is also true for the honorific expression. Especially, the style of letter writing and official documents is formulaic. So, despite an immense body of Japanese literature that facilitates research, it is highly possible that because of its conservativeness this literature does not reflect authentic honorific expressions of the time. This is the second reason I have limited my interest only to colloquial Japanese. But it is a matter of course that the honorific expression changes with time, even in official letters, even though change reflects not the actually used honorific expression, but the change of norm toward the honorific expression. I plan to do the same kind of study on literary Japanese.

Reference

Aan Pyounghuy. 1989. Keigo no taishō gengogakuteki kōsatsu. *Kōza nihongo 9, Keigoshi.* Tokyo:Meiji shoin.
Abe, Hachirō. 1990. Chikamatsu sewa zjōruri no shinwabun. *Kindaigo kenkyū 8.* Tokyo: Musashino shoin.
Akita, Sadaki. 1958. Chūsei no kenjōhō: kyōgen no 'mausu', 'itasu', 'zonzuru' nado. *Kokugo kokubun* 27-11.
Akita, Sadaki. 1976. *Chūko chūsei no keigo no kenkyū.* Tokyo: Seibundō shuppan.
Brown, Penelope & Stephan, C. Levinson. 1987. *Politeness: Some Universals in Language Usage.* Cambridge: Cambridge University Press.
Brown, R. and A. Gilman .1960. The pronouns of power and solidarity. *Style in language*, ed. by T. Sebeok, 253-76. Cambridge, Mass.: MIT Press
Bunkachō Bunkabu Kokugoka (ed.). 1998. Heisei 9nen Kokugo ni kansuru seron chōsa. Tokyo: Ōkurashō insatsukyoku.
Bunkachō Bunkabu Kokugoka (ed.). 1999. Heisei 10nen Kokugo ni kansuru seron chōsa. Tokyo: Ōkurashō insatsukyoku.
Chikamatsu zenshū kankōkai. 1986. *Chikamatsu zenshū.* Tokyo: Iwanami shoten.
Doi, Tadao, Morita, Takeshi & Chōnan Minoru (trans.) 1980. *Nippo jisho.* Tokyo: Iwanami shoten.
Fujiwara, Yoichi. 1978. *Hōgen keigo-hō no kenkyū.* Tokyo: Shun'yōdō shoten.
Furuta, Tōsaku. 1988. 'Tōkaidō yotsuya kaidan' ni oite kamigatafū no kotoba-zukai wo suru hito-tachi. *Kindaigo-kenkyū 7.* Tokyo: Musashino shoin.
Gunji, Masakatsu., Hirosue, Tamotsu., Urayama, Masao. & et al. (eds.). 1971-1974 *Tsuruya nanboku zenshū.* Tokyo: San'ichi shobou.
Hachiya, Kiyoto. 1970. Kyōgen no kotoba. *Nihon no koten geinō 4: Kyōgen 'Okashi' no keifu.* Tokyo: Sōgensha.
Hachiya, Kiyoto. 1977. *Kyōgen daihon no kokugogaku-teki kenkyū.* Tokyo: Kasama shoin.
Hachiya, Kiyoto. 1982. Kabuki no goi: koi no fūjime no baai. *Kōza nihongo no goi 5 kinsei no goi.* Tokyo: Meiji shoin.
Hachiya, Kiyoto. 1998. Kyōgen no kotoba no ryūdō ni kansuru kenkyū no shiten to kadai. *Kyōgen no kokugogaku-teki kenkyū.* Tokyo: Meiji shoin.
Hamada, Atsushi. 1970. *Chōsen shiryō ni yoru nihongo kenkyū.* Tokyo: Iwanami shoten.
Han, Mikyoung. 1995. *Shōkaishingo ni okeru keigo kenkyū.* Seoul: Pakiceng.
Han, Mikyoung. 1998. Shōkaishingo uy 'no, ga' uy yongpep: taigūhyōgen. *Nihon kenkyū 13.*
Hattori, Yukio. 1973. Jōruri, kyōgen no keigo. *Keigo kōza 4 Kinsei no keigo.* Tokyo: Meiji shoin.

Hayashi, Ōki. 1973. Kazoku to keigo. *Keigo kōza 6 Gendai no keigo.* Tokyo: Meiji shoin.
Hida, Yoshifumi. 1981. Shosei no keigo. *Kokubungaku* 26-2.
Hikosaka, Yoshinobu. 1975. Ōkuraryū kyōgen 'Toraakihon' kara 'Torahirohon' e: sono taigū hyōgen no henka. *Kokugogaku kenkyū* 14.
Ikeda, Hiroshi. & Kitahara, Yasuo. (eds). 1972. *Ōkuraryū Toraakihon kyōgenshū no kenkyū.* Tokyo: Hyōgensha.
Ikeda, Kikan. (ed). 1954. *Nihon koten zensho: Genji-Monogatari.* Tokyo: Asahi shinbunsha.
Ikegami, Akihiko. 1963a. Ninjō-hon ni arawareta ichi-ni ninshō daimeishi ni tsuite 1. *Tsurumi jyoshi daigaku kiyō* 1.
Ikegami, Akihiko. 1963b. Ninjō-hon ni arawareta ichi-ni ninshō daimeishi ni tsuite 1. *Tsurumi jyoshi daigaku kiyō* 2.
Ikegami, Akihiko. 1967. Ninjō-hon no taigū hyōgen kenkyū. *Tsurumi jyoshi daigaku kiyō* 4.
Ikegami, Akihiko. 1968. Ninjō-hon ni arawareta taigū hyōgen ni tsuite. *Tsurumi jyoshi daigaku kiyō* 5.
Ikegami, Akihiko. 1977. Shigiryū kyōgen-hon ni mirareru ichi-ni ninshō daimeishi no yōhō ni tsuite. *Matsumura Akira kyōju kanreki kinen kokugogaku to kokugoshi.* Tokyo: Meiji shoin.
Ikegami, Teizō. 1973. Gendai keigo no gaikan. *Keigo kōza 6 Gendai no keigo.* Tokyo: Meiji shoin.
Inoue, Fumio. 1981. Keigo no chirigaku. *Kokubungaku ichigatsu rinji zōkangō.*
Ishizaka, Shōzō. 1960. Koten kaishaku to keigohō, *Kōza kaishaku to bunpō* 1. Tokyo: Meijishoin.
Ītoyo, Kiichi. 1987. Taigai miuchi taigū hyōgen no chōsa. *Gaien* 565.
Iwabuchi, Etsutarō. 1937. Keigo no isshuno tsukahi kata. *Kokugo to kokubungaku,* 14-10.
Japanese linguistic department of Kyoto University. (ed). 1972, 1973. *San-pon taishō Shōkaishingo.* Kyōto: Kyōto daigaku bungakubu kokugo kokubun kenkyūshitsu.
Jinbō, Kaku. 1941. *Hyōjun-go kenkyū.* Tokyo: Nihon hōsō shuppan kyōkai.
Jugaku, Akiko. 1958. Muromachi zidai no 'no,ga': sono kanjōkachihyōgen wo chūshin ni. *Kokugo kokubungaku* 27-7.
Kaion kenkyūkai. 1977. Kinokaion zenshū. Tokyo: Seibundō.
Kajiwara, Masaaki & Yamashita, Hiroaki. (annotator.) 1991. *Heike-Monogatari,* Shin Nihon Bungaku Taikei. Tokyo: Iwanami shoten.
Kamei, Takashi. 1980. kyōgen no kotoba. *Nōgakuzensho* 5. Tokyo: Tokyōsōgensha.
Kamitani, Kaoru. 1976. Genji-Monogatari kaiwabun niokeru taiguuhyougen: kenkyū nōto. *Kōkazyoshitandai kenkyūkiyō* 14.
Kaneda, Hiroshi. 1952. Tōkyō-go ni okeru reru-gata keigo no seikaku. *Nihon bungaku ronkyū* 10.
Kang Seokwoo. 1997. Dōitsu-shūdan no naka de no daisansha ni taisuru taigū hyōgen.

Ōsaka daigaku nihon gakuhō 16.
Katō, Masanobu. 1977. Hōgen kukaku-ron. *Kōza Nihongo 11 Hōgen*. Tokyo: Iwanami shoten.
Kawatake, Shigetoshi. (ed.) 1924-1925. *Mokuami zenshū*. Tokyo: Shun'yōdō.
Kawatake, Shigetoshi. 1959. *Nihon engeki zenshi*. Tokyo: Iwanami shoten.
Kawatake, Toshio. 1966. (annotated.) *Meiji bungaku zenshū 9 Kawatake Mokuami shū*. Tokyo: Chikuma shobou.
Kikuchi, Yasuto. 1994. *Keigo*. Tokyo: Kadokawa shoten.
Kindaichi, Haruhiko. 1977. Hōgen no bunpō. *Nihongo hōgen no kenkyū*. Tokyo: Tokyōdō shuppan.
Kindaichi, Haruhiko. 1988. *Nihongo*. Tokyo: Iwanami shinsho.
Kindaichi, Kyōsuke. 1941. Joseigo to keigo. *Fujin kōron*. Tokyo: Chūōkōronsha.
Kindaichi, Kyōsuke. 1959. *Nihongo no keigo*. Tokyo: Kadokawa shinsho.
Kishie, Shinsuke. 1998. Keihan hōgen ni okeru shin'ai hyōgen kōzō no wakugumi. *Nihongo Kagaku3*. Tokyo: Kokuritsu kokugo kenkyūsho.
Kitagawa, Hiroshi & Tsuchida B, T. (trans.) 1975. *Heike Monogatari*. Tokyo: University of Tokyo Press.
Kitahara, Yasuo. & etc. (eds.) 1984. *Ōkuraryū Toraaki-hon kyōgenshū sōsakuin*. Tokyo: Musashino shoin.
Kobayashi, Chigusa. 1972. Chūseikōgo ni okeru gen'in riyū wo arawasu jōkenku. *Kokugogaku* 94.
Kojima, Toshio. 1974. *Kōki edo-kotoba no keigo taikei*. Tokyo: Kasama shoin.
Kojima, Toshio. 1979. Toraakihon kyōgenshū no keigo taikei: Taishō daimeishi no kōsei suru shujyutsu taiō. *Nakata Iwao hakase kouseki kinen kokugoronshū*. Tokyo: Benseisha.
Kokugakuin daigaku nihon bunka kenkyū-sho. (ed.). 1996. *Tōkyō-go no yukue*. Tokyo: Tōkyōdō shuppan.
Kokuritsu kokugo kenkyūsho. (ed) 1964. *Gendai no keigo ishiki ni kansuru ankēto chōsa*. *Tōkyō: Shūeisha*.
Kokuritsu kokugo kenkyūsho (ed.). 1967. *Nihon gengo chizu* Vol.2. Chart 95. Tokyo: Ōkurashō insatsukyoku.
Kokuritsu kokugo kenkyūsho (ed.). 1979. *Kakuchi hōgen shinzoku goi no gengo-shakaigaku -teki kenkyū 1*. Tokyo: Shūei shuppan.
Kokuritsu kokugo kenkyūsho (ed.). 1982. *Kigyō no naka no keigo*. Tokyo: Sanseidō.
Komatsu, Sumio. 1971. Kodai no keigo 2. *Kouza kokugoshi 5, keigoshi*. Tokyo: Taishūkan shoten.
Komatsu, Sumio. 1975. Kamigata buke-kotoba wa sonzai shitaka: kinsei zenki buke-kotoba ni tsuite. *Kokugo to kokubungaku* 52-3.
Komatsu, Sumio. 1985. *Kokugogaku ronsō 7 Edo-jidai no kokugo*. Tokyo: Tōkyōdō.
Koshimizu, Yutaka. 1977. Chūgokugo ni okeru keigo. *Kōza Nihongo 4 Keigo*. Tokyo:

Iwanami shoten.
Kotani, Hiroyasu. 1989. Kōbe-shi ni okeru teja-keigo no suitai:daigakusei no hōgen shiyō ni kanshite. *Kawaguchi Akira sensei taishoku kinen bunshū.*
Koyama, Hiroshi. 1960. introduction. *Nihon koten bungaku taikei kyōgen-jō.* Tokyo: Iwanami shoten.
Kurano, Tsuguhisa. 1967. Taishō no hitodaimeishi kara mita Toraaki-hon kyōgen no kotoba. *Yasudajoshidaigaku kiyō* 1.
Kurosaki, Yoshiaki. 1997. Hyōgo-ken katō-gun takino-chō hōgen no taigū hyōgen. *Hōgen shiryō sōkan 7 Hōgen no taigū hyōgen..* Hiroshima: Hōgen Kenkyū zemināru
Kuwayama, Toshihiko. 1972. Muromachi Edo shoki ni okeru 'no' to 'ga': taigūhyōgen men wo chūshin ni. *Bungei to hihyō* 3-9,10.
Kuwayama, Toshihiko. 1973. Muromachi Edo shoki ni okeru 'no' to 'ga': bunkōzō men wo chūshin ni. *Kokugogaku kenkyū* 39.
Lee Weonshik. 1984. Chōsen tsūshinshi ni zuikōshita wagakuyakukan: 'Shōkaishingo' no seiritsu jiki ni kansuru kakushō wo chūshin ni. *Chōsengakuh* 101.
Maeda, Isamu. 1977. *Ōsaka-ben.* Tokyo: Asahi sensho.
Martin, E. Samuel. 1964. Speech levels in Japan and Korea. *Language in culture and society,* ed. by D. Hymes, 407-15. New York: Harper and Row.
Mashita, Saburō. 1966. Chikamatsu ni okeru keigo. *kokubungaku* 5-2
Matsui, Toshihiko. 1974. Chūsei no fūzoku to keigo seikatsu. *Keigo kouza 3, Chūsei no keigo.* Tokyo: Meiji shoin.
Matsui, Toshihiko. 1988. Shosei-kotoba no tenkai. *Kokugogaku* 154.
Matsumura, Akira. 1957. *Edo-go tōkyō-go no kenkyū.* Tokyo: Tōkyōdō.
Matsushita, Daizaburō. 1928. *Kaisen hyōjun nihon bunpō.* Tokyo: Chūbunkan shoten
Mikami, Akira. 1953. Keigohō no A-sen. *Gendai gohō josetsu.* Tokyo: Tōkō shoin.
Minami, Fujio. 1987. *Keigo.* Tokyo: Iwanami shinsho.
Miyaji, Hiroaki. 1987. Kinki hōgen ni okeru taigū hyōgen unyōjō no ichi tokushutsu. *Kokugogaku* 151.
Miyaji, Yutaka. 1971. Gendai no keigo. *Kōza kokugoshi 5, keigoshi.* Tokyo: Taishūkan shoten.
Miyaji, Yutaka. 1981. Keigoshiron. *Kōza nihongogaku 9* Keigoshi. Tokyo: Meiji shoin.
Miyake, Takeo. 1944. *Gendai keigo-hō.* Tokyo: Nihongo kyōiku shinkō kai.
Mizutani, Osamu. 1989. *How to be polite in Japanese.* Tokyo: The Japan Times.
Mochizuki, Ikuko. 1970. Genji-Monogatari ni okeru keishou no settouji mi nituite, *Bungaku* 38-3.
Morino, Muneaki. 1971. Kodai no keigo 2. *Kōza kokugoshi 5, keigoshi.* Tokyo: Taishūkan shoten.
Morita, Takeshi. 1973. Shōkaishingo kaidai. *San-pon taishō Shōkaishingo.* Kyōto: Kyōto daigaku bungakubu kokugo kokubun kenkyūshitsu.
Naganokenshi kankōkai. (ed.) 1992. Naganokenshi hōgen-hen. Nagano: Naganokenshi

kankōkai.
Nagata, Takashi. 1986. Tōkyō hōgen no on'in henka. *SOPHIA LINGUISTICA* 20, 21.
Nagata, Takashi. 1988. *Wakamono no keigo ni taisuru iken ankēto*. Tokyo: Takashi Nagata.
Nagata, Takashi. 1996. *Chiikigo no seitai shiri-zu Ryūkyū-hen Ryūkyū de umareta kyōtūgo*. Tokyo: Ōfū.
Nakai, Seiichi. 1997. Nara-ken tenri-shi nagara hōgen no taigū hyōgen. *Hōgen shiryō sōkan 7 Hōgen no taigū hyōgen.*. Hiroshima: Hōgen Kenkyū zemināru
Nakamura, Eikō. 1961. Shōkaishingo no seiritsu, kaishū oyobi 'Wagoruikai' seiritsu jiki ni tsuite. *Chōsengakuh* 19.
Negoro, Tsukasa. 1992. Kenjōgo kara mita Genji-monogatari no bunshō. *Kokugo to kokubungaku* 11.
Neustupný, J. V. 1978. *Post-structural approaches to language*. Tokyo: University of Tokyo Press
Nihon Hōgen Kenkyū-kai. (ed.) . 1978. Nihon hōgen no goi. Tokyo: Sanseidō.
Nishida, Naotoshi. 1974. Heike-Monogatari no keigo. *Keigo kōza 3 chūsei no keigo*. Tokyo: Meiji shoin.
Nishida, Naotoshi. 1978. *Heike-Monogatari no buntaironteki kenkyū*. Tokyo: Meiji shoin.
Nishida, Naotoshi. 1995. *Jikei hyōgen no rekishiteki kenkyū*. Osaka: Izumi shoin.
Nishida, Naotoshi. 1998. *Nihonjin no keigoseikatsushi*. Tokyo: Keirin shobō.
Ogura, Shinpei. 1964. *Zōtei chōsengo gakushi*. Tokyo: Tōkō shoin.
Ōishi, Hatsutarō. 1989. Gendai keigo no tokushitsu, sono shōrai. *Kōza nihongogaku 9 Keigoshi*. Tokyo: Meiji shoin.
Okamura, Kazue. 1957. Heike-Monogatari rufuhon no keigo hyōgen. *Jissen joshi daigaku kiyō* 5.
Ōkubo, Kazuo. 1995. 'Go' no shiyō to yōgensei keigo no fushiyō. *Genji monogatari no keigohō*. Tokyo: Ōfū.
Okumura, Kazuko. 1989. Heike-Monogatari no jinbutsuzō to sono hensen: taigūhyōgen, katari no kyokusetsu wo chūshin ni. *Gobun kenkyū* 66,67.
Okumura, Mitsuo. 1966. Keigoji keifu kō. *Kokugo-kokubun* 35-5.
Otoha, Hiroshi. (ed.). 1960. *Nihon koten bungaku taikei 51: zyōrurishū*. Tokyo: Iwanami shoten.
Ōtomo, Shinichi. 1957. 'Shōkaishingo' no seiritsu jiki shiken. *Bungeikenkyū* 26.
Peng, Guozhuo. 1999. Bunkaku-chū ni okeru chūgokugo zettai keigo no fukkatsu to sono shakai-teki haikei. *Jinmon kenkyū* 137.
Peng, Guozhuo. 2000. *Kindai chūgokugo no keigo shisutemu: In'yō bunka ninchi moderu*. Tokyo: Hakuteisha.
Prideaux, G.D. 1970. *The syntax of Japanese honorifics*. The Hague: Mouton.
Rodriguez, Joan. 1955, Tadao Doi, trans. *Arte da lingoa de Iapam*. Tokyo: Sanseidō.
Sakaguchi, Itaru. 1978. Ōkuraryū kyōgen no taigū hyōgen ni tsuite. *Gobun kenkyū* 46.
Sakakura, Atsuyoshi & Asami, Tōru. 1996. *Ichi-go no jiten: Uchi*. Tokyo: Sanseidō.

Sakanashi, Ryūzō. 1970. Chuikamatsu sewa-mono ni okeru nidan katsuyō to ichidan katsuyō. *Kokugo to kokubungaku* 47-10.
Sakurai, Mitsuaki. 1966. *Konjaku-Monogatari no gohō no kenkyū*. Tokyo: Meiji shoin.
Sasaki, Shun. 1970. *Ōkuraryū kyōgen shiryō ni okeru taigū hyōgenhō no hikaku kenkyū: Toraakihon to Torahirohon. Kokubungakukō* 53.
Sanada, Shinji. 1973. Ecchū gokagō ni okeru taigū hyōgen no jittai. *Kokugogaku* 93.
Sanada, Shinji. 1983. Saikin jyūnen-kan no keigo kōdō no henyō: Gokayama Maki buraku de no zensū chōsa kara. *Kokugogaku* 133.
Seidensticker, Edward G. (trans.) 1977. *The Tale of Genji*. New York: Alfred A.Knopf.
Seki, Kazuo. 1976. Genji-Monogatari kaiwabun ni okeru keigo no mi, ohon no yōhō, *Gengo to bungei* 83.
Seo, Jeongjoo. 1984. Kankoku gendai keigo-hō. *Contaypep uy yenkwu*. Seoul: Hansin Mwun hwasa.
Shibata, Takashi & Suzuki, Taka. 1959. Haha to iu yō ni naru made. *Gengo seikatsu* 98.
Shibata, Takashi & Suzuki, Taka. 1961. Okā-san wa genki de ori masu. *Gengo seikatsu* 115.
Shibata, Takashi. 1978. Machino-chō no gengo seikatsu. *Shakai gengogaku no kadai*. Tokyo: Sanseidō.
Shimono, Masaaki. 1995. Biwa-ko tōgan no taigū hyōgen jyosetsu. *Kansai hōgen no shakai-gengo-gaku*. Tokyo: Sekai shisōsha.
Shin, Hyeykyoung. 1986. Kankokugo no keigo ishiki no chōsa hōkoku. *SOPHIA LINGUISTICA* 20,21.
Shinoda, Tōru. 1978. Heike-Monogatari ni okeru keigo: kore wo kanjō no hyōgen to toraeru. *Kokubungaku* 5-2.
Sugimoto, Tsutomu. 1967. Tenkan-ki no nihon-go. *Kindai nihon-go no shin-kenkyū*. Tokyo: Ōfūsha.
Sugimoto, Tsutomu. 1985. *Edo no onna kotoba : asobase to arinsu*. Tokyo: Kaitakusha.
Sugimoto, Tsutomu. 1988. *Tōkyō-go no rekishi*. Tokyo: Chūkō shinsho.
Sugisaki, Kazuo. 1988a. 'Haberitaubu' nitsuite. *Heianzidai keigohou no kenkyū*. Tokyo: Yūseidō.
Sugisaki, Kazuo. 1988b. 'Haberitaubu' saikō. *Heianzidai keigohou no kenkyū*. Tokyo: Yūseidō.
Takamure, Itsue. 1963. *Nihon koninshi*. Tokyo: Shibundō.
Takano, Tatsuyuki. (ed.). 1927. Chikamatsu kabuki kyōgenshū. Tokyo: Rokugōsha.
Tamagami, Takuya. 1952. Keigo no bungakuteki kōsatsu: Genji-Monogatari no honshō. *Kokugokokubun* 21-2.
Tamagami, Takuya. 1955. Genji-Monogatari no kaishaku bunpō. *Jidaibetsu sakuhinbetsu kaishaku bunpō*. Tokyo: Shibundō.
Tanaka, Akio. 1969. Keigo rongi wa naze okoru. *Gengo seikatsu* 213.
The National Institute for Japanese Language. 1964. *Gendai no keigo ishiki ni kansuru*

ankēto chōsa. Tokyo: Shūeishuppan.

Tochigi, Takao., Kusaka, Chikara., Masuda, Sou & Kubota, Jyun. (eds.). 1992. *Shin Nihon Bungaku Taikei: Hogen Monogatari, Heiji Monogatari & Zjōkyūki.* Tokyo: Iwanami shoten.

Tōdō, Akiho. 1974. Chūgokugo no keigo. *Keigo kōza 8 Sekai no keigo.* Tokyo: Meiji shoin.

Tokieda, Motoki. 1941. *Kokugogaku genron.* Tokyo: Iwanami shoten.

Tokieda, Motoki. 1954. *Nihon bunpō: Bungo hen.* Tokyo: Iwanami shoten.

Tomioka, Tokujirō. 1959. Heike-Monogatari no kaishaku to bunpōjō no mondaiten. *Kōza kaishaku to bunpō 5.* Tokyo: Meiji shoin.

Toyama, Eiji. 1977. Keigo no hensen2. *Kōza nihongo 4 keigo.* Tokyo: Iwanashi shoten.

Tsuchiya, Shin'ichi. 1986. Ukiyo-buro, ukiyo-doko no keigo ni-dai: naharu to tedegozaimasu. *Kagawa daigaku kokubun kenkyū 10.*

Tsuji, Seiji. 1997. *Chōsengoshi ni okeru Shōkaishingo.* Okayama: Okayama University Press.

Tsujimura, Toshiki. 1968. *Keigo no shiteki kenkyū.* Tokyo: Tōkyōdōshuppan.

Tsujimura, Toshiki. 1971. Keigoshi no hōhō to mondai. *Kōza kokugoshi 5, keigoshi.* Tokyo: Taishūkan shoten.

Tsujimura, Toshiki. 1989. Keigo ishiki-shi. *Kōza nihongo-gaku 9 keigo-shi.* Tokyo: Meiji shoin.

Tsujimura, Toshiki. 1992a. Keigo kankei yōgo kaisetsu. *Keigo ronkō.* Tokyo: Meiji shoin.

Tsujimura, Toshiki. 1992b. Shōkaishingo no 'iu' no keigokei: nihongo no keigo to kankokugo no keigo. *Keigo ronkō.* Tokyo: Meiji shoin.

Tyler, Royall. (trans.) 2001. *The tale of Genji.* New York: Viking Penguin.

Uno, Yoshikata. 1977. Gendai keigo no mondaiten. *Iwanami kōza 4 Keigo.* Tokyo: Iwanami shoten.

Watanabe, Eiji. 1974. Ji no bun ni okeru keigo hyōgen: Genji-Monogatari no keigo no yōhō. *Toyamadaigaku kyōikugakubu kiyō 22.*

Watanabe, Eiji. 1978. Hikaru Genji no taigūhyōgen: Genji-Monogatari tamakadurakei ji no bun no keigo hyōgen. *Kokugo kokubun kenkyū 59.*

Watanabe, Eiji. 1981. Chūko keigo to gendai keigo: kenjōgo ni tsuite. *Kōza nihongogaku 9 Keigoshi.* Tokyo: Meiji shoin.

Watanabe, Minoru. 1973. Jōdai-chūko keigo no gaikan. *Keigokōza 2, Jōdai-chūko no keigo,* Tokyo: Meiji shoin

Watanabe, Tomosuke. 1977. Kaisō to keigo. *Kōza nihongo 4 Keigo.* Tokyo: Iwanami shoten.

Yamagata, Hiroshi. 1982. Katsuyō no henka kara mita kamigata eiri kyōgen-hon: ra-gyo shimonidan katsuyō no yodanka no baai. *Bunken tankyū 11.*

Yamagata, Hiroshi. 1980. Kabuki kyakuhon ni okeru keigoji. *Okumura Mitsuo kyōju taikan kinen kokugo ronsō.* Tokyo: Ōfūsha.

Yamazaki, Hisayuki. 1959. Kinsei-zenki sanninshō no shutai taigū hyōgen. *Gunma-*

daigaku kiyō 8-8.

Yamazaki, Hisayuki. 1963. *Kokugo Taigū hyōgen taikei no kenkyū: Kinsei hen.* Tokyo: Musashino shoin.

Yamazaki, Hisayuki. 1964. Keigo no hensen. *Kōza gendaigo 2 gendaigo no seiritsu.* Tokyo: Meiji shoin.

Yamazaki, Hisayuki. 1990. *Zoku-kokugo Taigū hyōgen taikei no kenkyū.* Tokyo: Musashino shoin.

Yanagita, Kunio. 1938. Keigo to jidō. *Kokugo kokubun* 8-10.

Yasuda, Akira. 1973. Jyūkanbon kaishū shōkaishingo kaidai. *San-pon taishō Shōkaishingo.* Kyōto: Kyōto daigaku bungakubu kokugo kokubun kenkyūshitsu.

Yasuda, Akira. 1977. Joshi 2. *Iwanami kōza nihongo7 bunpō 2.* Tokyo: Iwanami shoten.

Yoshizawa, Norio & Hayashi, Kenji. 1973. Shokuba no keigo: ankēto ni yoru shō-chōsa. *Keigo kōza 6 Gendai no keigo.* Tokyo: Meiji shoin.

Zoku-Gunshoruijū-kankōkai . 1958. Shakkanki. *Zoku-Gunshoruijyū* 24.

INDEX

There is no exception to the rule that all languages change throughout time. This also applies to Japanese. In this book I have examined the linguistic change in honorific expressions over one thousand years, and therefore, the same words have changed in terms of pronunciation and inflectional endings. For example, while the [w] sound before the [i] sound has been omitted in modern Japanese, it was pronounced in the Heian period. The frequently-cited word [mawiru] 'come' came to be pronounced as [mairu]. The [p] sound has changed in the following way: [p] > [f] > [h] > [w]. The word [iu] 'say' has changed its pronunciation from [ipu] to [ifu] to [ihu] before finally dropping its [h] sound to become [iu]. In the index I have listed the current pronunciation at the beginning and then follow with the past pronunciation on the next line. In addition, Japanese verbs can be categorized into three patterns basically from the viewpoint of inflection: vowel stem verbs, consonant stem verbs and irregular verbs. Consonant stem verbs such as [iku] 'go' are inflected in the following manner; *ik-a-nai* 'don't go', *ik-i-masu* 'go (politely)', *ik-u* 'go', *ik-e-ba* 'if goes' and *ik-e* 'go!'. The 'u' form of the verb is considered the basic form that is indexed in a dictionary. I have, therefore, only indexed the 'u' form.

Subject index

a
absolute 21, 75, 99, 240
absolute honorifics 12-17, 68, 71, 76, 77, 79, 95, 98, 100, 147, 152, 198, 199, 223, 236, 241, 242, 261, 283, 290, 306, 309, 314, 317, 318
addressee-orientation 17, 145
addressee-oriented honorifics 5, 6, 75
addressee-oriented-ness 290, 314, 318
apjonpeop 320
asobase-kotoba 234
authorized textbook 271

b
ba 237
bamen 237
bikago 4, 5
buke-kotoba 176, 205, 206, 245, 257, 260, 263

c
cha-ya 234, 236
Chinese name 79, 311
chōnin-kotoba 206, 225, 229

d
daimyō 103, 133, 143, 145, 176
dialect geography 294, 296
dual expression 180, 197, 199, 284, 285
dual honorifics 21, 59, 69, 79, 80, 92, 96, 147, 316

e
Edo dialect 201, 245, 261, 313, 318
Edo period 318

g
geographical dialectology 294

h
hierarchical honorifics 17, 99-101, 151, 166, 171, 198, 199, 310, 311, 318
humble expression 22, 23, 26, 37

i
in/out group honorifics 100, 146, 147, 166, 167, 170, 171, 198, 199, 222, 227, 233, 236, 241, 249, 257, 259, 261, 283, 290, 295, 306, 312, 313, 314, 317, 318, 321
introduces oneself 88, 89

j
jochū-kotoba 199, 200, 242, 313

k
kamigata 175, 180, 201, 221, 241, 242, 261, 312, 313
kenjōgo 2, 3, 5, 6
kuge 8, 89, 101, 199, 311, 314
kuruwa-kotoba 234

n
nyōbō-kotoba 200, 313

o
o-yashiki-kotoba 242, 313

p
politeness 1-3

r
raru expression 22, 23, 26, 30-32, 37, 42
referent-orientation 17
referent-oriented honorific 5, 6
relative honorifics 12-18, 21, 68, 70, 75, 77, 79, 98-101, 146, 147, 152, 240, 318
respectful expression toward an in-group 306
respectful expressions for the natural world 296
respectful expressions toward in-group members 298
respectful expressions toward one's in-group 300

s

samurai 8-10, 75, 85, 143, 144, 161, 176
self-introduction 13, 82, 95, 100, 108, 148, 182, 205, 211, 223, 229
shitamachi-kotoba 263, 264
shōgun 127, 143, 154-156, 167, 168, 175
shosei-kotoba 258, 260
sonkeigo 2, 3, 5, 6
speaker-oriented honorifics 77
Standard Japanese 11, 15, 17-19, 151, 258, 263, 271, 289, 295, 298, 302, 303, 306, 308, 314, 317
status honorifics 17, 68, 71, 309, 310, 318

t

taboo 12, 309
teichōgo 4, 5
teineigo 2, 5, 6
tennō 154
Tokyo dialect 245, 246, 263, 295

u

uchi 312, 321

y

yamanote-kotoba 263, 264
yamato-kotoba 200
yūjo 221, 225, 231, 234-236, 240, 241
yūri 234-236, 239
yūri-kotoba 234, 235, 240

Author index

a
Aan 319
Abe 198
Akita 138
Asami 312

b
Brown 1
Brown 2

c
Chamberlain 260

f
Fujiwara 293, 299
Furuta 241

g
Gilman 2

h
Hachiya 104, 203
Hamada 152, 321
Hattori 202
Hayashi 283, 285
Hida 258
Hikosaka 104

i
Ikeda 25, 104
Ikegami 238, 287
Inoue 316

Ishizaka 13, 52
Ītoyo 298
Iwabuchi 14, 288

j
Jinbō 264
Jugaku 106

k
Kajiwara 75
Kamei 104
Katō 294
Kawatake 202, 246
Kindaichi 12, 13, 17, 18, 99-101, 296, 309, 321
Kindaichi 295
Kishie 298
Kitagawa 76
Kitahara 104
Kojima 238, 270
Komatsu 176, 177, 205, 229, 240
Koshimizu 320
Koyama 104
Kurosaki 298
Kusaka 76
Kuwayama 106

l
Levinson 1

m
Maeda 298
Mase 298
Mashita 198
Matsui 258, 310
Matsumura 263
Miyaji 4-6, 14, 15
Miyaji 307
Miyake 283
Morino 13, 21, 52
Morita 152

n
Nagata 277, 302, 315
Nakai 298
Nishida 13, 75, 77, 78, 318

o
Ogura 152
Ōishi 315
Okamura 76
Okumura 293

p
Peng 320, 321

r
Rodriguez 79, 105, 106, 112, 117, 124, 133, 135, 137, 138, 140, 142, 147, 159, 160-162, 165, 171, 185, 221, 240, 241, 317

s
Sakaguchi 104
Sakakura 312
Sakurai 77
Sanada 302, 303
Sasaki 104
Satow 221
Seidensticker 25
Seo 320
Shibata 237, 306
Shimono 300
Sugimoto 229, 258
Suzuki 237

t
Tamagami 12, 24
Tanaka 288
Tochigi 76
Tokieda 4, 5, 59

Toyama 14, 75
Tsuchida 76
Tsuchiya 241
Tsujimura 12, 15, 238, 240, 288, 309
Tyler 25

W

Watanabe 79
Watanabe 315
Watanabe 317

Y

Yamagata 202
Yamazaki 1, 14, 106, 133, 135, 137, 141, 142, 180, 184, 188, 229, 235, 238, 252
Yanagita 274, 283, 294
Yasuda 106, 167
Yoshizawa 285

Word index

a
agaru 255
ane 191, 192, 214
ane-ki 214
ane-san 216
ani 191, 192, 214, 215
ani-ki 179, 214
ani-san 216
aru 78, 79, 142
asobasu 78

c
chichi 12, 15, 100, 151, 179, 187, 188, 204-206, 237, 253, 255, 257, 272, 280, 281
  titi 78
chūn 302

d
desu 2
domo 3, 22, 78, 106, 112, 162, 164, 179, 204, 227
don 240
dono 13, 22, 52, 68, 71, 78-80, 85, 91-93, 96, 106, 117, 148, 160, 167, 179, 182, 185, 191, 192, 204, 206, 211, 227-229, 240, 250, 252, 285

g
ga 78, 79, 82, 86, 88, 94, 106, 111, 115, 120, 121, 129, 133, 135, 137, 138, 140, 141, 159
gata 164
go 23, 94, 184, 240, 248
goranjiraru 153
go-ran-nasaru 248
go-V-nasaru 255
gozaimasu 252
  gozarimasu 209, 250, 255
gozaru 106, 184, 191, 221, 293
go-zonji 231

h
haberu 57, 70
haha 78, 158, 179, 187, 188, 190, 205, 206, 231, 253, 255, 257, 272, 280, 281
haha-diya-mono 158
haha-sama 270
haru 15, 151, 298-300

i
iharu 113, 138-140, 146
ihaseraru 141, 143
ihasu 141
ihiyaru 141, 142
ihu 22, 108, 129, 136, 137, 143, 144
irassharu 204, 302, 318
itadaku 3
itasaru 117, 180, 196, 197, 199, 229, 317
itasu 3-5, 15, 106, 109, 129, 151, 179, 180, 193, 204, 227, 255, 257
iwa-reru 274

k
kaka-sama 188, 189
kaka-san 209, 232
kanpaku 154
keisu 12, 67
kikoyu 34, 37, 56, 60
kimi 78
kōgi 145
kou 78, 117, 160
kubō 154
kudasaru 193, 255
kuryare 257
kyou 78

m
mairaru 229
mairu 3-7, 82, 92, 96, 111, 115-117, 160, 179, 192, 204, 227, 228, 237, 302, 303
  mawiru 27, 59
mama 46
marasuru 79, 135
mashimasu 85, 188, 191
masu 2, 4-6, 252, 255, 302, 303
mausaru 42, 110, 113, 116, 119, 129, 137-139, 143, 146, 155, 159, 168-170
mausu 21-23, 46, 106, 115, 119-121, 134-136, 138, 144, 147, 148, 155, 157, 158, 160, 161, 168, 169
mēn 302
mensēn 302, 303
mesaru 109, 163, 184
mesu 78
mi- 36, 43, 51

mieru 302
mōsareru 228, 229, 284, 285
　mōsaru 180, 197, 229, 311, 317
mōshi-kike 222
mōshitsukeru 218
mōsu 193, 228, 255, 257, 311

n

naharu 298, 299
nansu 235
nasaru 156, 160, 191, 221, 293, 298
no 78-80, 94, 96, 106, 113, 116, 119, 122, 127, 129, 133, 135, 137, 138, 140-142, 159, 293
notamahu 22, 46, 57, 70, 78
nsu 221, 235, 293
nukasu 141

o

o 4, 200, 251
oboshiaru 163
oboshi-mesa-ru 168
oboshimesu 93, 153, 155, 197
obosu 78
ohasu 27, 70, 78
ohm 22
oho 321
ohoseraru 93
ohosu 22, 78
o-hukuro 231, 253, 270, 271, 280, 281
　ohukuro 205, 206
o-kā-sama 270, 272
o-kā-san 270, 271, 280, 281

okkā 232
o-kka-san 270, 271
o-mausu 80
o-me-ni kakaru 247, 256
on 91, 96, 115, 162
orareru 284
oriyarasu 148
oru 256, 257
ōseraru 108, 113, 124, 128, 129, 131-133, 136, 138, 141, 143, 146, 169
oshiraru 155-157, 168, 170
oshiyaru 139-141, 143, 146, 188
osshai 283
ossharu 248, 285, 293, 318
osshiyaru 190, 221, 274
otōsama 12, 100, 270, 272
otōsan 15, 229, 237, 270, 271, 280, 281
otsushiyaru 169
o-tot-tsan 253, 271
o-V-aru 293
o-V-asobasu 221
o-V-da 201, 232, 241
o-V-mōsu 249, 251
o-V-nansu 216
o-V-nasaru 168, 184, 188, 191, 197, 201, 209, 241
o-V-ni-naru 3, 318
o-V-ru 293
o-V-sasete-itadaku 318
o-V-suru 3
oya-diya-mono 158
　oyaja-mono 311
oyaji 188, 204-206, 270, 271, 280, 281

oyaji-dono 229

r

ra 161
raru 23, 42, 43, 54, 78, 79, 94, 110, 116, 128, 146, 147, 154, 157-159, 169, 171, 180, 182, 184, 185, 188, 191, 195, 197, 240, 241, 307, 312, 317
reru 3, 209, 212, 214, 216, 221, 229, 231, 241, 293
rou 160
ru 221, 298, 300, 307

s

saburahu 75
sai 293
sama 3, 6, 100, 106, 117, 160, 167, 170, 179, 185, 191, 204, 227, 228, 240, 248, 256
san 15, 151, 211, 228, 230, 240, 252, 254, 293
sansu 216
sanzu 82
sase-tamahu 52, 59
sashiraru 156
saurau 83
seraru 109, 113, 141
se-tamahu 22, 27, 60, 78, 80, 141, 316
sharu 293, 298
shi 240
shiraru 154, 161
shiroshimesu 93
shiyansu 209, 212, 216, 252, 259
shiyaru 179, 184, 221, 227, 231, 240, 241, 317
shū 124, 160, 162, 164
shujin 283

sōsu   12
　　sousu   67

t

tachi   22, 165
taikun   154, 155
taku   283
tamau   184, 188, 190-192, 197
　　tamahu   4, 21, 22, 42, 43, 54, 60, 78, 83, 87, 96, 114, 316, 317
tatematuru   94
te   212, 221, 228, 241
teja   191, 212
teya   191, 298
toto-sama   188, 270
tot-san   209
totsu-sama   188, 189
totsu-tsan   232
totsut-tsama   229
tsa   293
tsan   293

u

uesama   154, 155

v

vo   80
V-te   240

w

waseru   188

y

yaharu   298, 299
yan   293
yansu   293
yaru   293, 300, 307
yo   238

z

zo   237
zonjiraru   155
zonzu   4, 5, 155

【著者紹介】

永田高志（ながた　たかし）

1949 年神戸市生まれ
1990 年より現在まで　近畿大学文芸学部日本文学科
2005 年上智大学より　博士（言語学）

【主な著書・論文】
「ブラジル日系人の言語生活（アサイ日系社会を例に）」（『移住研究 28』国際協力事業団 1991）、『琉球に生まれた共通語』（おうふう 1996）、『第三者待遇表現史の研究』（和泉書院 2001）、「『広辞苑』第四版に見る外来語」（『日本近代語研究 3』ひつじ書房 2002）

Hituzi Linguistics in English No. 4

A Historical Study of Referent Honorifics in Japanese

発行	2006 年 3 月 20 日　初版 1 刷
定価	14000 円＋税
著者	© 永田高志
発行者	松本　功
装丁	向井裕一（glyph）
印刷所	三美印刷株式会社
製本所	田中製本印刷株式会社
発行所	株式会社 ひつじ書房
	〒 112-0002 東京都文京区小石川 5-21-5
	Tel.03-5684-6871　Fax.03-5684-6872
	郵便振替 00120-8-142852
	toiawase@hituzi.co.jp　http://www.hituzi.co.jp/

ISBN4-89476-271-4　C3082

造本には充分注意しておりますが、落丁・乱丁などがございましたら、小社かお買上げ書店にておとりかえいたします。ご意見、ご感想など、小社までお寄せ下されば幸いです。